Praise for *Building*

Economics has famously been called "the dismal science." Who knew, then, that a book about building a moral economy could be engaging, inviting, inspiring, constructive, pastoral, prophetic, therapeutic, and rich with stories? This one is, and it's Moe-Lobeda's finest writing and most important project to date.
—Larry Rasmussen, Reinhold Niebuhr Professor Emeritus
of Social Ethics, Union Theological Seminary

Practical, embodied and faithful, Dr. Moe-Lobeda has written a courageous guide filled with ideas, tools, and vision for the future of the planet.
—Raj Patel, award-winning filmmaker, author, and research professor,
Lyndon B. Johnson School of Public Affairs,
University of Texas at Austin

Building a Moral Economy is both a prophetic call to reshape our collective economic life for the sake of saving the future of human life on our planet and a practical and profoundly hope-inspiring road map for how each of us can do our part to close the gap between the brokenness of the world as it is and the world as it should be. I would recommend *Building a Moral Economy* to anyone who wants to know what they can do today to bring a better world into being.
—Rev. Adam Russell Taylor, president of *Sojourners* and author of *A More Perfect Union: A New Vision for Building the Beloved Community*

With morally muscled reason and touchingly brutal facts, Cynthia Moe-Lobeda lifts us to the joy of working together for personal, systemic, and consciousness transformation. Join others in, or strengthen your ties with, the liberating commitments of caring people to replace our socially and environmentally destructive economy. With brutal facts, hope-rousing stories, graceful reason, and moral-imagination awakening, Dr. Moe-Lobeda gently lifts us above despair, denial, and do-nothing acceptance of our exploitive economy. Engage, or more deeply engage, in liberating commitment to the many social movements transforming lives, the system, and our consciousness of the sacred. We can live in mutually supportive harmony with each other and all life.
—Richard B. Norgaard, ecological economist and professor emeritus
of energy and resources, University of California, Berkeley

This book is a tour de force of careful economic research integrated with rich theological perspectives and ethical norms. It outlines the systemic problems we face of widespread injustice and inequity, while pointing toward viable solutions. *Building a Moral Economy* is path-breaking and life-changing.
—Mary Evelyn Tucker, Yale Forum on Religion and Ecology

This luminous book brims with the spirited moral care and scholarly brilliance that mark all of Cynthia Moe-Lobeda's work. But *Building a Moral Economy* is her most personal, engaging, and capacious book—inviting readers to join the building of an already-emerging moral economy, and expressing her transformation from an anti-oppression framework, to an antiviolence framework, to a framework geared to healing ourselves and the earth of our fatally diseased conditions.

—Gary Dorrien, Reinhold Niebuhr Professor of Social Ethics at Union Theological Seminary and multiple-time award-winning author of more than twenty volumes

While nothing now materializes with more manipulative power than the global neoliberal economy, Moe Lobeda, almost impossibly, swoops us into the spiritual forcefield and healing beauty of a live alternative.

—Catherine Keller, George T. Cobb Professor of Constructive Theology, Drew Theological School, and author of *Facing Apocalypse: Climate, Democracy, and Other Last Chances*

What distinguishes this inspiring book is its insistence that our current civilization's crisis requires a range of actions that all cohere and are a matter of *whole sight* and a full integration of what we are used to thinking of as different categories of thought. Economic life as spiritual practice—this is Moe-Lobeda's holistic vision, described here with clarity and grace.

—Kim Stanley Robinson, American science fiction writer and author of *The Ministry for the Future*

Deeply personal and political, *Building a Moral Economy* invites us to a sacred journey of communal healing for a world beset by the climate crisis, economic inequity, and global racism. It is a hope-filled book that motivates us to act by offering many practical examples of social change.

—Kwok Pui-lan, author of *Postcolonial Politics and Theology: Unraveling Empire for the Global World*

Cynthia Moe-Lobeda's newest book is a healing gift for all who yearn and search for another model of meeting our socioeconomic needs that does not come at the expense of other people's rights and the health of our already beleaguered planet. Brilliant in holding together the community and the individual, the spiritual and the political, the transformative and the practical, Moe-Lobeda shines a light on stepping stones and paths toward economies that live out the divine call to love one's neighbours and to care for creation. The book brims with so much hope!

—Athena Peralta, director of the Commission on Climate Justice and Sustainable Development and leader of Living Planet—Economic and Ecological Justice Programme, World Council of Churches

Every once in a while, a book comes along and one thinks: *Why has something so desperately needed taken so long?* For just as we begin to think that everything about one of our greatest crises has already been written, too much talked about and too little done about, here is a book that takes away all the climate fatigue, all the silliness of the "what aboutisms," all the jadedness of "We've heard it all," all the frantic search for "something new." Cynthia Moe-Lobeda's wonderful book delivers everything it promises. Here is an invitation to the most intimate—and simultaneously most public and practical—spirituality, to a collective yet intensely personal journey to a new beginning, an inspired and inspirational way of living that spans the generations. Honest, open, and entirely persuasive because it is so entirely authentic, it embraces us all with a gentle and utterly irresistible inclusiveness, draws us into the book only to release us into the making of a different world. Seldom have I felt so fulfilled after reading a book, and I know why: this book was not simply written—it was birthed.

—Allan Aubrey Boesak, South African Black liberation theologian and human rights activist

Cynthia Moe-Lobeda offers a clear-eyed, openhearted, and Spirit-filled invitation to envision and work toward economies that are ecological, equitable, democratic—and moral. The journey she invites us on, toward the healing of a diseased economy and all its ways of life that violate our deeply held values, is a journey of freedom and communion. In [this book] is a sacred invitation to find the joy of putting our precious human gifts to use for the sake of our future.

—Pamela Haines, author of *Money and Soul: Quaker Faith and Practice and the Economy*

Cynthia Moe-Lobeda welcomes us, her readers, into a personal conversation about despair and hope, drawing us close with her own honest voice. This poetic volume resonates with emotional intelligence about readers' feelings about extreme inequality and the accelerating climate crisis, and offers prompts for reflection and action. It's an enlivening and empowering read, joyfully offering stories and voices of people of many faiths and nations who are carrying out varied efforts for planetary healing. If our society turns a corner toward healthy, life-affirming systems, this kind of interwoven calls to personal growth, moral challenge, narrative transformation, and collective action for structural change will have been among the catalysts that brought us there.

—Betsy Leondar-Wright, author of *Missing Class: Strengthening Social Movement Groups by Seeing Class Cultures* and coauthor of *The Color of Wealth: The Story Behind the U.S. Racial Wealth Divide*

What a feast of life! In this remarkable, impressive, timely, and disruptive yet inspiring volume, Dr. Moe-Lobeda speaks as a wayfinder for the global voyaging community and a voice of wisdom in the rough seas of the Anthropocene. To hold the voyaging canoe on course, the wayfinder points the way to a systematic rebuilding of equitable, ecological, and democratic economies. Slowly. Evenly. Without rushing into the future. For the sake of healing and restoration, the wayfinder pleads for the voyaging community to collectively raise the navigating sails of right relationships, neighborly spiritualities, and justice-seeking love, guided by the winds of Spirit, if its goal is to find a life-affirming economic route to the island of hope. Highly recommended!

—Rev. Dr. Upolu Lumā Vaai, principal and professor of theology and ethics, Pacific Theological College, Fiji

We can live in a world where everyone flourishes; it is what God intends. This life-affirming vision is at the heart of Cynthia Moe-Lobeda's book. Read this book if you find abandonment amid abundance and poverty amid plenty immoral and wrong, and to find a path that affirms that ending poverty is possible; indeed, it is what our God of justice demands.

—Rev. Dr. Liz Theoharis, director of the Kairos Center for Religions, Rights, and Social Justice, and co-chair of the Poor People's Campaign: A National Call for Moral Revival

Moe-Lobeda does a wonderful job laying out both the big picture and the small, practical steps on the way toward a spiritually informed new economy. Drawing the reader through her own beautifully written expressions of beauty, joy, and clear-eyed hope, she helps us recognize uncomfortable truths about the current environmental crisis while providing uplifting and empowering tools and resources to move us along together in a healing journey toward a better, more life-giving future for the whole earth.

—Kathryn Tanner, Frederick Marquand Professor of Systematic Theology, Yale Divinity School, and author of *Christianity and the New Spirit of Capitalism*

There is no shortage of books on the climate crisis or the economy. Few, however, so deftly weave robust analysis within an invitation to be part of an unfolding story of hope, courage, and justice in a world that sorely needs all three. Moe-Lobeda's book is both a challenge to us to consider the real environmental, social, economic, and human costs of "normal" behaviors and an inspiration to imagination and creativity. Her writing glides between the deeply personal story of her own journey as a scholar-activist and penetrating critique of economies that extract far more from our environment and lives than just tangible resources. Moe-Lobeda looks to art, religion, and social movements to find liberative "fragments" (a la David Tracy) that ground renewed hope, connect spirituality to socioeconomic activity, and invite readers to forge new "pathways for people

of courage." Moe-Lobeda's book is an engaging, challenging, accessible start to what should be a highly anticipated series.
—Ryan P. Cumming, program director, Theological Ethics and Education, Evangelical Lutheran Church in America, and senior lecturer, Loyola University of Chicago School of Continuing and Professional Studies

We people of faith need this book as a tender and brave reminder that there's still much for us to do to work for a more just world. Cynthia Moe-Lobeda's words invite us to dig into ourselves and then act in courageous, neighborly love. Read this book if you are ready to listen to your own heart and faith and then take bold action.
—rev. dr. abby mohaupt, director of the Garrett Collective, Garrett Evangelical Theological Seminary

The persuasive summons of this book is felt, first, in the inclusive and conversational manner through which Cynthia Moe-Lobeda makes her argument, and then, second, in the slow gathering of resources and voices that provide a distinctive praxis with which to reenvision economic life as a spiritual practice. Invoking the insightful recognition that diverse injustices are forms of disease that require healing, Moe-Lobeda conceptualizes a restructuring of economic systems to foster belonging instead of exploitation. Throughout this remarkably relational book, the reader is directly addressed and offered creative ways of participating in the collaborative journey of personal and systemic healing required for a moral economy as we work together in solidarity for change through resistance and rebuilding. We are summoned to delve into and discern within our faith traditions those redemptive resources with which to struggle for ecological and equitable ways of structuring local and global economic life.
—Gerald O. West, professor emeritus, School of Religion, Philosophy, and Classics, University of KwaZulu-Natal

Cynthia Moe-Lobeda offers a healing and hopeful message of economic life as spiritual practice, inviting us into a "sacred and healing journey to new ways of being human together." This is a blessing of a book.
—Marjorie Kelly, author of *Wealth Supremacy*, and distinguished senior fellow at The Democracy Collaborative

Communities of faith—and all individuals longing to live out a spiritual, moral, or ethical calling to create a better world—should read this book! This is a beautifully crafted testament to the joy, hope, and real possibility that people standing together with one another and the earth will create a future where all are cared for and none left to suffer alone. In these pages, we are encouraged that we can honestly and courageously face the harm we have done and decide to switch direction, like a beautifully coordinated flock of birds (one of the many powerful images Moe-Lobeda uses). Moe-Lobeda's wisdom, personal stories, and practical suggestions help us to first envision and then embody relational, empowering, caring economies that will be for the healing of all.

—Rev. Rebecca Barnes, coordinator of Presbyterian Hunger Program, Presbyterian Church (USA), and author of *50 Ways to Help Save the Earth: How You and Your Church Can Make a Difference*

Moe-Lobeda refreshingly and boldly juxtaposes a detailed critical appraisal of death-dealing economies based on exploitation and extraction, with a clearly defined constructive proposal of a moral economy built on "spiritual practices of awe, lament, holy anger, and gratitude" Replete with concrete examples of companions who are already on this sacred journey, this book is as contextually rooted as it is morally empowering and as conceptually nuanced as it is theologically accountable, firmly rooted in God's cosmic love.

—Rev. Dr. Kuzipa Nalwamba, program director for Unity, Mission, and Ecumenical Formation, World Council of Churches; adjunct professor, Bossey Ecumencial Institute; ordained minister, United Church of Zambia

Really loving one's neighbors—and constantly expanding the definition of who those neighbors are—will turn out to be the crucial practice of our overheated century, as these profound meditations make clear.

—Bill McKibben, author of *The End of Nature*

BUILDING A MORAL ECONOMY

BUILDING A MORAL ECONOMY

PATHWAYS FOR PEOPLE OF COURAGE

CYNTHIA D. MOE-LOBEDA

FORTRESS PRESS
Minneapolis

BUILDING A MORAL ECONOMY
Pathways for People of Courage

Copyright © 2024 Fortress Press, an imprint of 1517 Media. All rights reserved. Except for brief quotations in critical articles and reviews, no part of this book may be reproduced in any manner without prior written permission from the publisher. Email copyright@1517.media or write to Permissions, Fortress Press, Box 1209, Minneapolis, MN 55440-1209.

29 28 27 26 25 24   1 2 3 4 5 6 7 8 9

All Scripture quotations, unless otherwise indicated, are from the New Revised Standard Version Bible, copyright © 1989 National Council of the Churches of Christ in the United States of America. Used by permission. All rights reserved worldwide.

Library of Congress Cataloging-in-Publication Data

Names: Moe-Lobeda, Cynthia D., author.
Title: Building a moral economy : pathways for people of courage / Cynthia D. Moe-Lobeda.
Description: Minneapolis, Minnesota : Fortress Press, [2024] | Includes bibliographical references and index.
Identifiers: LCCN 2024011673 (print) | LCCN 2024011674 (ebook) | ISBN 9781506485195 (print) | ISBN 9781506485201 (ebook)
Subjects: LCSH: Economics—Moral and ethical aspects. | Economics—Religious aspects.
Classification: LCC HB72 .M543 2024 (print) | LCC HB72 (ebook) | DDC 174/.4—dc23/eng/20240514
LC record available at https://lccn.loc.gov/2024011673
LC ebook record available at https://lccn.loc.gov/2024011674

Cover image: Abstract Impressionistic background by Oleg Agafonov via Getty Images
Cover design: Kristin Miller

Print ISBN: 978-1-5064-8519-5
eBook ISBN: 978-1-5064-8520-1

To Ron, my precious lifelong lover, friend, and partner.

*To our splendid offspring, all of whom I love beyond measure and from whom I learn the beauty and wonder of life—
Jonathan Leif, Gabriel David, Emily Rose,
Erik Gabriel, Lila Rose, and any grandchildren yet to be born.*

To my ancestors.

CONTENTS

Acknowledgments   ix

Invitation   1

I
Our Moment in Time

1. Economic Life as Spiritual Practice   9
2. The Haunting Pathos of Now ... and the Courage to See   23
3. The Life-Giving Potential of Now   37

II
Treasure Trove of Good Medicine

4. Morally Empowering Seeing   55
5. Three Terrains of Liberative Change and Two Interflowing Streams   73
6. Vision and Guideposts   85
7. Morally Empowering Concepts   101

III
Fingers on the Hands of Healing

Setting the Stage   123

8. Fingers on the Hands of Healing: Build the New   129
9. Fingers on the Hands of Healing: Live Lightly   139
10. Fingers on the Hands of Healing: Change the Rules   147
11. Fingers on the Hands of Healing: Move the Money   157
12. Fingers on the Hands of Healing: Resist the Wrong   171
13. Fingers on the Hands of Healing: Build the Bigger We   177

14.	Fingers on the Hands of Healing: Practice Awe, Lament, Holy Anger, Gratitude	193
15.	Fingers on the Hands of Healing: Listen and Amplify	205
16.	Fingers on the Hands of Healing: Change the Story	213
17.	Fingers on the Hands of Healing: Drink the Spirit's Courage	243

IV
Religious Roots of a Moral Economy

18.	Religious Roots of a Moral Economy	253
19.	Ingredients of Freedom	269
	Moving On: Pathways for People of Courage	295

Notes 299
Index 361

ACKNOWLEDGMENTS

Many days, upon sitting down to work on this project, I lit a candle and prayed to the Spirit for guidance. On my best days, however, I first offered gratitude—gratitude for the gift of doing this work and for all who are supporting me in it. Oh what a throng of support it has been. From the tips of my toes to the ends of my hair, I thank all of you who have made the joyful, challenging, and at times painful journey of this book (and the series to follow it) possible.

To the trillions of microorganisms floating, flying, and frolicking about within and on my body—keeping these lungs pulsing, my heart throbbing, the blood flowing, my guts churning away, and my eyes moist, holding viruses at bay, cleaning up micro messes, concocting vitamins... whew, what a life-giving circus!

To the birds who bring sweet music to my soul, the blossoms and their luscious scents and glorious colors, the breezes touching my skin—all that bring beauty and joy upon stepping out the door each morning before I sit to write. And I thank the trees! For yielding oxygen and astounding melodies as winds sweep through your leaves, for your array of twinkling fluttering greens, for your quiet wisdom and tenacious life-force, I thank you elders, the trees.

I thank my human ancestors who brought me to life, and I thank the many living people without whom this book and the subsequent series would not be what they are. Thank you immensely to all who agreed to serve on the Wisdom Council advising this book, the subsequent volumes, and the accompanying online toolkits: Macky Alston, Betsy Leondar-Wright, Adam Russell Taylor, Athena Peralta, Liz Theoharis, Christopher Carter, Marjorie Kelly, Rebecca Barnes, Ryan Cumming, Pamela Haines, abby mohaupt, Aaron Tanaka, Emily Kawano, Obery Hendricks, Mateo Nube, Karyn Bigelow, Jeremy Lent, and Gary Dorrien. Your "yes" to that invitation has been more meaningful than you can know. It has given me confidence, perspective, and wise counsel. I am eager for your ongoing wisdom sharing. My deep gratitude goes to Christiana Zenner and Laura Stivers, who jumped in to say that they wanted to write a book for the forthcoming series, and to abby mohaupt, Michael Malcom, Derrick Weston, and Keisha McKenzie for accepting the invitation to join this writing team.

I am grateful to dear friend Steve Schultz for stepping forth to write grants to fund the digital resources to accompany this book series, and to Lauren Causey and Nathan Hickling of California Lutheran University for advising and managing those applications. Alicia Vargas, Ray Pickett, Larry Rasmussen, Paloma Pavel, and Carl Anthony, what would I have done without your gracious "yes" to my requests for letters of support to potential funding sources? I thank the American Academy of Religion and the Luce Foundation for the Advancing Public Scholarship Grant to fund constructing the website and digital toolkits that will expand the book series' reach, and Red and Susan Burchfield for their sweet offer to raise additional funds for bringing those resources into being.

California Lutheran University, thank you for the sabbatical that made this all possible. Thank you too to the MF Norwegian School of Theology, Religion, and Society and its Centre for the Advanced Study of Religion and its director, Liv Ingeborg Leid, for the splendid invitation to serve as Global Fellow in 2022. You afforded me a span of focused time to work on this project, a host of colleagues to engage it, and the lovely apartment, funding, and opportunity to explore Oslo and the beautiful woodlands surrounding it.

Athena Peralta, Philip Peacock, and Peter Cruchley, your invitation to serve on the Ecumenical Panel of the NIFEA Initiative—and Sudipta Singh and George Zachariah, your invitations to the original DARE gathering and to a month in India respectively—created relationships with a host of international colleagues, largely of the Global South, and the opportunity to learn from them. They have moved my heart and expanded my mind.

Precious lifelong friends, Rick and Robin Bissell, you were amazing to read the manuscript and offer your wisdom to strengthen it. Erika Katske, your editing was magnificent. Thank you, Pamela Haines, Rev. Collin Cowans, Meghan Sobocienski, Juan Carlos De la Puente, and Anne Hall for writing (or co-writing with me) a vignette for the book.

I am indebted to the many people who shared with me stories from their lives that appear in vignettes throughout this volume or who read vignettes in order to keep them true to the realities they conveyed: John Cummings, Bianca Vasquez, Kristen Kane, Kelly Marciales, Rev. Adam Russell Taylor, Jenne Pieter, the now passed William Stanley, Damon Mkandawire, Erin Powers, Rev. Collin Cowans, Neddy Astudillo, Jocabed Solano Miselis, Nikkeya Berryhill, Mary Lim, Lizette Tapia-Raquel, and companions in India who remain unnamed. A special word of gratitude to Sami theologian Tore Johnson for opening my eyes to the green colonialism faced by Sami peoples of the Arctic; Upolu Vaai for insight into the climate justice–related wisdom of Indigenous people of Pasifika; Dora Arce Valentin for introducing me to the legacy of Mercedes Sosa; and Noelle Damico for inspiration and knowledge regarding workers' rights. Pierre Savage, thank you for generously providing the words and sketch from your film, *Weapons of the Spirit*.

My framework of ten "fingers on the hands of healing change" is indebted to the articulation of six meta-strategies developed by the Climate Justice Alliance and Movement Generation, both based in Oakland. Thank you to the people of

Acknowledgments

CJA and MG for that creative work. This project and I are beholden to the host of people the world over, living and past, whose tenacious lived commitment to building more equitable, compassionate, ecological, and democratic forms of economic life have inspired and instructed me. Their witness is life-giving.

I am grateful beyond measure to Laura Gifford, the Fortress Press editor who guided this book with unfailing wisdom, savvy, patience, creativity, and kindness. She has been an angel. And so too has been Marissa Uhrina, the Fortress Press production editor who managed the book's production with such an eye for beauty, accessibility, and precision. Adam Bursi, also of Fortress Press, consistently gave the book and me his patience, keen expertise, and impeccable diligence. Kris Miller, Fortress's in-house designer, I thank you endlessly for bringing beauty, gracefulness, consistency, and nuance to the book design. I thank also Will Bergkamp for initially accepting this book and series for publication with Fortress Press.

Thank you to colleagues and students at Pacific Lutheran Theological Seminary and the Graduate Theological Union! Working with you brings me joy, and joy brings energy. Thus, you have nourished this project even without knowing it. Students in the two classes who read all or parts of this manuscript—thank you in particular.

Words cannot express my gratitude to my two sons, Leif and Gabriel; daughter-in-law, Emily; and two precious grandchildren, Erik Gabriel and Lila Rose, for inspiring me with the exquisite beauty of who each of you is. My heart's thanks is deepest to my lover and partner for life, Ron Moe-Lobeda. Your support for me in doing this work has taken so many forms, from indexing and editing to painting a purple wall in my study, to vision, wisdom of the heart, and love's encouragement. Ah, so good!

INVITATION

Dear Reader,

We humans are splendidly sensuous creatures.[1] We delight in the beauty of touch, taste, sight, sound, and smell. And we are hungry creatures. We hunger to belong. We hunger for joy, pleasure, beauty, trustworthy companions. These are holy hungers. They lead us to relish the gifts of being alive as Earth creatures in an extravagantly beautiful world—magnificent beyond imaging.

With this book, I invite you into (or further into) a sacred journey. It is a journey of healing. If you are anything like me, you will not stick to something for the long haul unless it brings you joy, or beauty, or something else for which you hunger. Just doing the right thing might not be enough to hold our commitment over time. So, I implore you: As you enter (or continue) the quest for more equitable and ecologically sane ways of shaping our life together, ask, "How can this bring me joy? Where in this may I find beauty?" I invite you—throughout the journey—to cultivate joy, bathe in beauty, honor your body and its wisdom, and feed your soul. Brief sections at the end of each chapter point in those directions.

You are at risk in reading the first two chapters of this book. They could lead to a sense of overwhelmed hopelessness. Fear not. We will protect against that landing. As one protection, I offer in chapter 1 what has fortified companions on similar journeys for millennia. It is a love story. You have a place in it.

And I offer you companions. I stand in awe of our companions in this journey—people close at hand and around the world—whose courage, wisdom, creativity, and fierce tenacity are the lifeblood of the movement to build more equitable, ecological, and democratic economies. Perhaps you are one of them already.

Gratitude and awe fill my soul in the fleeting moments when the stunning beauty of life on Earth and of ordinary human beings appears to my often-dullened heart. "Beauty will save the world." So claims Fyodor Dostoevsky. Beauty will not directly mitigate climate change or stop extractive, exploitative fossil-fueled economies. Nor will awe and gratitude. But beauty, awe, and gratitude will feed us for the great calling before us at this pivotal time in human history—to build a world in which all people and Earth's life systems may flourish.

An ancient Chinese proverb notes, "If we continue in the direction we are going, we will get where we are headed." Our current direction is toward death by climate catastrophe—for humans and for much of the other life on our planetary home. Earth's life-support systems cannot bear us, living as we do.[2] But we can change direction.[3] Indeed, we—and with us Earth's capacity to sustain life—hang in the balance. Our "now" is a turning point.[4]

Our children, grandchildren, and other cherished youngsters will ask, "What did you do when the world and my future were in dire risk?" What will we say? My hope is that this book might give you grounds to say, "My child, I was one of those who turned things around. Together with the Spirit, we rescued this garden Earth and its people."

This book and the series to follow are for people who want to live in ways that build justice, joy, and life-giving relationships, and who have a hunch that economies are utterly central to that quest. We created this book series and the accompanying Web-based resources for students, educators, business leaders, faith groups, activists, governmental bodies, community members, and all who hunger for economic lives that reflect values of social justice, compassion, ecological resilience, and shared, accountable power.

In writing, I have tried to offer you an odd combination. I speak to you in my voice, person-to-person, often from my heart and experience. Yet, all that I say rests on the high standard of scholarly precision and theoretical grounding that I believe you deserve.

Before we begin, I share a few tips for reading, a preview of the chapters to come, and a word about the Web-based resources that accompany this volume.

Reading Tips

Please consider not just reading, but interacting with this book. Engage it with your body, your heart, your gut, not only with your thinking mind. Perhaps these tips can help:

- When you sit down to read, begin with deep gratitude. Thank the trillions of organisms that live in your body, enabling you to function. Thank the nerves in your eyes and the muscles in your fingers that turn the pages or click the keys. Thank the ancestors who gave you life, and the trees of the Amazon that sustain it.
- Listen to your heart as you read. What do you feel? Where is pain or grief? How are you hiding from it or pushing it aside? Hear what your subtle inner voice might be saying.
- Listen to your body as you read. Notice where you are tensing up. What is that telling you?
- If possible, read this book with other people, a group, or a reading partner. You might call them an accountability group or accountability partner. Discuss what you read, think, and feel. More importantly, discuss the Sacred Journey Journal and the actions it invites at each chapter's end. We have more courage and sustained power for life-giving change when we have the support of others.[5]
- Try putting the ideas in this book into practice and see what happens. Talk about them with your friends, coworkers, children or parents or other kinfolk, or strangers you meet on the bus.
- We learn so much more by practicing the ideas we encounter and by conversing with other people about them. So, as you engage, I hope you will try out the ideas!
- Take an action that contributes in some small way to building a more ecological and equitable economy before going through the entire book. Taking even one small step in response to ideas can help them to come alive in our lives. Do so with other people—perhaps with your reading circle. You will encounter a multitude of possible actions. Action inspires our hope and courage. And action may be more fulfilling when done with other people.
- As you move along in this journey, build trusting relationships with others who share your values around social justice and ecological well-being.[6]
- Bear in mind the invitation (in chapter 1) to consider economic life as a web of relationships with people near and far.
- Explore the invitation (in chapter 1) to perceive economic life as a spiritual practice.
- Engage with the "Honoring Our Bodies" and Sacred Journey Journal sections at the end of each chapter if they are helpful to you.
- If you are one who hungers for action now, who is impatient with more reading, thinking, and reflecting when action is needed, then you might want to move immediately from part 1 to part 3, which outlines forms of action. Experiment with some of them, and keep cycling back to part 2.

Preview of the Chapters to Come

The journey from heartfelt longing for more equitable and Earth-honoring economic lives to realizing them voyages through landscapes of uncertainty and complexity. The diversity of possible paths is confounding. Some people en route may seem unfamiliar, even threatening. Daunting obstacles arise, as does awareness that the changes necessary are far beyond whatever "I" can do on my own.

How do we chart a course? How do we do so amid the demands of daily life? The complexity cries out for a set of tools. In this book we will call them medicines. The framework that unfolds in this volume provides a set of medicines useful for bringing in the new economy.

This framework—and the entirety of this book, the subsequent series, and the accompanying Web-based tool-kits—builds on the work of countless people around the globe who are creating more equitable, ecological, and democratic economies.[7] I have been fortunate to work with such people. They inform this book and the series it begins. You will encounter them in the pages of the book and its website.

Part 1 sets the stage and clarifies key assumptions that ground the book. Chapter 1 introduces the crisis, choice, and challenge before us. This chapter invites you to see economies as webs of relationships, and economic life as a spiritual practice. Economic transformation is seen as a healing process. Chapters 2 and 3 introduce the terrors and beautiful potential of our moment in time.

In part 2 we explore six essential healing medicines undergirding the journey. The first, in chapter 4, is an invitation to "see" in a way that enables facing the terrible truths of economic and ecological injustice woven into our lives, while maintaining profound hope and sense of moral-spiritual power to bring forth change.

Chapter 5 brings us to the second medicinal tool: acknowledging three terrains of human existence in which change takes place as we build a moral economy. These terrains are behavioral change, social structural change, and change in worldview or consciousness. From there we encounter the next medicine: the parallel streams of resistance and rebuilding that nourish and depend upon each other.

Chapter 6 introduces the fourth and fifth healing tools: vision of a moral economy and overarching guideposts for realizing that vision. Finally, in chapter 7 we encounter empowering concepts that expose what to avoid and what to embrace in order to foster moral economies.

In part 3 I invite you to join me in a "display that dazzles."[8] We explore ten "fingers on the hands of healing" economic life and the web of relationships that economies create. Each finger is a different form of action or way to embody neighbor-love in economic life. Traversing this landscape, we will encounter ordinary people around the world whose compassion and courage are giving birth to world-changing movements.

Invitation

This treasure trove of medicines in this book is far from comprehensive. That is not my purpose. Rather, I want to enable you and me to engage abundantly and courageously in the great challenge facing adults and youth alive now—constructing ways of life that enable Earth's community of life to flourish. The point is to take the seemingly impossible and render it possible by opening it up to see its various parts and how they already work.

My hope is that this set of medicinal tools will (1) make the complexity manageable rather than an obstacle to action; and (2) help you to clarify how you and your communities of companions may contribute to building moral economies. I invite you to augment these tools and adjust them to your particular terrain. Enhance this treasure trove through your own wisdom and experience.

Journeying into the world of religion as a vital—perhaps necessary—source of moral-spiritual power for the work of economic transformation is the purpose of part 4. The world's great faith traditions were born as a counterforce to predatory economies and other forms of oppression. This conclusion, borne out by recent scholarship, is startling and hope-giving.[9] If born of this root, then surely religion can be such a counterforce today. We will explore how religion and spirituality may be a seedbed of economic transformation toward more compassionate and just economies.

The word *religion* has multiple meanings. We will use it to signify organized efforts by human beings to perceive and relate to the great and intimate Mystery that some people call God. We will begin with the words of my friend, Rabbi Michael Lerner, who refers to God as "the transformative power of the universe." One focus will be the interplay between religious wisdom and other forms of wisdom such as the natural sciences, the arts, the social sciences, voices of Earth (trees, waters, animals, winds), and more.

The "Closing Words" section summarizes a few key themes and introduces the content and unusual nature of the small-book series that follows this introductory volume, as well as the online toolkits that accompany all of these books. The subsequent books in the series are based in stories of real people and their struggles and joys. The books face head-on the challenges on the way to moral economies, conveying hope and moral-spiritual power but not fraudulent optimism.

All chapters except those in part 3 end with a ritual intended to cultivate your power for liberative healing of economic life—personally and societally. The ritual entails honoring our bodies and reflecting on our sacred journeys toward economic healing. I encourage you to keep some record of the Sacred Journey Journal reflections so that you may return to them. They may reveal your own wisdom, resilience, strengths, weak points, fears, grief, holy anger, courage, and joys.

My aims in co-creating this series are three. The first pertains to people of the United States who desire more equitable, ecological, and democratic economic structures and lives but who are not yet actively engaged in seeking them. Here my aim is to plant and water the seeds of transformative engagement in movements to build the new economy. The second aim is to deepen the power and joy of people already engaged in those movements by enabling them to gain new insights, tools, and companions.

The third aim flows from my conviction that religion bears tremendous power for nourishing human efforts to achieve the good, especially where doing so is fraught with apparently insurmountable obstacles. I hope to convey the rich wellspring of moral-spiritual power for economic transformation that flows from the world's great faith traditions, with particular focus on Christianity and Judaism.

The Web-Based Resources

Your experience of this book will be richer if you also access the website that hosts the toolkit for this volume and will host more extensive toolkits for the subsequent volumes in the series. There you will find stories; art, music, and poetry relevant to economic transformation; videos; links to organizations and readings; zines; and connections to companions on the journey. See https://buildingamoraleconomy.org/

In companionship and hope,

Cynthia

I

Our Moment in Time

CHAPTER ONE

Economic Life as Spiritual Practice

> Most of the things worth doing in the world had been declared impossible before they were done.
> —Justice Louis D. Brandeis[1]

> Avoiding the most dire damages of climate change "requires transforming the world economy at a speed and scale that has 'no documented historic precedent.'"
> —Coral Davenport citing an IPCC report[2]

> A different economy is not just a theoretical possibility, or a distant utopia, but something already under construction in the real world.
> —Naomi Klein[3]

I am walking. The day is ordinary. The sky clear. My eyes drift upward. There, in the sky soars a flock of birds, resolutely heading together in one direction as though it is the only way to go. They seem bound on that path. Then, suddenly, with astounding grace, they shift and with a grand, unexpected swoop veer off in an utterly different direction! I gape. How did they do that?

Such a radical rapid shift is the challenge now facing humankind—or at least parts of it. Will we muster the moral courage to turn around and fly the other direction? Will we veer away from climate catastrophe and the stupefying economic and racial injustice that accompanies it? Will we soar instead toward a world in which all have the necessities for life with justice and joy and Earth's ecosystems flourish? This is the central moral and spiritual challenge of our time. This book and the subsequent series are one small response. You reading and engaging them is another.[4] "How," we ask, "do we catalyze and maintain a sweeping shift in direction?" Might the birds hold clues?

A splendid and vast worldwide movement to radically redirect economic life has unfolded largely unnoticed in the last three decades. Groups of people from all walks of life give rise to this creative and courageous undertaking. They are students, business leaders, fisherpeople, lawyers, peasants and other farmers, jobless people, scientists, nonprofit organizational leaders, artists, religious leaders, factory workers, healthcare professionals, retirees, engineers, homemakers, unhoused people, teachers, and more.

Earth's song of hope resounds around the globe in movements to build more equitable, ecological, and democratic economies at local, regional, national, and global levels.[5] These singers of hope say "no more" to economic practices that threaten Earth's livable climate. "No more" to economic practices and policies that drive some into anguished poverty so that a few can accumulate exorbitant wealth and many more can heedlessly overconsume.[6]

Like the birds, these ordinary economic changemakers fly in a life-giving redirection—from economies based on exploitation and extraction to economies that support flourishing for all, humans included. Hosts of people of all colors, creeds, continents, and cultures hunger for a world in which all people have food, water, homes, healthcare, and all that is necessary for flourishing and in which Earth's waters, air, soils, flora, and fauna once again sing a melody of life. In countless ways, ordinary people are living this vision into reality. In these pages—and in the subsequent book series and Web-based resources that accompany them—you will meet some of these people.

Perhaps you already are a part of this visionary and practical flock. If so, may this book strengthen your engagement. If not, then welcome! May your trip through these pages bring you joyfully into this community of hope.

I thank you for the moral courage to care and for the guts to wonder whether the "normal" practices of our economic lives—buying, borrowing, eating and drinking, investing, saving, selling, transporting and housing ourselves—and the public policies that structure those practices might be doing terrible harm to Earth, to others, and to ourselves. I ask you to dare to believe that more equitable, compassionate, and Earth-honoring ways of living are possible.

If you, like me, have glimpsed the dire realities of climate crisis or of economic violence and the strength of systems holding them in place, then you also may know the lure of despair or hopelessness. Its voice whispers seductively, "It is too late." Or "things will stay as they are, despite any efforts to build justice and save Earth's livable climate. The powers-that-be are too strong and devious. Let us just live as best we can and forget about matters too big for us to impact."

I know this voice. It is in me—seductively subtle and chillingly powerful. However, for reasons that will unfold in this chapter, that voice no longer has sway over me. Please join me as I share how I now live in the paradox of BOTH hope and despair, with hope leading and guiding my life. I must acknowledge the despair and not lie to myself. But it no longer has power; it gives way to active hope that energizes me.

Economic Life as Spiritual Practice

Each of us may choose to live as though it is too late, as though what we do does not matter. Or we may choose to hope and *to embody that hope in our actions—to act with all the power that the Great Spirit has breathed into us for enacting good.* Which will we choose?

If you are one who, listening to the climate science, realizes that it already is too late to avoid some degree of climate catastrophe, then I ask you this: How will you answer some years from now, when our children, grandchildren, or other precious youngsters ask with their eyes gazing at us, "Grandma, Grandpa, auntie, elder friend, what did you do when my world was being destroyed?"

Well, dear young one, I gave up because I knew it was futile, and I am a realist.

Or instead:

I—together with a whole host of people here and around the world—threw myself into building a future for you, even though many said it was impossible. "No," we said, "we will fight for life. We will embody a wild hope that we still can make a difference." And so it was; we built a regenerative relationship with God's garden Earth as creatures in it and of it; we forged new economic lives that enabled creation again to sing a song of life, and that enabled you, my dear one, to savor the glorious gift of life on Earth.

Which will we choose?

It is a strange wonder to be alive *as human beings now*, at this turning point in history. Our young and dangerous—yet infinitely precious—species will determine which way we go. Our decisions and actions will shape the fate of life on Earth. None before us have borne this moral weight. What we do matters! *It is, therefore, a good time to be alive.*

All realms of human endeavor, all forms of knowledge and wisdom—be they moral, spiritual/religious, scientific, aesthetic, or practical—are called to bring their gifts to the great panhuman work of our time. It is perhaps the most radical and urgent reorientation of society ever undertaken. That "great work"[7] is to forge ways of being human and living together on this planet that (1) allow Earth's life systems and life-support systems to thrive; and (2) enable life-giving relationships among and within human societies. Considering climate change, this "great work" will require "transforming the world economy at a scale and speed that 'has no documented historic precedent.'"[8]

Flocks of birds can switch direction. So can we. Changing direction requires seeing differently.

Here is an important preview of that re-seeing as it emerges in this book and in the subsequent short companion volumes: We will re-see economies as webs of relationships. We will re-view economic life as spiritual practice. We will locate economic life in the greatest love story ever told. And we will honor the collective work of economic transformation as a sacred journey—a journey of healing diseased and distorted relationships with Earth, with ourselves, with the Sacred Source whom some call God, and with neighbors far and near who are hurt by current economic systems. We will begin to understand our journey as one to freedom and toward claiming our right to live as we were created to live: that is, the right to live as beings in community—human community, geoplanetary community, community with the Sacred—contributing to the world's beauty and resilience. In reading and pondering these pages, we each embark or continue on this sacred journey.

Economies as Webs of Relationships

Imagine a different relationship in which people and land are good medicine for each other.

—Robin Wall Kimmerer[9]

"What if we saw the economy as a fabric of relationships?" What? I cocked my head. What? That is a profoundly biblical notion of economy, I thought with a smile. This proposal came from the New Economy Coalition, a network that claims no religious ties. Did they know that "economy" comes from the Greek *oikonomos*, the rules or guidelines (*nomos*) for how we are to organize and maintain the household (*oikos*), and that in biblical terms this household is the whole household of creation? Did they realize that God, according to the Hebrew Scriptures, gave two primary guidelines for ordering economic life—serve and preserve garden Earth (Gen 2:15) and love your neighbor with a love that seeks justice (Lev 19:18, later repeated by Jesus)—and that these two teachings are fundamentally guidelines for relationships? According to the biblical witness as well as the New Economy Coalition, *economic life is not just about numbers and money; economic life signifies actions within a web of relationships (many of them distant) that profoundly shape people's lives as well as the waters, air, soil, plants, and animals upon which life depends.*

I invite you to think of "economies" in this new way, a way that acknowledges a crucial reality generally ignored. It is that *our economic lives*—what we buy, consume, throw away, save, borrow, invest, sell, and how we feed, shelter, transport, and provide for ourselves and families—*are in essence about relationships.* These activities that make up daily economic life have tremendous indirect impact on other people and on Earth's other creatures. That impact may be damaging or life-giving.

For example, my savings account at a local cooperative bank that finances small-scale employee-owned businesses puts me in relationship with those employee-owners who now, perhaps for the first time in their lives, savor safe working conditions and a share in the profit from their work. On the other hand, if I put my money in Chase or another large, corporate bank, it will be used to finance the fossil fuel industry and thus the climate change that is killing and displacing people through fierce storms, drought, and hunger. My relationship with those people, through my investment, would be damaging, even deadly.

Buying tomatoes harvested by people forced to work in toxic conditions for far too little pay and no benefits puts me in a harmful relationship with those farmworkers. But by asking my grocery store to purchase only tomatoes produced by workers who are protected by a Fair Food Agreement,[10] I enter a life-giving relationship with those workers. Just imagine the difference in their lives! Moreover, think of the difference it makes in my life and the grocer's.

The economic activity of *systems* in which we are players also puts us into relationships that may either damage others or serve their well-being. A story from my life as a churchworker in Honduras illustrates:

> Her birth came at dawn. She emerged from the birth canal malnourished. Upon seeing Florita, I gasped. Was she too tiny to survive? Pale, frail, and eerily quiet, she lay with her mother, Floresmila. Four and a half pounds, said the midwife's scale. So unfair, my heart screamed. Florita was born malnourished because Floresmila and her husband were barred from access to land. They needed only un pedacito de tierra *(a small plot of land)* on which to grow food. But no—the land adjacent to the village had been taken over by global agribusiness to produce beef for Northern tables. International coffee companies owned other nearby lands. Floresmila and Juan Carlos—like many of the campesinos *in this village*—were forced to work other people's land for very poor wages. Oh, how they longed for their own land so that they could feed their children. The child born that morning did survive. But she entered toddlerhood frail and spindly, lacking the corn, beans, vegetables, and eggs that would have nourished her to strength and health had the villagers been able to plant their own crops. Economic policies—most notably trade agreements with the United States—had prioritized the interests of large agricultural corporations. I wondered, was my church invested in those companies? Was I paid from the profits of that investment and thus at the expense of Floresmila, her family, and other villagers who greeted me with smiles and buenos dias as I walked in the morning sun each day?

Economic policies, actions, and structures can determine whether people live or die, flourish or decline. They dictate who will have food, health care, and adequate education. Hunger, for example, often is not the result of insufficient food supplies, but rather results primarily from maldistribution of food and income or from land being accumulated by large companies instead of reserved for people who need it to grow food.[11] All who derive profit from those companies are in relationship with the people who need that land but no longer can use it—people like Floresmila, her child, and the other peasants of that area. The US citizens who ate the beef or whose mutual funds were invested in companies producing it were in relationship with these Honduran villagers. Did that include me?

Likewise, urban food deserts in the US are created by economic decisions of corporations and governments.[12] All who benefit from these decisions—investors, consumers, employees, and more—are in relationship with the people denied access to adequate food.

We human beings have the right, the calling, and the inner hunger to be in "right relationship" with human neighbors, far and near, and with the other creatures in this grand mystery called life on Earth. Right relationships enable both self and others to flourish, with particular attention to the well-being of marginalized people. *Reshaping economic life—as our journey through these pages will reveal—is a matter of reshaping relationships with neighbors far and near.* It is a matter of building new relationships, based not on exploitation and extraction but on mutual flourishing for self, others, and all of creation. Relationships are at the heart of spirituality. They manifest our spirituality and they shape it.[13] *Economy is a "fabric of relationships" and, thus, is a spiritual matter.*

Economic Life as Spiritual Practice— Enacting a Spiritualty of Neighbor-Love

In preparing to write this book, I have come to see economic life as a spiritual practice. This understanding seeped into me as I learned from revered spiritual leaders of the past and from courageous justice-seeking people in many lands. I hope that you too might come to see that economic activity and practices, by their very nature, enact a spirituality.

How odd—economic life as spiritual practice? *Spirituality* is a fluid, shimmering term. It has varied connotations to its users, and scholars define it in myriad ways. *Spirituality* as I use it here refers to an awareness and practice of being in relationship with something that transcends our material and constructed world but also flows within it, including within ourselves. That "something" is the sacred creating and energizing force or power that connects all things. Some call it *Yeshuvah*, God, Allah, Spirit, Creator, the Sacred, the Holy, the Divine, the Light, Ultimate Reality, a Higher Power, "Life Force of the universe ... connective tissue/energy of the universe that is God,"[14] or many other names and metaphors.

Spirituality is inherent in religion but is not limited to religion. It does not refer to something exotic, esoteric, churchy, otherworldly, or paranormal. One's "spiritual life" is not limited to times of prayer or contemplation. Rather, spirituality is at the heart of ordinary everyday life to the extent that ordinary life is lived with awareness of and in relationship with the Sacred. Spiritual practices—within religion and outside of religion—are practices that enable us to be more fully aware of and aligned with that sacred Spirit, to be nourished, encouraged, and guided by it. Thus, spiritual practices enable us to gain freedom *from* captivity by self-absorption, and gain freedom *to* align with something bigger than self. This astounding contribution of spirituality and religion will be central to our discussion in chapters 18 and 19.

From a Christian perspective, that spiritual "something" is the Spirit of the holy and intimate Mystery revealed in—but not only in—a first-century dark-skinned Palestinian Jew named Jesus and his people, the ancient Hebrews. Spirituality has to do with living in awareness of and in response to that Spirit, as it is flowing and pouring through and beyond all things. Spiritual practices help us align our lives with the ways and beckoning of this Spirit.

Of course, the nature of spiritual practice depends on what one understands that Spirit to be like. I believe that this Spirit is a force of Love that embraces all of creation, and each of us personally—a Love that will not desert us regardless of any evil we may do. This Love, according to the biblical witness, fiercely and tenderly seeks justice and well-being especially for the outcast, excluded, oppressed, and all on the margins of power and privilege. And *it calls people to live in accord with this Love*. Spiritual practices are what deepens our capacity to receive and trust this justice-seeking, Earth-treasuring Love and to live it into the world through activities of everyday life.

Thus we may see economic life as a spiritual practice, a way of either enacting a spirituality of neighbor-love or betraying it. Our economic practices, through the systems of which we are a part, may damage or destroy neighbors or they may serve neighbors' well-being. The latter aligns with the Spirit of God; the former betrays it. It is not by accident that religious institutions are the leading sector in divesting from fossil fuels; these religious institutions see investment in fossil fuels as dangerous to neighbors who are suffering from climate change, dangerous to nonhuman neighbors, and dangerous to ourselves.[15] Said differently, investment in fossil fuels (according to this perspective) betrays neighbor-love. Divesting is an effort to enact a spirituality of neighbor-love.

We have entered a "jungle of ambiguity" here, because so many words in the previous paragraph have multiple meanings. The most hazy and misleading may be *love*. As I use the word, it is not "love" according to common discourse. This distinction we take up later. It is crucial.

You will find spirituality and religious faith weaving through this book. Therefore, let me be clear. While I draw on some of the world's great faith traditions, I speak beyond the boundaries of religious traditions to all people of goodwill who hunger for more just and ecological economic lives. We take up the role of spirituality and religious faith more fully in part 4, but I want to note three points here.

First, I am painfully aware that religion, and particularly Christianity, has wielded vast power for terror and brutality throughout history and still today. It rests upon people of religious traditions to recognize and reckon with that reality. Doing so is integral to a life of faith, and particularly Christian faith, given its role in the atrocities of colonization—including genocide of Indigenous peoples, enslavement of African people, the Doctrine of Discovery—and other crimes against humanity such as the persecution of LGBTQIA+ people, the myth of white supremacy, and the Nazi reign of terror, to name just a few examples. We grapple with these crimes later in this book.

Second, I do not include religion for the purpose of convincing you to adopt a particular religious or spiritual practice, belief, or leaning. Rather, I appeal to religion because the forces lined up against economic transformation are monumental, and countering them calls for spiritual strength. Religious faith is one source of that strength, although not the only one. I believe that all of Earth's wisdom traditions—including the earth and biological sciences, behavioral sciences, religion, healing arts, and more—will be necessary to the great work of building economies that enable life to flourish. Religions indeed have many gifts of moral, spiritual, and practical power to offer. We explore them throughout these pages, especially in part 4.

Third, one of the most important gifts given by Jewish, Christian, and Muslim religious traditions is to situate economic life in a magnificent love story. This story is the foundation of my life, the motivating force behind this book, and—I believe—a light that cannot be overcome (John 1:5). Similar gifts are affirmed also in Dharmic traditions (using other terms such as compassion) as well as in many Indigenous spiritualities.

Let us take a closer look.

An Astounding Love Story

Some faith traditions offer a particularly precious gift to the work of economic transformation. This gift is to locate economic life—what we buy, consume, and throw away, as well as how we feed, shelter, and transport ourselves—in the greatest love story ever told. What do I mean by this?

Long ago, in my early teen years, I fell into self-loathing. I had learned that the economic systems providing food for people like me were preying on other people, using their lands and their bodies to make huge profits.[16] I had listened to survivors of that exploitation, and it made me despise myself for benefiting from those systems. I will reveal more of that story later. My point here is to share with you what helped to heal me from that dangerous self-degradation, and to nurture my power for responding to structural evil—such as economic exploitation and climate injustice—with self-love and neighbor-love.

Join me stepping back in time as I share with you from my personal journey.

I felt desperate, like I had no right to exist. Needing to confide in someone, I knocked on the dental office door of a former church youth-group leader whom I had not seen in years. He opened the door, saw my face, and closed his office. We walked to a nearby forest and sat down on a log by a creek. He read to me from the book of Romans (a book in the Christian Bible). I think that it was Romans 8:38–39. Suddenly, I was utterly engulfed by the love of the Great Spirit. My being was embraced by an unfathomable, radiant, and palpable reality that this Sacred Love would never leave me, regardless of whatever I might do or fail to do. I recall hearing my inner voice say, "I could sit like a bump on a log for the rest of my life and this One would love me no less."

That dazzling reality stayed with me with radiant intensity for some days. That knowing remains. It has become the bedrock of my faith, my life, and my calling to work toward a more just and compassionate economic order.

The love story is much bigger. It is cosmic. I realized with utter clarity that afternoon that not only I, but the entirety of creation, is enfolded by and imbued with a life-giving Force that ultimately will bring all to fullness of life in all of its beauty and goodness. Human creatures are created and called to embody this Force and to allow it to work in us to heal and liberate the world.

Monotheistic traditions call this Force "love"—the love given by the intimate Mystery that some call God. As revealed through the Hebrew Bible, what Christians call the First Testament or Old Testament, this Force is at work in humans as neighbor-love and is inherently both justice-seeking and Earth-honoring. In the life of the Palestinian Jew named Jesus of Nazareth, embodying this force meant resisting imperial Rome and experiencing death by torture at the hands of that imperial power. Oppressive power is threatened by justice-seeking love.

Whether you are situated in one of these religious traditions does not matter. What matters is to recognize this story of life-changing Love as one way of understanding economic life that could empower courage, wisdom, and spiritual strength for the great transition to economies of life for all. If you belong to another religious tradition, you might ask, "What are the life-giving claims that it offers for economic healing?"

Let us travel back further in time. Settle in for a story.

Imagine, if you will, a world of splendor and abundance beyond imagining... a dawn every twenty-four hours, sun called forth from deep indigo sky. Songbirds in myriad voices sing with abandon, the voice of beauty. Fragrance wafts from living beings in infinite shapes, colors, and sizes from the tiniest, most delicate blossoms to voluptuous deep purple floral extravaganzas. Drops of glistening water powder the land at the birth of each day. The air shimmers with fluttering leaves. Light rays dance. Everywhere is breath. Life is birthing. Luscious fruits hang from trees. In the soil, hearty grains emerge. And then dusk. Indigo of yet another shade deepens.

In this glorious circle of life, all that dies becomes sustenance for other creatures and elements. The weaving of interdependence is breath-taking, beyond full comprehension: a radiant ball of energy from eons past issues power sufficient to meet the needs of all life forms. What one gives off sustains the other. Birth and death. Days and planets, creatures and colors are born and die and bring new life. Decaying log nurses her young. Complexity and simplicity unite. Cycles of death and resurrection. And the trees . . . the trees watch, hear, guide, shelter.

It is a wild, raucous, birthing, fire-spewing, earth-quaking, fecund communion of life, joined in the "hymn of all creation," praising the Source and Sustainer of being. The splendor of this world is exceeded by one thing only: the radiant love of its Creator embracing Her creation and coursing through it. This world is beloved with a "love as a burning fire that will never cease in all the endless ages to come."[17] This love is more powerful than any force in heaven or earth. It will not desert you or our planetary home. Were we to end human life on this planet, we would still be in the embrace of that Love. You might pause for a moment to let that promise flood over you, fill every cell of your body, embrace you. You are now and, in every moment, beloved. Nothing you do or fail to do will change that. It is who you are. Your primary identity. Thou art beloved.

In the world's most recent moments appear creatures of particular consciousness. Self-aware temporally and spatially, they are able to reflect on the world and their place in it, to wonder, and to create. As all other creatures and elements, these human "mud creatures"[18] are crafted from the dust of long-past stars, fashioned as community, in community, by community, and for community—for communion. They depend for life itself on a web of interrelated beings and elements: the trillions of unseen organisms living on and in their bodies, the thousands of organisms in a foot of soil, the trees of the Amazon rainforest who produce our oxygen, the bees who beget life in the plants that give us food.

The plot thickens. The Sacred Spirit of Love—this holy and intimate Mystery—is at play in the world, breathing life into it. This Spirit is present within, among, and beyond us.

But that is not all. The Holy Mystery reveals to the human ones their lifework. They are called to recognize, receive, relish, and revel in this gracious and indomitable love. And then, they are called to love—to live this mysterious and marvelous love into the world. Forever beloved, they are to be bearers of the Creator's justice-making, Earth-relishing Love in its steadfast commitment to gain fullness of life for all, within a communion of all.[19] Ah, yes, the Holy One—speaking through prophet and story—is clear: where injustice blights life, this Love will see the injustice and move human creatures to undo it!

According to some interpretations of the monotheistic traditions, this is our life's work, our "vocation," our calling as humans: to receive and trust God's healing and liberating love and then to live it into the world. We are given this reason for being. The human creatures are created to be lovers—offering to God, self, others, and the entire creation the love that they are fed by the One who gives them life. For so doing, they are given, in the image of the Holy One, hearts of infinite compassion and minds equipped to seek justice. And into them, as into all creatures, is breathed the *Ruach* (breath, Spirit, air) of the Holy One. What an awe-invoking, Spirit-drenched, communion-weaving reason for being.

We will not love perfectly; to the contrary, we are, in the words of Martin Luther, God's "*rusty*" tools," utterly fallible and limited vessels of the Divine flame. In our efforts to love—including practicing neighbor-love as guide to economic life—our efforts will fall short. Knowing this can free us from despair at our own shortcomings and the shortcomings of the policies, institutions, and networks that we build.

Pause for a moment. Take a breath. Notice a danger. Though quiet as a whisper, it wreaks havoc. It is this: we (humans) tend to be miserable at authentic self-love. Authentic self-love is a deep affirmation of the infinite goodness, worth, and gift that is oneself. It frees us for loving others.[20] The journey to healing economic life, then, includes the journey toward embracing the true beauty and gift of oneself.

This is the *oikos*, the household of God. The Holy One, hungering for its well-being, gave to our species guidelines for household management, *oikonomia*, and the intelligence to develop those guidelines in multiple ways as the complexity of social life unfolds. The *oikonomia* (economy) was grounded in two rock-solid foundations: we are to love neighbor as self (Lev 19:18 and Matt 22:39) and we are to serve and preserve God's garden Earth (Gen 2:15). According to the first of these guidelines, Earth's bounty is to be shared. None should have too much where it cast others into want.

However, rejecting the *oikonomos* of God, some crafted contrary rules. Those new rules enable a few—largely descendants of the tribes of Europe—to use up most of Earth's bounty. The species created to love and to serve the garden now lives out the opposite. We live in strata. For those at the bottom, "poverty means death."[21] The wealthiest 10 percent of the world's people, which includes the middle class in rich countries, owns 76 percent of the world's wealth.[22] We "consume" Earth's wealth, eating it up before it can be replenished. The pathos of our situation stuns. Though we may long to heed God's call to love, we are complicit in ecocide and economic brutality, not by intent or will but by virtue of the political economy that shapes our lives. The Holy One "set before [the human ones] life and death, blessings and curses" and commanded us to "choose life so that you and your descendants may live" (Deut 30:19). We have chosen death. Unknowingly, unintentionally, unwittingly, a portion of humankind has chosen death for the living world. Under our weight, all "creation has been groaning" (Rom 8:22). We are at a turning point. "If trends continue, we will not."[23]

We can change direction. We can "choose life so that we and our descendants may live." We can heal from predatory economic life and create an economy of life abundant for all.

What a life-giving and encouraging story in which to live.

The sacred love story continues. You are in it. In a world writhing with injustice, with huge swaths of human earthlings threatening Earth's livable climate, we, dear readers, are daring to ask what it means to "love neighbor as self."

The Jewish, Christian, and Muslim Scriptures are clear. Relationships with neighbors are to be guided by this unwavering light. It is God's commandment, invitation, and calling to love neighbor as self. This is crucial: neighbor-love, according to these traditions, pertains not only to interpersonal relationships, but also to the social structures that determine our indirect relationships with neighbors. Moreover, neighbor-love is not principally an emotion, a feeling of affection or goodwill. While it may include such feelings, they are neither its centerpiece nor an essential component of it. At the heart of neighbor-love as a biblical reality is a steadfast commitment to serve the well-being of the one who is loved, empowered by the Spirit. *Nothing could be more important for glimpsing the world-changing power of the call to love neighbor as self.*

Two thousand years ago, the geographic scope of an ordinary person's impact was much smaller. A person living in North America did not have a life-giving or a life-threatening impact on a person living in Asia or Africa. Given the global economy, that scope has exploded; it is planetary. The way I live my life impacts the communities from whose land comes the oil to produce my polyester bedsheets, fly my food from other continents, and fuel my car. My desire for a sweet beverage impacts countless people in India whose water has been taken or poisoned by a Coca-Cola plant. My greenhouse gas emissions impact those who now must flee their homelands in Central America as climate refugees.

What form, then, does neighbor-love take in this context? Certainly it involves seeking to transform our neighbor-relations so that my life does not harm or kill others nor threaten Earth's ability to sustain life. To transform neighbor-relations in the globalized world means to transform the economic policies, practices, and principles that shape those relations. *Avoiding the most dire damages of climate change "requires transforming the world economy at a speed and scale that has 'no documented historic precedent.'"*[24] This is the sacred healing journey on which we embark.

A necessary but truly uncomfortable step in that healing is facing what is beneath the surface of economic structures and practices assumed to be normal. If you are anything like me, you long to flee from such knowledge. However, James Baldwin's words ring true: "Not everything that is faced can be changed, but nothing can be changed until it is faced." So, let us muster the courage to face what most of us—me included—long to ignore. We do so in the next chapter.

* * *

Honoring Our Bodies

Pause. Breathe deeply. Ask yourself, How do I feel? What is my heart saying? Then notice from where in your body the answers emerge. Where are you tense? Allow the tense muscles to soften. Breathe a sigh of pleasure at that softening. Now rise and stretch as you are able. You might bend over slowly and, allowing your torso to incline forward, forward, forward . . . let your head sink down, hanging loosely. Breathe. Feel the sweetness of your back extending, unconstricting. When it feels right, lift again by pulling in your butt, keeping your back straight. Then draw back your shoulder blades deeply until the stretch feels rich and intense and let them slowly loose again. Now drink in a deep, slow, delicious lungful of air. Let it out slowly. Again. How beautifully ancient is that air. How sweet the drink of it.

Finally, you might thank the trees for giving you air to breathe. Thank the trillions of organisms that creep and crawl and swim around in your body—allowing your guts to work, your lungs to breathe, your eyes to see. What a miracle it is to be alive—alive as a teeming bustling communion of microorganisms "singing" together to keep your miraculous body animate.

Sacred Journey Journal

Please choose one of the following options that speaks to you:

- Return to the "astounding love story." Sit for a moment with it. Behold yourself with the eyes of "God" seeing you as primarily—first and foremost—precious, beloved. Imagine yourself embraced by this love. Perhaps it is a blue light, gentle wings, or a golden glow. Imagine knowing that it will never leave you, regardless of what you do or do not do. Imagine yourself at age ninety, still beloved. How do you feel? What images come to mind? Perhaps write or draw or hum the feeling.

- Imagine a precious young person in your life asking you some years from now, "Grandma/grandpa, auntie/uncle, elder friend, what did you do when my world was on the brink of destruction by climate catastrophe?" What do you hope you will say in response? Write it. What could you do now and in the future to make that response true?

- Listen for your inner voices. What are different parts of you saying? If there is a voice that you are not proud of, or even ashamed of, give yourself a break! Drop the shame. You are a human being. All of the following examples are within me. Is there a voice in you of powerlessness or hopelessness: "It is too late. We cannot really do anything to change the mess we are in." Is there a voice of avoidance: "Good grief, I just want to live my life. I don't have time for this. Let someone else handle these messes!" Is there a voice of fear? Confusion? Anger? Is there a voice of hope, determination, and courage? Write down some of the messages you hear within. All are important, especially the voices that could sabotage your power. Acknowledging them is the best first step to freedom from their influence.

CHAPTER TWO

The Haunting Pathos of Now . . . and the Courage to See

> Our children die of hunger because our land, which ought to grow food for them, is used by international companies to produce strawberries for your tables.
>
> —A Mexican strawberry picker speaking to a group of US citizens[1]

> In El Salvador, poverty means death, and people are not poor by chance. They are poor because the systems that make you wealthy make them poor.
>
> —Jesuit priest Jon Sobrino[2]

> Please ladies and gentlemen, we did not do any of these things [lead high carbon-emission lifestyles], but if business goes on as usual, we will not live. We will die. Our country will not exist.
>
> —Mohammed Nasheed, former president of the Maldives[3]

I HONOR YOU for the courage it will take to let the three voices above sink in.

We (you, dear readers, and I) share a holy longing. It is the longing to live in ways that give rise to joy and flourishing for all—ways of life that do not leave others in deadly poverty or threaten Earth's life-sustaining climate, waters, and air. It is a holy hunger. Yet, most of us—myself included—are, as of yet, ill-prepared to live into that calling. This chapter and those to come will help equip us to do so.

I beseech you: do not hear the voices of the strawberry picker, Jon Sobrino, Mohammed Nasheed, or this chapter itself as a call to guilt, blame, or shame. That would serve no good purpose and might nudge you into denial, powerlessness, or self-deprecation. I speak here from my heart and painful experience—the experience from my early years that I shared in the last chapter.

If you are going to trust me, you may need to know a little more of my story. For me, it is uncomfortable to share it. But I can hardly invite you on this journey without giving you some glimpse of what has made me who I am and set me on this path. The following scene occurred nearly a decade before the scene from my life in chapter 1:

> *I entered the auditorium, took a seat on the bleachers, and waited for the film to begin. An hour later my life had changed forever. I was fourteen. The film was an evening event at a regional gathering of the church-based youth organization in which I was an elected leader. That film tore my heart apart. It revealed that the multinational corporations providing my food were brutally exploiting people in Latin America and the Caribbean to maximize corporate profits. I was aghast at the suffering of those workers and its links to what we North Americans eat. It seemed so horribly wrong.*
>
> *I became an activist. But, as I learned more and more about the complex webs of exploitation enabling our extravagant consumption, I fell into self-hatred, shame, and powerlessness that lasted for years. It led to self-destructive behavior that could have cost me my life; my self-despising led me into the wasteland of severe anorexia. I felt I had no right to exist.*
>
> *Years later, the experience of God's grace in the woods by the creek began my healing journey. Decades of unraveling what had happened to my spirit and psyche taught me that such self-abuse has no place in the work of liberation and healing. It does no good and it does not reflect the great truth that, despite our complicity in unjust social structures, God holds us beloved, and we are to see ourselves as God sees us—precious beyond measure.*

This chapter is likely the most painful part of the book. When you face the realities named in it, you too may feel the sinking pull of powerlessness and shame. Or you may feel the seductive lure of denial and the false peace it offers. Perhaps they already, in a subterranean way, eat away at you. But I bid you to refuse these lures. Instead, we together will weave garments of collective power, power for building relationships that enable life with justice and joy for all.

So, read with raw honesty, courage, and hope. Know that you are not alone. Remember who you are: beloved beyond measure. If you like, you might start by taking a quick look at the stories that close this chapter. They foment hope.

As you read, recall two things:

- We are talking about the *impact* of our lives, NOT our intent. Most of us do not want to damage others or our home, Earth.

- We are talking about the impact of our *collective* lives, not our individual lives. As individuals or households, we do not have this devastating impact.

Fierce Urgency of Now

Today, we know the terrible truth: we, people of the high-consuming world, are living in ways that will destroy us if we continue them. By fueling climate change, we are dismantling the conditions for life in our habitat. And our lives as we currently live them depend on economic systems that impoverish many.

The 2019 "World Scientists' Warning to Humanity" of a climate emergency highlights the link between the world's high-consuming societies and the climate crisis. "The most affluent countries are mainly responsible for the historical greenhouse gas emissions and generally have the greatest per capita emissions." Among "profoundly troubling" factors, they note per capita meat production,[4] fossil fuel consumption, air travel, and per capita CO_2 emissions.[5]

This is not merely a matter of consumer choice. We are programmed by the marketing industry to consume as much as possible, to buy, use, throw away, and buy again. Brilliant minds are sucked away from meaningful purpose by the lure of lucrative marketing careers. While teaching undergraduate students, I recall the sinking feeling of realizing that some of my brightest students would dedicate their splendid minds to devising ways to make people buy more things. Moreover, countless products are designed to become obsolete ensuring more consumption and waste. My friend, Kelly Marciales, became a climate activist when her young daughter paused during a trip to the dump, gawked at the wasteland of discarded stuff, looked at her mother, and asked simply, "Can't we do better than this?"

And what of impoverishing other people? As Pope John Paul II and Pope Francis have pointed out, poverty is directly related to an economic order that enables a few to build vast wealth at the expense of other people and Earth.[6] Former banking executive Lim Mah-Hui cuts to the quick: "The disproportionate wealth of the elite still depends on cheap labour."[7]

This is a haunting reality if we take seriously the suffering that comes with "cheap labour." Cheap labor often means wages so low, and working conditions so dangerous, that people die.[8] It means leaving people in Detroit without jobs to access "cheaper labor" in Asia or elsewhere. But cheap labor builds profit and wealth for others. A 2022 report examining three hundred publicly held US corporations found forty-nine firms with a compensation ratio of over 1,000-to-1. What happens to families when parents are paid only eight dollars an hour? How can we accept this as normal? After giving a public lecture in Norway some years ago, a person in the audience approached me and said with sadness that inequity had risen in Norway so much that now many CEOs made as much as fourteen times what their lowest paid workers make. "Did you say fourteen times?" I asked him. "Yes," he nodded grimly. He was shocked beyond words when I revealed that some CEOs in the US make five hundred times what they pay their lowest-paid workers.[9] The words of Jesuit priest Jon Sobrino at this chapter's outset are searing. *"In El Salvador, poverty means death, and people are not poor by chance. They are poor because the systems that make you wealthy make them poor."*

Sobrino's words could be adapted to show the racialized nature of economic relations, and especially the racialized wealth gap, within the United States: "In the United States, poverty can mean death, and Black, Brown, and Indigenous people are not poor by chance; they are poor because economic systems have exploited them and excluded them from specific rights granted to white people." Even the conservative-leaning Brookings Institute reports "staggering racial disparities" in wealth in the US.[10]

Economic decisions throughout US history have produced searing poverty and inequity. American history begins with the brutal use of enslaved African people and stolen Indigenous lands to build the wealth of some white people. It continues with patterns of restricting land acquisition in the West to whites through the Homestead Act of 1862, the wrongful appropriation of Black farmers' land through discriminatory USDA lending policies and forced sales, the denial of home loans and college tuition to Black people under the GI Bill, and legal segregation that barred many Black people from higher paying jobs. Black poverty was further entrenched by policies excluding agricultural and service workers from the New Deal's Fair Labor Standards Act, redlining, gentrification, and racist hiring practices.[11]

I challenge you (as I challenge myself) to have the guts and the moral honesty to let the words of Sobrino, the Mexican strawberry picker, and Mohammed Nasheed take on flesh and blood. For white readers, may we recognize the horror of economic violence levied against Black, Brown, and Indigenous bodies and lives. For all, may we allow global and local realities such as these to sink in; refuse to be blinded by the denial and numbness that can protect us from the pain of knowing. What does it truly mean to our souls that the overconsumption by some (including oneself) is bought in part by life-choking impoverishment of others?

For me, the anguish of knowing was seared into my soul and began to shape my life as a young teen with the experience I described above. In the ensuing years, living and working in Latin America and working with people in Africa, Asia, and the United States has reinforced that ways of life in the US, and the economic policies that make them possible, contribute to severe, even deadly, poverty and ecological degradation. Never will I forget the face of the woman picking strawberries whose voice you hear in the quote above. She said those words to a delegation of local elected officials that I led on a trip to the Mexico-US border. Nor will I forget the woman living in my church in Seattle who had been forced into homelessness by a job that paid a minimum wage and failed to provide health insurance. The low wages paid to her and to countless others allow my consumer goods to remain inexpensive, enabling me to consume or save, but leaving many workers too poor to pay rent or to adequately feed their children. A companion from Africa recounted the devastation to innocent families in his country who had owned small successful textile businesses, when US companies dumped cheap textiles into their market. The small businesses were destroyed, and with them the owners' means of sustaining their families. Were my pension funds invested in those companies?

The moral and spiritual travesty crashes in upon us. The daily activities of the world's high-consuming sectors (both the ultrarich and the relatively well-off like me and many of my readers) are enabled by economic systems that exploit people and Earth. My daily doings that are inherently good—making dinner for my family, visiting a distant friend—in concert with billions of other such acts, through their carbon footprints, imperil life chances for my grandchildren. The utterly unthinkable is the normal. We are complicit *without* wanting to be, and often without knowing it, because the global economy hides the consequences from us.

This is a deadly disease. It defies the spiritual and moral calling to love neighbor as self, to live by compassion. Healing requires acknowledging the disease and choosing freedom from it. *This book is an invitation to do so, and to enter (or continue) a healing journey.*

The Vexing Complexity of Now

Matters would be much easier if there were clear "good guys" and "bad guys," if everyone was either exploited or exploiter, oppressor or oppressed. But that is not the case.

> *"Dr. Moe-Lobeda, you don't understand, I live in my car." The undergraduate student in my class suffered from the economic violence of a nonliving wage paid by a local fast food company. Yet her scholarship came from a fund invested in the mining company that poisoned the river in Zambia. "My cousin died after swimming in that river," declared a colleague from Africa whom I met years later. My student was* BOTH *exploited and the financial beneficiary of exploitation.*

Various forms of economic oppression intersect and intertwine so that many of us are both exploited and exploiter in the complexities of the global economy. The racialized nature of capitalism means that an African American woman in the United States may live in poverty due to the history of racist policies denying Black people access to wealth. Yet by buying a cellphone or computer, this woman "benefits" from exploitation of cobalt miners in the Congo.

This is not to say that we all are in the same boat. For example, in the present and the near future, North Atlantic countries are, in general, more protected from climate change than nations of the Global South. People with money are far more protected from economic exploitation and from death and destruction by climate change than are people without money. This means that, in general terms, white people are more protected than people of color. And—as we will see in discussions of climate debt, climate colonialism, and climate racism—some people are vastly more responsible for greenhouse gas emissions and financial profiteering than others. However, the fact remains that the lines of exploiter and exploited are far from clear at all times.

We All Are Damaged

For decades, I saw the predatory economy as injustice wrought by the "haves" upon the "have nots." In more recent years, I have realized that those of us who benefit materially from the extractive, exploitative economy, also are damaged materially and spiritually by it. That damage comes in many forms.

One is economic vulnerability. The United States' economy leaves not only poor people but also middle-income people materially vulnerable. A colleague from Switzerland was serving as a ministerial intern with my congregation in San Francisco. When she chose fear as the subject of a study group for young adults, I asked her why. She said, "Americans live in fear. You fear that you will lose your job or that you will become ill and not be able to afford good health care and necessary medications or that you will be impoverished in your elder years or that your company will be purchased by another and will downsize you out or that your rent will become untenable." Yes, an economy that prioritizes maximizing shareholder returns and CEO salaries over people's well-being leaves even those of us who appear to be economically secure vulnerable.

People of all economic strata are damaged, too, by the manipulation of our desires to foment buying. "Consumer culture … train[s] us from infancy to never cease desiring."[12] Maximizing growth and maximizing profit means convincing people to consume as much as possible—to buy, throw away, and buy again.[13] The irony is mind-numbing; maximizing consumption means spewing forth ever more greenhouse gasses. And that, in turn, is destroying the climate on which you, I, and our loved ones depend.

And what of the impact on our health, psyche, and spirit?[14] Advertising to children has exploded in recent decades.[15] How does the relentless marketing of junk foods impact the health of young people? How is our emotional health assaulted by the barrage of images telling us we are not good enough unless we buy some beauty product, article of clothing, or tech device? The sinister world of marketing to women, and especially the creation and exploitation of insecurities around women's body image, demonstrates the power and danger of psychological manipulation in marketing.[16] Cultivating body dissatisfaction through advertising is lucrative for the weight loss, clothing, and cosmetics industries. It damages us, and yet some people profit from that damage.

Wealth inequity itself damages. The United States has one of the highest levels of wealth inequity in the world. Ample evidence shows that happiness and sense of well-being are significantly lower in high inequity societies.[17] High degrees of inequality in a society negatively "affect the wealthy and the middle classes, not just the poor."[18] Studies show that "bigger inequalities make class and status more important and strengthen the belief that some people are worth much more than others."[19] People "in more unequal societies are less likely to trust others... are less willing to help each other," and "higher levels of inequality give rise to much more violence—as measured by homicide rates."[20]

Finally, we are damaged by the "moral injury" of knowing on some level that we are locked into ways of life that imperil Earth's life systems and damage so many people. What happens to us and to our souls over time when we profoundly, but unwittingly, violate our values in the way we live? What happens when we come to accept as *normal* the brutal exploitation that buys our cheap goods? What does it do to our integrity, to our capacity to live fully? Theologian Deanna Thompson notes that living in ways that betray one's values evokes shame.[21] Shame is a destructive emotion that eats away at one's core.

Constant and pernicious betrayal of values, especially when we feel powerless to do otherwise, corrodes. We may

- Deny or ignore the betrayal, numbing ourselves to escape acknowledging it—pretending, for example, that there are not violated workers behind the food I eat.
- Resort to declarations of moral outrage but avoid moral action.
- Hide under the cloak of privatized morality, doing good in charitable terms but sidestepping accountability for systemic injustice.
- Blame ourselves and become self-loathing.

Or we may join with others; learn the emotions, tools, and strategies to resist and rebuild; and enter (or engage more fully in) the great movement to build more equitable, earth-honoring, and power-sharing economies. That is my hope for you and for me. I believe that this will bring us all deep joy.

In short, the reigning form of economic life[22] and its basis in carbon-based energy poses five deadly dangers:

- It is destroying the climate conditions necessary for life on Earth to thrive and threatens many of Earth's other life-support systems.[23]
- It concentrates wealth in very few hands through policies and practices that impoverish many.[24]
- It undermines democracy (understood in terms of accountable and distributed power) by concentrating economic power in a few hands and "freeing" it from accountability to the wider public.[25]

- It damages those of us who profit materially from the global economy.
- It forces people into ways of living that hurt or kill others, thus betraying our sacred calling as human beings, heard throughout the world's spiritual traditions as a call to live by compassion (Buddhism and other Dharmic traditions), love neighbor as self (Judaism, Christianity, and Islam), or live in kinship with all creatures (many Indigenous traditions).

Therefore, living according to the norms and practices dictated by this form of economy poses profound moral problems for those of us who, like me, and probably many of you, benefit materially from it and have at least some capacity for seeking to change it.

For people following many of the world's religious traditions, the moral problem is also a spiritual problem. Living in ways that contribute to tremendous suffering and that undermine Earth's capacity to sustain life defies a central spiritual and moral calling of the human being. According to Jewish, Christian, and Muslim traditions, that call is to love God and to love neighbor as self, with a love that is both justice seeking and Earth honoring. From the perspective of Buddhism and some other Dharmic traditions, it is the call to live by compassion. For many Indigenous spiritualties, it is the call to honor Earth's web of life and to live as kin with other-than-human parts of creation.

Many voices of secular society have called for religious communities to step up to the plate in facing climate change and the economic systems that fuel it. Christian traditions bear a unique moral responsibility due to the church's role in establishing both the colonial enterprise and the norms of Western society that undergird today's economy. The church is called to rebuild economies that are more consistent with the "kindom"[26] of God into which Jesus calls us—a world in which all people have the necessities for fullness of life, none gain excessive wealth at expense of others, and Earth's life systems flourish.[27] Religious teachings and practices are rife with resources to heed this calling. We will consider them in part 4.

The spiritual problem extends beyond people situated in religious traditions. Complying with the dictates of a dangerously exploitative economy betrays values that many United States Americans hold dearly in private life but have learned to ignore in relationship to our collective economic lives. Three of those values are providing for a viable and healthy future for our children and grandchildren, contributing to the well-being of other people, and not killing people. Climate change—fomented by fossil-fueled capitalism—and economic exploitation betray these values.

The pathos of this contradiction stuns. It reverberates in my soul. I long for a future for my precious children and grandchildren, Lila Rose and Erik Gabriel. I would give my life to save theirs. And I hunger to be a force for good in others' lives. You, I imagine, share similar passions. This is the pathos, the hidden agony, of being players in economic systems that damage people and Earth's life-systems. This contradiction is the horror of the "good life."

How then shall we heal? That is the life-saving question we pursue herein. An initial step is to face squarely a paradox haunting the paths to healing economic life. Unfaced, this paradox may sabotage that healing.

The Paradox of Knowing

On the one hand, countless concerned people, including business people, faith leaders, activists, scientists, farmers, and others, have argued for decades that we must leave behind exploitative, extractive economic practices, policies, and principles.[28] A 2020 poll found that only about a quarter of US Americans "believe our current form of capitalism ensures the greater good of society."[29]

Yet—at least in the United States—the sense that radical change in economic and financial power structures at the macro level is impossible pervades public consciousness. "The economy as we know it is inevitable," common knowledge whispers convincingly in people's ears. "We have no power to rein in the forces behind this wealth-concentrating form of economic life." Indeed, corporate- and finance-driven capitalism would have us believe that this form of economy is inevitable. How would we produce computers, vehicles, food, clothing, medical supplies, and other necessities without it?

Simply stated, the paradox is this: the viability of life on Earth and the ability of societies to approach equity among people require radical economic change. Yet, many people assume—on an unconscious level—that such change is impossible.

A related paradox affirms this initial contradiction in the collective psyche: people of relative economic privilege in the United States (and elsewhere) need to recognize the extent of economic and ecological violence wrought by today's economy in order to collectively challenge it. Yet, the more people know, the more powerless and hopeless we tend to feel, and thus the less we are inspired to act. "It is easier to imagine the end of the world, than the end of capitalism."[30] The world we long for may seem an impossible dream. The iron-clad grip of financialized capitalism, having infiltrated into all arenas of life, seems impenetrable.

It is not. That is the premise of this series of books and online tools.

A Reality in the Making Now

Widespread systemic change toward more equitable, ecological, and democratic economies is not an impossible dream. It is a reality already in the making around the globe in a host of creative ways. Whether we find our way to economies of life that replace economies of extraction and exploitation hinges on how we respond to any sense of powerlessness and inevitability we feel. "Our choice," writes Eric Liu, "is about whether we as free people respond to a sense of powerlessness by claiming our full actual power—or by surrendering it altogether."[31]

Notice a crucial assumption that underlies my assertion: economies are shaped and maintained by human decisions and actions. Any system constructed by people can also be deconstructed and transformed by people. Human decisions and actions build and change economies. Let us sear this reality into our hearts and minds.

How will we do so? That is the question we pursue in this book series and its web-based resources. The reader will encounter people envisioning and acting toward a moral economy. Savor a tiny preview, starting in the Basque region of Spain:

Alasne awakens, snuggles her young son Markel. After breakfast, she heads off to work at a cooperative company of the Mondragon Corporation, a federation of worker cooperatives founded more than fifty years ago by a young Catholic priest. Alasne is new and relatively low on the pay scale, but she makes a good living: plenty to support her family. At Mondragon, she is an employee-owner, and the wage ratio is at most nine to one—compared to seven hundred, or even one thousand, to one in some US-based corporations. Instead, at Mondragon, profits go to employee-owners, capital improvements, and causes that the company supports. Alasne works at a banking cooperative within Mondragon. Mondragon is no small-scale entity. The seventh largest company in Spain, it hosts ninety-five cooperatives and fourteen research and development centers with sales in over 150 countries. It boasts annual revenue of fourteen billion and employs nearly one hundred thousand people. The businesses in this federation of cooperatives range from banking and insurance, to a wide range of consumer goods including construction equipment and industrial components, to services such as business consultancies, architecture, and engineering, to a university. Mondragon's mission includes personal and professional advancement of workers as well as community development, all in the name of transforming society through business development and employment. Mondragon is solidly committed to grassroots democratic management and fair distribution of wealth, proving that worker coops are viable on a large scale.[32]

* * *

Meanwhile, in the US...

His silver-gray hair practically glowed. The wrinkle-carved face grinned at the young man who held the door and then took his arm. They joined a small cadre from their congregation, merrily sipping away at steaming mugs of fair-trade coffee and glasses of locally produced wine. Celebration time it was. Last year for Lent, the whole congregation had studied Jesus's call to "Love your neighbor as yourself." The pastor convinced members to examine how their practice of the Eucharist (holy communion) and their brunch following the Easter sunrise worship service impacted neighbors far and near. This inquiry meant learning about the industrial food system, including the Farm Bill and trade policy. Whew! They decided to continue this study of neighbor-love way past Lent.

Congregants were horrified by what they discovered. The bread for the Eucharist (for them, the body of Christ) was produced by agro-industry in ways that created harmful greenhouse gasses and polluted land and water with pesticides and petroleum-based fertilizers. The eggs, sausage, and milk used for brunch came from Concentrated Animal Feeding Operations (CAFOs) that devoured water supplies, tortured chickens, spewed refuse, and introduced growth hormones, herbicides, and other chemicals into their bodies through their food. Moreover, the workers—mostly Black and Brown people including immigrants, minors, and prison labor—were underpaid, lacked benefits, often abused, barred from organizing, and sickened by exposure to toxins.

"What? This is how we celebrate the risen Christ?" they had wondered with heavy hearts. Some felt powerless. Joe, a middle-aged tech worker, said, "There's nothing we can do. This is just reality." Julia, a member of the congregation's young adult group, had nightmares about chickens in cages with their beaks cut off. One young couple, new to the congregation, declared, "Politics is not our thing. If this congregation carries on in this way, we will find a different faith home." "Politics is not your thing," responded the old silver-haired man with a piercing look, "but love is." The young couple stayed. It was that young man who took his elder's arm as they entered the room.

A year has passed—a difficult but also joy-filled year. The congregation has joined hands with a mosque, two synagogues, a Buddhist monastery, and a handful of Christian congregations to support two local CSAs, one of which is a small local Black-owned farm. One of the farmer-owners has joined the congregation. This new interfaith coalition also supports a worker-owned grocery store where these faith communities purchase food and other supplies. Through Bread for the World, the coalition actively advocates for changes to the Farm Bill to ensure policies that subsidize small farms practicing regenerative agriculture instead of large-scale monocropping by agribusiness. Most recently, the coalition joined the Fair Food Program (FFP) of the Worker-Driven Social Responsibility movement. The FFP, along with the Coalition of Immokalee Workers, launched the Campaign for Fair Food in 2001 to educate consumers about exploitation in food production processes. The result has been a powerful alliance of consumers and farmworkers that push retail food outlets "to only purchase from suppliers who meet fundamental human rights standards and to pay a small premium to help improve farmworkers' falling incomes. This alliance has won Fair Food Agreements with more than a dozen of the world's largest food companies."[33] Members of the congregation and their interfaith partners were thrilled to read a report in *Harvard Business Review* that the Fair Food Program is one of the "most successful social-impact stories of the past century."[34] According to the MacArthur Foundation, the FFP's work is a "visionary strategy with potential to transform workplace environments across the global [food] supply chain."[35]

But this is only the beginning. This vibrant interfaith coalition is now debating their focus for the coming year. Support the development of a local banking cooperative? Push for local legislation requiring the school district to purchase food from local, small farms? Advocate for living wages and benefits for agricultural workers?

* * *

Across the sea in Amsterdam...

Nine-year-old Fleur smiles as she ambles toward a playground made from recycled wood and metal. Her third-grade class had won the school's contest for "no-waste" classroom. Two years ago, her city, Amsterdam, made a radical leap to become the world's first city to commit to building a circular economy, eradicating waste and enacting public policy aimed at improving well-being, especially for marginalized people.[36] Their Earthshot Prize citation notes, "By 2030, the city will halve its use of new raw materials. By 2050, its economy will be fully circular.... Most importantly, the city is changing the way its residents and companies think, shifting people from a 'use-and-dispose' mindset towards one of 'rethink-and-reuse.'... Two years into the city's

'Circular Strategy,' things are already changing, with a blizzard of small acts leading to society-wide transformation."[37] Evaluation of the project "shows that the transition to a circular economy is realistic and profitable."[38]

Many such stories of hope and moral-spiritual power span the globe. You will read more of them as we move forward in these pages.

* * *

Honoring Our Bodies

How do you feel? Where is that feeling in your body? Where in your body do you feel tension? Fear? Guilt? Focus your heart on those parts of your body. Allow them to soften. Now gather a piece of paper, a pencil (not a pen), and a hard surface for writing. Walk to a mirror. Look at yourself for at least one minute. Recognize the courage that is in you. It took courage to face—even partially—the haunting realities described in this chapter. You have courage that you might not know you have. See it in the mirror. Breathe deeply.

Now, practice the art of contemplative drawing. Do not look at what you are drawing; the aim is not accuracy. The aim is to gaze softly and reverentially at what you are drawing. What you will draw—while sitting or standing in front of the mirror—is your face. Draw your beautiful soul shining out of your face. (You might recall the love story and be gazing at yourself as the beloved creature you are in that story.) Finally, choose one small item that symbolizes your courage. It must be small enough to carry in your pocket and hold any time that you want to be reminded of your courage. (It might take some time over the next couple of days for that object to appear to you. No problem. You will find it.)

Sacred Journey Journal

- What is one thing from this chapter that you hope to recall for years to come?
- As you move forward in this journey toward economic transformation, who is one person or small group in your life whom you might call upon to walk with you in some way? It might be to read this book with you and reflect on the Sacred Journey Journal responses. It might be someone with whom you would share what you are learning, thinking, and feeling. Ask yourself, Why would it be meaningful to share with this person or group? Consider inviting her/him/them to be part of your journey. What would prevent you from doing so? How might you overcome those obstacles?

CHAPTER THREE

The Life-Giving Potential of Now

> Ours is the first generation to deeply understand the damage we have been doing to our planetary household, and probably the last generation with the chance to do something transformative about it.
>
> —Kate Raworth[1]

> Tikkun Olam (a Jewish concept)—"to heal, repair, and transform the world... that's what you're here for."
>
> —Tzvi Freeman[2]

Disease and Healing

For nearly four decades, I saw economic injustice, racial injustice, and (later) climate injustice as forms of oppression. Over time, I came to see them also as forms of direct and indirect violence.[3]

In recent years, however, my understanding has expanded even further. I now see these realities also as matters of *disease in need of healing*. An economy that is rooted in and depends on the foul soil of exploitation and the relentless destruction of our habitat is a disease.[4] Economic lives that violate God's call to build life and societies based in neighbor-love and Earth care are diseased. Maximizing consumption and growth—despite the damage this causes—reveals a diseased understanding of economic life. Diseased too is the assumption that unlimited extraction of Earth's goods is normal, good, and even part of God's plan.[5]

Building the new economy—a moral economy—is a matter of healing. Healing from the unacknowledged violence of lifeways that violate deeply held values. Healing from the ways in which our identities and sense of self-worth are distorted by beliefs that we are what we own or how we look. Healing our children from their allegiance to companies and their logos. Healing from diseased and distorted relationships with Earth and with communities of people who are hurt by our economic lives. *This is a journey of healing as individuals, as societies, as a species, and as the Earth community.*

When my young son broke his arm in the mountains of western Washington, I journeyed with him into the closest small city. After hearing the emergency room doctor say that the break included a slightly dislocated bone, I asked, "Aren't you going to put it in a cast?" He said, "No, the human body has such a drive to heal that it will heal itself, and the bones will realign without the cast." They did. Since then, I have observed the abounding human drive to heal. It is afoot now in movements to build moral economies.

Ancient religious wisdoms, from multiple faith traditions, hold that the destiny of human life, and of the world itself, is union with the Sacred Source and communion among all. How striking that recent years have seen social theorists, physicists, biologists, and other experts making similar claims: that, in the imagery of physicist Karen Barad, the cosmos is wired for communion; connection is the orientation of life and of the very elements from which life emerged. We are swimming in a vast communion that we tend not to see![6] Said differently, we are created and called into "life together."

Communion or belonging is our destiny—not only after death but here on this Earth.[7] Theologian Willie James Jennings argues that what "God wants" for human beings is "communion," and that the "deepest struggle for us all is a struggle for communion," for "belonging." God's dream, he avers, is "to gather together ... reforming us as those who ... gesture communion with our very existence."[8] Jennings reflects the ancient faith claims within Judaism and Christianity that human beings are to shape our life together (our societies, communities, institutions, and households) in ways that build community. Eastern Orthodox theology—as explained by theologian John Chryssavgis—holds that humans are to think "in terms of communion. . . . That is our truth as humans within the created cosmos. That is what we are called to 're-member.'"[9] Biblical texts instruct the human creature into two primary paths of communion-building: serve and preserve garden Earth (Gen 2:15) and love your neighbor (Lev 19:18, Matt 22:39)—the two metarules that should guide our economic lives (the *nomos* for the *oikos*).

As human beings and communities, we are diseased when we do the opposite, making rules for life together (*oikonomia*) that enable some to maximize profit by exploiting others and Earth and that drive us apart, alienating us from one another and Earth. In our alienation from communion, I believe that God wills healing and restoration for us into the humankind God created us to be. That healing includes restructuring economic life to foster belonging instead of exploitation. It also means adopting profound shifts in our perceptions of the world.

This notion is the impulse behind this book and the subsequent series. If we are called into being for communion or community, and if the reigning form of economic life thwarts that, then we are also called to heal and transform economic life.

This healing journey to reform economic life is already afoot in our communities and around the globe.

The Life-Giving Potential of Now

Wearing jeans and tee-shirts, three women walked into the meeting room. A little boy bounced between two of them, swinging from their outstretched arms. I smiled, recalling my small sons bouncing that way when they were young. I had come to listen. And listen I did, carefully.

The women looked tired but resolute, even animated. They were employee-owners of Dulce Hogar, a worker-owned house-cleaning cooperative. Their caring for one another and their pride in their business was palpable. Building Dulce Hogar had changed their lives and the lives of their children. They had been mistreated while working for other house-cleaning companies that paid them only a small percent of what the customers paid, offered no job security, and gave them no control over their work schedules which wreaked havoc on their young families. Some had experienced wage theft. These women had hungered to have a say in their hours, working conditions, and wages.

This evening they met in their headquarters at Luther Place Memorial Church in Washington DC, the congregation where my family had been members for ten years and where my children had been baptized and nurtured by a loving community. Two decades after moving to the West Coast, I was back to learn.

In 2016 the community had launched a listening campaign guided by Bianca Vasquez and Kristen Kane, two young organizers connected to the congregation. The goal was to listen to neighbors, with a focus on the most marginalized, to build community and discern possible partnerships. At listening sessions with immigrant neighbors, the congregants and these neighbors shared deeply from their lives. They shared dreams for their families, their workplaces, and their communities. The congregants learned of their neighbors' experiences with low wages, wage theft, and abusive work environments.

The response was transformative. Some of the immigrant women collaborated to launch a worker-owned business, with the congregation as an ally. Dulce Hogar was born. Like most births, it was a challenge! Creating Dulce Hogar required enormous work, tenacity, and leadership. The women learned to run a business, to make collaborative decisions, and to find time while also raising families in an expensive city with little income. The effort was supported by the original listening team which had evolved into an incubator for cooperative business focused on economically marginalized people.

Inspired by the Dulce Hogar success and committed to a broad vision of worker ownership, the Beloved Community Incubator launched in 2018 as a nonprofit focused on incubating and supporting cooperatives.

BCI, still based at the congregation, now supports fifteen worker co-ops and solidarity economy organizations and has partnerships with worker-owned co-op networks around the country.[10] Countless people in the area now support these co-ops by employing the workers, buying their products, building relationships, and advocating for public policy that favors small business and worker ownership.

Alive as Human Beings Now

To be a human being is "rare, precious and infinitely meaningful."[11]

A sense of awe, mystery, and sacred purpose enveloped me while at a Buddhist temple some years ago, when I learned that to be human is "rare, precious and infinitely meaningful." While humans have a moral obligation to rectify the problems that we have caused (such as climate change and social injustice), that responsibility is not the only basis of our calling to build economies that serve life rather than wealth concentration. Another basis of that calling is a sacred invitation to use our rare and precious gifts as humans for the sake of the future. Those gifts include meaning making, cognitive brilliance, the capacity to hold paradox, moral consciousness, the ability to perceive systems at work, and the willingness to invest in shared narratives that enable broad cooperative moral action. Consider the last four of these gifts in reverse order.

Shared Narrative Imagination

Noah Harari argues that the most significant difference between humans and other animals are in the ways we act collectively. Humans, he writes, are the only animals that can cooperate both flexibly and in very large numbers (for good or for evil). According to Harari, this capacity stems from our ability to create shared stories that guide community action according to common beliefs and values. Shared stories can bend the course of history. Humans, he avers, use language not only to describe reality but to create new realities.[12] I refer to this as *narrative imagination*. We can recognize the culturally produced narratives that shape our lives, assess them, and—where needed—imagine new narratives. This story-creating and story-sharing capacity is tremendously powerful for enabling both individual and societal change.

Life-shaping narratives operate largely on subconscious—or semiconscious—levels. They function in us as individuals and as collectives. Recognizing them is vital.

I recall vividly the moment I realized the sabotaging power of a culturally produced narrative that was running my personal life—and the liberating power of naming it. I was pregnant and planning to return to full-time work at a job that I loved soon after our first child was born. A few months into the pregnancy, my partner told me that he would like to stay at home to be a full-time dad for the first year of our baby's life. My immediate response shocked me. I am a feminist who—one would expect—would welcome such a declaration. Our child would have a full-time parent—and a tremendously loving and compassionate one at that. Yet I was distraught and angered. "No!" my heart cried out. After days of processing this unexpected reaction, I realized that my psyche was living out the culturally produced *story* according to which I had been shaped: my partner should play the role that my father had played during my childhood—a man having a respected professional role in the world. Recognizing that I was embodying a particular cultural narrative, and that caving into it would damage my marriage and my child, enabled me to rewrite it. I realized what a tremendous blessing it would be for our little one to have an active, adventuring, nurturing man to be with him full-time in his first year of life.

The socially constructed story of white supremacy illustrates the power of narrative on the societal level. Kelly Brown Douglas traces the "story" and language of white supremacy from one of its roots in a first-century treatise written by the Roman historian Tacitus to the consequent murder of Black people by white people today. That story, especially as told in the last five hundred years, has convinced people that Black, Brown, and Indigenous bodies are less human than white bodies and thus less deserving of human rights. The story is a lie and has wrought unfathomable suffering. Its power lies in its invisibility to those not suffering directly from it. White people have tended not to see the myth of white supremacy that shapes everything from city planning and housing policy to entertainment, health care, policing, education, religious belief, and much more.[13] To debunk and refute that deceptive, terrorizing story, we must name it.

Recognizing the stories that shape us—as individuals and as societies—is key to assessing them. Do they tell the truth or distract us from it? Do they free us to be more compassionate, inclusive, courageous, and wise? Or do they trap us in fear, exclusiveness, and narrow allegiance to our perceived self-interest alone? Do they nurture our self-respect and sense of self-worth or lead us into self-loathing or self-aggrandizement? Do they limit our potential for the good or stifle it?

Seeing and assessing the malformative narratives of our cultures and lives is essential for escaping their stranglehold and for rewriting them. Seeing them can be a mighty challenge. They are hidden because they "do your thinking for you."[14] In nearly all of the classes I teach, I ask students to walk through their daily lives for the duration of the term with a question in mind: *"What in any given situation is uncritically presupposed to be inevitable, natural, normal, or divinely mandated that might be, in fact, just a cultural construct?"* This question is a tool for perceiving life-shaping stories, both personal and societal. It opens the door to assessing those stories and re-writing them. The ability to do so is one of the gifts of narrative imagination.

Culturally produced narratives function like "strings attached to our minds and hearts," pulling us this way and that.[15] They shape—among other things—our sense of what makes us worthy, and this sense impacts economic life. Imagine people freed from seeing their worth through the lens of possessing the right clothing, shoes, tech gadgets, cars, or homes. Culturally produced assumptions also shape our sense of what is possible. Raised in a neoliberal capitalist culture, it can be too easy to assume that this form of economy is inevitable.

Rewriting the dominant story about the purpose of the economy is integral to reshaping it. The purpose of economies, according to the neoclassical economic story, is to maximize the production and consumption of goods and services. Doing so is perceived as morally good. At this point in history, however, continuing to follow that purpose would destroy us. It presupposes no limits to growth and to Earth's carrying capacity. We will talk more in chapters 5 and 16 about the power of naming, assessing, and rewriting cultural narratives. For now, the point is this: our ability to build a moral economy depends on our capacity to identify and change the shared stories driving our current economy.

Systemic Imagination

Linked to this capacity for cooperation based on shared stories is our ability to see systems. The twentieth-century sociologist C. Wright Mills called this capacity "sociological imagination." I use the term *systemic imagination*. We can think about our lives not only as individuals but also as parts of the social systems through which we impact other people and Earth's web of life. We have the ability to consider, for example, the impact we have on others through systems in which we are players such as electoral systems, taxation systems, wage structures, policing practices, and energy policy. We can imagine serving the good not only in our interpersonal relationships, but also in our voting and other work that shapes our neighborhoods and cities. We can recognize that culturally shaped stories—operating on a societal level—can justify or normalize systems that might in fact be morally abhorrent. The story of women's inferiority or of Black people's inferiority, for example, justified systems that denied them the right to vote.

Seeing systemically is a vital human capacity for changing economic systems, policies, and practices. Indeed, the capacity to perceive the impact of social systems on our lives and to perceive the impact we have on other people through social systems, including economic systems, is key to assessing and changing those systems.

Moral Imagination

A third human gift is *moral imagination*. Human beings are blessed and cursed with moral consciousness, an awareness of "the tragic gap" between the way things are and the way things could and should be.[16] Moral consciousness is a blessing because it enables us to choose and press for the latter.

Moral consciousness requires truth-telling—acknowledging the consequences of life as we live it. This includes recognizing the horrors of climate change for millions who are not causing it, and admitting the anguish that results from unjust employment practices, polluted neighborhoods, and predatory speculative investment, to name a few examples.

Moral consciousness also requires moral imagination—the capacity to imagine how things could and should be, to recognize what is possible. Moral imagination is born of collective wisdom; we may come to see what is possible by witnessing the possible coming to life in what other people are doing or saying. For example, employee-owned businesses enable people to have control over their work lives and to share profits. I had always assumed them to be exceptions to the standard of large corporations not owned by their employees. The religious studies scholar-activist Jeremy Posadas, however, introduced me to the idea of a radical reversal. Imagine, he said, a society in which it was *normal* for businesses to be owned by the employees![17] He helped me to recognize a possibility that I had not previously realized.

Paradoxical Imagination

I recall the moment when I realized the gift of embracing paradox.

> *My mother had been killed three years earlier. My father, who had loved her dearly, was filled with grief. I hungered with all my heart for him to find happiness again. I stood with him in front of the door to a house. He knocked. It was the home of a woman he was seeing and who later would become his second wife. As she opened the door, I saw the joy on my father's face—joy that I had not seen since my mother's death. Contradictory emotions flooded my being: joyful relief that there was happiness in my dad's life again, and searing pain that the woman who stood before us was not my mother. (She did become, I must add, a beautiful second mother to me.)*

We humans are blessed with the capacity to embrace paradox. A key to moral power for rapid reorientation of economic life is to accept jolting paradox. "Paradox is ... a way of holding opposites together that creates an electric shock that keeps us awake."[18] Paradox allows truth-telling. Holding paradox allows us to acknowledge one truth without denying another equally valid, but seemingly opposite, truth. Paradox ushers into our lives possibilities that we once thought did not exist.

The experience of joy and sorrow illustrates the value of embracing paradox. Profound anguish and equally profound joy coexist. Grief need not destroy my joy, and savoring my joy does not require repressing my grief. Thus, there is no need to bury my grief, for example, about climate change.

Life is both brutal and infinitely beautiful.[19] I am awed and fed by life's beauty, while also being horrified by its brutality. Facing the brutality does not diminish the beauty. Relishing the beauty does not deny the brutality. I need not run from facing the brutalities undergirding economic life as we live it nor deny myself the joy of letting beauty flood over me.

Despair and hope reside together in my being. Yes, I do feel despair. Yet even while knowing despair, my hope is unceasing and endures beyond the despair. For me, this hope is a gift of faith. For many people it grows out of other soil. Different religious traditions articulate the grounds of hope differently. My roots in Christianity guide me to find hope in the resurrection promise that *all* of life will—in some way that we cannot fathom—arise from death and destruction. Nothing can ever "separate us from the love of God" (Rom 8:38–39).

What seems impossible is yet possible. Holding this paradox is, in my experience, at the heart of power for liberative change, including economic transformation. You might allow yourself to notice and accept other paradoxes that open doors for daring action.[20]

These Four Human Gifts Held Together

This basket of gifts, unique to the human creature, supplies us with collective moral capacity and obligation. Failure to use these gifts feeds moral inertia—doing nothing in the face of moral travesty. Moral inertia traps us, leaves us paralyzed in the "tragic gap" between the way things are and the way things could and ought to be. One thing is certain: a great enemy of creating more life-giving economies is the moral inertia of otherwise caring and compassionate people. Cultivating moral-spiritual power is at the heart of the journey to heal our economic lives. Thank you for daring to nourish and tend to that power in yourself and your communities.

The Life-Giving Potential of Now

September 24, 2022 slipped into history as an historic day. At the 77th session of the UN General Assembly, the president of Vanuatu called upon the nations of the world to establish a Fossil Fuel Non-proliferation Treaty to stop the expansion of all new fossil fuel projects and manage a global transition away from coal, oil, and gas. *EnviroNews Nigeria* reported, "The President of Vanuatu, Nikenike Vurobaravu, made the historic call on the floor of the UN General Assembly."[21] In his speech, President Vurobaravu said, "Every day we are experiencing more debilitating consequences of the climate crisis. Fundamental human rights are being violated, and we are measuring climate change not in degrees of Celsius or tons of carbon, but in human lives.... Our youth are terrified of the future world we are handing to them through expanding fossil fuel dependency, compromising intergenerational trust and equity. We call for the development of a Fossil Fuel Non-proliferation Treaty to phase down coal, oil, and gas production in line with 1.5 degrees Celsius and enable a global 'just transition' for every worker, community and nation with fossil fuel dependence."[22]

Momentum toward this moment had been building since 2015, when the Suva Declaration by Pacific Island Nations called for an internationally binding moratorium on the extraction of fossil fuels.[23] As reported by Canada's *National Observer*, "Vulnerable Pacific island states have long been at the forefront of climate leadership.... The Fossil Fuel Non-proliferation Treaty Initiative... launched two years ago with support from civil society organizations... has grown quickly, and today is backed by more than 750 organizations; cities like Toronto, London and Los Angeles; thousands of scientists, academics and politicians, as well as over 100 Nobel laureates."[24] "The proposal has also been supported by the Vatican and the World Health Organization."[25]

The treaty aims at international cooperation to stop new production of fossil fuels, phase out existing production, and fast-track a just transition to renewables for workers and communities. Citizen activists around the world are advocating for cities, states, and nations to endorse the proposal.

Within six months of this historic day, the Intergovernmental Panel on Climate Change (IPCC) released the Synthesis Report for its most recent Assessment. The Report confirmed what the Non-proliferation Treaty insists—that to limit global warming to 1.5 degrees Celsius and thus prevent catastrophic climate change, humankind must immediately begin its global transition away from fossil fuels. This includes ending new production, and financing the rapid and equitable shift to renewable energy sources.

On March 29, 2023, 132 UN member states voted to adopt a landmark Resolution for climate justice. The Resolution requests an advisory opinion from the International Court of Justice (ICJ), clarifying the legal obligations of states—under international law—to address climate change and the rights of people impacted, especially in more vulnerable developing countries. The initiative was inspired by young law students in the Pacific Islands who brought it to the Vanuatu government in 2019. The initiative has spurred a movement around the world. A ruling by the ICJ would lend enormous weight to developing countries' insistence that nations historically responsible for greenhouse gas emissions are obligated to help finance vulnerable countries' efforts to protect themselves, adapt, and recover from climate related disaster and transition to renewable energy-based economies.

The music of hope echoes from sea to mountain, from Indigenous Pacific Island climate warriors to scientists in India, from African tax justice advocates to North American advocates for universal income. Hope reverberates in the vast and multifaceted movement to build more equitable, ecological, and democratic economies at local, regional, national, and global levels.[26] These efforts go by many names, including the new economy, the solidarity economy, a democratic economy, economic democracy, the new democracy movement, an economy for life, an economy of life, a moral economy, the new restoration economy, a wellbeing economy, sustainable economies, local living economies, democratic socialism, green economies, climate justice economies, and a new financial and economic architecture.[27] Different parts of this movement focus on the ten different forms of action that we examine in chapters 8–17.

Many people involved in one dimension of this movement are unaware of its other dimensions and of its historical roots. All who work toward moral economies are more powerful if aware of their "companions" on the journey and of how their particular form of action opens doors for other forms to bear fruit. To that end, in this text we will trace five sets of connections, focusing on how they depend upon each other in vibrant, but often unrecognized, ways:

- Connections between various "forms of action" ("fingers on the hands of healing change").
- Connections between local, national, and global change.
- Connections between behavioral change, systemic change, and consciousness/worldview change.
- Connections between small practical steps and larger systemic change.
- Connections between resisting and rebuilding.

The story of the Fossil Fuel Non-proliferation Treaty demonstrates all of these connections.

In their book *Assembly*, Michael Hardt and Antonio Negri iterate the striking potential of now. Movements, they insist, have emerged with the potential to wrest power from the concentrated hubs of finance and corporate worlds to the multitudes. These movements do not all claim economic transformation as their primary focus. Some aim primarily at climate justice, others at racial justice or gender justice, others at decolonization, and still others at strengthening democracy.

The Life-Giving Potential of Now

The beauty and power of our moment emerges from the interdependence among efforts to usher in racial, gender, economic, political, and climate justice. To me, a hope-giving feature of our time in history is the convergence of these movements in a common sense that justice in any of these arenas requires economic transformation. To illustrate: the Black Lives Matter movement has brought into public awareness the racist nature of capitalism. This movement and other voices shed light on the first large-scale manifestation of the links between racism and capitalism in the cotton industry, sustained by the Atlantic slave trade, and highlight how those links continue to the current day. For example, the disproportionately white investing classes in the United States profit financially from enterprises that exploit Black and Brown lives. Those enterprises include privatized prisons that use prisoners, who are disproportionately Black, for cheap labor and—in some states—require monetary payments from them upon leaving prison; manufacture and sales of weapons that kill people of color around the globe; and companies using contingent labor and paying unliveable wages.[28]

Another example of the interface between related and overlapping social movements is climate justice.[29] The climate justice movement(s) arose because some efforts to mitigate climate change actually harm people who already are marginalized by race, class, and gender injustice. Climate justice insists that cutting greenhouse gas emissions cannot be done in ways that create "sacrifice zones" (areas in which some communities and their lands are damaged by the efforts).[30] Climate justice means freedom from pollution for farmworkers, industry laborers, miners, and the people who live proximate to oil refineries and other industries. And it means reparations for the climate damage done by high-carbon-emitting sectors. Also known as "loss and damage" payments, those reparations include assisting climate vulnerable communities and nations as they protect against and recover from climate induced disasters.

In short, much work of economic justice, racial justice, gender justice, climate justice, democratization, and decoloniality bears rich fruit in others among these six arenas. All reveal that unfettered neoliberal capitalism, like industrial capitalism, denies fullness of life for many and shapes life such that a few benefit from the exploitation of many. Since economic power translates to political power, we know that for democracy to be real, its principles of accountable and distributed power must apply to economic as well as political systems.

The impetus toward a moral economy includes many economists from various perspectives who agree that currently reigning economic theories and systems "are fueling the rise of a global one percent and simultaneously driving us towards climate breakdown and ecological collapse." Within the discipline of economics, an "emerging global movement of new economic thinking... is rising" to promote transition to economies that are regenerative, re-distributive, and democratic.[31] This amplifies the potential inherent in our time.

The convergence of movements creates new "conditions of possibility."[32] May knowing or knowing of this convergence nourish your hope and sense of moral-spiritual power. Religious or faith traditions hold invaluable resources for feeding and watering that power for the good, especially where doing so is fraught with apparently insurmountable obstacles.

Religion for Now: Transformative Power

Our goal should be to live life in radical amazement.... Get up in the morning and look at the world in a way that takes nothing for granted. Everything is phenomenal; everything is incredible.... To be spiritual is to be amazed.

—Rabbi Abraham Joshua Heschel

An extraordinarily potent configuration of forces presents formidable obstacles to the work of building moral economies. Some of those obstacles are intentionally constructed by brilliant minds for the sake of maximizing profit and concentrating wealth regardless of human and environmental costs.[33] Other obstacles are not the result of ill intent, but rather are grounded in the everyday lives of good people. Escaping the magnetic pull of "the way things are" is difficult. The force of habit and "paths of least resistance" are compelling.

Wherein lies the moral-spiritual courage to acknowledge the suffering caused by the reigning economic order and the complex forces aligned to keep things as they are? Where can we find the capacity to stare into the abyss and not be engulfed?

That heroic capacity is the purview of the human. It is our birthright. The beauty of the human shines in the moral courage to see clearly what threatens to burn the soul, strangle the spirit, and blow hope to the winds, and still choose to enact hope toward the good.

For this we must be well fed with moral, spiritual, and material sustenance. Here is the strength of truly supportive community and—for some people—the power of religion. Among fields of human endeavor, religion holds a particular sway. It has power to cultivate the good in people as well as the evil—and all that flows between the two. Religion has enspirited some of humankind's most noble moments, including the civil rights movement in the US; India's movement of nonviolent resistance to British colonialism; the South African anti-apartheid struggle; Buddhist resistance to imperial powers in Viet Nam; the abolitionist movement in the US; courageous freedom struggles in Central America, South America, the Philippines, and elsewhere; and resistance to Hitler's fascism in Scandinavian countries, France, Germany, and other lands.

The Life-Giving Potential of Now

The obvious irony screams. Religion often has done the opposite. In many of the instances noted above, religious groups also undergirded the oppressive structures. Religion has led people en masse to commit terrible crimes against humanity and against Earth. Religion—in particular Christianity—has contributed to the mindsets and worldviews that rationalize and justify the worst of human economic behavior: slavery, indentured servitude, prison labor, colonialization, theft of Indigenous peoples' lands, and devastation of air, soils, waters, and climate conditions. This reality led me, for many years, to walk away from Christianity. I was livid at the church (and rightly so) for its complicity in some of humanity's great atrocities, including the construction of race and white supremacy. (I describe how and why I "returned" in chapter 18). Any appeal to religion to serve the good must also acknowledge where religion has instead betrayed it.

Today, many in civil society are calling religious communities to step up to the plate in countering climate change. They suggest that the spiritual depth and moral energies of faith traditions are invaluable for addressing the climate crisis.[34] Countless religious groups have emerged that are dedicated to climate justice or other dimensions of ecological healing.[35] Several global religious networks vehemently critique the neoliberal global economy and support those building alternatives.[36]

In part 4, we will acknowledge the contradiction between religion as an ingredient in the exploitative and extractive ethos behind industrial and financialized capitalism and their predecessor, colonization, on the one hand, and religion as an ingredient of healing from that ethos on the other. We will consider gifts that religion can offer to the work of economic-ecological transformation. We will look at ways that faith communities can be seedbeds for the new economy.

Our Freedom, Our Right, Our Healing

The journey to economic healing is a journey of freedom—freedom from the logic of predatory capitalism; freedom from bondage to its stranglehold over our values and relationships; freedom from being forced, by the way economies are set up, to participate in damaging other people and Earth's life-support systems. We are not free if our way of life requires killing people and dooming our grandchildren.

It is also a journey to claim our right to live as we were created to live, as beings in community, both human and geoplanetary. Increasing evidence in the evolutionary sciences and ecological studies suggests that the basis for life's development is symbiosis and that humans evolved because of lifeforms' capacity to collaborate at the cellular, interspecies, and group levels. This idea resonates with claims that God's dream for all is communion.[37] The economy in which we are players denies us the right to live as positive members of the Earth community. We—creatures created and called to love—are cast into structured enmity with Earth and our neighbors.

Finally, this journey is one of healing from a diseased economy. We will heal from a diseased orientation that normalizes ways of life that destroy our habitat and other people. Healing is both of ourselves and of larger systems—personal healing and systemic healing.

Plastic brought home to me the reality of the ways in which my freedom and rights are betrayed. Single-use plastics are everywhere in this country—plastic silverware, cups, bags, medical packaging, even microparticles in our face cleanser and hand soap. A relentless stream of plastics. Imagine that plastic degrading into tiny particles. They make their sinister way into our water systems and from there into our bloodstreams and cells. Some filter with menacing invisibility into infants as they drink their mother's milk. Other plastics (including a plastic island the size of Texas) float on the oceans' surfaces and into the bellies of sea life eventually killed by it. Imagine the subsistence fisherpeople whose livelihood and food supply are then dangerously diminished.

The strategic marketing of single-use plastic packaging is ominous:

> In 1956, Lloyd Stouffer, the editor of the US magazine Modern Packaging, addressed attendees at the Society of the Plastics Industry meeting in New York City: "It [is] time for the plastics industry to stop thinking about reuse packages and concentrate on single use. For the package that is used once and thrown away, like a tin can or a paper carton, represents not a one-shot market for a few thousand units, but an everyday recurring market measured by the billions of units." Stouffer was speaking at a time when reuse, making do, and thrift were key practices reinforced by two US wars.[38]

Creating single-use plastic products was a tool for maximizing profit. Stouffer's vision was realized. We live in a world of single-use plastic. My right and freedom to live as a positive member of the Earth community is betrayed by the colonization of life by single-use plastic. Through it, I am damaging Earth's ecosystems. Building economic systems that do not reward industries for such predation on Earth's ecosystems is a move to reclaim my freedom and rights—and a move towards healing.

In Closing

I offer to you the image with which we began in chapter 1. Have you ever seen that dance in the sky—a flock of birds soaring together in one direction when, abruptly, in a grand and graceful arc, they veer off into an utterly different direction? Such a radical shift is the challenge we now face. It is a central moral and spiritual calling of our time. How will we garner the moral courage, spiritual strength, political will, and inspired wisdom to turn our economies around and fly in the other direction? Grappling with this book and its on-line resources—and perhaps the subsequent series—is a step on that journey.

At the heart of this calling is healing. Healing our selves, our souls, and our structural relationships with neighbors and all of creation. Healing in the direction of communion—a holy communion that is messy, imperfect, clumsy, and perhaps tentative, yet far closer to fullness of life for all than is life under predatory capitalism. We now step (fly) more fully into that sacred journey.

* * *

Honoring Our Bodies

It is time for a beauty walk. It would be lovely to give yourself some time for this—perhaps twenty minutes. But if that cannot be, no problem; even a two-minute beauty walk will feed your body-soul. Step outside if possible. If not, inside will work. Walk slowly and gaze at the beauty around you. Soak it in. Let it filter into your pores and cells. It may be visual beauty—the sky, leaves blowing in the wind, a tiny plant rising through a crack in the concrete, the face of an elder walking down the sidewalk, a particular color or shape or photo in your home. It may be beauty of touch—the breeze on your skin, the sun on your back, the feeling of the soles of your feet caressing Earth. It may be the beauty of sound—music, birdsong, laughter. It may be beauty of smell—the scent of plants, of coffee, of food cooking in the apartment next door. It may be beauty of taste—perhaps you take with you a piece of ripe fruit or a special tea. You are surrounded by beauty—let it feed you.

Sacred Journey Journal

What is one narrative that functions in your life in a harmful way, "pulling you this way and that like a string attached to your mind and heart?" It may be one operating in your personal life (such as a narrative insisting that your body is ugly or that people would not love you if they really knew you). Or it might be one functioning on a societal level (like the narrative of white supremacy). Write down, sketch, or diagram this narrative, and what harm it causes to you or others. Nourish your power by rewriting that narrative in a life-giving or freeing way. What does the new narrative say? How might this new narrative be healing for you? (You might begin by rereading the brief section on "Shared Narrative Imagination.")

II

Treasure Trove of Good Medicine

CHAPTER FOUR

Morally Empowering Seeing

> Attention or seeing is "the effort to counteract illusion ... false pictures of the world ... to come to see the world as it is."
>
> —Iris Murdoch[1]

IMAGINE YOU AND trusted friends gathered around a fireplace for a hearty, simple meal. You and your companions hunger to live in ways that help people and your planetary home flourish. You grieve for millions of climate refugees fleeing to the shores of lands they do not know. You long for your children and other young ones to have a future with decent air, water, and food.

Now, imagine your daring band of friends opening a treasure chest of medicine for healing toward a moral economy. Medicine is a revealing metaphor. Medicines or remedies do not work alone. A body does not heal from grave disease with a single remedy. The medicine of adequate rest works together with medicinal tea, abundant water, healthy food, prescription medications, loving attention, and more.

Let us now unwrap one of these treasured medicines. I call it morally empowering seeing or critical mystical vision. This way of seeing has freed me to face the terrible truths of economic and ecological injustice woven into my life while maintaining hope and a sense of moral-spiritual power to work toward change.

In chapter 2, I shared about my own descent into despair, self-loathing, and powerlessness as a young teen when I learned that my food comes through systems that brutalize people in Latin America and the Caribbean. Decades of unraveling what happened to me in those years of despair have taught me this: while I do believe it is a moral obligation of people who benefit from systemic injustice to see it clearly, such awareness can be devastating and hence dangerous. My seeing led me straight to the wasteland of despair and shame. I do not wish that desolation on anyone. I believe, therefore, that clarity about "what is going on" must be accompanied by seeing something else as well.[2] In this chapter, we unfold that "something else."

Our quest is for a way of perceiving reality that is medicinal—one that will help us heal so that our lives are not toxic to our planetary home, and our material well-being is not bought by the blood of others. What would enable recognizing the devastating impact of our current economic reality without sinking into denial or self-loathing or powerlessness? What conditions of seeing will lead from awareness to liberative action?

After introducing the concept of morally empowering seeing, we will look briefly at each of its four parts. The first is seeing "what is going on." I call this truth-telling. The second is seeing "what could and should be," that is, more equitable, compassionate, and ecologically sound alternatives. I think of the third mode of perception as "mystical vision." By this I mean recognizing sacred powers at work enabling life and love ultimately to reign over death and destruction. And the fourth? It is seeing the infinite and life-giving beauty that imbues and surrounds us.

This fourfold vision is subversive. It exposes and disrupts "the way things are." It reveals a better future in the making and breeds hope and moral-spiritual power for moving into that future.

A guiding challenge runs through these four forms of seeing. It is to see with both fierce, raw honesty and also with generosity and grace. Yes, we are complicit in structural violence with terrible consequences, but simultaneously we are beloved beings with boundless capacity for compassion and the work of justice-making love.

Seeing What Is: Truth-Telling

Ours was a time when most forms of art and literature were drawn into the modes of concealment that prevented people from recognizing the realities of their plight.

—Amitav Ghosh[3]

There is no getting away from the fact that humanity needs to come to grips with the truth if it wishes to contain a monster of its own creation.

—Christiana Figueres and Tom Rivett-Carnac[4]

The great liberation theologian Dorothea Soelle once said that an unjust society must hide the suffering of its victims. James Baldwin said as much in his call "to bear witness, to allow suffering to speak, to tell the truth" of the suffering wrought by white supremacy in the United States.[5]

To build a moral economy, we must "tell the truth" about the "the incalculable anguish"[6] and the ecological peril caused by economic practices and policies common in the current economy. And we must unmask the links between that anguish and peril on the one hand and "our" wealth and material comfort on the other. Both—the anguish and its connection to our lives—are crucial aspects of truth-telling about "what is."

Honesty of this sort may seem to be a breeding ground for hopelessness. To the contrary, it is an excursion of hope and into hope. The quest itself is born of the firm conviction that human beings bear moral power. It is the power to see and resist what is wrong and destructive. Using that power requires stark honesty, truth-telling. It is subversive honesty. Some see this power as the enlivening breath of the Sacred within and among us.

The purpose of this truth-telling is NOT to cast shame. Rather it is for the sake of building more humane, life-giving, and equitable alternatives.

A brilliant and courageous Filipina theologian once described how impoverished women in her country suffered at the hands of the exploitative global economy. When someone in the audience, disturbed by the account, confessed "I find this nauseating," the theologian acknowledged the man's honesty and replied, "I am truth-telling." The truths about human anguish caused by a predatory economy, and the links of that suffering to our material wealth, are hard to face. When I pick up my smartphone, I do not want to see the rape, child trafficking, brutal working conditions, forced labor, and warfare fueled by coltan mining in the Democratic Republic of Congo which supplies much of the global electronics industry.[7]

From such truths we long to flee. While I was teaching at Seattle University, the university decided to focus on the links between wealth and poverty as a theme for the year. Professors were asked to address this theme in courses, and at the end of my ethics course, one student declared, "There is no value in this course at all, because I do not believe there are links between wealth and poverty." He was a finance student whose sole aim was to make money, and he did not want to see any connection between his goals and the poverty and suffering of other people.

Art—in its many forms—created by people negatively impacted by neoliberal capitalism powerfully reveals the realities of "what is going on." I learned about art's impact more than three decades ago at a church in El Salvador. The display of truth-telling artwork depicted young bodies tortured by the repressive and terrorizing regime supported by the United States and working to protect US corporate interests in that region. Those people were "sacrifice zones." Their deaths were considered either necessary or immaterial. Never will I forget those paintings. They fuel my commitment to build economies based on mutual flourishing rather than on exploitation and violence used to maintain it.[8]

Truth-telling—getting a clear sense of what is going on—is vital for designing better policies and practices and for building moral accountability. Carbon inequity illustrates both the moral accountability and the problem solving engendered by truth-telling. In both senses, recognizing carbon inequities is central to addressing the climate challenge."[9]

Carbon inequity is calculated along three axes: inequity based on company emissions, individual emissions, and national emissions. Consider each briefly.

Companies: The 2017 Carbon Majors Report shows that one hundred companies are responsible for 71 percent of global industrial GHG emissions since 1988.[10]

Individuals: The "World Scientists Warning of a Climate Emergency" vividly paints the unequal carbon emissions between relatively wealthy and impoverished individuals: "The climate crisis is closely linked to excessive consumption of the wealthy lifestyle."[11] (Note that in global terms, the "wealthy" includes middle strata people living in industrialized nations.) The scientists highlight the high emissions produced by meat production and air travel in particular as well as other uses of fossil fuels. According to the World Inequity Report, "the richest 10% of people on the planet are responsible for nearly half of all carbon emissions."[12]

Nations: The comparison between nations is reported by the Club of Rome: "Today's rich countries are responsible for nearly 80% of all human-related carbon emissions from 1850-2011." Yet, these countries "account for only around 14% of today's global population."[13] Let that disparity sink in. Those emissions are destroying the habitat, of humans and others.

This kind of truth-telling opens doors to more effective public policy for reducing emissions. It also lays the groundwork for holding high-emitting countries, sectors, and industries morally accountable. That accountability—translated into public policy—is a matter of life and death. It means, among other things, that high-emitting nations are morally obligated to higher levels of emissions reductions than are low-emitting nations. And it means that high-emitting nations ought to finance climate change adaptation and mitigation in low-emitting countries. These are primary sticking points in international negotiations around climate policy, and are key points of advocacy for people committed to climate justice. (We will come back to this in chapter 10.)

Truth-telling about "what is" necessarily includes seeing the historic roots of our current realities. For example, we must tell the truth that colonialism was (and neocolonialism continues to be) an environmental assault that leaves many colonized lands and peoples more vulnerable to climate change.[14]

Seeing those historic roots reveals the intersection of economic injustice and racial injustice, and the ways in which both are intertwined with ecological destruction. These links are not always obvious in the public consciousness. Yet they are crucial for building equitable and ecological economic life. Law professor John A. Powell says it clearly: "Deeply structured economic inequity cannot be fully addressed in the US without understanding how race and racism has shaped our political economy."[15] [16]

We—at least I—often flee from seeing fully the links between my life and the ecological peril and human suffering that results from it. How is that moral oblivion possible? Brazilian feminist theologian Ivonne Gebara offers a clue.

Social evil, she writes, escapes into obscurity by being accepted as fate, or as God's design, or as punishment for sin, or as the normal. It is "not easy to spot evil's presence," she notes, when it is "intermingled in our culture, education, and religion—events or behaviors regarded as normal, common, even good."[17]

Let us heed her prescient warnings. I invite you in the days to come to notice where the consequences of a predatory economy may be hiding behind masks of the normal, God's design, necessity, or fate. To illustrate: It may seem normal, inevitable, or even good that most of "us" drive around individually in large, heavy vehicles that spew enormous quantities of greenhouse gasses. Some years ago, Amsterdam utterly dislodged my sense of this as normal. While there I beheld city streets filled with seas of bicycles, bike parking lots, and people carrying huge loads on their big, old bikes! Imagine that you are a person on Mars looking down on Earth, gazing at cities filled with large metal vehicles holding single persons. With shock, you wonder, "Are these earthlings a suicidal species? How is it that they transport themselves individually in those huge containers that are destroying the climate conditions that give them life?" It would be perfectly possible, I realized after about one minute in Amsterdam, to recalibrate what is normal. Normal could be cities in which one stepped onto widely available, public, electric trams or settled into very small electric transport pods or (for able-bodied people) onto bikes or scooters. (Remember this illustration moving into chapter 5 when we will talk more about the role of consciousness change in economic transition.)

Truth-telling about Earth's climate is key to our survival as a species. Our era "will come to be known as the time of the great derangement," suggests award-winning Indian literary figure Amitav Ghosh. This is a time, he avers, in which humanity has been "drawn into the modes of concealment that prevented people from recognizing the realities of their plight."[18] Yes. Therefore, learning to reveal what has been concealed is crucial. That is the work of "seeing what is." It includes re-cognizing (bringing to the surface of our cognition) our unacknowledged assumptions about economic life. We have been taught, for example, to assume that maximizing profit within the limits of the law and buying products as inexpensively as possible are normal, natural, even preferable practices that ultimately make us all better off.

The sacred work of truth-telling is a boundless task. It is the work of a lifetime and is filled with beauty and goodness. It is both necessary and perilous. Perilous because it can suck us into despair or self-condemnation. Necessary because failure to see what is going on prevents effective action. Twenty laureates of the distinguished Blue Planet Prize state in a report that to prevent "climate catastrophe... will require recognizing, understanding, and acting on interconnections between the economy, society and the natural environment... redesigning the economic system... and behavioral change." Then with great insight they insist that *inadequate understanding of reality is preventing our acting.*[19] That is, they call for truth-telling about what is.

Seeing What Could Be and Is in the Making: Healing

If there is any one thing that global warming has made perfectly clear, it is that to think about the world only as it is amounts to a formula for collective suicide. We need, rather, to envision what it might be ... to imagine other forms of human existence.

—Amitav Ghosh[20]

Gazing too long into these economic fires may leave us burning with shame, guilt, powerlessness, hopelessness, or a toxic mixture of all four. Yes, have the courage to see the fire, *but look not on it without gazing also at the amazing healing underway and the hope that it spawns.* Be sure to see also the antibodies, the cells, the muscle and sinews that are tenaciously gravitating toward healing. They bring healing from a "civilization based on wealth accumulation to one that is life-affirming: an ecological civilization."[21]

What may seem impossible is not. In early nineteenth-century United States, most aspects of economic life were in some way linked to slavery. The institution of chattel slavery seemed (at least in the minds of many white people) inevitable, normal, reality, or even God's will. By midcentury that had changed. Enough people said, "No, this is NOT inevitable, normal, natural, or God's will. It is wrong. We can change it."

Seeing what could be—seeing healing in process—is like drinking fresh, cool sparkling water when one is gasping with thirst. It entails acknowledging

- key reasons why building more equitable and ecological economic life on a systemic scale is possible now even if it was not in the past;
- the worldwide organism of healing—that is, the movement of people headed tenaciously toward more equitable, ecological, and democratic economies;
- one's own unfolding place and roles in this organism of healing and the role that one's communities (religious, educational, neighborhood, vocational, etc.) may play.

But first, do have a brief taste of the feast! Glimpse what happens when healing is underway. Meet the people in West Detroit and feel the joy bouncing off the walls of their gathering place. You will find them at the outset of chapter 8. Turn next, for just a moment, to the first couple of pages in chapter 6. Encounter there folks whose lives have been restored through "community wealth building." Imagine lives being transformed as that model becomes more mainstream. Now, we touch on the three dimensions of seeing what could be that are noted above.

Building More Equitable, Ecological Economic Life Is Now More Possible

A fascinating set of dynamics converge to make our time ripe for restructuring economic life. This is cause for celebration. I hope that recognizing this convergence will water seeds of hope in your soul.

One dynamic is the increasing public dissatisfaction with capitalism. According to the Pew Research Center, among the youngest voters (ages 18–29) in the United States, more people view socialism positively than view capitalism positively.[22] A Harris poll found similarly that "Generation Z has a more positive view of the word 'socialism' than previous generations and—along with millennials—are more likely to embrace socialistic policies and principles than past generations."[23] David Callahan, cofounder of Demos, writes, "Contemporary capitalism is under growing fire, with a rising chorus of critics making four main points: first, that the current incarnation of capitalism produces too much inequality; second, that it is too unstable and prone to crisis; third, that capitalism in its current form is at odds with the planet's ecology; and fourth, that capital has hijacked government, subverting democracy and winning too many special favors." Callahan goes on to note a fifth critique: "That extreme market forces are corrupting us *as individuals*—morally and ethically."[24] New York Times commentator David Brooks notes that "since the financial crisis of 2008, more and more Americans have concluded that the US system needs fundamental realignment."[25] The Club of Rome in discussing its widely acclaimed postpandemic release *Earth4All: A Survival Guide for Humanity*, notes that "74% of people in G20 countries want transition to wellbeing economies."[26]

A second and related dynamic is the growing number of critiques of capitalism from *within* the corporate world and the discipline of economics. Marc Benioff, the co-CEO of SalesForce, declared at the 2020 World Economic Forum, "As a capitalist, I believe it's time to say out loud what we all know to be true: capitalism as we know it is dead." Earlier, in a 2019 *New York Times* opinion piece, he had written,

> Capitalism as it has been practiced in recent decades—with its obsession on maximizing profits for shareholders—has also led to horrifying inequality. Globally, the 26 richest people in the world now have as much wealth as the poorest 3.8 billion people, and the relentless spewing of carbon emissions is pushing the planet toward catastrophic climate change. In the United States, income inequality has reached its highest level in at least 50 years, with the top 0.1 percent—people like me—owning roughly 20 percent of the wealth while many Americans cannot afford to pay for a $400 emergency. It's no wonder that support for capitalism has dropped, especially among young people. To my fellow business

leaders and billionaires, I say that we can no longer wash our hands of our responsibility for what people do with our products. Yes, profits are important, but so is society. And if our quest for greater profits leaves our world worse off than before, all we will have taught our children is the power of greed.[27]

While one may question whether Benioff's practices match his words, his articulation marks a potential for change from within.

Benioff is not alone. Indeed, a rising moral impetus from within the corporate and finance worlds is one gateway for protecting people and ecosystems from unrestrained corporate profit seeking.[28] Consider the growing movement by corporations to transition to worker-owned entities. Growing too is the movement to establish (or transition to) B Corporations.[29] In contrast to conventional corporations that only measure the financial bottom line, Certified B Corporations are measured by a triple bottom line: ecological, social, and financial.[30]

A third dynamic that makes economic transformation more possible today is a growing awareness that the relentless drive to maximize profit (especially by fossil fuel industries and industrial agriculture with its petrochemical components), and the throw-away consumerism required for that profit, are fueling climate change. Many voices, including scientists and economists, argue that the economy as we know it has put us on a "collision course with our own extinction."[31] More and more, the movement to curtail climate change is converging with movements to build economic equity.

The fourth dynamic is the movement of some alternative economic models from the margins to mainstream economic thought. As noted by the United Nations Research Institute for Social Development, "Once positioned on the radical fringe or considered not to have systemic or structural significance, alternative ways of thinking, living, and organizing—including alternative economies such as the social and solidarity economy—are attracting more attention *within mainstream knowledge and policy circles.*"[32]

Yet another dynamic (as noted in chapter 1) is increasing acknowledgement that racism and capitalism are inextricably linked. Early capitalism in the United States, for example, was inseparable from the enslavement of African people and the genocide and land theft executed against Indigenous peoples. Today, as we have noted, the wealth gap in this country is highly racialized, and many involved in social movements for racial justice understand their movements to include economic justice.

Sixth is the historic knowledge that societies are capable of pivoting their economies almost instantly if the need is recognized by political leaders and the public to be a matter of dire urgency.[33]

Finally is the breadth, depth, number, and vast diversity of people and movements throughout the world who see economic transformation toward more equitable, ecological, and democratic economies as integral to their goals. These include racial justice, climate justice, water and food justice, and decolonial movements. The array of people finding alliances and supporting each other's work is a feast.

These seven dynamics converge at our moment in time. Together they create the hope-giving potential of now. It is possible that the world that we pass on to our children and grandchildren may not be ordered and shaped by the logic of predatory capitalism.

The Worldwide Organism of Healing—the Movement of People Headed Tenaciously toward Moral Economies

Let us look more closely at the last dynamic identified above. What a brilliant dawn it heralds. World renowned scientists, grassroots activists, environmentalists, legislators at local and national levels, public health professionals, homemakers, students, investors, educators, lawyers, elders and youth, Indigenous and settler people, scholars, people of countless ethnicities, global and local faith communities, business leaders, subsistence level farmers, and so many more are joining in a fervent commitment to shift from economies based on extraction and exploitation to economies based on ecological wholeness, equity, and democracy. In my experience, becoming aware of this convergence, and seeing the astounding presence of it on every continent is food for hope.

We meet many of the players within these movements in more depth in part 3. For now, take a moment to sample the beauty of this intercontinental, intergenerational, multiethnic, interreligious, cross-class network of healing. To begin, settle in for a story.

Monica and some friends in her congregation were fed up. They were fed up with seeing the lines at their church's food bank grow longer, fed up with knowing that kids in their city were going hungry, fed up with realizing that the carbon footprint of their own food was destroying their future, fed up with knowing that parents in resource-rich countries of Africa had no money to feed their children because global companies had absorbed the profit from their resources and their labor. They were furious knowing that the bank was investing their money in global agribusiness that wiped out small-scale farms around the world and guzzled petrochemicals—and that some people were getting richer as a result. They felt like their food, cars, and so much more was covered with blood, and they were sick of it. "Enough!" they declared. "Enough of this madness." They took the flock of birds as their inspiration for changing direction, and the Hebrew prophets, including Jesus, as their guiding lights. "This coming year," they decided, "we are dedicated to healing these broken relationships imposed on us by 'the way things are' in this economy." They dedicated twelve months to a collaborative reset; they would reorient so that God's call to love neighbor as self could become the basis for their economic lives. They knew full well that this transition entailed addressing root causes of the wealth gap and of ecological degradation, not just fixing the symptoms. And they knew also that they could not do the work alone or even as a whole congregation. No, they would need to work with others!

First, they decided to "build a team." They called it "Love in Action: Eco-economic Justice." The team orchestrated a listening campaign in the congregation and in the surrounding community. Each of the members scheduled one-to-one conversations with more than twenty individuals or small groups, asking how they felt about their economic lives and the bigger economic picture. The Love in Action team wanted to know whether other people also were fed up with being part of systems that seemed to be making some people poor and others rich and that were hastening climate change.

After three months of listening, they invited more folks to join in collaborative planning, formed a study group, and conducted some basic training in talking about controversial issues as people of faith. With this foundation, the congregation mapped a path forward. They decided to act for change in three arenas, all aimed at economic-ecological justice: lifestyle changes for households and their congregation, systems change, and change in worldviews including theology.

Looking back three years later, Monica grins:

"We had no idea what astounding friends we would make along the way. For many of us, life will never be the same, and we now have companions around the globe. My daughter Sarah is 'best friends by Zoom' with a young woman in Samoa who calls herself a 'climate warrior.' As a result—thank God—Sarah is much less depressed about climate change. She is helping to start a 350.org chapter in her high school.

"Our church joined an interfaith coalition pushing the city to adopt a Community Wealth Building plan modeled after the 'Cleveland Model,' and our mayor has met with the minister for Community Wealth Building in Scotland.[34] It feels like a minor miracle, but one part of that plan will be requiring city offices to do their procurement with local worker-owned businesses where possible. You know in

Morally Empowering Seeing

Cleveland, the hospitals and universities now use the local Evergreen Cooperative Laundry, rather than big global corporations to do their laundry. Can you imagine what that means for the worker-owners? We talked with some of them. They had been jobless before, partly because some were formerly in prison and that makes getting a job horrible. A guide from the Democracy Collaborative is helping our coalition imagine and organize.

"Our legislative advocacy team hooked us up with the state-wide interfaith advocacy group, and with them, we helped to pass a living wage law. In the coming year, the aim is local legislation calling on the school districts to buy food from local farms and to prioritize the network of Black-owned agricultural coops. It might mean the kids can actually visit the farms like they do in New Mexico.[35]

"Our next move, and we are launching it in about a month, is to join the Fair Food Program and use its model of 'Worker-Driven Social Responsibility.' Yes, I know it is a long name, but you would not believe what it enables us to do. We can work with workers all over the world to get fair wages and decent working conditions! No more toxic worksites! We want to get the state to sign on. Who knows.

"It has meant a lot for our worship life here, and for confirmation classes and adult education. The kids in confirmation did a two-month thing on what it means to follow Jesus's call to 'love your neighbor as yourself.' As a result, many things changed. Believe it or not, the kids demanded that we do a 'justice audit' of our eucharistic practice to find out if the bread and wine, candles, cups, flowers, and all were made in ways that hurt Earth or people. Well, that changed things around here. It also really opened people's eyes. And since the confirmation class insisted that Earth is also our neighbor (they got this from the Bible), we decided to 'fast' from single-use plastic for Lent. Most of us have just kept on with that.

"Now people keep coming up with more ideas—join the state-wide Poor People's Campaign, connect with the Solidarity Economy Network, divest from fossil fuels. But ... one step at a time, I say—or maybe a few steps at a time.

"Sometimes it has been hard. People want to go in different directions and we have a bit of trouble getting agreement. But it is worth it; we are closer as a community than we have ever been and it seems like other people are finding out about this 'Love in Action: Eco-economic Justice' congregation and are starting to show up to join us. Some have not been inside a church in a long time!"

Many religious traditions and interfaith networks are addressing poverty and climate change by challenging contemporary capitalism.[36] In the world of Christianity, the World Council of Churches (WCC) began work for justice in global economic systems in the early 1970s. A major WCC report, *Economy of Life*, locates the "root causes" of the wealth gap and the ecological crises within the dominant model of capitalism, in its cultivation of greed and short-term profit seeking, and in the lifestyles of the world's wealthier people. The report also insists, "Churches should not confine themselves to designing projects that will help poor people ... nor should they believe that capitalism as an economic system is beyond interrogation." Noting the need to ask, "Why is there a need for aid in the first place?," the report explains, "A rice farmer whose livelihood is destroyed because of the influx of imported and subsidized rice from the US ... may need aid in the short run to survive. But the fundamental issues to be tackled are injustices in global trade and financial systems including relentless capital flight from poor to rich countries." "What is needed," the document finds, "is for churches to work for global justice by critically and prophetically addressing capitalism, which, despite numerous mutations, cannot eradicate poverty, inequality, and ecological destruction.... The answer lies in a participatory search for alternatives that are centered on the people and the earth."[37]

In 2013, the WCC and three other major global ecumenical networks initiated an ongoing project entitled NIFEA (New International Financial and Economic Architecture). It calls for and equips member churches to engage in building "An Economy of Life."[38]

Likewise, many denominations within US Christianity are complementing their service and development work with efforts aimed at systemic change such as advocating for public policy, participating in community organizing, engaging in food sovereignty networks, and creating resources for worship and theological education. Increasingly, seminaries and other programs to prepare pastors, priests, and other church leaders include training in social justice and eco-justice leadership and ministry.

Social movement networks are mobilizing people, providing peer support among innovative organizations, and producing excellent guides for a just transition toward economies that prioritize human and ecological flourishing.[39] Examples from this table in the feast include the following:

- The Poor People's Campaign bringing together economically poor people with their middle-class allies to build, in their words, a "moral economy."
- The Solidarity Economy Network enabling communication and collaboration among many organizations, businesses, and individuals dedicated to building economies that value people and Earth over profit.
- The movement in the United States building momentum to enact reparations for the enslavement of African people and the subsequent history of exploitation.

- The landback movement seeking to reestablish Indigenous authority in territories that tribes claim are theirs by treaty rights.
- The food justice movement, including the Black food sovereignty movement, working for food access and democratic control of food systems.[40]

The movement to build worker-owned coops and other worker-owned businesses is thriving. It is closely linked to efforts at "community wealth building" emerging in major cities around the country.

The movement to develop alternative finance—such as public banks, social purpose investing, and local credit unions that re-invest in their communities—helps to finance the development of worker-owned business, renewable energy, and local energy companies. It prioritizes small-scale business owned by people in economically marginalized groups. These efforts are capturing the allegiance of investors who want their money to be a force for justice and ecological wellbeing.

Engaged "think tanks" and training labs offering conceptual frameworks and public education for different dimensions of the new economy abound. They provide tools for systems-wide endeavors to build the new economy. Many are working with cities to implement innovative policies and programs. Among these are the Democracy Collaborative, the Doughnut Economics Action Lab, Class Action, the Next System Project, the Wellbeing Economy Alliance, the Solidarity Economy, the Global Commons Alliance, and the Global Citizens Initiative.

Many city governments are seeking innovative ways to build wealth in marginalized communities and to reduce carbon emissions.[41] New frameworks for conceptualizing economic life—such as doughnut economics—have gained attention and are becoming resources for policy makers. They build on earlier thinkers in the field of ecological economics such as Herman Daly, Hazel Henderson, and Richard Norgaard.

Some nations are adding rights and principles of nature such as *buen vivir* (Bolivia) and *sumac kawsay* (Ecuador) to their constitutions, providing legal and ethical platforms for legislation that curtails damage done by extractive industries. Other nations are adopting alternatives to the Gross Domestic Product as a measure of economic well-being.

United Nations agencies help people push for social justice in the transition to low-carbon and zero-carbon economies.[42] The United Nations Alternative Economies for Transformation Programme explores alternative, financially viable economic models that are both egalitarian and ecologically sound.[43]

Direct action groups raise consciousness about the urgency of the issues and mobilize people to act. Many also make specific public policy demands. Youth have become especially prominent and powerful in these movements that are fighting for their futures.[44]

In the academy, programs that push toward the new economy have emerged across disciplines, from theology to sociology to economics to environmental studies. Scholar-activists who are teaching, writing, and speaking in service of more equitable and ecological economies are now found in the sciences, behavioral sciences, fine arts, cultural studies, law, education, and more. Kate Raworth, author of *Doughnut Economics*, describes a "revolution in economics" fomented by graduate students "from India and the US to Germany and Peru." They are "revolting" against the narrow and conservative confines of mainstream economics curricula.[45]

These players do not all hold the same ideological frames or political commitments. The people involved span significant political and conceptual terrain. But they do share the realization that the current "outdated economy," is morally bankrupt and is driving us all into devastation.

More importantly, they share a threefold vision of what is possible: (1) that human economies can operate within the limits of Earth's economy of life; (2) that economies for wellbeing can generate equity, rather than concentrate wealth; and (3) that economic life can be governed by democratic ideals of shared and accountable power. These three principles—ecological, equitable, and democratic—call for dramatic revision of business, finance, agriculture, water and energy use, and transportation. And for the high consuming among us, these principles also mean changes in everyday life. We explore these three principles more fully in the following chapter.

How would you illustrate this sacred convergence in your heart-mind? What metaphor captures its healing power, its courage, and its creativity?

Your Place in This Organism of Healing

Which of these networks entices you? About which would you like to learn more? With which might you or your community engage? What categories or kinds of players have I missed in this sketch? What else would you add?

As you continue through this book (and perhaps the series that follows it), may you develop a vision for your place in this organism of healing. And may you also envision the roles that different communities, institutions, and businesses in your life could play.

In part 3, you will encounter a wide array of "fingers on the hands of healing," or forms of action. Perhaps you and your communities already are deeply engaged in some of them. Perhaps they are new to you. Most likely you fall somewhere in between those poles. As you discern which forms of action fit, may you see yourself both building on your current gifts and abilities and daring to tread new terrain—to venture where you feel uncomfortable, inexperienced, or uncertain. May you know yourself to be part of a vast and sacred movement. You will find yourself in the presence of splendid and often unexpected companions.

In this foray into "morally empowering seeing," we have looked at two of four forms of seeing—seeing "what is going on" and seeing "what could be and is in the making." We move now to the third form of seeing.

Seeing Presence and Power of the Sacred

Seeing both what is and what could be (both our diseased economic reality and the healing that is already underway) is vital. For many of us, a third mode of vision accompanies these two and brings with it tenacity, hope, and strength. It is the choice to recognize a sacred force *present with and within this world* and luring all of creation—including us, the human creatures—toward a destiny of life in its fullness for all. This form of vision evokes "hope that our efforts on behalf of our planet are not ours alone but that the source and power of life in the universe is working *in and through us* for the well-being of all creation, including our tiny part in it."[46]

Different spiritual, religious, and secular traditions understand this force or power differently. Some know it as Yahweh, God, Allah, Creator, or divine Love. But it goes by many names and metaphors. I relish Rabbi Michael Lerner's imagery of "the transformative power of the universe."

The point here is not how the sacred is named, but rather the strength, hope, insight, and courage that can come with practicing this third mode of vision—keeping the heart's eye attuned to power within and beyond creation that works to transform death and destruction into life and love. Secular as well as religious voices hold that attending to a sacred force or energy is invaluable for nurturing and guiding the journey towards more life-giving ways of living. Canadian biologist David Suzuki avers, "All cultures have believed in power beyond human power.... These beliefs restore our sense of belonging, of being-with."[47]

Because my knowledge and experiences lie within Christian traditions, I draw most of my illustrations from them—while noting that there is no singular Christianity. There are Christianit*ies*. And they are monumentally varied.

Many streams of Christian tradition, together with other religious wisdoms, hold that the destiny of human life, and of the entire universe, is union with the Sacred Source and communion among all of creation. Further, they hold that the Sacred Spirit is—despite all evidence to the contrary—leading and luring us toward that destiny. This is not a destiny for life *after* death alone, but a destiny for life on Earth. That power for wholeness and healing is known in many Christian traditions as the Holy Spirit, and in some contemporary Jewish Renewal circles as the *ruach* of God.

One astounding understanding is that this Spirit of power for right relationships is breathed into us and "is flowing and pouring through all things."[48] In the words of one fourth-century Syrian church leader, God's "fire of compassion" abides within us and has its "voice in our ears."[49] The material world is drenched with the transformative power of the universe. By many it is known as divine Love. Writes Suzuki, "Spirit is a powerful, mysterious word.... It is the power of divine creation... and it is divinity itself."[50] Five centuries earlier, Martin Luther declared that the Spirit may evoke courage. "The Hebrew word for 'spirit' might well be rendered 'bold, undaunted courage.'"[51]

Our role as humans is to recognize this presence and to cultivate our "responsiveness to holy presence in the world."[52] In fact, many Eastern theologians "perceive salvation as an awakening to the whole world illumined by the brilliance of divine presence."[53] Cultivating this third form of vision is drinking from wellsprings of power for building economies based in life-giving relationships instead of exploitative ones. We will explore this more fully in chapter 17's section on "drinking the Spirit's courage."

This form of vision is dangerous. Throughout history, and still today, people interpret the hand of God in ways that, at best, justify narrow self-interest and, at worst, underwrite cruelty, oppression, and domination. Religion has been a force for terror and brutality—both subtle and blatant. The dangers in turning to religion abound. But those dangers do not mean we ought to give up the ancient human hunger to be guided by a sacred force for good that comes from within and beyond.

The fourth form of seeing in this framework of morally empowering vision is recognizing, attuning to, and being fed by beauty.

Seeing Beauty

My friend was dying. She was far too young to die. The cancer was not yielding to her noble efforts to claim life. I walked with her one afternoon in autumn. It was a normal-seeming afternoon. To my normal vision, nothing struck me as extraordinary—no vivid or exotic plants, no riveting sunset, no distant mountain scape. My friend, however, stopped every few minutes, astounded by the beauty that she beheld. "Oh, Cynthia, do you see those clouds?" Moments, later: "Ah, what a gentle breeze—I would love to feel that forever!" Perhaps a block down the road: "Have you ever heard the birds singing like this?" At one point, she simply laughed. It was a laugh of wonder at the beauty around us, in the sounds, smells, sights, and fleshly feelings. She saw the beauty, and it fed her soul. It gave her joy.

I have come to realize that in times of great challenge, grief, confusion, or chaos, we may choose to be fed by beauty—by perceiving it and being humbly thankful for it. How is it that the human creature is so profoundly sensual, that we have so many invitations to relish beauty? Our sight, smell, touch, hearing, taste, emotions, and interpretive capacities dangle beauty before us. The touch of a breeze on skin, the twinkle of leaves in sunlight, the taste of good coffee, the subtle smell of the air after rain, the sound of birdsong or human voice, the beauty of small kindness, a loving look from an ancient face.

Even where beauty seems absent, it is present. It may be above in the womb-like grayness of the sky or in the distant sound of laughter. It may be in a look of sympathy from an unknown face. In the ugliest of times, beauty may emerge. In brokenness, pain, and loss, beauty may seep through the cracks. A friend once said to me that she did not want to awaken in five years and find that joy had been all around her but that she had failed to grasp it. I feel the same about beauty.

When my mother was brutally raped and murdered by three young white men, it was the beauty of human love that saved my father, sister, and me. When my second mother was recovering from a head-on collision that nearly took her life, a friend who was a pianist asked her what he could do to help her. "Come to my home and play the piano," she said. He came weekly, and the beauty of the music helped her heal.

Beauty can open the heart. At one point, when I was deep in despair at the virulence and overwhelming power of structural violence, I heard a young person from East Germany playing the piano. In that splendid moment, my hope was restored. A composer from centuries past had heard beauty in his heart and transferred it to notes on paper; people preserved those notes for hundreds of years; and now in the twenty-first century a young person who had experienced much pain in his life played that beauty. In turn, it rescued me from despair.

The ancient Greeks claimed that beauty (*kallos*) evokes "deep yearnings for justice, healing, and peace."[54] Perhaps Dostoevsky was not quite right that "beauty will save the world."[55] However, certainly if we choose to perceive it and drink from it, beauty will nourish courage to heed the great calling of our time—to build ways of life that allow Earth's community of life to flourish. Attuning heart and mind to beauty nurtures power for subversive love.

Morally Empowering Vision in Sum

"Morally empowering seeing," then, is a phrase to signify the union of vision in these four forms:
- seeing "what is going on," especially unmasking systemic injustice masquerading as good
- seeing "what could be and is in the making," that is, alternatives
- seeing ever more fully the Sacred Spirit of life coursing throughout creation and leading it into fullness of life for all
- seeing the beauty surrounding and within us

These lenses together allow us to acknowledge that, while we are entwined in structural violence, we are also beloved beings with boundless capacity for compassionate justice-making love.

Keep, then, *the eyes of your intellect, your heart, and your gut alert to all four. Doing so is at the heart of economic life as a spiritual practice. Morally empowering seeing is a spiritual practice.*

The next medicine in our treasure chest of healing remedies is the ability to recognize three "terrains" in which change takes place in the transition from extractive to life-giving economic life.

* * *

Honoring Our Bodies

Imagine one ancestor in your life whom you respect and whom you would like to accompany you on this journey. It might be an ancestor in your blood line or in your faith community's legacy or from history. Invite this ancestor to accompany you through the journey of this book and wherever else it takes you. Imagine her, him, or them sitting with you or walking with you or holding you or holding your hand or looking you in the eyes or whatever other posture feels life-giving for you. What do you want to tell this person now, at this point? Or what do you want to request from her, him, or them?

Sacred Journey Journal

- Sit in silence for a few moments. Recall the feelings that emerged as you read the section on "Seeing What Is: Truth-Telling." What feelings emerged with "Seeing What Could Be and Is in the Making: Healing"?
- What is one small way in which "Seeing What Is: Truth-Telling" connects to your life?
- What is one small way in which you (or a community or group to which you belong) could practice "What Could Be and Is in the Making: Healing"? In other words, how might you enter into (or more fully into) the movement for a more equitable and ecological economy at a local or global level?

CHAPTER FIVE

Three Terrains of Liberative Change and Two Interflowing Streams

> I knew my grandchildren confronted the harrowing challenge of moving from industrial to ecological civilization. The Great Transition, it's called. Epic times.
>
> —Larry Rasmussen[1]

YOU HAVE EMBARKED on a sacred and healing journey to new ways of being human together on this Earth, ways that will hoist us back from the precipice of peril on which we hover. You walk with a host of marvelous companions, far and near, most of whom you will never meet in person. You walk with courage—the courage to recognize hidden horror and to choose life, freedom, and healing instead. The audacious courage to believe that we can heal selves and societies from the rapacious age of exploitative economies into an age of economies for life. You walk too with the courage to act on this belief, to practice it. I applaud your courage. May you cultivate it, rejoice in it, and beckon others into it. May you recognize this as spiritual practice—enacting economic life as spiritual practice.

Three Terrains

When I set out to heal from self-destructive behaviors that were linked to the culture around me, I moved forward in two terrains—changed behavior and changed worldview. I had to change not only the self-destructive behaviors of entrenched anorexia and self-degradation, but I also had to shift how I perceived reality. The latter felt daunting. I recall thinking that I must dislodge one by one the bricks in the wall of false security that I had built around me—my way of thinking about what gave me value, what was important, and what my future held.

Neither the behavioral change nor the worldview change alone would have brought long-term healing. They needed each other. Now, I realize that change in a third terrain—social structures—also would have been invaluable. If, for example, health care and mental health care had been fully available at low or no cost, my healing could have happened sooner in my life.

As you join the "cloud of witnesses" building a moral economy—or as you strengthen your already existing role in that cloud—few concepts are more important than recognizing the enlivening interplay among change in three terrains of human existence. Those terrains are
- practices or behaviors—daily activities of individuals and households
- social structures or systems[2]—shifts in institutions together with change in the larger economic, political, or cultural systems formed by institutions working together[3]
- mindsets/consciousness/worldview/guiding narratives—individual and societal patterns of perceiving, thinking, and understanding reality[4]

Keep in mind two points. First, transformation of economic life requires change in all three terrains. Second, change in one of them opens doors to change in the others.

Often people assume that change in one terrain is the most important, and they sideline the other two. I recall a fascinating argument between my Christian Ethics students working on their "interrupting injustice project." One argued that what individuals do in everyday practice (riding bikes or busses instead of driving, giving up beef or single-use plastics, buying fair trade items, shopping at coops and farmers markets, etc.) is relatively ineffective and insignificant. What is needed, she contended, is structural change including public policy, legal mandates, and large-scale institutional revamping.

The other student insisted that we should prioritize individual behavioral change. Social structural change, he averred, will not occur to the extent that we need it. What is needed is individual people and households shifting to live in ways that are ecologically sound and economically nonexploitative.

Yet another student pushed further, pointing out that we had been studying the power of narrative in shaping lifeways. That student argued that we need a new narrative, a new way of perceiving reality. We need a new story that holds other-than-human parts of creation as sacred, revises the purpose of economic life away from maximizing profit, and changes our understanding of what is normal and possible. Only then, with changed consciousness, will we change our economic systems, this student insisted.

As the term went on, it was a delight to help this class unearth the synergy between change in these three arenas.[5] To illustrate, imagine city streets in the United States filled with bicycle riders, as are many streets of Amsterdam. How could this come to pass? People are more likely to commute by bike (behavioral change) if city policy (structural change) makes bike riding safer, more convenient, and affordable to people with no or low incomes.[6] Such policies are more likely to pass if people are changing their mindsets—if we are coming to perceive hopping on a bike as the normal mode of transport. The influence of the three terrains on each other is not one way; it is circular or spiraling. Changed

Three Terrains of Liberative Change

behaviors, and thus more bikers, press cities to enact policies making biking safer and more affordable. And seeing a sea of people on big, old, black bikes in Amsterdam, for instance, shifted my mindset about what is normal and possible for human transportation.

Another example also illumines how change in one of the three terrains opens pathways for change in the others. Speculative investment in the global economy has terribly destructive impacts.[7] Public policy (structural change) that disincentivizes speculative investment would encourage people to invest in other, longer-term ways (behavioral change). This shift, in turn, would prevent some of the damage done by financial speculation. Such public policy would go hand-in-hand with change in consciousness or worldview; it would begin to reorient us from the assumption that finance should aim singularly at maximizing short-term profit to prioritizing a "triple bottom line"—social, ecological, as well as financial. This change would entail a shift in the assumption that maximizing profit is a human right. Said differently, investment would be guided not only by the question "Will this make me the most money?" but also by the question "Will this build social and ecological well-being?"[8] This change in worldview would, in turn, invite further structural and behavioral change. Many recent efforts to mitigate climate change encourage change in all three terrains.[9]

Dangers of Focus on Individual Behavioral Change Alone

Maina Talia comes from Tuvalu, a small country of low-lying islands in the South Pacific. As a young theologian and climate activist, he wrote an op-ed for the *Guardian* entitled "My Home Is Being Swallowed by the Sea." Climate change may soon render Talia's homeland unlivable. We have worked together on two projects, and I have listened carefully to his wisdom. In his piece "Am I Not Your (Tu)Akoi—Neighbour?" which calls on neighbors from around the world to respond, Talia declares,

> We are wary of the impacts of sustainability proposals such as planting trees, changing light bulbs, tapping renewable energy sources, and the like. Are they aimed ... at safeguarding the prevailing exploitative economic model? ... The reality is that without radical reorganization of the economic system that robs mother earth of her ability to sustain life, we will not find answers to the prevailing problems created by climate change.[10]

Dr. Talia is warning against the danger of focusing on lifestyle or behavioral change alone as the solution to climate change. "I will get my own life in order, live as green and clean as I can. I will switch to an electric car, buy fair trade products and locally grown produce, conserve water, eat less meat, foreswear single use plastic, move my banking to a local bank that supports minority owned business." Yes! Socially just and green lifestyle choices are vitally important. However, "we can't shop our way to a better world."[11] Martin Lukacs says it well:

> *Of course, we need people to consume less and innovate low-carbon alternatives—build sustainable farms, invent battery storages, spread zero-waste methods. But individual choices will most count when the economic system can provide viable, environmental options for everyone—not just an affluent or intrepid few. If affordable mass transit isn't available, people will commute with cars. If local organic food is too expensive, they won't opt out of fossil fuel-intensive super-market chains.... This is the con-job of neoliberalism: to persuade us to address climate change through our pocket-books [only], rather than through power and politics.[12]*

We are in danger if "our outrage is channeled away from collective political action and toward 'green consumerism' alone."[13] Systemic problems require systemic responses as well as individual ones. Failure to recognize this is the great fault line of the green lifestyle movement when it is not combined with collective effort to change social structures and worldviews/consciousness/mindsets.

It turns out, for example, that the idea of a "carbon footprint" (which countless people have used to help reduce household carbon emissions) was conceived and promoted by British Petroleum (BP). The author and activist, Rebecca Solnit, reveals that

> *British Petroleum, the second largest non-state owned oil company in the world, with 18,700 gas and service stations worldwide, hired the public relations professionals Ogilvy & Mather to promote the slant that climate change is not the fault of an oil giant, but that of individuals. It's here that British Petroleum, or BP, first promoted and soon successfully popularized the term "carbon footprint" in the early aughts. The company unveiled its "carbon footprint calculator" in 2004 so one could assess how their normal daily life—going to work, buying food, and (gasp) traveling—is largely responsible for heating the globe.[14]*

Talia, Solnit, and Lukacs invite you and me to honor an empowering paradox: behavior (lifestyle) changes are necessary but not adequate unless accompanied by change in systems and worldviews. I believe that heeding this paradox—and insisting on action in all three terrains—embodies neighbor-love as well as self-love. It is enacting economic life as a spiritual practice.

The Value of Change in Consciousness/Worldview/Mindset

Let us dwell for a moment on the third terrain of change—shifts in consciousness, worldview, or mindset. We human creatures perceive and act in response to worldviews into which we have been socialized.[15] Being raised in a particular society and in subcultures of it, we come to assume certain things to be natural that are in fact beliefs constructed by our society or subculture.[16] These "culturally produced assumptions" shape what we think, feel, value, strive for—in short, how we live.[17]

In chapter 3, while exploring narrative imagination, I wrote about the importance of examining our unconscious and semiconscious assumptions about what is natural, normal, inevitable, or divinely ordained. A function of mature adulthood is to become aware of those guiding presuppositions, assess them, and choose which to retain, revise, or reject.[18] Not recognizing them deadens our power for change. What is natural, inevitable, or divinely mandated, after all, is not subject to human decisions and actions; it cannot be changed.

The danger, of course, is that unexamined mindsets, assumptions, and worldviews undergird our perilously destructive ways of life. They render as "normal" what—if carefully examined—might be considered abominable. We will return to this thought and experiment with it as we explore "changing the story" in chapter 16.

A close friend was expelled by the apartheid government of South Africa for his work in the anti-apartheid movement. Later, he told me that many people in the anti-apartheid movement said that if they had three books, one would be the Bible, one would be Paulo Freire's *Pedagogy of the Oppressed*, and one would be *Prophetic Imagination* by Walter Brueggemann, a Hebrew Bible scholar. "Why?" I queried. It was because this groundbreaking book calls people of faith to recognize and challenge the consciousness or worldviews undergirding oppression and to nurture alternative consciousness and perceptions. This, Brueggemann insists, is essential for moving from oppressive ways of life to liberative and life-giving ways. Such is the power to be found in challenging society-shaping worldviews!

A diverse body of literature speaks of encultured mindsets or worldviews as narratives, stories, or life-informing myths. This literature suggests that human beings create stories and then order life to be players in that story. The story gives meaning and guides behavior. It explains how things should be, what is right and good, who counts and how much, what is worth living and dying for, who we are, what our purpose is, and how we ought to organize our lives. David Suzuki writes that the human "brain creates a narrative.... The brain selects and discards information to be used in the narrative, constructing connections and relationships that create a web of meaning.... When the mind selects and orders incoming information into meaning, it is telling itself a story."[19] Yuval Harari argues that *homo sapiens*'s ultimate dominance over other species was due in part to our capacity to tell grand narratives that are shared, believed, and enacted by vast numbers of people.[20]

Guiding narratives shape our lives, both for better and for worse, on the individual and the societal levels. The two are related. My individual mindset is shaped in part by the mindsets around me. Thus, mindset or narrative change pertains to the mindsets of both individuals and societies. Take a moment to think of narratives or guiding assumptions that have informed your society and many people in it. For a very long time, the guiding mindset of many societies—including Western society—was that women are less than men. Shifting this worldview societally was intertwined with a corollary shift in individuals' worldview.

Colonialism has shaped the guiding narratives for people in the US (and in most other parts of the world). We assume as normal or natural the worldview that undergirded and justified European domination of peoples and exploitation of their lands. This worldview holds that some people are less fully human and less entitled to basic human rights. It renders land as property to be owned and as a commodity to be bought and sold. It assumes the cultural superiority of Euro-based literature, art, and music. Thus, for example, the "classics" have been the classics of the Greco-European world. Coloniality rendered Western European cultures as civilized and African or Indigenous American cultures as not. We all are shaped, largely unconsciously, by the vestiges of these presuppositions that were transmitted as truths.

This does not make us "bad people." Rather it means that a moral life—and the work of building a moral economy—depend upon decolonizing our minds, hearts, actions, institutions, and public policies. Depend on? Yes! Changes in structures and practices will not lead to lasting transformation of our societies, let alone our economies, if we do not also change the fundamental mindsets that normalize exploitation and inequality. Ethicist Christopher Carter says it well in relationship to Christian faith: "As Christians who are directed by the Greatest Commandment to embody love and pursue just relationships with all of our neighbors, I want to suggest that we are all charged with the task of decolonizing our minds, as well as our religious, social, and political institutions."[21] This is a call to recognize, assess, and change our mindsets—that is, our guiding narratives.

Probing the "how" of change in consciousness, mindsets, or guiding narratives is fascinating and fertile. So, too, is uncovering the particular narratives that shape economic life. What unconscious narratives or assumptions in the US, for example, make it seem *normal or acceptable for a company to compensate some people with the equivalent of thousands of dollars per hour while not paying others enough to feed and house a family?* Recall the story in chapter 2 of the man in Norway who was so disturbed that the pay ratio in many companies in Norway had climbed to 14-to-1 between the highest and lowest paid employees. In his world, and according to its worldview, 14-to-1 was far too large a gap; it was unjust. In ours, that ratio is more than 1,000-to-1 for at least forty-nine firms.

What guiding narrative regarding human worth and human rights shapes our strange sense of normal?

Later, in discussing the ten "fingers on the hands of healing" for economic transformation, we will look further at "changing the story" as a strategy, including the re-formation of narratives shaping economic life. For now, the point is this: transformation of economic life—of economic practices, structures, and truth claims—entails change in three terrains of human existence:

- practices (of individuals and households),
- social structures, and
- mindsets/consciousness/worldviews/guiding narratives (of individuals and of societies).

This third terrain is a marvelous landscape, pulsating with potential for moral-spiritual power. "Changing the story" is a fruitful way of conceptualizing this terrain. Changing the story may also be seen as a matter of inner healing. Imagine our society healing to renarrate the economy's purpose as serving fullness of life for all rather than maximizing profit for a few! Imagine collective healing to break free from bondage to myths that constrain our decency in economic relationships with one another and with Earth. This terrain is also a matter of imagination—imagining and then adopting new, more equitable and ecological narratives. If our heart-minds "can conceive of an ecological and equitable economy, then we can act to make it a reality."[22]

Two Intertwining Streams: Resistance and Rebuilding

The third healing remedy is recognizing two intertwining streams in the current of economic change—resistance and rebuilding. They go by many names. Gandhi knew them as "two strings [in the] nonviolent bow" of *satyagraha*,[23] *noncooperation with evil* and *cooperation with good*.[24] The International Alliance for Localisation uses the terms *resistance* and *renewal*. They write, "We believe that effective action to localise our economies comes from working on two complementary fronts—resistance **and** renewal."[25] The World Council of Churches and its global ecumenical partners refer to these two streams as "exposing and undoing unjust financial and economic structures" and "building life-giving alternatives," insisting that the two be held together.

Resistance takes many forms. Christiana Figueres, a Costa Rican diplomat who has led national and international climate policy negotiations, highlights public protest as one form of resistance, referring to it as "a moral choice" and "the most powerful way of shaping world politics." She recounts an example:

> *In April 2019, the group Extinction Rebellion . . . seized the moment and began a series of global protests, the first of which was to take over*

Central London for ten days in non-violent protest. Thousands of first-time activists, people who had never marched or signed a petition in their lives, blocked roads, linked arms, and planted trees on Waterloo Bridge.[26]

She goes on to note the "rebuilding" that this "resistance" helped to catalyze. "Within two months of that initial protest, the UK declared a climate emergency, adopted a target of net-zero emissions by 2050 . . . and established a citizen assembly to look at how it could be achieved."

"Resistance" includes refusing to participate in some aspects of exploitative and extractive economies. You are resisting when you decide not to bank at Wells Fargo because it invests in new fossil fuel exploration or not to stay in a hotel that refuses to unionize. Resistance also includes creating poetry, music, and public art that exposes corporate greed; preventing megacorporations from entering a community; divesting in fossil fuel pipelines; and so on.

"Rebuilding" is a dazzling array: the urban farms erupting around this nation and world, the fast-growing number of employee-owned businesses, the New Economy Coalition's more than two-hundred-member businesses and networks, the networks of Black farmers, the multitudes of people doing business with these local alternatives. Rebuilding also means advocacy for laws that hold capital accountable for its impact, support renewable energy, prioritize small business, and so much more.

"Resisting and rebuilding" are anchored in Christian theology as repenting for damaging lifeways and turning instead to what furthers human and ecological well-being. This work is grounded in the life of Jesus and in the Hebrew prophets' clarion call to reject oppressive systems and to live according to the ways of Yahweh. Both the First Testament (known as the Old Testament by many Christians) and the Second Testament (or New Testament) of the Christian Scriptures see repentance (*teshuvah* in Hebrew and *metanoia* in Greek) as a powerful move to turn the other direction—to move from orienting actions and consciousness around sinful ways to orienting in ways that align with God's justice-seeking, Earth-honoring love.

Perhaps most important is recognizing that resistance and rebuilding depend upon and strengthen one another. Neither will get far without the other.

Hidden Harm—Healing Beckons

Imagine being on a distant planet and watching the daily life of people in the United States with a fine-tuned lens that reveals consequences and connections, invisible threads running between us and each person and non-human creature whom our lives impact or on whom our lives depend. It is the lens of "what is going on," the first dimension of morally empowering vision that we examined in chapter 4. The curious viewers from a distant planet look in on one household. It is the home of Katy.

First, they see inside Katy's heart. "She is a kind person," one of them remarks. "She finds joy in making other people's lives better. Let us watch her day."

Katy awakens, lying on sheets purchased at low cost from a large chain store that pays some cashiers less than eight dollars per hour. The extra-terrestrial viewers see one cashier and her two kids rising from sleep in a homeless shelter because that wage is not enough to cover rent. Katy draws a tomato from a plastic bag to put in her morning omelet. The puzzled spectators see the bag over time. It disintegrates into tiny particles that find their way into fish that children eat daily in the island nations of Oceania. The tomato is covered with chemicals and was shipped from hundreds of miles away. The viewers begin to count the greenhouse gas emissions behind this breakfast.

After breakfast, Katy goes online to pay the bill for a recent trip by drawing on a mutual fund invested in many firms, including Exxon Mobile. Exxon Mobile has used those investments to systematically spread doubt about the truth of climate change and to lobby Congress for the rights to unfettered drilling in the Arctic. Both moves have contributed inexorably to climate change. The extra-terrestial watchers see climate change causing villages in Alaska to fall into the sea, setting towns in California ablaze, and sending climate refugees from the drought in Honduras fleeing to the US border. Katy does not know that her mutual fund is financing climate change.

Checking her bank account, Katy sees that her paycheck has been deposited and her retirement fund has grown slightly. Little does she know the reach of those monies. The bank's investments and the retirement fund both include funds that speculate in food prices. The speculation has rendered profits for the funds while also driving up the cost of basic food staples in the Philippines. Rosario, a Filipino mother of three, can no longer afford the food her family needs. She is devastated.

Before lunch, Katy is relieved to see her most recent purchase from Amazon delivered. That afternoon her child comes home with a project for her high-school ethics class. She is to trace the ecological and social justice impacts of a recent purchase on Amazon and draw lines connecting the product to the people impacted by producing and transporting it. She starts with the pay and health care benefit differential between Amazon's CEO and the Amazon warehouse workers. She cannot see all of what the interplanetary viewers see over time—chemicals from the production plant have shown up in the breast milk that Katy's sister is feeding her young daughter.

The wondering watchers on the distant planet trace the connections and consequences of Katy's activities in a day. They are stunned. Nearly every moment has consequences of indirect violence. "Why 'on earth' are they living this way?" query the incredulous observers. Again, they peer into Katy's heart. There they see a Katy who does not want to damage other people.

This is bondage to structural violence. Let us uncover paths to freedom. This is a diseased economic life. Let us uncover healing medicine. This is betrayal of our right to live in ways that serve the good. Let us reclaim that right.

As we move through the remaining chapters, we chart a freedom trail. We encounter healing medicines. We reclaim our right to live in ways that enable well-being for people and Earth.

* * *

Honoring Our Bodies

If I were you, I might be weary after processing the material in this book thus far. Grappling with this chapter alone could make your brain and heart hurt. It may be time for the spiritual practice of rest. This is a term given to me by a friend, Nancy, who began a "resting practice" as a part of her recovery from cancer. I thought it so wise that I formed a spiritual practice group for students at the seminary where I teach. The group was called "Rest as Spiritual Practice." I invite you to find a comfortable place to lie down. Have a warm blanket if your place is cool. Be sure your feet are warm. Have something to serve as an eye mask to create darkness. Be utterly comfortable. Remind yourself that rest is a human right and that the Great Spirit wants rest for the creatures, including the human creatures. (According to some traditions, including Christian and Jewish faiths, God mandates keeping the Sabbath to ensure rest.) Set an alarm for whatever time you can give yourself—half an hour? Ten minutes? Even five minutes makes a difference. Imagine putting your concerns into a chest on a shelf and telling them that you are taking a temporary break from them; they are not to bother you! Then close your eyes and sink into blissful rest.

Sacred Journey Journal

Which of the three "terrains of liberative change" (behaviors, social structures, worldviews) seems most foreign to your life? In which does it seem most difficult for you to act? Focus on that terrain. What is one thing that your household (or a group or community to which you belong) could do in that terrain towards healing economic life? If it is hard to imagine one thing, do not be discouraged! Note that difficulty, and return to this question after you have begun part 3 of the book. You might now just glimpse through part 3 and read the small section called "Setting the Stage." Does an idea emerge for an action you might take?

CHAPTER SIX

Vision and Guideposts

> Where there is no prophecy, the people cast off restraint.
> —Proverbs 29:18

> Imagine a world where everyone has enough.
> Where housing is a human right.
> Where there is no difference between "worker" and "owner."
> Where our financial system puts people over profits.
> Where we face the realities of our changing climate and relearn to live in balance with nature.
> Building this world is possible. It has already begun.
> —Pathways to a People's Economy[1]

> Imagine a different relationship in which people and land are good medicine for each other.
> —Robin Wall Kimmerer[2]

Fourth Medicine: Vision of a Moral Economy

THE POTAWATOMI BIOLOGIST Robin Wall Kimmerer calls us to "imagine a different relationship in which people and land are good medicine for each other." We might also say in which people are good medicine for other people, nearby and around the globe. *What a vision: our economic lives breeding well-being for others and for Earth instead of devastating them indirectly through systems that we tend not to acknowledge.*

A Tale of Transformation

Shanine (name changed) worked for minimum wage at two part-time jobs. Neither offered benefits. She had done all she could to find better work, but no good jobs were available. With her low wages, she was unable to afford rent, so Shanine moved between a shelter and friends' couches. She was exhausted and had been for months. She longed for a job with a livable wage and a place to call home.

Two years later, Shanine, along with more than two hundred other formerly impoverished people, is an employee-owner in Evergreen Cooperatives. She makes a strong, livable income, has healthy working conditions, participates equally in the Cooperative's decision-making, and is part of a collaborative community. She volunteers at the shelter where she had slept and bakes delicious pies for the friends who had taken her in. What happened?

In 2008, a group of Cleveland-based institutions convened by the Cleveland Foundation launched the Evergreen Cooperative Initiative. They partnered with the Democracy Collaborative's innovative Community Wealth Building (CWB) program.[3] The aim was to create local, shared wealth within impoverished and disinvested neighborhoods such as Glenville. The initiative would develop new cooperative business ventures enabling low-income people to gain financial security, exercise democratic control in their workplaces, and participate as employee-owners.

They did it! Evergreen Cooperatives now is a thriving employee-owned and controlled businesses: Evergreen Energy Solutions, Green City Growers, and the Evergreen Cooperative Laundry. Many of the employee-owners are Black. Many are formerly incarcerated or otherwise justice impacted. All live in nearby underserved neighborhoods with chronic unemployment and underemployment.

Evergreen Cooperative Laundry was first. Large hospital systems commonly launder with a corporate service that ships laundry to a centralized location to keep costs low. Their system ignores greenhouse gasses emitted in the shipping as well as the human suffering stemming from the inadequate wages and poor working conditions it produces. Such was the case in Cleveland. No longer! Cleveland Clinic (Ohio's largest employer) is now an anchor institution with Evergreen Cooperatives. Evergreen Cooperative Laundry does the clinic's laundry right there in the neighborhood, a green business owned and run by its employees. And it does the laundry also for other local hospitals, hotels, and other institutions.

The Cleveland model and the Democracy Collaborative's CWB programs are inspiring other community wealth-building endeavors across the country, in England, and in Scotland. Scotland appointed a Minister for Community Wealth and has CWB initiatives in more than thirty municipalities. Community wealth building—as demonstrated in these initiatives—is one strong pathway to democratic economies that serve people ("the many not the few") and planet. They are building economic democracy from the ground up.[4]

Sarah McKinley, the CWB Program's intrepid leader, is clear: the long-term intent is that community wealth building will become mainstream. "CWB is where the next [economic] system begins," she avers. It "prefigures a more regenerative economic system ... a larger systemic transformation of our global economy away from an economy of extraction that benefits a few to an economy that is regenerative, recirculatory, sustainable, and beneficial to the planet, to each other, and to social thriving. . . . Community wealth building is one way of showing us how we can do it."[5] Says the Evergreen Cooperatives Board Chair, "Our goal is equitable wealth creation at scale."[6]

The Power of Moral Vision

What we assume to be normal determines a great deal! Imagine a few shifts in what is considered "normal" in economic life. Today it is assumed normal for a business to be large, global, controlled by a small number of people, dedicated solely to maximizing shareholder returns regardless of consequences, and unaccountable to the people or natural world it impacts by outsourcing its services to where labor is cheap and environmental standards low. (Of course, this does not describe all business, but it does reflect typical business priorities.) It is normal for me to drink a can of Coke that was produced by depriving communities in India of their water supply, and normal for you to buy for your daughter a soccer ball that was made in Bangladesh by an eight-year-old who lost his vision sitting for hours a day stitching in order to survive. It is normal for a person in the United States to work five full days a week, yet not earn enough to pay for a roof over her head, while another person in the same company is paid in an hour what most other employees are paid in a year. It is normal for an oil company to make vast profits, while taxpayers foot the bill for the ecological damage they cause, including paying for recovery from climate-change fueled fires, floods, and storms. *What a bizarre and perilous normal!*

How different would life be if it were considered normal for businesses to be owned and controlled by employees and to be dedicated to ensuring no ecological damage, including carbon emissions? Do read that sentence again! What if it were considered normal for all people to be paid a living wage for their work, normal for the highest paid employee to receive no more than ten times the lowest paid? How different our world would be if we shifted our vision of the normal.

Imagine that the economy as we now know it is "a temporary thing; a barely surviving remnant of old ways of being; not the immovable immutable truth it presumes itself to be."[7] Imagine breaking free from the strangling grip of an economy that is slowly sucking life out of Earth and many of its people. Imagine healing, reclaiming in new forms the two ancient *nomos* (rules) for the *oikos* (household of creation): serve and preserve the garden Earth and serve your neighbors' well-being as your own (love your neighbor as yourself).

Moral vision is our vision of the good.[8] A moral vision—conscious or not—tells us what is good, right, and true. In general, we assume moral vision unconsciously; we are not necessarily aware of it. It is shaped by the values and practices of the family, society, and any subgroups in which our lives unfold. It is taught to us through the narratives of history, advertising, religious traditions, and other aspects of culture.

By "*economic* moral vision" I refer to the vision of what would be good, right, and true for economic life. George H. W. Bush articulated and reinforced an economic moral vision in 1992 at the Earth Summit in Rio de Janeiro with his infamous statement: "The American way of life is not up for negotiation."[9]

Moral vision shapes how people live. An economic moral vision in which people are affirmed or further rewarded for accumulating as much wealth as possible encourages people to do just that. If, in contrast, according to the prevailing moral vision, wealth accumulation beyond a certain point was considered morally repugnant, people would be far less likely to pursue it as a goal.

When what is considered to be moral shifts and begins to be seen as immoral, human behaviors, policies, norms, and institutions change. In the United States, for example, excluding women from voting gradually changed from being considered moral to immoral in the span of a few decades. It was a shift in moral vision that resulted in changed behavior, public policies, institutions, and norms for human relationships.

When moral vision changes, what we perceive as *possible* also changes. A few centuries ago in many Western societies the legal equality of women and their legal right to freedom from nonconsensual sex was widely assumed to be impossible. The moral vision shifted, and with it the seemingly impossible became possible.

It is wise to be aware of the kind of economic moral vision that guides you, your family, and your society. Many important life decisions flow from an economic moral vision. My undergraduate students who understood that their families would be proud and consider them "better" people if they were able to make a lot of money, buy a luxurious house, and drive an expensive car, tended to make certain choices during their college years, such as majoring in finance, marketing, or pre-med degrees. (According to many students' accounts, these were not necessarily the choices that they wished to make.) Students who sensed that their parents envisioned for them lives of service or artistic production—and who might be a bit chagrined by conspicuous signs of excessive wealth—tended to make different choices. The two sets of students were guided by differing economic moral visions.

An account of a young Cherokee boy growing up in the early twentieth century describes the hunting philosophy of the boy's people. As the boy's grandfather explained, they were to hunt only the animals that they needed for food. The approach embodied an economic moral vision, and it shaped the community's way of life.

In short, an economic moral vision manifests and reinforces values. The economy as we know it demonstrates and reinforces the primary value of maximizing profit and wealth, and pays scant attention to the cost to workers and to future generations. It weaves those values into the fabric of our society. A moral economy, in contrast, will demonstrate and reinforce the values of Earth care, racial and economic equity, and democracy, weaving these values into our perceptions of right and good living.

What economic moral vision guided the Cleveland model? What economic moral vision influences you, your children, or other children in your life?

Cognitive linguist George Lakoff insists that critiquing a guiding vision or moral framework leads to change only if an alternative exists. It is not adequate to simply recognize that the current economic vision—maximizing growth, consumption, and profit, and ignoring or accepting the suffering it imposes—is outdated and perilous. An alternative economic vision needs to replace our outdated and perilous one for it to lose its grip on us.

Emerging Visions for Life-Giving Economies

Alternative visions for economic life have surged in recent years. They include a fascinating convergence of both religious and secular articulations of hopes for new systems. Perhaps the most well-known religious vision is the encyclical released by Pope Francis in 2015, *Laudato Si'*. The text reverberated around the world, giving rise to movements, teaching, and advocacy in religious communities (both Christian and beyond) and in the secular world. Pope Francis is vehement in his critique of "the neo-liberal market that kills." His vision resonates with the visions noted below of many secular organizations seeking economic change.

I am grateful to others, both individuals and organizations, for their careful work in crafting economic moral visions. I share several of these visions here to offer a fuller picture of what is possible than would be painted by hearing only one or two of them. As I write them, my skeptical voice kicks in: "These are worth their salt only if people are trying to realize them." If you share that voice, join me in testing these vision statements. As you read on in part 3, look for where the organizations or networks noted below are enacting their visions.

- The "World Scientists' Warning to Humanity" (1992), signed by over 1,700 leading scientists including 104 Nobel laureates, envisions "the transformation of our global economic system from a chaotic, deeply unjust and unsustainable free-for-all into a well-managed, equitable vehicle protecting and restoring climate stability and biodiversity while ensuring adequate livelihoods for all."[10]

- The vision and aim of the Center for Economic Democracy is "to transform American capitalism into a more just, sustainable, and democratic economy."[11]
- The Climate Justice Alliance envisions "building a Just Transition away from extractive systems of production, consumption, and political oppression, and towards resilient, regenerative, and equitable economies.... The process of transition must place race, gender, and class at the center of the solutions equation in order to make it a truly Just Transition."[12]
- The New Economy Coalition works toward an economy "where capital (wealth and the means of creating it) is a tool of the people, not the other way around... a new economy that meets human needs, enhances the quality of life, and allows us to live in balance with nature."[13]

Visions developed by religious communities and interreligious coalitions will be particularly relevant for people with religious leanings. One of those articulations, representing Baháʼí, Buddhist, Christian, Hindu, Islamic, Jewish, and Rastafarian traditions, sees "provisioning and care for human beings and all of life, rather than profit" as "the center of any economic system."[14] The World Council of Churches and other global ecumenical networks express similar visions.

Do not make the mistake of perceiving these as utopian dreams. While achieving them in full may be beyond human capacities, substantive movement into them is indeed within our reach—and is already underway. The "new economy is bursting forth through the cracks of the current system as people experiment with new forms of business, governance, and culture that give life to the claim that another world is possible."[15] Recall the story of Shanine and the Community Wealth Building movement, and attune yourself to the stories that will appear in coming chapters. Allow them to shape your vision of what is possible.

These visions for a moral economy and the organizations embodying them share five key perspectives. First, that *transformation toward economies of life is truly possible and is underway*. Equally significant is the shared conviction that this process must be guided by perspectives and voices of communities who have been oppressed or marginalized by the dominant form of economic life. Third, they all consider economic well-being and ecological well-being to go hand-in-hand.

Next, all visions seem convinced that systemic economic change requires a dramatic shift in our understanding of the purpose of economic life, including the purpose of business. (This we discuss in chapter 16, "Change the Story.") Neoliberal capitalism insists that the economy's purpose is to maximize economic growth, short-term profit, and consumption. Unfolding visions of a new economy focus on a radically different purpose—to enable all people to have the necessities for a healthy life, while restoring the health of Earth's ecosystems and diminishing the wealth gap. This radically reformed purpose is in line with the ancient meaning of the term *oikonomos* (economy) and with the two rules for economic life: neighbor-love and creation care.

Finally, alternative visions seem consistent in their embrace of three lynchpins of a moral economy: *ecological, equitable, and democratic*.[16] These are guideposts for an economy that is a web of relationships in which people and Earth are good medicine for each other and in which people are good medicine for one another.

Fifth Medicine: Overarching Guideposts—Ecological, Equitable, Democratic[17]

Guideposts are powerful. They are plumb lines, signaling whether a practice or policy is in line with intended values.

These three primary guideposts for economies are healing! They would set us on a path of healing from economies that hurt many people through climate change, wage deprivation, toxic waste and working conditions, contingent labor, and more and deprive our children and grandchildren of a livable future. These three guideposts would uphold deeply held values—such as treating other people decently—rather than betraying those values.

In our contexts, what do these guideposts mean? We look here at a short and simple version of each. If you want to dig more deeply, please read through the toolkit for this book on the series website.

Ecological

Whether or not our society—or human civilization—can survive intact will depend in large measure on whether we take ecological limits seriously.

—Stan Cox[18]

"I was stunned," writes Kimmerer. As Distinguished Teaching Professor of Environmental Biology at SUNY, she had surveyed two hundred university students in a general ecology class, asking them to "rate their knowledge of positive interactions between people and land. The median response was 'none.'... When we talked about this after class, I realized that they could not even imagine what beneficial relations between their species and others might look like."[19]

Close your eyes for a moment and imagine how it would feel to know that the economy of your city, town, or rural community and everything in it—the industry, the transportation, the agriculture, other businesses—had no negative impact on the air, water, soil, and biodiversity of your region! Imagine that your home region is carbon neutral. The trees, streams, and critters rejoice. What does this feel like? To me, it feels peaceful, rich, whole, miraculous. This is possible. Some cities are working toward it.[20]

The guidepost of "ecological" calls for economic practices, policies, and systems that build the health of the eco-systems they impact, directly or indirectly. For many years, "ecological" has meant that the economy and economic activity would be "sustainable." That is, they would not deplete Earth's resources faster than Earth could rebuild them.[21]

Scientists now say, however, that sustainability is no longer adequate. We have so damaged Earth's life-support systems (soil, waters, climate, air) that economic activity must be restorative or regenerative, not merely sustainable. We must "reverse the widespread ecological damage that has been done in pursuit of economic growth—damage that reaches well beyond global warming."[22] This means, among other things, that greenhouse gas emissions must fall rapidly and immediately.[23]

Fossil fuel industries have fought against one vital point for three decades: that rapid reduction in emissions requires more than the development of renewables and incentives such as cap and trade. Rather, it requires mandatory caps on fossil fuel extraction and use, caps that are lowered yearly. Stan Cox argues this point well: "Fossil-fuels cannot be suppressed solely through the expansion of non-fossil energy or through market interventions such as carbon pricing; eradicating emission will require a statutory limit on all fuel extraction, one that lowers quickly year by year.... It will require a transformed economy that operates on less, not more, energy."[24]

For this reason, varied means of reducing greenhouse gas emissions, working in concert, are necessary. Switching to renewable energy sources is crucial. Yet alone, it is inadequate and dangerous. Renewable energy sources can profoundly damage vulnerable communities, creating "sacrifice zones."[25]

Therefore, a second method for reducing emissions, decreasing energy consumption, is necessary for people of the Global North. We cannot persist in our energy-consumptive mode of living, even when we do shift from fossil fuels to renewables.[26]

A third means of reducing greenhouse gas emissions is through legislation to eliminate fossil fuel subsidies and halt exploration for new fossil fuel reserves. "Governments around the world are still subsidizing fossil fuel investments with taxpayers' money to the tune of more than $5 trillion per year."[27] [28]

A fourth method for reducing greenhouse gases is reducing methane emissions. While CO_2 is the major greenhouse gas, a close second is methane, especially as produced by the cattle industry.[29] Reducing methane means reducing

Vision and Guideposts

the amounts of meat and dairy products in our diets. Reducing meat and dairy consumption would also help with a fifth method for gas reduction—stopping massive deforestation.

The final method involves various technological solutions. These will help, but technical solutions alone are not capable of resolving the issue. The belief that they can obstructs movement toward reducing energy use.

Note that all three terrains of change explored in the previous chapter (behavior, social structures, and worldviews/mindsets) are powerful for heeding the ecological guidepost. Imagine the impact of *structural change*: cities could decide to make public transportation renewable and to purchase only renewables produced under conditions of "just transition." Laws could require corporations to:

- replace the financial bottom line with a triple bottom line of ecological sustainability, financial viability, and social impact;
- be accountable and responsible for any social and ecological costs their operations incur;[30]
- measure profit and loss not only by quarter—and in monetary terms—but also by long-term, nonmonetary measures.

The impact of *worldview change* on realizing the ecological guidepost is no less dramatic. For example, our worldview that values overconsumption will shift to the valuing of sufficiency, enough, or frugality. Our mindset that globally traded food products are the norm will be replaced by valuing locally and regionally produced goods. A mindset that assumes the normalcy of disposable goods will give way to valuing and using enduring, repaired, and reused goods. We will discard the presupposition that growth is an adequate and accurate measure of economic well-being.[31] And each of these changes in social structures and worldviews have corresponding *changes in the third terrain—behaviors* as individuals, households, and institutions.

Equitable

> *I think the economic logic behind dumping a load of toxic waste in the lowest-wage country is impeccable and we should face up to that. ... Just between you and me, shouldn't the World Bank be encouraging more migration of the dirty industries to the less developed countries?*
>
> —Lawrence Summers, then chief economist and vice president of the World Bank and former Harvard University President[32]

I must confess that I do not draw a sharp or any distinction between economics and ethics. Economics that hurt the moral well-being of an individual or a nation are immoral and, therefore, sinful. Thus, the economics that permit one country to prey upon another are immoral. It is sinful to buy and use articles made by sweated labour.

—M. K. Gandhi[33]

Inequality, it turns out, is not an economic necessity; it is a design failure.

—Kate Raworth[34]

While "ecological" pertains to relationships within the broader Earth community, the "equitable" guidepost refers primarily to relationships between and among humans. Equitable economic practices and policies in today's context help to diminish the wealth gap. They also privilege the well-being of those who have been on the losing side of extractive wealth-concentrating economies.

What does this mean in the three terrains of lifestyle/behavior change, structural change, and worldview change? We will unpack this much more fully in chapter 7's discussions of just transition, energy equity, tax justice, and climate reparations. For now, we illustrate with one example. Replacing the ubiquitous goal of "maximizing profit" with the goal of "making a profit conditioned by the social and ecological good" illustrates the shift provided by the guidepost of equity.

An economy that rewards—or even mandates—maximizing profit, rather than simply making adequate profit, can never be equitable; it privileges people who have the means to maximize profit at the expense of others. In the neoliberal economy, corporate charters mandate corporations to maximize profit in the form of shareholder returns. The impact can be devastating when maximizing profit requires such behaviors as moving production plants out of one community in order to hire lower-paid workers in other nations, paying wages so low that workers must live on the streets, avoiding providing health insurance, or leaving wastelands in the wake of mining or logging.

The move to B Corporations, whose charters include attention to the triple bottom line, illustrates structural change.[35] So too do new policies that support worker-owned businesses accountable to local communities. Worker-owned business and B Corporations make a profit, but they do not concentrate on maximizing profit. They are accountable for meeting other criteria, as well, such as adequate wages and benefits.

What other kinds of economic policies cohere with the guidepost of equity? Note a few that have been or will be enacted in different communities:

- legislation classifying necessities—such as water, shelter, electricity, health care, and education at levels necessary for well-being—as human rights, not to be denied for the sake of profit;

- laws restricting the pay differential between the lowest and the highest paid person in a company or public entity;
- programs that provide financial incentives and training for transitioning to employee-owned and employee-managed businesses and local, small-scale agroecology;
- requirements for businesses of a certain size to assume costs for righting their social and ecological impacts;
- statutes requiring businesses of a certain size to produce no carbon emissions;
- initiatives that make truly affordable health care available to all.

These policies illustrate the terrain of structural change. What of the behavioral/lifestyle terrain? I step into a store and am sucked like a magnet to my long-held practice of buying the least expensive version of everything. But, the guidepost of equity stops me in my tracks; it has me replace items on the shelf. Instead, I tell myself, "Go find the fair-trade coffee, the bread produced by a local small bakery, the eggs produced by humanely raised chickens, the jars not made of plastic, biodegradable cleaning products." This, in turn, means a worldview change—away from seeing "getting a good buy" as a virtue. (Recall that this lifestyle move pertains to folks who have sufficient financial resources to do it without compromising the real needs of self or dependents. If I were stretched to afford food and other necessities, then "getting a good buy" might very well be a virtue.)

The guidepost of equity brings with it the gift of a racial equity lens. In terms of food systems, for example, agriculture and food production have exploited and marginalized Black, Brown, and Indigenous people in what became known as the Americas since before the birth of this nation.[36] A racial equity lens asks of any policy or practice, "What is the impact on Black, Brown, and Indigenous people? Will it exploit food workers or benefit them? Will it reinforce or break down the scourge of food deserts? Will it support Indigenous farmers and farmers of color?"

Why is equity such a crucial guidepost for building an economy of life? Surely it is important for the simple moral imperative. Poverty, especially amid wealth, can be anguishing. We are to bring it to an end. However, is there more reason? Yes. Ample evidence shows that wealth inequality makes for less stable, more violent, and less satisfied societies.[37] All sectors are hurt. Still newer evidence adds yet another imperative: "Large income and wealth differences—both within and between countries—reduce the chances that our societies will respond adequately to the environmental crisis."[38]

Democratic

You can have wealth concentrated in the hands of a few, or democracy. But you cannot have both.

—Louis Brandeis[39]

Corporations have been enthroned.... An era of corruption in high places will follow, and the money power will endeavor to prolong its reign ... until wealth is aggregated in a few hands ... and the Republic is destroyed.

—Abraham Lincoln[40]

The evils of capitalism are as real as the evils of militarism and racism. The problems of racial injustice and economic injustice cannot be solved without a radical redistribution of political and economic power.

—Rev. Dr. Martin Luther King Jr.[41]

The "democratic" guidepost calls us toward distributed and accountable power. Accountable economic power means that economic systems and players are accountable to the people and communities who are negatively impacted by them. What a colossal change from the norm in advanced global capitalism in which enormous corporations are accountable only to shareholders—and effectively only to the large shareholders! Consider the anguish in Detroit when automotive companies closed plants and moved them to other countries with far lower wage, environmental, and safety standards. What pain and suffering would have been avoided had those companies been accountable to their workers in Detroit?

Distributed economic power means that workers in Detroit would have had power in the decision whether to move the plant. "Economic democracy" or a "democratic economy" are terms describing a reorientation that ensures economic power is widely shared, including, most importantly, shared by people most impacted by the long history of extractive systems and practices. It includes the flourishing movement to build or transition to employee-owned businesses in various forms. This burgeoning movement is at the heart of an economic democracy movement.

Historically in the United States, democracy has been limited to the political realm, with the economic realm "free" from democratic constraints. Yet many respected leaders from both Republican and Democratic parties have cautioned against the dangers of concentrated economic power, warning that it would ruin social well-being as well as democracy. Abraham Lincoln, for example, warned that "corporations have been enthroned.... An era of corruption in high places will follow and the money power will endeavor to prolong its reign ... until wealth is aggregated in a few hands ... and the Republic is destroyed."[42] So too did Franklin D. Roosevelt. "Americans," he declared, "must forswear that conception of the acquisition of wealth which, through excessive profits, creates undue private power." These warnings recognized that "inequalities in economic power lead to inequalities in political power."[43]

The Three Guideposts Held Together

It is crucial to hold all three guideposts together as a foundation for building moral economies and as criteria for decisions and actions to mitigate climate change.[44] Why? Because one guidepost alone can lead to *policies and actions that work against the others*. An example is initiatives that reduce carbon emissions but damage people already vulnerable to climate devastation or already suffering from economic violence; such initiatives uphold the ecological guidepost but work against the equity quidepost. Many Indigenous leaders, for example, cry out that efforts to develop renewable energy (mining lithium for batteries among them) threaten their communities and livelihoods. Their communities become "sacrifice zones," people and lands "sacrificed" in order to produce renewable wind and solar power or batteries for electric vehicles. We look more closely at this danger in the next chapter.[45]

These guideposts do not imply any opposition to markets per se. Markets existed long before capitalism. They are a means of exchange and come in many forms. Nor do these guideposts oppose business. Businesses have a profound and integral role to play in building a moral economy. Likewise, these principles do not oppose profit. The guideposts oppose (1) maximizing profit without regard to the costs to people and the Earth community; and (2) business and markets that work against equity, ecological regenerativity, and democracy.

These changes toward ecological, equitable, and democratic economies are *not* simply idealistic dreaming! Countless people, businesses, governments, and other groups in the US and around the world enact them daily. They bring life-giving change in the terrains of individuals/households, social structures, and worldviews.

We will meet many of these people as these pages unfold. The coming chapter introduces companions in Denmark, Pacific Island nations, and the United States. What a host!

A Label?

You likely have noticed that we have not given a formal label to a moral economy. That is for good reason. In the jungle of ambiguity created by economic change and the varied connotations of many terms, some labels may do more harm than good.

"Democratic socialism," for example, is used by many. However, that label evokes in some people's minds the specter of state socialism, even though this is a false correlation. *Democratic socialism diametrically opposes state socialism and its concentration of economic power.*

"Post-capitalist," too, could be a viable label, but it triggers negative reactions in some people. Moreover, the term presupposes a definitive meaning of capitalism, whereas in reality, capitalism comes in many and extraordinarily diverse forms.[46] A capitalism that maintained, for example, a maximum pay differential of 10-to-1 between highest and lowest paid employees in an industry, a triple bottom line, and a requirement that companies absorb social and ecological costs of operations would be a different type from the neoliberal capitalism prevalent today. (The father of modern economics, Adam Smith, would roll over in his grave if he heard the current economy labeled as "capitalist," for it transgresses many of the conditions that Smith argued as necessary to healthy economic systems.) Moreover, advocates of a new economy are often unclear about whether they advocate "moving away from capitalism" or "moving away from a form of capitalism that is built on the exploitation of people and the planet."[47]

For those who want a label for the new, moral form of economy, we may use "democratic economy" or "economic democracy." These work very well, as indicated in the discussion of economic democracy above. What is said there about economic democracy pertains to democratic economy as well.

However, far more important than a term or label are the medicines we are exploring here in part 2 of the book:

- a morally empowering way of seeing (seeing what is going on, what could be, the Spirit's active presence, and beauty);
- three terrains of life in which social change takes place (behavior/lifestyle, social structures, and worldviews);
- two interflowing streams that drive change (resistance and rebuilding);
- vision for a moral economy
- guideposts for a moral economy (democratic, equitable, and ecological);
- a set of concepts that guide action and outline what to avoid.

Taken together, these lay the groundwork for building a moral economy. If applied seriously in public and corporate policy and in people's lives, they "form a political economy entirely different from capitalism as generally practiced."[48]

*　*　*

Honoring Our Bodies

Hear again the Buddhist teaching from chapter 3: "To be a human being is rare, precious, and infinitely meaningful." Now allow yourself to contemplate this teaching and let it land in your body. I invite you to close your eyes, and then to repeat these words slowly. Does an image or a feeling come to you? If so, just sit with it for a minute or two. Invite your body to feel what it is to be rare, precious, and infinitely meaningful. Now imagine the ancestor whom you identified earlier in your Sacred Journey Journal, conveying to you with her, his, or their eyes the truth that your particular life is in fact "rare, precious, and infinitely meaningful." Again, sit with this message.

Sacred Journey Journal

- Re-read all of the epigraphs in this chapter (at the outset and at the beginning of sections and subsections). What in them or in the chapter itself speaks to your heart?
- Do you know a business—large or small—that follows the vision and the three guideposts set forth in this chapter? What enables it to exist? What could you (or your household or place of employment or worshipping community or other group) do to strengthen it? If you do not know such a business, imagine one. Describe it. In what sense is it ecological, equitable, democratic? What does it need from the community to thrive? What public policies would help it to thrive?

CHAPTER SEVEN

Morally Empowering Concepts

I WAS VEHEMENT: "Paying attention to concepts and theory is little more than playing in an intellectual candy store—fun but frivolous and of no real use!" So I thought earlier in my life.

One of my mentors, Beverly Harrison, and Black women theorists such as Patricia Hill Collins taught me otherwise. A new concept can reveal possibilities that one did not know exist. It can unearth hidden horrors that must be seen to be undone. Theory and concepts can shine light through the vexing, swirling pool of reality.

The French sociologist Pierre Bourdieu argued that the "power of preserving or transforming the social world" rests in "preserving or transforming the categories of perception of that world."[1] That is, the concepts that we use for seeing what is going on, and what could happen instead, have tremendous power in preserving or transforming "the way things are." Concepts, thus, can be tools for healing and for liberation.

Here we consider, in short form, a few such concepts. Some shine light on where to head as we build moral economies. Others expose what to avoid. Take heed.

As you read, I ask you to engage these concepts not only as ideas, but *also as realities that already are at play in your life, even though you might not recognize their presence*. Ask of each concept, "How is my life connected to the reality that this term names? If it is a damaging connection, how might my life be connected to this reality in a different way, a way that heals or liberates?"

May you use these concepts as good medicine on your journey toward healing the economy. May they be medicine for healing relationships—relationships with self, with others, with all of creation, with God—through changing the systems and worldviews that shape these relationships. May these concepts be food for our souls.

Climate Justice/Climate Injustice[2]

Calm fierce determination. It flowed from her eyes. She was the youth among us. Maima's words during the three-day gathering in Bali were few but gripping.[3] Her people in the low-lying Pacific Islands, she said, were losing their livelihoods—traditional fishing and agriculture—and their homes to climate change. This meant also losing culture and identity. Terrible losses. The countries causing this devastation, she averred, must help to finance relocation and recovery. But, this young climate activist went on to insist, her people were not victims; they were protectors of the oceans. This commitment pulsated within their identity. "We Indigenous people are the custodians that have been given the role to protect and care for our oceans and our land. Not only for us but also for our future generations."[4] Indigenous People of the Pacific Islands are reweaving the ecological mat.

I had met Maima some weeks earlier. On stage with a microphone in Karlsruhe, Germany, Maima and other Indigenous youth led a rally for climate justice at the General Assembly of the World Council of Churches. Languages, garb, and religious symbols from distant lands graced the space. As delegates or speakers at the two-week assembly, the young Indigenous trailblazers cried out to faith leaders from around the world to step up to the plate—to convince their communities and governments to vastly lower emissions and help finance recovery and relocation for Indigenous communities wracked by climate change. Climate injustice fueled their passion. Climate justice was their hearts' desire.

Climate Injustice

"Climate injustice" signals four things:
- the climate crisis does not impact all communities equally;
- not all people bear the same amount of responsibility for causing it;
- climate-privileged sectors and societies often respond to the climate crisis in ways that protect themselves but severely damage more vulnerable communities;
- those of us in the high-emitting world bear moral responsibility to address the climate crisis in ways that account for our role in causing it.

Let us unpack this a bit. The world's impoverished people—who are disproportionally people of color and Indigenous communities—suffer most from the ravages of climate change.[5] They are also least responsible for causing it. The world's high consuming people, who are most responsible contemporarily and historically for the climate crisis, are more able to protect themselves from the devastation wrought by it.

This does not play out only between nations, but also *within* nations. Economically impoverished communities (again, disproportionally communities of color and Indigenous people) are most vulnerable to climate-intensified storms, wildfires, drought, food insecurity, heat waves, and disease.[6] A University of California study calls this the "climate gap." Researchers found, for instance, that "African Americans in Los Angeles are nearly twice as likely to die from a heat wave than other Los Angeles residents."[7]

This is the first layer of climate injustice. Recognizing the deeper layers is crucial for moving toward climate justice. A second layer is the tendency of climate-privileged societies and sectors to respond to climate change with policies and practices that enable them to survive with some degree of well-being while relegating others—the most "climate vulnerable"—to devastation.[8] Third, climate mitigation measures designed by privileged sectors often further endanger climate-vulnerable people.[9] Increasingly, Indigenous people and people of the Majority World refer to this as "green and blue colonialism." Examples span the globe. We consider some of them shortly. Fourth, the world's high-consuming people have benefitted materially from economic systems that have produced the climate crises. These four layers of climate injustice are intra-generational.

The fifth layer is intergenerational. High-emitting sectors limit the life-chances of future generations. The final layer of climate injustice is interspecies. Climate change and associated ecological devastation extinguish species and destroy habitats.

For me, and perhaps for you if you too are from the high-emissions world, realizing the magnitude of climate injustice and our place in it—the searing agony of lives lost and of our culpability, the millions of climate refugees thrown from their homes despite their innocence in causing the crisis, the future that awaits our children—invites despair. That is, unless we also see pathways for addressing the wrong and preventing some of the suffering. *For this reason, I thank God for the climate justice movement. It heralds a way forward.*

Climate Justice

Climate justice is the cry of youth delegates from the Pacific and other climate vulnerable parts of the world at international climate summits and in local communities around the globe:

> *Climate change is a lived reality for our Pacific communities.... These small island nations are threatened by a changing climate that awaits to swallow the land and the lives of many who call the Pacific their home.... As frontline communities of the Pacific, we believe that sharing our stories of resilience will call on high emitting countries to take responsibility for their actions and enable change. We believe we are not victims but communities*

who are fighting for the future of our home in the face of climate change. We believe in climate justice for all.[10]

"Climate justice" implies at least three dimensions of a moral response to climate injustice. The first is that the people most responsible for the climate crisis bear a moral responsibility to address it in ways that account for their role and for the fact that their material wealth comes from systems that have caused the crisis. Countless faith-based and other civil society networks point to this fact. It has been a sticking point in climate negotiations since the first COP conference.[11]

Secondly, climate justice signals that efforts to mitigate climate change must incorporate racial, economic, and gender justice lenses. Those frames prompt critical questions: How will an action impact Indigenous people and people of color, impoverished people, and especially women of impoverished communities or BIPOC communities? How do we implement a "just transition" rather than simply a transition from fossil fuels?

Finally, climate justice calls for climate reparations, including responding ethically to the millions—possibly billions—of climate refugees evacuating areas hit hardest by heat, floods, and drought.

The 2022 Statement for Climate Justice by the Global South issued by the Inter-religious Climate and Ecology Network illustrates both climate injustice and climate justice:

> *On the day of Global Climate Strike, September 23, 2022, we, a network of faith-based and civil society organizations in the Global South, demand developed countries in the Global North to recognize their historical role in the devastating climate disasters felt around the globe and take responsible action.... The recent flood damage at an unprecedented scale in Pakistan that killed more than 1,100 people and displaced 33 million confirmed yet again that the first and most severely hit by climate change are those in the Global South. In fact, it is the poorest 50 percent of the world's population that emit only 7 percent of the global greenhouse gas emissions that are at the forefront of climate change. The exploitation of natural resources and human lives in the Global South, however, continues to this day by multinational corporations from the Global North.... We demand developed countries to take conscious actions. Developed countries should phase out fossil fuels by 2030 and support the developing countries' transition to renewable energies. They should provide financial, technological, and capacity-building support for developing countries to adapt to the effects of climate change. [We specifically call for those nations to] cancel financial debt of the developing countries considering the ecological debt the Global North owes to the Global South.*[12]

Green and Blue Colonialism

The enterprises of green energy are activating colonial paths of extraction ... creat[ing] sacrifice zones.

—Myra Rivera[13]

The Indigenous Southern Sámi are a reindeer-herding people. Reindeer, explained my friend Tore Johnson, a Sámi theologian, are integral to their identity and economic well-being. Large-scale wind energy projects implemented by the Norwegian government are "dispossessing Sámi herders of their pasturelands,"[14] and thus endangering their livelihoods, culture, and identities. For these people, reindeer herding is already subject to increasingly unstable winter weather caused by climate change. Large-scale wind power facilities multiply that damage. Aili Keskitalo, the Sámi parliament's president, refers to this as "green colonialism" and an extension of the colonization of Sámi by the dominant culture and political economy of Norway.

For many Pacific Islanders, identity, livelihood, and purpose are intimately connected to the sea. "We are its guardians. We recognize its significance and its essence as the basis of our Pacific identity and wellbeing. We Are the Ocean. In its preservation, we are preserved."[15] In 2009, the first-ever permit for deep-sea mining was issued to a Canadian company, Nautilus Minerals, to operate near Papua New Guinea. Part of the project's purpose is to mine minerals used in renewable energy production, including electric car batteries. Significant opposition arose among Pacific Islanders, conscious of the damage that would be done to the ocean floor, the waters, the marine and land-based ecosystems, the food chain, and their fishing livelihoods.[16] Some people refer to the damage to waters and their ecosystems caused by sustainability efforts as "blue colonialism."

Transitioning from fossil fuels is essential. Wind and solar energy are key to that transition. Yet, the specter of continued exploitation emerges. Thus, the gift and challenge of truth-telling or seeing more deeply "what is going on" is invaluable. Truth-telling asks, What are the consequences, especially for climate-vulnerable people?

In 2022, an alliance of Pacific region parliamentarians issued the Pacific Blueline Statement. This call to protect the oceans from deep sea mining was endorsed by multiple organizations and leaders who see extraction as continuing the legacies of colonialism and nuclear testing that made their islands and seas into "sacrifice zones." The parliamentarians write,

> *Our forebears have ... stood firm against the ruinous incursions of nuclear testing, driftnet fishing and bottom trawling, and marine pollution. Against impossible odds, they united to move a world to adopt*

a nuclear test ban treaty, a ban on driftnet fishing, and the London Dumping Convention. Deep sea mining (DSM) is the latest in a long list of destructive industries to be thrust into our sacred ocean. It is a new, perilous frontier, extractive industry being falsely promoted as a proven answer to our economic needs. . . . We call for a total ban on DSM within our territorial waters and in areas beyond national jurisdiction.[17]

Green colonialism on Sámi lands is not isolated from people of the United States. The increase in wind energy development, while driven by European energy consumption, is linked to the demands by global companies, including Google and Facebook, to purchase renewable energy. "Through renewable energy purchases, these industries can 'green' their activities and gain market shares."[18] So too with blue colonialism in Pacific Islanders' waters. The electric vehicle industry feeds the push to mine copper from the ocean floor. *Electric vehicles use copper. I know; I drive one.*

Green colonialism happens around the world, through hydroelectric dams, destruction of crop lands to grow biofuels, mining for minerals needed for electric car batteries, and more. In short, *the move to renewables may be done in ways that further damage or destroy people.* "The 'green' energy industry promises to build a sustainable wonderland with electric cars and bullet trains powered by limitless renewable energy supply. It reinforces the dangerous idea that we can maintain our addiction to high-energy lifestyles in a sustainable way."[19]

Green colonialism also occurs within the United States when investment in renewables damages marginalized communities. Nuclear energy and hydroelectric dams, to illustrate, have come at tremendous costs to Indigenous communities in the US. More recently, carbon offset projects involving Indigenous peoples' lands have caused internal conflicts and have limited Indigenous communities from using their lands for medicine or other cultural purposes.[20]

The world's Indigenous communities who are fighting green and blue colonialism teach us three valuable lessons:

▶ First, a green future must also be a just future. The key is to view all renewable energy policy and projects through a decolonial lens. We need to ask, "Do these policies or project continue the colonial legacy of extraction and exploitation?"

▶ Second, getting free from fossil fuels depends NOT ONLY on transitioning to renewables. It also requires the world's high energy consumers to reduce energy use. This is an ever-present message from the Global South to the Global North:[21] "You cannot solve the problem of your sky-rocketed emissions only by replacing fossil fuels with renewable energy sources; you also must reduce your consumption!"

▸ A third lesson is equally clear: listen to the people who stand to lose the most and support their struggles. This includes listening to Indigenous communities who have been nurturing their ecosystems for centuries.

With these lessons, the concept of just transition jumps to the fore.

Just Transition[22]

Just transition is a framework for a fair and sustainable systems shift from an old extractive economy to a new regenerative economy that is fair and just.

—The Center for Story-Based Strategy[23]

Cedar walls radiated welcome. A vibrant crowd exuded joy. The Duwamish people's longhouse in Seattle overflowed. His pen poised, Washington's Governor Jay Inslee, standing in the Longhouse, signed the HEAL Act into law.[24] This moment in 2021 marked years of tenacious organizing by community-based groups, led by people of color and Indigenous people.

The landmark law requires action and funding for a just transition. That is, a transition *from* economic ways that have damaged people of color, Indigenous people, low-income people, and Earth. And a transition *to* more equitable, democratic, ecologically-sound economic practices. The people were also wary. Says Front and Center, a lead network in this coalition,

"We know a Just Transition won't come easy. White supremacy and the 'dig, dump, burn' consumer economy are still a reality for all of us to navigate. . . . Change takes time and can be frustrating. But we believe we can persevere through these obstacles and make change if we work together."[25]

Just transition is a stunningly beautiful concept. Though it comes from the secular world, it is theologically profound, for it is a means of practicing both "rules" for living in the household of Earth offered by the God of biblical faith—"love your neighbor" and "serve and preserve garden Earth."

"Just transition" signifies the commitment to transition from extractive fossil-fuel based economies to low carbon (or zero-carbon) regenerative economies in ways that (1) serve the well-being of marginalized people who could be damaged by that transition; (2) make space in the decision-making process for people at risk of damage by the transition; and (3) address inequities caused by the current extractive and exploitative economy. This stands in contrast to ways of making the transition that ignore matters of social equity, and thereby may damage vulnerable people.

Originating in activist communities, the term has become mainstream.[26] Passage of the HEAL Act in Washington state demonstrates this.[27] So too does a recent groundbreaking move in Denmark. In 2020, Denmark "passed a binding law for climate-neutrality by 2050, and the planned phase-out of its oil and gas sector is central to meeting these commitments." The law states that *"a just transition is central* to this transformation. Denmark is committed to helping workers transition to new and well-paying jobs and supporting those regions and communities that are most impacted."[28] The move is significant; Denmark is "the world's largest oil producer to commit to ending oil and gas extraction." Many states of the US and cities in various countries incorporate just transition into planning. Scotland, New Zealand, Canada, Spain, and Denmark have governmentally appointed just transition task forces, commissions, or initiatives, and the European Union has a "just transition fund."[29] Of course, the extent to which this rhetoric will be lived out remains to be seen.

Varying Contexts and Emphases

Just transition is complex and has different emphases depending on context. The measures called for by just transition are as varied as the measures for mitigating climate change. The following illustrations offer a glimpse of that range.

Phasing out coal could devastate coal workers. Just transition includes provisions to enable displaced coal workers to obtain decently paying jobs with benefits.[30]

For the people of mineral-rich regions of Africa, Latin America, the Pacific Islands, and Indigenous lands in Turtle Island (North America), just transition means protecting the lands and communities targeted in renewable energy initiatives. In many cases their people are being exploited—sometimes terribly—in the extraction of those minerals.[31] Just transition prohibits mining practices that harm people or damage their environment, and requires that profits from mining go primarily to the people impacted rather than primarily to mining corporations. Principles of just transition also require participation of local people in decision-making about mining in their regions.

In yet another arena, just transition affirms the principle that nations historically responsible for carbon emissions are mandated to reduce emissions more than nations with low emissions levels.[32] Likewise, just transition requires that nations that have benefited materially from the carbon-intensive economy (wealthy nations) provide financing for climate mitigation and adaptation to impoverished nations.[33]

Other advocates of just transition point to the problem of carbon offsetting. This is the practice of businesses or countries paying for emissions to be reduced elsewhere, instead of cancelling their own emissions. In effect, those who have the money can keep on emitting greenhouse gasses. To make matters worse, some carbon offset projects damage Indigenous, subsistence, and other frontline communities.[34]

The Indigenous Environmental Network (IEN) offers an eloquent description of just transition from an Indigenous perspective. You might give yourself the gift of reading it before moving on.[35] See https://www.ienearth.org/justtransition/.[36]

The Climate Justice Alliance, together with Movement Generation, also provides an excellent explanation of just transition on their website and in the paper "Just Transition Principles" that incorporates most of the emphases outlined above.[37] Building a moral economy includes assessing public policy proposals for alignment with just transition values.[38] These principles and resources are invaluable for that important work.

Low-Emissions Economy/Low-Carbon Economy

If we attempt to construct a wind- and solar-powered society that replicates today's high-energy living arrangements and transportation systems, the result will be the creation of "green sacrifice zones" in nations that have large deposits of cobalt, lithium, and other metals that go into the mechanisms essential to renewable electricity systems.

—Stan Cox[39]

Inherent in a just transition is the concept of a low-emissions economy or low-carbon economy.

For me this concept was a relief, a breath of hope. It countered the sense of futility that arose when I first began to learn about green and blue sacrifice zones. One "teacher" for me has been a colleague from Zambia. "My cousin was hospitalized and died from swimming in a river that the mining company had poisoned," he said. "That mining company poisoned my cousin." I learned more. The company mined lead, which is used in back-up batteries for solar and wind power and in the creation of wind turbines.[40] Many children suffer brain damage from constant exposure to the toxins left in the soil and water by companies mining lead.[41] The agriculturalist Stan Cox's warning rings true.

The goal of a renewable energy economy bears big problems. Many renewables depend upon minerals, the extraction of which has harmed and even killed people. A "just transition" lens for assessing efforts to mitigate climate change says "no" to sacrificing marginalized people to produce renewables.

Enter here the value of shifting the goal from renewable energy economies to "low-emissions economies" (also called "low-carbon economies"). This concept points to a far more equitable goal. *It aims both at moving from fossil fuels to renewables and at consuming less energy.* Friends, hear this well! It is key to saving lives.

The principles of just transition and of a low-emissions economy are closely linked to the term *postextractive economy.*

Postextractive Economy

Climate change will unequivocally defeat economies that are based on constant taking without giving in return.

—Robin Wall Kimmerer[42]

God forbid that India should ever take to industrialism after the manner of the West. If an entire nation of 300 million took to similar economic exploitation, it would strip the world bare like locusts.

—Gandhi[43]

People gathered to listen. Leonora (name changed for the sake of security), a leader in the tax justice movement in Africa, spoke with passion: "Africa is not getting a fair deal for its mineral resources. The impact on the people is terrible." She went on to declare, "When the mining companies come, they displace the people. The people are pushed out to the hills where they cannot even grow their food."[44]

This leader was speaking about extractive economies. The term refers to economic practices, policies, and structures that (1) extract resources without equitable compensation or any protection against ecological damage; or (2) extract wealth from economically marginalized communities; or (3) extract labor from people without equitable compensation or safe working conditions.

The rapidly growing global tax justice movement partially addresses these extractive travesties. The Global Alliance for Tax Justice, a coalition led by people of the Global South, promotes taxing corporations that extract resources from countries of the Global South to prevent the companies from amassing revenues by leaving behind exploited lands and peoples. The movement for tax justice spans five continents. It is one means of curtailing the power of extractive industries to decimate people and lands where they operate.

Two British organizations—War on Want and the London Mining Network—provide a framework for moving to post-extractive economies in their "A Just(ice) Transition Is a Post-extractive Transition." They write that "clear limits must be set on the extractivist model.... The livelihoods, rights, and cultural survival of thousands of frontline communities—and the integrity of countless ecosystems—depend on placing these boundaries on the extractive industries."[45]

Recall the three terrains of change entailed in building moral economies. The third was change in consciousness, mindset, or worldview. What a vast shift in consciousness to assume that companies are not "free" to extract lumber, minerals, waters, labor, and communities' wealth without limit. Freedom to extract has been a foundation of life in the modern West. One primary purpose of European colonization was to extract gold and other minerals from what became known as the Americas and Africa. Westward expansion in the United States was fueled by extraction. The fossil fuel era of human society is the era of extracting oil, gas, and coal. Efficiency in parts of the business world depends upon extracting as much free and low-cost labor as possible. The construction of the modern human might be seen as the construction of *homo extracticus*. Transitioning to a post-extractive economy will mean a new (or perhaps ancient and reclaimed) consciousness regarding human freedom and human rights in relationship to creation and other people.

Real-Cost Pricing/Full-Cost Pricing

Sending humans to the moon was difficult and unprecedented. Surely a species who can travel from Earth to the moon has the smarts to measure real costs of our earthly activities. The World Scientists' Warning to Humanity is clarion:

> [One] step humanity can take to transition to sustainability is revising our economy to ... ensure that prices and taxation take into account "real costs." [That is,] prices should reflect not only the internal costs of producing a good or providing a service, but also all external costs—like increased unemployment or climate change—that are currently passed on to society.[46]

This is no easy move. Current economic practices do not measure, for example, the real costs of food produced by industrial agriculture (costs of depleting soil of its nutrients, polluting watersheds, salination, petrochemical production for pesticides and herbicides, etc.). These costs are considered "externalities," meaning that they are external to a company's bottom line or a nation's GDP. Nor do we yet have metrics for the public health costs of exploitative and toxic working conditions, or ways of including costs of fighting storms and wildfires in the bottom lines of fossil-fuel companies whose emissions bear much responsibility for the climate change that intensifies these disasters. Yet, as the world scientists imply, the fact that this is difficult or unprecedented is no reason not to do it. Surely it is not more difficult than traveling to the moon!

Economic Democracy

There can be no real political democracy unless there is something approaching an economic democracy.

—Theodore Roosevelt[47]

The underlying illness is . . . the corporate drive to make profits for shareholders, no matter who pays the cost. . . . The solution is economic democracy.

—William Greider[48]

Economic democracy, or expanding democracy to the economic realm, is a move to rescue democracy from the control of money. The founders of the United States had differing notions of how far democratic power in the nation should extend. Most sought to build democracy in government, but not in the economy.[49] In limiting the principle of democracy to government, some of the nation's founders assumed that economic powers would be constrained by market forces or by the state.

This has not proven true. Economic powers, and in particular large limited liability corporations and the finance industry, have been "free" to concentrate wealth in the hands of their shareholders. Judicial and legislative decisions have given corporations the legal rights to exercise tremendous influence in the political realm.[50]

The shapers of the post–World War II global world order were strategic in protecting wealth from democratic governance.[51] They were the theorists and power brokers who built the current neoliberal global economy.

Many of the neoliberal theorists were explicit about the *dangers of what they perceived as too much democracy* and the dangers of curtailing the "freedom" of the wealthy—and particularly the freedom of large corporations and finance institutions—to do as they pleased within the market.[52] From its earliest years, the United States has seen an ongoing conflict between democracy and property rights.[53] Neoliberalism is a decades-long win for property rights over democracy.

Economic democracy describes an array of policies and practices in systems impacting everything from small companies to nations. While we cannot elaborate the breadth of this movement here, we will simply note its essence: the idea that power—be it political or economic—should be relatively *distributed* and should be *accountable* to people impacted by it.[54] "Economic democracy" stands in contrast to the power-centralizing dynamics inherent in both capitalism and state-centered socialism. Economic democracy precludes the recent unaccountable economic power moves that enabled a few billionaires and other exorbitantly wealthy individuals to profit financially from the suffering of others during the COVID pandemic.[55]

Economic democracy embeds the democratic principles of shared and accountable power into economic structures.[56] It calls for people and communities to have a role in the economic decisions that shape their lives. Its basic conviction is this: decisions that shape people's lives (including those about wages and benefits, access to water and food, availability of jobs and safe working conditions, and the impact of industry on the environment) must not be made only by a few very wealthy people who will not experience the consequences of their decisions and who will likely profit from decisions that hurt other people. Small business owner and advocate of economic democracy Marjorie Kelly describes economic democracy as "a healthy economy—rooted not in the unsustainable wealth of a few but in the enduring prosperity of the many."[57]

The movement toward economic democracy—while not highly evident in the public discourse—is robust and growing. Three aspects mutually enhance each other: (1) businesses that practice economic democracy; (2) public policies that encourage it; and (3) efforts to raise awareness of economic democracy as a more life-giving alternative. Let's listen in and then view a bit of history.

Businesses and Other Projects Enacting Economic Democracy

Do you recall chapter 2's story from the Mondragon Cooperative in Spain? That initiative is a large-scale example of economic democracy. Recall, too, Shanine and the Cleveland Cooperative Initiative, which has made more than two hundred formerly impoverished people into employee-owners of their business. Says the Atlas of the Future about Cleveland's experiment in economic democracy,

> *[The] initiative is beginning to build serious momentum in one of the cities most dramatically impacted by the nation's decaying economy.... The success and impact that a simple model has had on Cleveland—and the dignity it has restored to local communities—is truly inspiring. And other cities are taking note, replicating and adapting this innovative approach to economic development, green job creation and neighbourhood stabilization.*[58]

One city following Cleveland's lead is Chicago. The Windy City, led by the Mayor's Office of Equity and Racial Justice (OERJ), launched a Community Wealth Ecosystem Building Program "to invest in the organizations that start, sustain, and scale CWB models." "Community Wealth Building," declares the Mayor's Office, "promotes the local, democratic, and shared ownership and control of community assets." The primary goals are to create worker cooperatives, low-income housing cooperatives, community land trusts, and community investment funds. The city is investing heavily in this undertaking, advised by leaders of community-based organizations.[59]

Meanwhile, in Boston, a coalition of Black, Indigenous, other people of color, and working-class people created the Boston Ujima Project, an ecosystem of cooperative business, arts ventures, and investment funds. The project offers technical support, low-interest financing, marketing assistance, advocacy, and networking to small, democratically controlled businesses. It helps solidify procurement contracts with large local anchor institutions such as universities and religious institutions. Its partner businesses include farms, restaurants, production companies, retail outlets, recycling firms, and more.

Chicago, Cleveland, Boston—these are the tip of the iceberg. Businesses enacting economic democracy are flowering in many forms around the nation. They include consumer cooperatives, worker owned or managed businesses, publicly accountable local or regional banks, community supported small-scale farms, publicly owned energy companies, community-based land trusts, and more. They serve as experimental workshops and leaven for a more just economy.

A key factor across all of these initiatives is governance and ownership by a broad spectrum of *stakeholders* rather than a small group of corporate executives and major *shareholders*. "Power is relocated into the hands of those who are actually doing the work ... and whose interest is tied to their local communities and the natural environment where they live."[60]

Public Policy

Public policy can either obstruct or enable economic democracy and can incentivize or discourage transition to worker-owned business. Illustrations are countless. In 2022 California passed the Employee Ownership Act, which equips workers to become co-owners of the companies where they work. Seven years earlier, the California Worker Cooperative Act created a legal entity for worker-owned coops.

Raising Awareness

Efforts to raise awareness of economic democracy abound, and yet most initiatives still operate beneath the radar in public discourse. Organizations supporting worker-owned businesses are at the forefront of public education. The Center for Economic Democracy, for example, hosts a fountain of initiatives to launch, steward, and finance projects in economic democracy and identifies one of its primary strategies as to "educate and inspire."[61] So, too, the New Economy Coalition and the US Solidarity Economy Network include education as a principle strategy.[62] We will encounter these and other organizations in chapter 8's foray into "building the new" as a form of action.

A Bit of History

Economic democracy has a rich history "extending back to the cooperative and guild socialist movements of the nineteenth and early twentieth century" in Europe.[63] Countless leaders have warned that amassed wealth would undermine democracy. The Nebraska Supreme Court, for example, ruled in 1889 that "it is doubtful if free government can long exist in a country where enormous amounts of money are allowed to be accumulated in the vaults of corporations, to be used at discretion in controlling the property and business of the country against the interest of the public and that of the people, for the personal gain and aggrandizement of a few individuals."[64]

In the United States, the movement to build economic democracy began decades ago and has gained momentum in the last decade. The movement insists that democracy will be compromised if economic power is exempt from the democratic norms of accountable and distributed power. Democracy is also at risk, this movement avers, when economic "freedom" generates extreme economic inequality. The subordination of democracy—rule (*kratia*) by the people (*demos*)—by powerful economic players flies in the face of democracy's ideals and jeopardizes it.[65]

This position has been on the table since theories of classical liberalism and of democracy developed in the seventeenth and eighteenth centuries.[66] The current, robust economic democracy movement is a next step in the great project of democracy—to replace rule by a few with rule by the people.[67]

The impetus toward more democratic forms of economy has a solid history in Christian ethics from its inception as a discipline in the early twentieth century. Various voices in the Social Gospel movement espoused democratization of the economy in different forms. All were rooted in the conviction that unfettered capitalism—because of its inevitable inequality and exploitation—is contrary to the way of Jesus and the reign of God.

The future of economic democracy is "yet to be written."[68] It is a hopeful future precisely because the need is so dire and the worldwide movement against concentrated economic power is growing strong.

Climate Reparations

Dr. Moe-Lobeda, what are we to do? It is too horrible; it is unbearable. I am screaming inside—just looking into the eyes of those people ripped from their homes by climate change, and to think that WE *are causing it.*

> *I wish I had never seen that film or the faces of the people in it. What are we to do?*
>
> —Student after seeing the film *Climate Refugees*

> *The impacts of climate change . . . demonstrate a grand irony: Those who suffer most acutely are also those who are least responsible for the crisis to date. That irony introduces a grand dilemma, one that our systems of law and governance are ill-equipped to accommodate. . . . I introduce a theory of climate reparations to meet the great and disproportionate injuries that will result from anthropogenic climate change.*
>
> —Maxine Burkett, professor of law[69]

For me, while the realities of climate injustice and the suffering they bring are soul searing, the notion of climate reparations is profoundly hope giving. Reparations is an avenue for "justice-making neighbor-love" where it had seemed impossible.

We will pause a little longer on this concept because it is so gnarly, loaded, and difficult to fathom; it wants to escape into the abstract, slip into the shadows. Our ancestors and guides from the past did not reckon with this reality. We must consider varied voices and muster courage not to run.

So, let us hear from some who are bearing the brunt of the climate's fury and whose people stand to lose lives, livelihoods, or homelands to it, and who also bear tidings of reparations as a means to repair terribly wrong relationships and build "right relations." (Recall from chapter 1 that the biblical norm of neighbor-love includes justice, which pertains to right relationships, relationships in which all may flourish, and especially those who are marginalized and vulnerable.) One of these voices relates this call to the Bible's Good Samaritan story.

Calling for Climate Reparations

Angelica Navarro—Bolivian diplomat, climate negotiator, and ambassador to the WTO—brought to the world's attention the call by nations of the Global South for climate reparations, payment of the climate debt owed to them by the wealthy world. Navarro argued in 2009 at COP 15 that Bolivia is owed a debt because its people are endangered by climate change that is caused disproportionally by people of the wealthy world.[70] The appropriate response, she argued, is reparations by the wealthy nations for the harm it has done.

People of the Global South and Indigenous peoples have insisted since the first UN climate conference nearly thirty years ago that payment for climate-caused "loss and damage" is owed to nations suffering from climate changes they did not cause.[71] As early as 2009, legal communities began arguing for, and articulating the complexities of, climate reparations.[72] With COP 27 (in November 2022 in Egypt), "loss and damage" payments or financing (also known as climate reparations) appeared on the COP formal agenda and featured prominently in the negotiations for the first time.[73]

Like Navarro and countless others, the Alliance of Small Island States (AOSIS), a group of thirty-nine small island and low-lying developing nations largely from the Caribbean and South Pacific, emphasizes that finance for loss and damage is not "a favor" but rather payment due for what has been done to them.[74] For this reason, many refer to "loss and damage payments" as "climate reparations," although the term "loss and damage" is more common in international climate negotiations. ("Loss and damage payments," "loss and damage finance," and "climate reparations" may be used interchangeably.)

Rev. Dr. Gordon Cowans of Jamaica links these reparations to the history of colonization. He argued in an eloquent address to a team assembled by the World Council of Churches that "indiscriminate exploitation of natural resources [by colonizing countries] left Caribbean nations more vulnerable to climate shocks.... Time has come for repair through reparatory justice." Reparations, he went on to explain, must include funding to Caribbean nations to recover from climate-related damage and to rebuild their economies. He insists that reparations must also include cancellation of the external debt that is sucking so much sorely needed money from these nations. We will hear more from Rev. Cowans in chapter 12.

Tuvaluan theologian and activist Maina Talia, in a presentation on a Tuvaluan interpretation of the Good Samaritan story, challenges economically privileged people of the Global North to convert from being what he calls "robbers" who "enjoy the loot of the capitalist system" to being good neighbors. Speaking of the two wounds of poverty and assault on Earth, Talia writes, "These two open wounds are the work of the robbers."[75] He goes on to note that "the demand from the robbers . . . for profit" results in the enormous amount of greenhouse gases released by burning fossil fuels. Talia's voice, from a people and a nation who will be drowned by climate changes it did not cause, is an invitation for those of us who "enjoy the loot of the capitalist system" to become Good Samaritans by engaging in climate reparations.[76]

Forms of Climate Reparations

What forms might climate reparations take? Many Indigenous and Global South activists propose ways climate reparations are to be paid and warn against untenable methods. The Via Campesina, an international network of small farmers, articulates a perspective of many Indigenous peoples in insisting that loss and damage payments NOT take the forms often promoted by wealthy nations, such as carbon offsets and net zero efforts. Carbon offsets and goals of net zero emissions allow corporations to continue emitting greenhouse gasses by paying for projects that fight climate change. Often those projects end up hurting people, albeit unintentionally.[77] Via Campesina insists that offsets and net zero initiatives are "false solutions," arguing,

> *The legacy of carbon offsetting schemes so far has included environmental crimes, conflicts, corporate abuse, forced relocation, and threats to food sovereignty and cultural genocide, particularly for Indigenous Peoples, smallholder farmers, forest dwellers, young people, women and people of colour. Carbon offsetting schemes are responsible for atrocities inflicted upon vulnerable populations around the world, and we reject them as a form of climate colonialism. . . . We demand that rich countries stop shirking their responsibilities. . . .* **We demand solutions that deliver emissions reductions at [the] source** *and lead us toward a more just and equitable world. We demand real, additional, public finance from rich countries so that developing countries can transition towards just energy systems, adapt to climate impacts, and be compensated for irreparable loss and damage as stipulated under article 6.6.*[78]

Another face of reparations may well be the acceptance and support for climate refugees forced to flee lands made unlivable by rising seas, intense heat and drought, and climate-intensified storms. Estimates vary, but they are arresting. Some estimates foretell refugees in the billions if we allow an increase of more than 1.5 degrees Celsius.

Many appeals from the Global South promote three broad forms of climate reparations or "loss and damage" payments:

- funding for climate mitigation that would enable impoverished nations to bypass dirty energy and move to renewables, reducing their national emissions;
- funding for climate adaptation including relocation;
- cancellation of debt owed by many impoverished countries to finance institutions and governments of wealthy nations.[79]

A recent example comes from Alaska. "Newtok, Alaska, a remote Yup'ik Alaska Native Village, has been battling erosion and flooding resulting from climate change for over twenty years. Due to rapidly increasing water levels in the Arctic, the entire village of Newtok was forced to relocate to Mertarvik. . . . In November 2022, the Biden-Harris Administration announced that the Village of Newtok was one of three communities selected for a $25 million relocation grant. . . . Relocation grants are provided to communities, such as Newtok, who are severely impacted by climate change and in a position to implement and manage relocation and retreat plans."[80]

The situation in Pakistan after the 2022 floods as described by the general secretary of a network of twenty-six peasant organizations in Pakistan illustrates both the case for climate reparations and two of the three types of reparations noted above:

> [As of Sept 2022,] more than one-third of Pakistan is under water. Flash floods, generated by abnormal monsoon rains have so far claimed the lives of 1350 people. One million residential buildings are totally or partially damaged, leaving more than 50 million people displaced from their homes. . . . These impacts are undeniably a symptom of an accelerating climate.
>
> Despite producing less than one per cent of global carbon emissions, Pakistan bears some of the worst consequences of the climate crisis globally. The nation has consistently ranked in the Global Climate Risk Index as among the top ten most vulnerable countries in the world over the past twenty years. As Julien Harneis, the UN humanitarian coordinator in Pakistan says: "This super flood is driven by climate change—the causes are international."
>
> The people of Pakistan are the latest victims of a global crisis to which they have contributed almost nothing—and which has instead been driven by the excess emissions of rich countries and corporate polluters. This fundamental injustice is at the root of increasing demands for climate reparations from Pakistan and the wider Global South.
>
> One such demand is debt cancellation. Debt injustice and the climate crisis go hand in hand. As extreme weather events intensify, countries on the frontlines, such as Mozambique, and island states in the Caribbean, are facing increasing economic damages. After these events, low-income (and often already heavily indebted) governments face a shortfall in funding and have little choice but to take out further loans to rebuild livelihoods and communities.
>
> If the West intends on supporting Pakistan through this crisis . . . a first step should include comprehensive debt cancellation, alongside greatly increased climate finance to support communities to adapt to the impacts of climate change. . . . Why should Pakistan have to take out any loans at all to pay for the impacts of a crisis it has not caused?[81]

David Wallace-Wells, editor at large of *New York Magazine*, sums up the case for climate reparations in a cover story entitled "Climate Reparations." Climate change, he writes is "a moral catastrophe—engineered by the sheltered nations of the global North . . . and suffered by those, in the global South, least responsible for it and least prepared. The rich are rich today because of development powered by fossil fuels." "The responsibility for the climate crisis doesn't lie with humanity, it lies with the global rich."[82]

The Concepts as a Whole

We return to where we began this foray into concepts—concepts as good medicine for the sacred work of healing economic life. May they be medicine for the healing of relationships—with self, others, and all of creation—through changing exploitative economic systems and the worldviews that shape them. May these concepts guide you in the spiritual practice of healing these relationships. May these concepts be food for your soul.

Moving On

I invite you in part 3 to explore a final medicinal tool. It is a set of ten forms of action. We will call them "fingers on the hands of liberative change" and also "fingers on the hands of healing." I hope that you relish the possibilities that they open for the transition to more life-giving forms of economic life.

* * *

Honoring Our Bodies

The musician Betsy Rose sings a beautiful song: "I am daughter of the Earth, and I surely know my worth." Move to a place where you feel comfortable, at ease. Try singing that line to any tune that you treasure. Imagine: you are a child of Earth and therefore you are of infinite worth, and you are a vessel of healing, liberating life-force. Sit with that reality; how does it feel in your body?

After a few moments, imagine a person who is significant in your life and who would not appreciate many of the concepts in this chapter. What is one concept about which this person would be particularly antagonistic? Imagine going to visit this person and sharing why you value this concept and talking about it. How does it feel to knock on her, his, or their door with the intention of having this discussion? How does your body feel? Now imagine that you are accompanied by the ancestor you identified previously in this journal. The ancestor is joining you in the conversation. Perhaps the ancestor is even doing the talking, and you have just come along. How does your body feel now?

Sacred Journey Journal

Recall that the concepts you have explored in this chapter are meant to be good medicine for healing economic life. Choose one of them and enter into it as a healing medicine. Is this concept—or rather the reality it describes—connected to your life? If so, in what way? If this concept describes something good, how might you enact this concept in your life (or enact it more fully in your life)? If it describes something to avoid, how might you (or your household or a group of which you are a part) actively counter or avoid the reality it describes?

III

Fingers on the Hands of Healing

Setting the Stage

> We've got lists upon lists of the things we need to reform but not enough about how to accomplish those reforms. I think no one should mention a reform/next step/needed change without also discussing how to get from here to there.
>
> —Valarie Kaur

> It is healing behavior, to look at something so broken and see the possibility and wholeness in it. . . . We are all healers too—we are creating possibilities, because we are seeing a future full of wholeness.
>
> —adrienne maree brown[1]

WHAT MARVELOUSLY COMPLEX wonders we accomplish with our hands. Creating splendid music on a piano or a reed flute, carving a piece of wood, scribbling a poem, planting a seed, changing a diaper, crafting a simple scrumptious meal. Each finger plays a different role in the complex system that is the human hand. One finger alone does not accomplish much. Yet what magnificent creations they render when dancing in collaboration.

This is the way with great movements to heal society of terrible wrongs, from abolishing chattel slavery to dismantling economic exploitation. Many different forms of action—different fingers on the hands of healing—are needed. The beauty of this is that every person and group has a role to play; differing gifts and propensities chime in, from art and music to legal strategies, from financial acuity to public protest, from liturgy to listening, from legislative action to education and more. You may not be drawn to one form of action, but your gifts will fit with others.

In the following ten short chapters, we sketch this fertile array—"ten fingers on the hands of healing"—in relationship to building the new economy. They are ten different forms of action that, working together, will enable us to transform predatory forms of economic life into economies that serve life. (We refer to these also as "ten fingers on the hands of liberating change.")

- ▶ Build the New
- ▶ Live Lightly

- Change the Rules
- Move the Money
- Resist the Wrong
- Build the Bigger We
- Practice Awe, Lament, Holy Anger, Gratitude
- Listen and Amplify
- Change the Story
- Drink the Spirit's Courage

In sketching this panorama, I have drawn on the work of various movement groups. I am grateful beyond words for their creative, visionary, and practical work toward forging life-giving economies. Especially significant for me has been the framework provided by the Climate Justice Alliance in their six "meta-strategies" (stop the bad, build the new, change the rules, move the money, build the movement, change the story).[2]

In exploring this rich array and recognizing its diversity and interdependence, may you gain a clearer sense of what may be your roles and your groups' roles in the movement to build more compassionate and Earth-honoring economies. You might imagine yourself in new roles. Be in dialogue with what you read and the people and groups you encounter in the process. Let yourself imagine: "Oh, I could see myself in this!" Or "My synagogue could take on something like this." "Ah, this would challenge me so much, but if I had a team of companions."

Vital Links

As you prowl around in this fertile terrain, bear in mind that no one of these ten forms of actions is "the" main one or "the" most important. Multiple forms of action are *necessary, interdependent, and inadequate apart from other forms*. A dangerous mistake is made when practitioners of one form imply or assume that it alone is adequate or is the most important. For example: In some accountings, the new economy is equated with the burgeoning movement to create alternative forms of business that are worker owned, local or regional, ecologically sound, and equitably managed. While that is one crucial strategy (we call it "building the new), it could not flourish without other strategies such as public policy change, moving the money, and more.

I recall well my conversations in Washington, DC, with the Beloved Community Incubator that we met in chapter 3. They recently had won a huge victory by helping a group of low-income immigrants to buy their apartment complex that was going to be sold out from under them in a gentrification process. They taught me that their work to create that new housing option ("building the new") would not have been possible without public policy advocacy ("changing

Setting the Stage

the rules") a decade earlier that gave first rights of purchase to tenants. The point is simple but profoundly important. Deep social change cannot be achieved by one form of action alone. All fingers on the hands of change or healing are needed.

The connection between forms of action is one important link that we will trace in the upcoming chapters. Be alert also for four other key links. They are the interplay

- among global, national, and local change,
- between resisting and rebuilding (chapter 5),
- among change in behaviors, social structures, and consciousness or worldview (chapter 5),
- between small practical steps and larger systemic change.

These connections are vital to building power for healing our shared economic life. They are bridges to a more compassionate, just, and ecologically sane future.

You may recognize a paradox. We are claiming an extraordinary vision for economic life, while also moving toward it in highly pragmatic steps. Let not the practicality of the steps obscure the extraordinary and transformative nature of the vision. Nor let the astounding nature of that vision lure us from the need for practical steps to enact it. The two sides of this paradox go hand in hand. They need each other. Holding them together is vital; dropping one would suck the power out of the other. Why? The practical steps alone will not change the economy on the large scale. But if they are seen as part of the larger vision and movement toward it, then they are seeds of splendidly more life-giving ways of life in garden Earth.

A story illumines these links.

Eight-year-old Stefano Castro, born in Mexico, was eager to tell his mother about his recent farm trip:

"First I saw Fidel and his friends dancing to bless the land. To start the dance, they blew into a shell and made a fire in a bowl. The dancers have a lot of things to put on, like white robes with sashes.... I have seen clothes like that in Mexico. Next I helped plant some seeds. It's a lot of work.

At the greenhouse, my friend Andrew showed me how to harvest the lettuce.... There were about 800 million plants in there. It was the most fun thing I ever did.

The next day I helped him load the salad on a truck so he can drive it to the school.... Now when I eat salad at school I remember all the people and the work that goes into making it, and it tasted really good too."[3]

The people of largely Latino/a and Indigenous communities in New Mexico and a Quaker organization—together with a great deal of deep listening, Indigenous people's spirituality, and vision of an economy that nurtures communities' well-being—gave rise to a vibrant network of agricultural cooperatives. It provides fresh organic produce for countless communities, and more than half of New Mexico's school children. The network engages elders and youth, and enables year-round food production through passive solar hoop houses. This cooperative food economy enables small farmers to thrive and build power "without getting caught in the traps of competitive capitalism."[4] They support each other rather than competing against each other. For example, "With very different growing seasons in the north, center, and south of the state, by working together the co-ops can complement each other's efforts and provide a broader range of foods throughout the year." The farmers and new farmers involved learn "skills in running cooperatives and marketing."

Clearly these innovators are "building the new" and "building the bigger we." But other fingers on the hands of liberative change are equally important. Public policy advocacy ("change the rules") moved the state to fund public schools to purchase from local farmers. Now, school districts, including the two largest in the state, receive "thousands of dollars to pay for school lunch ingredients from local farms—which predominantly benefits low-income children."[5] Without deep listening ("listen and amplify") this network would not have been born. And, says one observer, the success of this food economy "cannot be fully explained or understood without attention to the spiritual foundation" ("drink the Spirit's courage"). Ancient spiritual rituals and prayer sustain the people, the land, the plants, the cooperative network. These people are rewriting the purpose of business and economic life ("changing the story"). The purpose becomes the well-being of all, not just the wealth of a few. A prayer at planting time says as much. "This seed is for myself and my family, this seed is for my neighbor, this seed is for the animals, this seed is for the thief" (knowing that the thief might very well be a person in great need).

A young Latina involved in the cooperatives' training program voices the global-local links as she reflects on "other farmers from across the world who are doing exactly what I'm doing, trying to create an alternative to the industrial food system, and trying to feel the connection with those people."[6] The three terrains of change—structural change, change in worldview, and change in lifestyles—are integrally intertwined.

Finally, and perhaps most important for our purposes, a statement by one Quaker woman describing this endeavor reveals the link between practical steps on the one hand and the vision and movement toward large scale systemic economic change on the other.

> *"This work is starting to change the economic landscape of the area, as it shifts the locus of food production away from agribusiness and toward local communities. . . . A network of cooperative enterprises, founded on community empowerment and individual transformation, is building up the soil from which a completely reimagined economy can grow. These fundamental shifts in economic dynamics, already transformative on a small scale, contain the seeds of a very different world."*[7] This network is cultivating *"the soil from which a completely reimagined economy can grow."*[8]

A Map of the Chapters in Part 3

Here is the plan. Each of the ten fingers on the hands of healing receives a short chapter. In each chapter, we follow a similar path:
- A pithy summary of this form of action.
- A longer narrative description.
- Life-Giving Links (how this "finger" links to other "fingers on the hands of healing").
- Sacred Journey Journal: Practicing this Healing Medicine.
- Resources for Digging Deeper.
- Woven in, at different places in different chapters, are illustrative vignettes.

In continuing your Sacred Journey Journal by "Practicing This Healing Medicine," I invite you into the power born when reflection (including reading) weds with practice. It is the power that comes from a decision to "live out your values in public, and do so repeatedly."[9]

CHAPTER EIGHT

Fingers on the Hands of Healing: *Build the New*

> Can we imagine an economy in which firms are typically owned in large part by the people who work there?
>
> —William Greider[1]

> In scattered experiments—disconnected, often unaware of one another—unsung leaders are building the beginning of what many of us hunger for but can scarcely imagine is possible: an economy that might enable us all to live well, and to do so within planetary boundaries. They're laying pathways toward an economy of, by and for the people... one that takes us beyond the binary choice of corporate capitalism versus state socialism into something new.
>
> —Naomi Klein[2]

The Essence

Build or support small-scale businesses, finance institutions, farms, energy companies, and community land trusts that put the well-being of everyday people and Earth over endless growth and profit.

Vignette

Joy bounced off of the walls. Children scampered about. Voices in Spanish and English greeted our ears as we entered the room. Luscious smells of tortillas and onions on a grill filled the air. A dark-haired elder scooped up a small child, and beckoned us to have a seat in one of the folding chairs. Community art work decked the walls. This was a weekly gathering to eat together and simply celebrate the joys and trials of being a community.

This neighborhood in southwest Detroit was known in the larger world as a place of poverty and need. Yes, there were needs. Young people needed jobs. Families needed income, food, internet access, rent control, childcare, and more. What many outsiders did not see was also the beauty and strength of the people. In this neighborhood, the people built Grace in Action Church and Collectives, a movement of people creatively living out the radical love of Jesus in ways that were rooted in the gifts and needs of the community. They believe that the gospel of Jesus includes creating a better life for people, especially people in need. This life, Grace in Action says, is "not only about spirituality and community but also about economics."

They have put that belief into practice. They have built a network of worker-owned cooperatives and youth run collectives, as well as a worshipping community. One youth collective, Radical Productions, designs and develops websites, software, and digital assets for small to mid-sized businesses and nonprofits. Another, the Equitable Internet Initiative, makes high-speed community-based internet access available to the many low-income households in Southwest Detroit. These two are joined by three other collectives. Lives have been transformed. Youth have jobs, invaluable training, leadership skills, and access to higher education. Households have incomes, internet access, and collective power. People have trustworthy community and joy. Worship is wed to the everyday lives of people. Oh yes, it has been challenging! Tenacity, deep listening, learning from mistakes, and starting over have marked the trail. And in the process, they are "building the new," new forms of economy that breed justice, life, and belonging.

Fuller Description

A vibrant face of the new economy movement—in the United States and globally—is the host of people building and supporting alternative forms of business, finance, agriculture, and energy companies, as well as community land trusts, that put the well-being of everyday people and Earth over endless growth and profit. "Islands of sanity," says Margaret Wheatley. These initiatives still attend to the financial bottom line. However, it is held along with two other bottom lines. They are human well-being and ecological well-being. It's called a triple bottom line: people, planet, profit.

Emerging with blazing energy, this movement to build the new goes by many names: solidarity economy, local living economies, local regenerative economies, sustainable economies, and more. It is a "moving river of alternative systems that are operating, growing, and being imagined around the world." These alternatives are germ cells of an equitable, ecological, and democratic economy. The movement to "build the new" shows us that "a different economy is not just a theoretical possibility, or a distant utopia, but something already under construction in the real world."[3]

"Wait a minute," you may say, "I am not going to be building a new business or farm!" That is true for most of us, me included. Our role then is to shift our daily practices to support these alternatives by using them instead of their unaccountable profit-maximizing mainstream counterparts, and to support legislation that favors these small-scale alternatives, especially when owned by marginalized people.

Let us tour five manifestations of "building the new." They are worker-owned business, locally rooted socially responsible finance, small-scale local or regional regenerative agriculture, community-owned energy companies, and community land trusts.

Employee-owned Business

The forms of business in the new economy are many. Foremost among them is worker-owned (or employee-owned) businesses.[4] They are run and owned by the employees.[5] This movement is rapidly growing and becoming more sophisticated.[6]

Do you recall meeting the employee-owners of Dulce Hogar in chapter 3? Remember the people of Evergreen Laundry in chapter 6 and of Mondragon in chapter 2. (Notice the range in size, from 89,000 employee-owners of the Mondragon to around twenty in Dulce Hogar.) They are but the tiniest tip compared to the large iceberg of worker-owned businesses that have grown in recent decades.

Building a cooperatively owned business is not in my personal future. If that is true for you also, then have a glimpse at the vital role that people like you and me can play in supporting this transition to business being owned and managed by the people who work in them. We head back to Grace in Action in Collectives in Detroit with a question for its director, Meghan Sobocienski.

CYNTHIA: Okay, Meghan, I believe that worker-owned business is a truly good thing. I think it is a path to a democratic economy. I am all for it. But, I am not going to be starting a business! Do you and people like you who are starting worker-owned businesses need people like me? If I lived in Detroit, would I have a role to play in supporting the Grace in Action collectives? If so, what is it? I mean, can you give me some examples of how people outside of your collectives support them? Or maybe examples of how you support other worker-owned businesses of which you aren't a part?

MEGHAN: Cynthia, this is a really important question. There are many ways for people who are not directly a part of a cooperative to support worker owners and organizations like Grace in Action that support worker ownership. Here are a few ideas:

Recognizing the power we have as individual consumers is really important. Recognizing the power we have as collective consumers is even more important. Think of what could happen if faith communities—from national headquarters to local congregations—did an equity and community impact inventory of every single investment being made, every dollar spent on buildings, supplies, and food, and at every gathering and meeting, and then committed to spending those dollars in local communities, using local talent and alternative economic models like cooperatives and small businesses rather than large corporations that are familiar, fast, and cheap. The economic impact would be massive. Cynthia, it would be so powerful. Can you imagine all of the worker-owned businesses this would help to thrive!

As our economy becomes faster moving and more digitally based, companies like Amazon and Shien have more and more of a monopoly on the goods and products we buy. But they have absolutely no concern or reinvestment back into any community. Investing our individual and collective money locally, in cooperatives, in Black-, Brown-, queer-, and women-owned businesses rooted in communities and neighborhoods becomes really important. Building and investing in alternative economic systems is a moral and Christian response to the massive building of economic empire happening all around us.

Many of the cooperatives that Grace in Action supports in Detroit are service based which is really common in communities where relationships are valued over productivity. We are starting to talk a lot about Artificial Intelligence (AI) and the way that the ramping of AI with very little regulation or moral deliberation could leave some of our businesses in really difficult situations. For example, if an AI chat can translate a document as well as a human, there's a good chance AI will corner Bridging Languages (the translation cooperative that GIA helped support) and others like it out of the market. Asking difficult questions personally and publicly about the services we use individually and collectively becomes really important here. We can choose to invest in services and businesses directly rather than opting for AI technology in certain situations, even if it's easier, cheaper and faster.

Standing up and voting with our collective and individual dollars really matters a lot.

And of course, any cooperatives benefit from back office supports, especially in the beginning. So, if you have legal, financial, graphic design, marketing, businesses expertise, then approaching an organization like Grace in Action and asking whether that type of support would be helpful might be mutually beneficial.

If someone is interested in supporting a cooperative in Detroit you can learn more about Grace in Action at www.giacollectives.org. Every dollar spent locally goes back into the local community and lifts whole communities up.

CYNTHIA: Meghan, thank you!

Historically, worker-owned companies have aimed at transforming local economies to reflect two aims: equity (especially through life-supporting wages and benefits) and democratic control (shared power and responsibility). In recent years, a third aim is present in many: ecological well-being. This third aim appears especially in communities long plagued by industrial environmental degradation.

Widespread support for the movement to put control and ownership of business into employee/owner hands is rapidly growing. It includes local governments and "anchor institutions." Anchor institutions are large institutions like universities and hospitals that are grounded in the community and not likely to leave it. They agree to buy goods and services from the worker-owned business, which in turn trains and employs—at a living wage—local low-income people, thus building wealth for the community rather than extracting it.[7]

Lives are changed for people when they no longer are at the mercy of a mega corporation that may refuse to pay a living wage and benefits, and may "let them go." But new alternative businesses require finance.

Finance Institutions

What is your money doing after you send it to the bank or into saving? It is active. It does things. It affects people's lives. It may be funding new oil drilling in the Arctic, a mining company that is toxifying Indigenous people's rivers in Columbia, or a sweatshop in Bangladesh. In contrast, your money may be financing a new community-based organic farm, an employee-owned grocery store in a food desert neighborhood, a Black-owned solar company in your city, or a family-owned micro business in Kenya. What do we choose to DO with our money?

Finance is vital! One manifestation of building the new is redesigning finance to do good rather than ill. Finance institutions in the new economy take diverse forms. You may be familiar with socially responsible investing. Or you may know of regional credit unions and banks that invest in the local community, and especially in businesses owned by marginalized groups. Other forms are the public banking movement modeled in part after South Dakota's long-standing public bank, and community-based revolving loan funds. The common denominator is "moving the money" to build equitable and ecologically regenerative economies. We will explore alternative finance more fully in chapter 11 ("Move the Money").

Alternative Agriculture

A creative tenacious surge of agricultural alternatives is arising around the world, from India to Iowa. They are the fruit of people experiencing industrial agriculture as a dead end and deciding to do something about it. They grew sick and tired (many of them literally sick and tired) of the toxic work environments, enormous carbon emissions, high use of petrochemicals, exploitation of workers, immiseration of animals, soil and water depletion, obliteration of small farms, and more that come with industrial agriculture and the global food supply system. "Enough," they cried by daring to engender life-giving small-scale ways of working with Earth to produce food.

These alternatives come in a tapestry of forms. They are a foretaste of the future in which all people have adequate healthy food, and eating does not cripple the food supply of generations to come or create misery for others. Foremost among these alternatives in the United States are community supported agriculture (CSAs), small-scale organic farming, farmers' markets, farm-to-school programs, and the growing network of Black and Indigenous food sovereignty initiatives.

Let's taste the feast:

- In upstate New York Soul Fire Farm teaches and practices Afro-Indigenous farming. They are regenerating eighty acres. Pay them a visit, in person or virtually. There you will meet Black and Brown food growers in agro-ecology trainings, youth immersed in food justice workshops, organizers leading reparations and land return initiatives. Fields of vegetables, fruits, and medicinal plants in healthy soil will fill your vision. You will see honeybees and pasture-fed livestock. Some folks will be heading out with doorstep delivery bringing the harvest to people living with food insecurity. Ancestral farming practices are increasing topsoil depth and sequestering carbon.
- Urban farming is erupting across the country. Detroit, for example, hosts some 1,500 urban farms and gardens. One study, led by the University of Michigan, finds that by using more of the city's vacant lots for growing food, "Detroit could meet 75 percent of its vegetable demand and 40 percent of its fruit demand."[8]

- The faith community plays a role. To illustrate: My students have visited Urban Adamah (integrating Jewish practices with educational urban farming), the Zen-based Green Gulch Farm, and Abundant Table (an immigrant-led farm founded as a ministry of the Lutheran and Episcopal communions). The Faithlands program of the Agrarian Trust assists faith communities in making their land available for farming and community gardening, donating it to Black and Indigenous farmers as an act of reparative justice, or creating ecological land-use.
- Agrarian land trusts protect farmlands from development and from industrial agriculture, and make it available instead to small-scale farmers (current and next generation farmers).[9]
- The National Black Food and Justice Alliance is a coalition of nearly fifty Black-led projects, some of which aim at supporting Black farmers. Simply reading the list of its member organizations is a dance with inspiration and hope.[10] Most of them build Black food sovereignty in one way or another.
- Via Campesina is at the heart of a robust global movement to build small-scale, local agriculture aimed at local or regional food sovereignty. Spanning five continents, this network represents some 200 million small-scale farmers in over eighty nations. They advocate for policies that support small-scale community-based farms, and they defend peasant land rights, seed rights, and water rights.

These are just a few sprouts of a fast-growing plant: regenerative, small-scale, democratically controlled agriculture. It is a plant that will feed the future.

Community-Owned Energy Companies

The rallying cry is "energy democracy." The energy democracy movement supports community-owned and -controlled clean energy initiatives to replace corporate-controlled, fossil-fuel energy producers and utility monopolies. Context shapes the form. One form is municipally owned energy service providers. Another is renewable energy coops in low-income communities. A distinct benefit is the ability to prevent enormous power plants from emitting pollutants into vulnerable neighborhoods. Where energy providers are controlled by the community, they can prioritize the health of the community.

Community-Based Land Trusts

Some community land trusts address the affordable-housing crisis. With community land trusts, a nonprofit, governed by a community board, buys property to preserve it as affordable housing for working-class and low-income people, and to give residents more say over what happens in neighborhoods threatened by gentrification. Other land trusts advance urban agriculture, or the transfer of farmlands to Black, Brown, and Indigenous farmers. The Central Virginia Agricultural Commons, for example, conveys ninety-nine-year leases to Black farmers for chemical-free farming, provides produce and farm education for local school children, and mentors new farmers.[11]

The Common Denominators

A common denominator among the five (business, finance, agriculture, energy, and land trusts) is the commitment to foster local or regional rootedness and accountability, shared control and ownership, and ecological regenerativity. They share, too, the dedication to build local wealth that is distributed rather than concentrated in a few hands.

Importantly, many also have the intent of helping to catalyze the larger-scale transformation of our economy from a predatory economy to a new life-giving economic system, and see themselves as one part of that transition starting at the local level.[12] They open the door to a more just future by modeling it. *Just imagine locally rooted, democratically accountable business, finance, agriculture, energy supply, and land trusts as the default model!* The notion seems as strange as living on planet Mars. But no, this reality is being born in our midst. While on the surface, initiatives to "build the new" may seem like disparate and lone endeavors, in reality they are "evidence of a sophisticated network of enterprises building a new world right here in the shell of the old."[13]

These initiatives are rooted in a proud legacy of worker-owned business, socially responsible finance, and commonly held agriculture, in the United States and globally. This legacy has gained momentum in the recent decade, in part because worker ownership benefits not only the workers but also their communities.[14] As expressed by Rosemarie Hinkle-Rieger, cofounder of the Southeast Center for Cooperative Development, "Worker cooperatives are likely to form relationships with other local business, hire local workers ... and reinvest their profits back into the neighborhood. Worker-owners are interested in generating profit, but they are also invested in ensuring that they work in a healthy environment, have job stability, safe business practices, and fair wages and benefits."[15]

While many are small-scale, others are large. Perhaps the most well-known large-scale employee-owned cooperative is the Mondragon Cooperative that we met in chapter 2. This business—with its nearly 100,000 employee-owners—proves that worker coops are a viable option on a large scale.[16]

Emily Kawano, an economist, popular educator, and innovator who has spent much of her life in efforts to build equitable alternatives to predatory capitalism, offers a provocative metaphor to describe this emerging body of business, agriculture, finance, land trusts, and energy alternatives.[17] Her image conveys also the challenges and opposition sometimes faced by this movement to "build the new."

Emily: "When a caterpillar spins its chrysalis, its body starts to break down into this nutrient-rich group, and within that nutrient-rich group are what are called imaginal cells. Those cells have an imagination of what it could be that's different from the caterpillar, and it's so different that what's left of the caterpillar's immune system starts to attack these imaginal cells and to kill some of them. But many of these imaginable cells survive. They find each other and they begin to clump, they begin to survive the attack of the immune system. As they continue to clump and come together and recognize each other, they start to specialize into a wing, an antenna, an eye, and a leg until they emerge as a butterfly, a transformed creature. And so, this is a nice metaphor for the solidarity economy right now.

"If you think about this . . . we're sort of like imaginal cells. We don't all recognize each other, we're not really clumping yet, and we're not pulling together in the same direction to give birth to this transformed economy, society, and world. But that is the role of the solidarity economy, to provide that framework to get us recognizing each other and building together."[18]

Moderator: "Thank you so much, Emily. Never let it be said that economists can't also be poets!"

Life-Giving Links

We cannot leave behind exploitative business, agriculture, and finance unless we have alternatives. As someone once said, "I can tell you that your 401(k) is probably invested in private prisons, but you aren't going to change unless you have a reasonable expectation that you will be able to survive in retirement. . . . Unless we have clear alternatives . . . we will remain complicit participants in the very systems we criticize." For this reason "building the new" is an indispensable ingredient in transforming the economy.

Yet, alone, "building the new" is not adequate. The scale of the ecological-economic crisis and its systemic roots call forth the other fingers on the hands of healing change as well. The reasons are many: without action on the broader political level, small-scale alternatives may be wiped out by large corporate moves (recall Kawano's metaphor of the imaginal cells being killed); buying goods at alternative businesses may be too expensive for low-income people (until increasing customer base lowers costs); too few people may be motivated to engage with the alternatives; financing might not be available; and other barriers may come into play. We cannot "build the new" on a large scale for the long term without also "changing the rules" (through public policy, legal structures, etc.),[19] "moving the money," "changing the story," "resisting the wrong," and other aspects of healing economic life. For this very reason, many people creating new business, finance, agricultural, and energy enterprises are also engaged in public policy advocacy work and resistance work. As ethicist Karen Baker-Fletcher notes, once we begin the local projects, "it seems we must gradually move on to concretely address the larger issues."[20] Builders of the new economy "should also place a high priority on influencing the mainstream debate and policies over the long term," write two leaders in the field.[21]

Sacred Journey Journal:
Practicing This Healing Medicine

What possibilities for your life, integrity, and joy are created by responding to the questions below?

- Where do you see "building the new" happening in your community? If you are not sure, then you might enjoy a quest to find out. You could begin by googling "worker-owned business in [the name of your area]," or "cooperative banks," "CSAs," "housing trusts," or other key phrases in (the name of your area).
- How might you and your group (congregation, friend group, book club, game group, circle of parents, neighborhood, etc.) support some of those initiatives?
- What kind of "building the new" is needed in your community that you and your companions might instigate or join others in developing?

Then consider one of the following, choosing whichever speaks to you:

- How might practicing this healing medicine bring you joy?
- In what ways would it align your life more fully with your real values?
- How would you feel five years down the road if you practiced this means of healing our economic life and building a moral economy?
- In what sense would it be "loving your neighbor as yourself" with a love that seeks justice and liberation?

Resources for Digging Deeper

See the toolkit for this book on the series' website at: https://buildingamoraleconomy.org/.

CHAPTER NINE

Fingers on the Hands of Healing:
Live Lightly

We are told the economy only changes through big shifts, like those that require policy actions.... But what if that's only part of the picture. What if we can be ensnared in the barbed briar, and still make choices each hour and each moment from a set of values that are different from the set of values from which the current economy is derived? Could we start to practice the everyday, rote realities of the future we want, now?

—Jess Rimington[1]

Practice your values publicly and repeatedly.

—Kelly Marciales[2]

Before you finish eating your breakfast this morning, you've depended on more than half the world. This is the way our universe is structured.... We aren't going to have peace on earth until we recognize this basic fact of the interrelated structure of reality.

—Martin Luther King Jr.[3]

The history of farm labor in the United States is a history of exploitation. Most people have no idea that they're connected to this system every time they buy fresh fruits and vegetables.

—Eric Schlosser[4]

The Essence

Changes in the daily practices of individuals, households, and institutions so that daily practices contribute to more ecological, equitable, and democratic economic lives, communities, and society. That influence may be direct or indirect.

Fuller Description

Perhaps you can learn with me from one of my big mistakes as a professor.

> *The students in my class at Seattle University were completing their "Resisting Economic Violence" assignment. One aim of the assignment was to open students' eyes to the impacts, on people and on Earth, of products that they used regularly. We began with Dr. Emilie Townes's question: What is "for our enjoyment at the expense of other people's lives?"[5] What is the "true cost of low prices"?[6]*
>
> *Student groups traced the impacts of an object that was common in their lives—a tomato, a shirt made of synthetic fiber, a plastic water bottle, a soccer shoe, and so on—and then presented their findings to the class. Group after group presented. By the end, the cumulative impact was sorely disheartening. "My God," one student said, "I had no idea that so much harm comes just from my daily habits." I was heartsick. The assignment had left these students feeling guilty and powerless.*
>
> *We made a quick pivot in the class plans. I gave students the option to do a part 2 to the assignment instead of writing a paper on another topic. In part 2 the students sketched paths to undoing the negative impacts that they had revealed in their initial presentation. These were paths of economic transformation. They were to use "fingers on the hands of healing" (forms of action) explored in this book. One of those fingers or forms of action is changes in daily lifestyle practices, shifting from habits and customs that depend upon exploitation, and choosing alternatives. For example, the student group whose presentation had been on tomatoes, shifted to buying tomatoes only from retailers who had signed on to the Fair Food Program that protects tomato pickers' rights.*

In this book, we refer to this form of action as "living lightly." You probably are well familiar with it. Many of you have been practicing it for years.

Let's have a look at one household, spurred on by a child anxious about climate change.

For months, Tamisha had been talking about climate change, scared about the future. But recently, she had fallen silent. Nightmares had begun. Her mothers knew her well, and they sensed what was going on. She was in climate despair, feeling powerless and hopeless. They talked with Tamisha. After much conversation, the family made a climate pact; they agreed to make three immediate changes in how they lived, and then each month to add a new change, and to maintain each new practice in the months to come. The changes would lower their carbon footprint. And, even more important, they agreed to be "public" about it—to talk about this with other people, to invite others to join them, and bring this to their synagogue. One of Tamisha's moms also agreed to bring the idea to her workplace. (Tamisha's parents later confessed that they had groaned inside initially about making this climate pact with their daughter. They both worked at low-paying jobs, and had no extra time for this. But they needed to help Tamisha come out of despair.)

Their first immediate change was to move their small savings account out of Chase Bank and into a local cooperative bank that had no investments in fossil fuels. Tamisha went online to help find a local bank. They stopped cold turkey using new plastic bags for groceries and lunches. (For lunches, they used empty bread bags.) Their third immediate change, eating less meat, seemed like a good idea anyway, given the cost of meat.

As a few months went on, plastic containers in their home were largely replaced by glass and metal. They reduced electricity use, and with it, their monthly electricity bill. Food bought in bulk from the local coop and from a Community Supported Agriculture farm took the place of much processed and packaged food. "When changes are taken one step at a time, it's not that big a deal," one of Tamisha's moms explained. "If you try to do it all at once it's self-defeating."

A year down the road, this household is quite a different place! Moreover, Tamisha's youth group at the synagogue got wind of an organization called Dayenu and were drawn to its purpose of enabling "American Jews to confront the climate crisis with spiritual audacity and bold political action."[7] They convinced the synagogue community to form a Dayenu Circle. As I see it, Tamisha and her family were teaching themselves and others new ways to practice of neighbor-love.[8]

The Paradox of Practice

We need to look more closely and honestly. A paradox haunts the commitment to change daily habits. On one hand, change in everyday practices regarding fossil fuel use, food, and other consumer choices are crucial; we of the Global North need to learn to live lightly—to consume less, consume ethically, and produce fewer greenhouse gas emissions. Every "system of evil requires personal actions to make it work."[9] Thus, overcoming those systems requires people to resist their own and others' participation in them. Corporate permission to extract and exploit continues because "so many players, right down to individual human beings, facilitate its operation."[10] That "facilitation" includes buying products and using services produced through extraction and exploitation. Lifestyle changes are necessary for that permission to be revoked.

Yet, on the other hand, a focus on behavioral change is deceptive and distracting if it leads us to think that such actions *alone* will solve the problem or absolve us of our role in exploitation. "We cannot buy our way into a more just and restorative economy." Other forms of action toward systemic change are the necessary complement to behavioral change. (Recall the discussion of "three terrains" in chapter 5, in which we noted the dangers of focus on behavioral change alone. We noted efforts by the fossil fuel industry to lure people into believing that the solution to climate change lies solely in individuals' lifestyle changes, not also in changes to the fossil fuel companies' unbridled extraction. The industry did this by developing and promoting the carbon footprint measure for individuals and households.)

A Morally Empowering Response

This paradox invites two possible responses. One is to give up on lifestyle changes, concluding that they make no difference. The other is to claim and relish the power that comes with making lifestyle changes if we also (1) magnify their impact by making them publicly visible and (2) link lifestyle change to other fingers on the hands of healing change.

What does this mean? Let's return to the students in my class, and in particular the group that examined the social and environmental impacts of a buying a tomato. In researching the impacts, they unearthed a long trail of farmworker exploitation.

> Monica worked long hot days in a Florida field picking tomatoes. She made only forty cents for a thirty-two-pound bucket of tomatoes, working in horrid conditions. Monica rose at 4:00 to drop her toddler at the sitter's home and catch the company's morning bus for workers, but then she waited for unpaid hours until the dew dried before picking could start. Last month, she had collapsed, weakened by no rest break in ninety-five-degree heat. Her husband, who used to work with her, was fired a few days ago. They said it was poor performance, but really it was because he had been organizing their coworkers to try to form a union. No longer having him near her, Monica was terrified by the

groping hands of her manager who also was demanding sex just to keep her job. To make matters worse, she had become ill, and feared it was COVID. But she could not stay home; there was no sick leave, and if she lost her job, she was terrified of what would become of their two small children. This was normal, the way things were. On occasion, she was a victim of wage theft by her employer, which made her income even less.[11] Monica lived in fear of her bosses in these tomato fields, which one US attorney called the "ground zero for modern slavery."[12] The company made great profit selling these tomatoes.

Scant months later, Joey, preparing dinner for his kids in Minneapolis, made lasagna with canned tomatoes picked by Monica. Joey had no idea of what lay behind those tomatoes.[13]

Human rights abuses are ubiquitous in global and national supply chains, and seem to be ignored by many people who benefit from the low prices or the investment profits (me, for example, and perhaps you also). Perhaps we are aware of these abuses, but consider them inevitable and apparently acceptable, sacrifice zones in corporate-and-finance driven capitalism.

Corporate Social Responsibility (CSR) calls companies to voluntary commitments. But CSR has largely failed to rectify the ongoing human rights crisis in supply chains. It does not include legally binding requirements to enforce standards, and monitoring is often in-house. To illustrate, since 2005, "more than two thousand workers have been killed in factory fires and building collapses" in the Bangladesh garment industry.[14] *Many companies that outsourced through these factories had publicized explicit commitments to Corporate Social Responsibility. Yet they had not corrected the dangerous working conditions.*

"How, then," these students asked, "can we get food and clothing, and everything else we need without destroying people? Where is freedom from that supply chain violence against neighbors?"

Pursuing this question, they discovered Worker-Driven Social Responsibility (WSR), a newer model for dismantling the human rights abuses abiding in many supply chains. It corrects for the faultlines in CSR. WSR entails legally binding agreements between brands or retailers and their workers' advocacy organizations. And it requires "rigorous workplace inspections that are effectively independent of brand and retailer influence, public disclosure of the names and locations of participating brands and suppliers, and a complaint mechanism that ensures swift and effective action when workers identify abuses."[15] WSR builds workers' power to protect and enforce their own rights.

The model has seen success in highly exploitative working contexts, including Florida's agricultural fields and the garment sweatshops of Bangladesh.[16] A global campaign based on this model produced the landmark Accord on Fire and Building Safety in Bangladesh.[17]

The Fair Food Program (FFP) is another internationally recognized success of WSR. According to the *Harvard Business Review*, the Fair Food Program is one of the "most successful social-impact stories of the past century."[18] The Macarthur Foundation acclaims the FFP as a "visionary strategy with potential to transform workplace environments across the global supply chain."[19] The program has received national and international awards.[20]

The FFP uses consumer power to prevent human rights abuses in food-related industries and to chop off some roots of farmworker poverty. The program, launched in 2011 by the Coalition of Immokalee Workers, educates consumers on the exploitation and suffering behind the food they eat, and mobilizes their support for fair treatment of workers. The result is a powerful alliance of consumers and farmworkers to incentivize retail food companies to (1) purchase only from suppliers who pay fair wages and meet basic human rights standards, and (2) pay a very small premium to improve farmworkers' incomes.[21] Based on legally binding agreements, the FFP gives farm workers leveraging power for gaining decent working conditions including water and shade, protection from sexual harassment in the workplace, and the right to file complaints and organize without retaliation.[22] These gains have changed lives.

WSR would not work without people who buy these goods standing up to say, *"We will have no more of this! No more of devastating other people to gain our food, clothing, and other needs.!" "We will buy only products that are sourced equitably."* This is a declaration of freedom. It is neighbor-love in action. Here is the power of "living lightly" as a tool for economic healing.

The student group in my class employed it. They proposed the lifestyle change of buying tomatoes only from retailers who had signed on to the Fair Food Program, or from local small farmers. Good!

"Now," I challenged them, "how can you multiply the impact of that move by linking it to other fingers on the hands of change, and by 'going public?'" The results were unforgettable. First, taking to heart the principle that we are more powerful with others than alone, they determined to "build the bigger we." Contacting the Coalition of Immokalee Workers (CIW) led them deeper into the Fair Food Program (FFP), which the CIW had initiated.[23] They learned that the CIW had helped to form the student/Farmworker Alliance, which did leadership development with young people, especially on college campuses.[24] The students in my class learned that college students had "helped the Fair Food Program take off. College campuses banned Taco Bell and McDonald's until they agreed to join the program. The pressure worked, and both fast food giants signed on.... Wal-Mart, Burger King, Subway, Trader Joe's, Whole Foods and Yum Brands, which owns KFC and Pizza Hut in addition to Taco Bell, have all joined the Fair Food Program, as have many others." The farmworkers, their student

Live Lightly

allies, and other allies had achieved this through hunger strikes, marches, and other demonstrations to bring public attention to the cause. This was "resisting the wrong," another finger on the hands of change.

"Change the rules, change the rules, change the rules," I heard one member of the group insist in a planning meeting during class. "We need to look at public policy!" They began exploring a statewide bill that would require all agencies receiving state funds to buy food only from companies that had signed on to the FFP's agreement. What about "build the new," one member of the group asked? How about pushing for a campus policy that has food services buying half of its produce from local organic farms with fair labor practices? We would be "building the new" agricultural system. Hearing the group's presentation, someone else in the class piped up, "I work with campus ministry, and we could bring a speaker from the FFP to campus." "Oh, that is 'listen and amplify,'" I inserted from my listening position in the back row.

Ideas abounded. They got it! *These students saw the power of linking lifestyle changes (such shifting where one buys tomatoes) to other fingers on the hands of change.*

Channels of Impact

Let us look more closely at the ways lifestyle changes can have broader impact if we make them publicly visible and link them to the other forms of action.[25]

- Letting others know what you are doing sets an example. People learn by modeling. Research, for example, shows that when one household puts in solar panels, others tend to follow.
- Making lifestyle changes visible influences the public moral climate, paving the way for policy change and institutional change.
- Practicing justice-making and Earth care in daily life counters powerlessness, denial, and despair for oneself and for others who see that practice. (Tamisha's mothers moved their family into climate activism specifically to help free their daughter from climate despair.)
- Individuals' practices alert corporate players that opposition exists and lend material support to workers seeking better conditions. The Coalition of Immokalee Workers would not have won better working conditions for farm laborers had consumers not supported them by boycotting tomatoes grown in farms with abusive working conditions.
- Practicing alternatives, and doing it publicly, reveals to the world that alternatives are possible. Taking one's money out of Chase Bank or Wells Fargo opens that door for others who did not realize that alternative banking was alive and well.

The classic feminist adage *the personal is political* rings true. Personal lifestyle changes and structural change are inextricably related. Change in the one catalyzes change in the other. Choices in personal life ultimately can impact larger economic systems. Few concepts are more important to moral power for changing systems than recognizing the constructive interplay between these two terrains.

Life-Giving Links

This chapter has been replete with links between fingers on the hands of liberative change. Here we note one more. Lifestyle change ("living lightly") is closely aligned with "building the new." Many people change lifestyle practices in part by switching to local banks, employee-owned business, and local agriculture.[26]

As this description reveals, for many people who are practicing "living lightly," these lifestyle changes are not experienced as "giving things up" in a burdensome way that sucks joy out of daily life. Rather they are experienced as enabling more relationally rich and community-based modes of everyday life. This is important. The changes may enliven rather than deaden joy.

This does not mean that such changes are necessarily easy or simple. Often, they are not; they are messy, complicated. Relationships and community-based efforts may be cumbersome and conflict laden. Yet such moves away from dependence on the megamarket and its imperatives seem to bring with them a deeper sense of aliveness, community, and security.[27]

Sacred Journey Journal: Practicing This Healing Medicine

You already may be well along the path of "living lightly." If so, how might you be more public about what you are doing, or how might you link it to one of the other fingers on the hands of healing? If you are new on this path, what are two immediate steps that you and your household might take? And how will you bring this to other people or a group of which you are a part?

Then consider one of the following, choosing whichever speaks to you:
- How might practicing this healing medicine bring you joy?
- In what ways would it align your life more fully with your real values?
- In what sense would it be "loving your neighbor as yourself" with a love that seeks justice and liberation?
- How would you feel five years down the road if you practiced this means of healing our economic life and building a moral economy?

Resources for Digging Deeper

See the toolkit for this book on the series' website at https://buildingamoraleconomy.org/.

CHAPTER TEN

Fingers on the Hands of Healing:
Change the Rules

Poverty is a policy choice.

—Dylan Matthews[1]

Economies are "shaped by the rules and regulations made through the political system."

—Joseph Stiglitz[2]

All over this country we are using policy to rewrite the rules and build pathways to a people's economy.

—New Economy Coalition[3]

The Essence

"Change the rules" indicates efforts to change public policy so that it
- reduces the gap between rich and poor;
- supports ecologically regenerative business, transportation, food systems, recreation, households, and more; and
- enables power to be distributed and accountable.

No doubt you recognize our three guideposts at play: equitable, ecological, and democratic. Change the rules means public policy advocacy through legislation—local, state, national, or international. Changing the rules also includes legal advocacy and work to elect public officials who support policies that build equitable, ecological, and democratic economies.

Vignette

"I don't do politics; I want to keep my hands clean of all that. I believe that people of faith should be neutral in divisive political matters, and be active in helping people." Max was a faithful member of a congregation and had a deep heart of care for people in poverty. His hard work and kind countenance sustained the congregation's food bank. His laugh kept folks going. Max's "I don't do politics" was responding to my suggestion that, as a part of his Christian practice of neighbor-love, he join a campaign to pass a law in Washington state to establish a wealth tax.

After this conversation, we began, over a period of months, to talk further. He attended an intergenerational Bible study on the meaning of "Love thy neighbor as thyself." (It was an experiment bringing together confirmation kids and adults to probe the meaning of neighbor-love in our world today. They volunteered together one Saturday morning and did this class for two months on Sunday.) In the class we looked at roles that public policy—including tax policy—plays in creating poverty and concentrating wealth. We explored the role that public policy could play in undoing poverty and the gap between rich and poor. We looked too at what some faith groups were doing locally in their political advocacy for tax laws that would benefit low-income people, and at what faith-based public policy advocacy had achieved in other countries.

One Sunday morning in class, Emily, one of the confirmation kids involved, read aloud Desmond Tutu's words: "If you are neutral in situations of injustice, you have chosen the side of the oppressor. *If an elephant has its foot on the tail of a mouse and you say that you are neutral, the mouse will not appreciate your neutrality.*" The room went silent. Then an elder—we knew him as Mr. Androwski—asked, "What elephants are standing on the tails of the people who come to our food bank?" I will never forget Max's face. He did not come back to the class the following week.

Later we talked. Max said that his world was shattered when he heard Emily and Mr. Androwski. Four months later, Max was a leader in the community-organizing campaign to pass a wealth tax. He saw this as being a Good Samaritan to many people in the state who were victimized by a tax system that favored wealthy people and penalized very low-income people. "Go Max," I said to myself! "Go Holy Spirit," replied my friend Susan when I told her this story.

Fuller Description

Long ago, in my youth, I thought that legislative and electoral advocacy did not matter. Laws would never be passed nor people elected that would really try to make our society more just. Regardless of whom we elected, I thought, things would pretty much go on as they were. Later I learned my lesson, as I saw the devastation that can be wrought by poor choices of elected officials, and as I witnessed the power of laws to change society, for the better and the worse.

The Climate Justice Alliance says as much: "Building the new" is not enough, they aver. But why? Why is it not enough just to build new equitable, ecological and democratic business, finance, and agriculture? Why worry also about legislation and laws?

> *"We must change the rules," the Climate Justice Alliance goes on to say. "We must identify the legal and structural barriers to the economy we need to build. We must . . . write the rules that need to be written to facilitate constructing the Just Transition economy."*[4]

In this sense *public policy advocacy is a spiritual practice*. It is attuning one's heart to perceive why people are suffering, what is causing the suffering, and then stepping in to stem those root causes. It is building the conditions for life to flourish.

I am reminded of Emily Kawano's metaphor of the imaginal cells forming the new butterfly. Some of the "caterpillar's immune system starts to attack these imaginal cells and to kill some of them," she warned. Public policy can protect those vulnerable imaginal cells, allow them to gain strength and scale. In 2020, for instance, when BIPOC-owned businesses—already hampered by the lack of access to capital that plagues new small Black-owned business[5]—suffered the additional impact of the coronavirus, some state and local governments stepped in with protective public policy.[6]

Imagine, for a moment, the life-saving impact that changing the rules through public policy could have in the United States.[7] I picture the lives that would be saved from poverty or death-by-poverty if a living wage and good health care benefits were mandated for all people. For families who are malnourished and live in cars because the parent's fulltime work is underpaid, consider what it would mean to earn a living wage. What if we determined as a society that the maximum wage ratio between highest and lowest paid workers was to be ten to one? Picture the children who could eat well if laws required health care, decent wages, and nontoxic working conditions for farmworkers.

Public policy can open doors to local agriculture or block it, and the impacts of local agriculture are astounding. Locally grown food travels far fewer miles between producers and consumers and thus reduces carbon emissions. Local jobs are created. Food deserts are transformed. Food insecurity decreases. The exploitation and environmental degradation associated with industrial agriculture is reduced. Let your heart's eye see the food produced when cities or states use public policy to incentivize urban agriculture on vacant lots.

In other senses, as well, public policy advocacy is a crucial element in building a more equitable, compassionate, and ecological economy. As argued by the renowned climate justice advocate Bill McKibben and others, changes at the individual behavioral level alone will not enable our nation to reduce emissions enough and soon enough. *"Climate change must be fought also through public policy."*[8]

So too with the struggle against poverty and inequity. Public policy may determine who lives and who dies. Whether people will have health care, have access to medications and clean water, and be able to feed their families is determined by public policy. Public policy determines whether public banks can exist, and worker-owned cooperatives can thrive. Imam Omar Suleiman marks the import: "It is," he declares, "time to move out of the domain of charity and into the domain of policy. . . . Take an active role in shifting the policies that make charity necessary."[9]

This is the terrain of legislative, legal, and electoral advocacy. *It is the core of democracy—people taking part in establishing the laws that will govern our life together. In essence we are talking about laws that align the economy with basic values*—that all people are created equal and have equal rights to food, water, and other necessities for life; that future generations, our children and grandchildren, have the right to life; that preserving and restoring Earth's ability to sustain life is essential.

These values are "real" only when we enact them as a society. That requires laws because people do not always voluntarily act to serve the greater good.

We have done this in the past. Our forebearers fought for laws to abolish chattel slavery, and laws prohibiting child labor. It was through changed laws that women won the right to vote. Advocacy to change laws transforms values into lived reality.

Rosario, a Filipina economist and member of a small global team advising the World Council of Churches on its economic justice work, identifies international speculation on food staples in the stock market as a virulent cause of hunger in the Philippines. She declared with calm passion, "Food trade is speculative and globalized. This drives up food prices. Then, in my country, people cannot afford basic food." For poor people in many nations, speculation in food products may be devastating. Laws and the budgets they establish enable that speculation to happen. Laws are needed to stop it.

How, you might ask, are we to know which policies to support and which to reject? Criteria are key. They are found in the three guidelines discussed in chapter 6: equitable, ecological, and democratic. Key questions help in using these guidelines. In my classes, we call them "reality revealing questions." Have a look.

Change the Rules

Reality Revealing Questions

Equitable
- Will this policy—directly and indirectly—help to reduce the gap between rich and poor?
- Who will benefit from this policy in the long and short terms?
- Who will suffer due to this policy in the long and short terms?
- Will this legislation promote jobs for low income or unemployed people?
- Will it result in "sacrifice zones?"

Ecological
- Will this policy—directly or indirectly—reduce carbon emissions or increase them?
- In what senses, if any, will this policy—directly or indirectly—cause ecological degradation?
- In what senses, if any, will it—directly or indirectly—cause ecological regeneration?

Democratic
- Will this policy result in more widely shared and accountable power?
- Will this policy counter the power of the rich to influence decisions?
- Whose voices will this policy engage and amplify?
- Whose voices will this policy ignore or suppress?
- What mechanisms are built into this policy to ensure accountability to the public?

"Changing the rules" through public policy happens on the local, state/provincial, national, and international levels. Needless to say, the examples are endless. Enjoy with me a sampling.

Local Level

We return to Amsterdam. In 2019 the city passed landmark legislation to have no fossil-fuel vehicles in the city by 2030, to have "reduced CO2 emissions by

55% below 1990 levels by 2030,"[10] and to have a completely circular economy by 2050. Amsterdam formally adopted doughnut economics in 2020 and may be the first city worldwide to do so.[11] Other major cities, such as Brussels and Barcelona, have followed suit. Many cities are leading the way in public policy to reduce emissions. New York, for example, announced its "commitment to a 33% reduction in food-based emissions by 2030" after learning that food consumption and waste produce carbon emissions. "We've already made great strides in reducing our food emissions by leading with plant-based meals in our public hospitals and introducing 'Plant-Powered Fridays' in our public schools," declared then Mayor Eric Adams.[12] Advocates in some cities are calling upon their municipality to change the rules governing its investments to ensure that pension fund investments and other city monies are divested from fossil fuels and reinvested in clean energy, socially responsible funds, and finance institutions that reinvest in communities. Linda Sarsour, cofounder of Until Freedom, implores, "Do local politics—elect district attorneys, mayors, city council members."[13]

State/Provincial Level

Recall the story in "Setting the Stage" of the network of small cooperative farms in New Mexico. Public policy advocacy helped to enable these small farms to thrive and thirty thousand school children to have organic produce for lunch. The state funded school districts to buy from the small-scale local farmers.

Advocates in some states are seeking legislation to change the legal mandate of corporations. This is a function of state law regarding the obligations of corporate boards of directors. Originally corporations were mandated by charter to serve the public good. That has changed to a mandate to maximize stockholders' returns.[14] Efforts are underway in some states to make a powerful shift, from requiring that corporations measure only the financial bottom line to a requirement that they measure a triple bottom line: financial, ecological, and social equity.

National Level

Legislation in line with the Green New Deal exemplifies legislative moves on the national level, as does the letter signed by the Circle of Protection, a coalition of church bodies and related ministries representing a diverse swath of Christianity in the US with close to 100 million members. They wrote to President Biden on March of 2021, asking him to prioritize "policies providing a living wage for all workers, international aid to address hunger, increase taxes on corporations and high-income Americans," and a host of policies aimed at keeping people out of poverty.[15]

International Level

Increasingly climate and economic justice advocates call upon ordinary citizens to "change the rules" on international levels. Some advocate for international laws requiring corporations to pay for the social and environmental costs of their greenhouse gas emissions. Imagine the impact if Chevron and Shell had to bear the cost of their extractions, costs that now are borne by people from Pakistan to Haiti who are ravished by climate-enraged storms! Twenty laureates of the distinguished Blue Planet Prize insist, "The fundamental market failure is the unpriced 'externality' of the impact of emission."[16] Changing the rules through public policies that required internalizing those costs would be a major game changer in the fight against climate change.

> *She stood up boldly. I watched her glance at her notes and move to the microphone, clear her throat, and wait until the floor was open. "Norway will be promoting the Robin Hood Tax," she declared, and went on. "It is a tax on short term international financial transactions. Join us; call upon your governments to push for the Robin Hood Tax." This youth leader spoke at the World Council of Churches General Assembly in 2022. People listened.*

"The Robin Hood Tax would curb the speculative investment that damages so many small vulnerable economies, . . . [and it] would raise an estimated $500 billion in revenue per year to support public services, including education, infrastructure and research funding."[17] In Europe, a similar tax on short-term financial transactions, known by some as a Tobin Tax, is already a reality in eleven nations and the movement is advancing in the EU.[18] (The following chapter looks more closely at advocacy related to tax justice.) Internationally—as well as nationally and locally—public policy advocacy is a powerful finger on the hands of healing change.

All Levels

"I do not have time to weave public policy advocacy into my life," I thought honestly some years ago. "It will take more time than I have. The kids need me. My job needs me. My sister, parents, friends, church need me. I do not have time." A few weeks later I heard the announcement in my church: "We have become an 'Advocating Congregation.'" That meant a small group from the congregation would organize letter writing to Congress and to the state legislature after Sunday service, during coffee hour. They would bring stamps, pens, and sample letters. They would sign us up to get policy alerts from the Faith Action Network of Washington State. Not only that, they would make it easy to join a throng of faith-motivated people going to the state capital yearly to advocate around particular issues. The good news went on: they would organize information sessions about any legislation or issues that people in the congregation requested. *The point is this: we are not an I, we are a we. If I depend on a community, not just on myself, to engage in "changing the rules," then it becomes doable, maybe even a joy.*

Life-Giving Links

The links between "change the rules" and the other fingers on the hands of healing change pulsate with energy. Examples abound. We view a few.

"Building the new" in the form of worker-owned co-ops depends upon public policy that channels finance and other support to them.[19] The New Economy Coalition (NEC) demonstrates. Its reason for being is "building the new." So, in meeting with one of its leaders, I expected her to focus our conversation on their network of innovative new enterprises. To my surprise she began by telling me excitedly about their emphasis also on equipping people for public policy advocacy. Working with other organizations, they had developed a toolkit for generating and supporting "new economy policy." The NEC writes,

> *"All over this country we are using policy to re-write the rules and build pathways to a people's economy."* Their toolkit, *Pathways to a People's Economy,* *"provides tools for communities and organizations to make concrete policy demands to advance a new economy—an economy for, by, and with the people."*[20]

Tax justice (a part of our next finger in the hands of change, "move the money") also depends on "changing the rules" through legislative action. To illustrate, the organization Patriotic Millionaires promotes legislation that would restructure the tax system so that wealthy people pay a greater share of their income in taxes.

In the Poor Peoples Campaign (PPC), we see the deep connection between "changing the rules" and movement building ("building the bigger we"). While the PPC aims primarily at movement building, its Moral Agenda and Moral Budget are all about public policy. Calling for "visionary social and economic policy," they write, "What we need is long-term economic policy that establishes justice, promotes the general welfare, rejects decades of austerity and builds strong social programs that lift society from below."

Sacred Journey Journal: Practicing This Healing Medicine

Ideas can change the world when they are practiced. Practicing ideas breeds moral power. And it can bring joy, the joy of living one's values in public. Dare to practice the ideas in this chapter.

How might this "finger on the hands of healing" ("change the rules") look for you or your group (congregation, friend group, chat group, book club, circle of parents, neighborhood, etc.)? What are one or two faith-based or other advocacy organizations in your community or state? Select one and learn a bit more about it. You might sign up for its "advocacy alert" or other electronic information vehicle. You might invite someone else to join you in exploring this medicine, to be your accountability buddy.

Then respond to one of the following, choosing whichever speaks to you:
- How might this bring you joy?
- In what ways would it align your life more fully with your real values?
- In what sense would it be "loving your neighbor as yourself" with a love that seeks justice and liberation?
- How would you feel five years down the road if you practiced this means of healing our economic life and building a moral economy?

Resources for Digging Deeper

See the toolkit for this book on the series' website at: https://buildingamoraleconomy.org/.

CHAPTER ELEVEN

Fingers on the Hands of Healing:
Move the Money

The key to disrupting the flow of carbon into the atmosphere lies in disrupting the flow of money to coal and oil and gas.
—Bill McKibben[1]

Our belief that stock gains are bloodless ... is deluded.... The truth is, when a company ... pursues shareholder gain with a laser-like focus, someone pays the cost.
—Marjorie Kelly[2]

The Essence

Transform finance to serve human well-being and Earth's flourishing. Replace the single bottom line of maximizing profit with a triple bottom—*people, planet, and profit*—for all investments and other financial transactions.

Vignettes

They were young. They were elders. Some were rabbis. One blew the shofar.

"Dayenu! Enough!" they cried, lifting the matzah as a symbol of urgency. Gathered in front of Chase Bank, Wells Fargo, Bank of America, and other major fossil fuel investors, these faithful Jews marked the ancient call for freedom from the Pharaoh—this time the "Carbon Pharaohs."[3] Their Passover meal in 2022 was a street Seder in front of major financial institutions! They called on the institutions to move their money and stop funding fossil fuels.

"Move your dough," sprang from the lips of an elder propped up by a cane and the arm of a youngster who echoed the old man's call.

Twenty-one Passover actions across the continent drew over one thousand Jews and allies to call upon the leading investors in coal, oil, and gas to move their money. "Fossil fuel companies have hardened their hearts," cried one woman, referring to the ancient Hebrew accusation against the Egyptian Pharaoh for hardening his heart.

"What is going on?" quizzed a curious bank customer. A woman—her head covered by a yarmulke embroidered with flowers and vines on soft mahogany cloth—stepped over to respond. "This is the All Our Might Campaign," she explained. "We must bring freedom from the fossil fuel era and inaugurate a new era of clean energy![4] For the sake of our kids," she added, pointing to a curly-haired little girl bearing a sign clearly penned by a child's hand. It commanded, "Stop ruining our future!" "We have been working with all our hearts and all our souls on this," continued the woman. "We are living through climate plagues." Seeing interest in the bystander's eyes, she went on: "There is some success. The Inflation Reduction Act, you know, invests over $360 billion in clean energy and transportation. But that is only a start. Join us?" she added with a smile.

* * *

More than a decade earlier, in 2010, a band of hearty Pennsylvania Quakers launched their Bank Like Appalachia Matters (BLAM!) campaign. Within five years they had convinced PNC Bank to divest from mountain-top removal mining (PNC had been a primary financier of that practice, which has destroyed more than five hundred mountains, two thousand miles of flowing water, and countless lives in Appalachia.) Revisiting their five-year struggle, the Earth Quaker Action Team shared stories. We listen in.

"Remember our two-hundred-mile walk from Philadelphia to the bank's headquarters in Pittsburgh, gathering supporters along the way, and telling the PNC Board that we'd risk arrest if they didn't stop funding mountain-top removal mining?" "Yes, I still can hear us singing the old union song 'Which Side Are You On?' to each member of the board during their 2013 shareholder meeting. They shut the meeting down in seventeen minutes!" "Remember when a PNC board member traveling to England to lead a garden tour, was met by British Quakers bearing chocolates and signs demanding that PNC stop their complicity in blowing the tops off mountains?" "What I relish is that we pulled off thirty-one actions against PNC in thirteen states and the District of Columbia within twenty-four hours!" "It was thrilling to see us grow from a small band of Quakers to a multifaith network. PNC saw that we were gaining power and would not go away until they changed."

These Quakers and their interfaith companions moved the money![5]

* * *

Across the Atlantic youth activists, dressed for a summer tennis match, commenced their tennis game inside Credit Suisse branches in Geneva and Lausanne. Their aim? Getting the Swiss tennis star Roger Federer to reject his sponsorship deal with Credit Suisse in protest of its fossil fuels investments, as a step in motivating Credit Suisse to divest from fossil fuels. The youth were fined, and Credit Suisse agreed to stop financing new coal-fired power plants. During their court hearing, the youth refused this offer, saying that this was not enough. No more fossil fuel investments, they insisted.[6]

* * *

Nearly six thousand miles away, a graduate student in theology at Pacific Lutheran Theological Seminary pondered her "interrupting injustice project" for the ethics course. She must choose a form of injustice from which she gains, and plan a public move to interrupt that injustice. She chose to interrupt finance-rooted injustice. Hers was a twofold move. She moved all of her investments (a mutual fund and a small retirement account) into funds that refused to invest in fossil fuels. Then, in order to be public and thus have more impact, she called on her congregation and national denomination to do the same, and she wrote to the companies from which she had divested and explained why. What would happen if all theology students, religious leaders, and congregations, synagogues, mosques, and temples took similar public moves? Indeed, as of this writing, faith-based organizations are a lead sector in the movement to divest from fossil fuels.

* * *

On Juneteenth, 2023, 140 economists and policy experts from around the world signed a letter calling Global North leaders to transform the global financial system, starting by redirecting trillions in public finance to curb the climate and inequity crises.[7] They "propose that Global North leaders shift funds away from the parts of our economies that are most dramatically driving our current crises:
- *Stop funding fossils — instead make companies pay for their damages.*
- *Cancel illegitimate Global South debts.*[8]
- *Tax the rich."*[9]

(These steps are at the heart of this chapter's understanding of "move the money.")

Fuller Description

Recall that flock of birds in chapter 1, soaring through the skies, seemingly intent on their course. Suddenly, in an arching swoop, they veer off in a new direction. Imagine: the vast financial expertise and resources of the world, with a rapid swoop, shifting direction. From being lured magnetically in the direction of profit-maximizing, growth-maximizing, consumption-maximizing finance, they sweep off in the opposite path—financing a just and ecologically healthy future. What soaring potential.

For years I taught undergraduate students from all disciplines of the university. I grieved to see business students and marketing students sharpening their wonderful young minds into tools primarily for promoting consumption and maximizing short-term profit. How I longed for them to use their young brilliance to innovate a sustainable, equitable, and power-sharing economy!

Neoclassical economics has taught that the movement and investment of money is not a moral matter or a spiritual matter. This is false. Finance plays a major role in determining who has food, water, education, health care, and more, and whether we will continue to spew greenhouse gasses into the air. Thus, *finance shapes relations with neighbor, the world over. For this reason, finance is a deeply spiritual and moral matter.* In Jewish, Christian, and Muslim scriptures, the movement or use of money is subject to God's commandment to love neighbor; money ought to serve neighbor's well-being (recalling that neighbor is whomever my life impacts, directly or indirectly) and meet the needs of self and ones dependents.

This is why no less than four major global ecumenical organizations came together in a process called NIFEA—developing a coherent strategy of action for working toward a New International Financial and Economic Architecture.[10] This may seem audacious. Perhaps, but if the current financial system is funding the destruction of Earth's life systems, then the aim of dramatically reorienting the flow of money is smack in line with God's call to "serve and preserve" garden Earth (cf. Gen 2:15) and to love neighbor as self (Lev 19:18, Matt 22:39).

We consider four winds pushing the shift to "move the money." The first is finance. The second, divestment and reinvestment, may be seen as a subset of the first, but we will examine it in particular. The third is tax justice or "pay your dues," and the fourth is canceling the debt of highly indebted impoverished countries.

In this chapter, we highlight the role of faith communities. They have been key players in the quest to bring the flow of money in line with basic values of human dignity, justice, and Earth care.

Finance[11]

It is now time for financial service providers to accelerate the shift to renewables. They have the power—and the responsibility.

—Antonio Guterres, UN Secretary-General[12]

The global financial system is ... outdated. ... It acts as a means of wealth accumulation for a narrow elite, whilst disregarding the negative [consequences] of environmental damage and social inequalities. A new, sustainable finance system will be a core pillar of a new economy which serves both humanity and the planet.

—Club of Rome[13]

When Ron and I married decades ago, we decided to keep our savings in socially and ecologically screened funds. Next, we switched our banking from a large corporate bank to a local credit union and a community bank. Both reinvested in marginalized parts of the community. Never have I regretted those moves.

Decades later in October 2012, I felt viscerally the spiritual power of decisions regarding finance. Gathered around a large table in a rather sparse meeting room were the General Secretaries of the World Council of Churches, the Lutheran World Federation, the Council for World Missions, and the World Communion of Reform Churches, as well as key staff from each and an "Ecumenical Commission" of thirteen theologians and economists assembled to advise these organizations on their faith-rooted work to help build a more just and ecologically sane global economic and financial architecture—the NIFEA Initiative. Members of that commission from Africa, Asia, and Latin America testified fervently of the suffering wrought by the current systems of finance that drained money from their lands. Many also pointed to the role of finance in ecological destruction that damaged their people.

The geophysical scientist David Archer expresses what many in that room decried: "Money flows toward short term gain and toward the over-exploitation of unregulated common resources." These tendencies, if unchecked are guiding "toward inevitable doom."[14] Surely the God of life is filled with grief and holy anger, the NIFIA group declared. People of God, in the name of God, must interrupt this flow.

The NIFEA initiative is firmly grounded in theology. "God," the initiative affirms, "loves this good Earth and all people with a love that will never cease. That life-saving love intends fullness of life for all now. Therefore, this divine love seeks to free human beings and the rest of creation from exploitation and oppression, including exploitation by finance. God's love seeks to free both the perpetrators and the victims of financial violence."

Collaboration between religious and secular groups marks the movement to finance that serves people, planet, and profit.[15] This movement is marked also by strong collaboration between faith traditions, including traditions with historic antagonisms.[16] A small book (available online) initiated by the World Council of Churches Child Rights Programme, *Cooler Earth—Higher Benefits*, is an array of best practices, strategies, and illustrations from faith communities and secular organizations around the world using finance to address climate change.[17]

Imagine the impact if all religious institutions including schools grounded in faith traditions were to say, "How we use our money is a moral and spiritual matter. No longer will our money betray our calling to love neighbor and serve and preserve the earth." And with a swoop like the flock of birds, they shift direction, putting their money into firms that cultivate equity and Earth's well-being.

Divestment / Reinvestment

Have you ever had that icky feeling when you believe in certain values, but know your money is supporting all the things you hate?

—Morgan Simon[18]

The scientific and moral imperative is clear: there must be no new investment in fossil fuel expansion, including production, infrastructure and exploration.

—Antonio Guterres, UN Secretary-General[19]

"What's the most dangerous building in your town? Probably the new bank branch . . . because if it's connected to one of the big national banks—Chase, Citi, Wells Fargo, Bank of America—that branch is deeply enmeshed in the destruction of God's creation that climate change represents. It's taking your money and turning it into carbon. . . . Those four banks . . . are the main lenders to the fossil fuel industry," writes Bill McKibben. He goes on: "If you want to build a new gas pipeline, if you wish to frack a well, if you hope for a shiny new LNG port, all you have to do is apply and chances are you'll get your cash. Consider Chase. . . . In the last three years it handed the industry $196 billion. For deep-sea drilling, for Artic exploration—you name it."[20]

Are we powerless against this? No; people and institutions the world over are divesting from fossil fuels and reinvesting in clean energy. That includes taking our money—personal money, institutional money, and public funds—out of banks and investments that fund the fossil fuel industry, and putting that money into alternatives, alternatives that aim not only at profit but also at human and ecological well-being.[21]

This divest/reinvest movement began in 2011 on US college campuses and grew rapidly into a global movement. While catalyzed by universities, faith-based organizations, and foundations, it has spread to "new sectors, including large insurers, pension funds, and banking institutions . . . as [they] recognize the reputational, financial, and legal risks of remaining invested in fossil fuels."[22] Today, religious communities remain the largest sector of divesting groups.[23]

Indigenous communities and youth also are raising public consciousness regarding divestment and reinvestment. The Indigenous Women's Divestment Delegations, for example, enables Indigenous women leaders to meet management of European and US financial institutions to explain how their fossil fuel investments drive climate change and climate injustice, and to pressure for divestment.[24]

A 2021 report by DivestInvest tells the story of this movement.[25]

The fossil fuel divestment movement is a source for tremendous optimism. Ten years in, the divestment movement has grown to become a major global influence on energy policy. There are now 1,485 institutions publicly committed to at least some form of fossil fuel divestment, representing an enormous $39.2 trillion of assets under management. That's as if the two biggest economies in the world, the United States and China, combined, chose to divest from fossil fuels. . . . The true amount of money being pulled out from fossil fuels is almost certainly larger since not all divestment commitments are made public.

Major new divestment commitments from iconic institutions have arrived in a rush over just a few months in late 2021, including Harvard University, Dutch and Canadian pension fund giants PME and CDPQ, the U.S. city of Baltimore, and the Ford and MacArthur Foundations. . . .

One of the most important victories for the movement has been the financial elite's gradual acceptance of the movement's core financial arguments. Fossil fuels are a bad bet financially. It was once considered a fringe position to argue that the fossil fuel industry's value is dependent on "stranded assets"—fuel reserves buried in the ground that will become worthless in a clean, renewable energy future. Now the concept is cited by BlackRock, the largest investment house in the world, as a reason to divest. . . . Surveys and analyses by Wall Street firms support it.[26]

Two years before this report was issued, the large body of scientists who published the "World Scientists' Warning of a Climate Emergency" noted as an "encouraging sign" the movement of "institutional fossil fuel divestment." This, they say, is vitally important because "the world must... replace fossil fuels with low-carbon renewables and other cleaner sources of energy.... We should leave remaining stocks of fossil fuels in the ground."[27] The *Financial Times* reports that the investment community also is recognizing the long-term liability of assets based in fossil fuels.[28]

Many organizations and leaders committed to the new economy stress divestment not only from fossil fuels but also from other exploitative or extractive industries such as private prison corporations, the extractive mining industry, and other corporations whose practices exploit people or Earth's goods.

Reinvestment includes investing in clean energy, but also in local endeavors that are democratically controlled, ecologically regenerative, and equitable. That may be local loan funds, minority-owned or cooperatively owned business, and the many forms of small-scale alternatives explored earlier under "building the new." The Movement for Black Lives, for example, encourages not only divesting from private prison corporations but also investing in Black-owned business and other Black community endeavors. Likewise, Mazaska Talks, a network rising out of the Indigenous-led resistance to the Dakota Access Pipeline, encourages individuals, cities, and institutions to divest from banks funding pipeline and tar-sands projects and to reinvest in local credit unions and native-owned banks.[29]

The New Economy Coalition articulates the divest-reinvest link well: "In recent years we've seen enormous energy from movements working to divest the money of individuals, institutions, municipalities, pension funds, and more out of the extractive economy of Wall Street banks, private prison corporations, and the fossil fuel industry, and reinvest those funds into the New Economy."[30]

Tax Justice (Pay Your Dues)[31]

A tall African woman rises slowly from her chair. The room hushes. Her voice is riveting: "Africa is not getting a fair deal for its mineral resources! The impact on the people is terrible.... We are very rich in natural resources and mineral wealth. We are asking global corporations operating in African countries to pay their taxes! Taxes are the lifeblood of the country. They are needed to build schools and health care. But the multi-nationals are experts in avoiding paying taxes."[32]

The speaker is a leader in Tax Justice Network Africa (TJNA). It includes thirty-two national or regional organizations.[33] Her words send my heart spinning. I envision the threads connecting children without healthcare in African nations with the corporate profits accrued through tax evasion. Did those profits—working their way through the global finance system—help to fund my salary?

A recent ground-breaking report documents the suffering that corporate tax evasion and abuse cause for impoverished people around the world:[34]

> **"Poorer countries are hit harder by global tax abuse."** *In fact, "lower income countries' tax losses are equivalent to nearly 52 per cent of their combined public health budgets." The lost money is enough to pay 34 million nurses annual salaries.*[35] **"South Africa's tax losses could lift over 3 million people out of poverty."** *Yet* **"rich countries are responsible for almost all global tax losses."** *(Bold is in the original.)*

While launching this report, economists and other advocates urged citizens to push their governments to pass tax reform measures that "clamp down on global tax abuse and reverse the inequalities and hardships exacerbated by tax losses." The global movement for tax justice is a third element of "move the money."[36]

Prominent religious voices describe tax justice as a vital tool for building more equitable and ecological societies, and for enabling right relationships with "neighbors" far and near. Rev. Rowan Williams, former archbishop of Canterbury, says as much: "Many of the world's largest companies seem to have forgotten that they have moral duties, as well as legal ones. They must support human flourishing, not least by paying their fair share of taxes in all the countries where they do business."

Church Action for Tax Justice (based in England) writes,

> *Returning a percentage of our wealth to the public sphere for the benefit of all is an acknowledgement that we are part of society, and that we all depend on one another. Our riches are not ours alone. . . . Yet in rich and poor countries alike it is still too easy for large companies and wealthy individuals to avoid paying their fair share of tax. Too often, tax is seen as negative: a burden to be minimized. We can tell a different story about tax. That it allows us to contribute to services and infrastructure shared by all, and that paying it is not just a duty but a privilege.*[37]

The Zacchaeus Tax (ZacTax), launched by the NIFEA Initiative described above, calls faith communities around the globe to join their campaign.[38] That means aligning their faith communities' funds with principles for just taxation, and pushing national governments to support tax justice measures. Foremost among those measures are the following:

- Requiring global corporations to pay taxes to the countries in which they operate. (This includes penalizing corporate tax dodging.)
- Enacting progressive wealth taxes at global and national levels to curb the growing concentration of wealth.[39]
- Enacting progressive carbon and other pollution taxes.
- Enacting a financial transaction tax on trade in equities, currencies, and derivatives to rein in speculative investment with its devastating impact on vulnerable economies.[40]

Imagine the impact if faith communities—Buddhist, Jewish, Christian, Muslim, and many others—around the world determined to push for these measures as a way of honoring the call to compassion and neighbor-love. Take a moment to see in your heart's eye the lives that could be saved by such a moral and spiritual force.

While more active in the Global South and in Europe, the tax justice movement is present too in the United States, and decries the growing wealth inequity in this country.[41] Former Secretary of Labor Robert Reich explains how current tax policy tends to syphon money into the hands of the wealthiest people. As of April 2022, he writes, "One man—Elon Musk—owns more wealth than the bottom 40% of (U.S.) Americans.[42] In [one minute] Jeff Bezos will have added about 30,000 to his wealth.[43] *But virtually none of that wealth growth—the main source of billionaire income—may ever be taxed.*[44] . . . That's because income tax doesn't cover billionaire wealth: Bezos's salary is just $81,840. Musk's is $0. *In many years, they've both avoided paying any federal income tax at all.*[45] If we want billionaires to pay what they owe, we've got to tax their wealth—not just their income."[46] He goes on to cite budgetary and legislative moves to increase wealth taxes.

The movement to create a Billionaires Income Tax (BIT) in the US is growing. In 2021 over sixty national organizations sent a letter to Congress recommending the BIT legislation proposed by Senator Ron Wyden be adopted.[47] It would tax billionaires' increase in wealth as income. Thus, their income through increased wealth would be taxed as is the paycheck income of workers. The revenues could be invested into sorely needed public goods such as education and healthcare.

Taxation as a move to build a more moral economy is not new. It has a long history. Wealth tax in particular, so feared in the United States, has been far more present in Europe.[48]

What does this have to do with ordinary people in the United States who would like corporations to pay their taxes but who see no way of making that happen? I was shocked to hear the South African Lutheran leader Uhuru Dempers say, "Faith-based organizations are key players in working toward tax justice." What would happen if congregations concerned about hunger decided—as a part of their anti-hunger ministries—to join the Zacchaeus Tax movement or to collaborate with the Global Alliance for Tax Justice? Consider now the fourth element of "move the money."

Canceling Debt of Highly Indebted Impoverished Countries

"I am Bishop Bernardino Mandlate, Methodist bishop of Mozambique, and I am a debt warrior."

He uttered this single sentence, his voice exuding quiet power. When asked to address a United Nations meeting concerning the causes of poverty in Africa, Bishop Mandlate identified the external debt as a primary cause. *The debt, he declared, is "covered with the blood of African children."*

I will never forget this man. With five words ("I am a debt warrior"), he revealed to me a world that I lived in but did not see. It is the world of people in impoverished nations suffering because their country's money is siphoned off into the finance systems of wealthy nations like my own.

The small child awakening in Jamaica did not borrow any money, but she pays the price for her country's heavy debt burden. Her country received loans packaged with the promise of development and immediate poverty alleviation. But the lenders demanded austerity conditions—such as reduced spending on health care, education, and basic food subsidies—that plunged her family and many others more deeply into poverty. Yet this child's creditors still demand payment.

The stupefying cost of debt repayment, while stunting the growth of many impoverished countries, contributes to the wealth of wealthy countries. Bishop Mandlate's words ring a note of horror in the heart for those of us whose economies benefit from debt repayments by economically poor nations.

A global coalition of faith-based groups and other NGOs, beginning in the late 1970s, championed the reduction or cancellation of the foreign debt of highly indebted poor countries (HIPC). Known as the Jubilee 2000 campaign, this movement used the biblical notion of the Jubilee year to press for a "jubilee" for HIPCs; the foreign debt would be canceled or reduced, and funds freed for alleviating poverty.[49] The Jubilee campaign helped to achieve substantial debt relief for many countries.

However, now again, with echoes of that time, debt threatens lives in many poor countries.[50] Rev. Adam Russell Taylor, executive director of Sojourners, formerly led the Faith Initiative at the World Bank Group and is no stranger to the anguish wrought by this debt. He writes,

> *I know talking about international lending policies makes most people want to yawn, but the Bible takes debt — and the people who profit from it—seriously.... So, if you care about truly addressing the dual crises of*

> *extreme poverty and climate change, stay with me on this. . . . If we're serious about addressing the dire effects of climate change, we need to tackle another problem: a worsening debt crisis that has left many nations needing exponentially more resources to recover from climate disasters and invest in sustainable development.* [51]

Taylor explains why low- and middle-income nations have so much debt, unraveling the complex of "mutually exacerbating crises" including "energy prices, rising interest rates, . . . the pandemic," and drastic weather worsened by climate change such as hurricanes, earthquakes, flooding, droughts:

> *When one of these natural disasters devastates a small, low- or middle-income country, that country generally needs to take out a loan to repair the damage and help their population recover. Because private lending institutions generally view these loans as risky investments, they offer exceptionally high interest rates that make such loans non-starters for these countries. Instead, nations needing a loan for disaster relief often turn to one of the multilateral development banks (MDBs) like the World Bank or the Inter-American Development Bank. . . . Unfortunately, borrowing from MDBs often comes with challenging interest rates and stipulations that the recipient nation must tighten its spending to ensure the loan can eventually be repaid. For many nations this means they must prioritize repaying their debts instead of making critical investments in their nation's sustainable development. So, when the next hurricane, or earthquake, or flood strikes, they're once again not prepared. It's become a devastating cycle of debt and disaster.*

Rev. Taylor invites people of faith to enter a growing global movement for reforms that would make money available to low- and middle-income countries to help relieve their foreign debt, recover from effects of climate change, and prepare for future disasters. The movement is made up of ordinary people who care enough to step up to the plate. Groups in the United States may link with siblings around the world in this endeavor ("build the bigger we") by joining with the Jubilee USA Network. *"For those of us who are people of faith,"* Taylor, insists, it's *"a powerful expression of the Jubilee vision of restoring right relationship."*

Rev. Taylor expresses eloquently what we contend in this book series: that economies are a web of relationships and thus are subject to the two overarching *oiko nomos* (rules for managing the household of Earth) given by God—to "love neighbor" and to "serve and preserve" creation. Today, canceling the debt is one piece in the puzzle of building a moral economy that honors these two *oiko nomos*.

All Four Winds Blowing Together to "Move the Money"

If you have financial resources, perhaps you had not before considered the finances that support your life (bank account, savings account, pension fund, investment funds, employer's investments) as spiritual matters. They are. They shape our relationships with neighbors and with Earth. The child who dies from lack of health care in Jamaica might not have died had the global corporations at work there paid their fair taxes to Jamaica. Do I receive dividends from investments in those corporations? Billions of people will be saved from devastation by climate change if the human community divests rapidly from fossil fuels and invests in clean energy and energy conservation. People employed in worker-owned co-ops in Cleveland might still be jobless if people had not invested in the Cleveland project instead of in Chase Bank.

May it become a joy for you and for me to "move the money" for the sake of human beings and our planetary home.

Life-Giving Links

Moving the money is impossible on large scales without also "changing the rules"—building public policy that incentivizes morally responsible finance or removes barriers to it. Likewise, "changing the story" by reframing the purpose of financial activity is critical. "Moving the money" through divestment is a means of "resisting the wrong," and reinvesting is means of "building the new."

Sacred Journey Journal:
Practicing This Healing Medicine

Have a look at the "Resources for Digging Deeper" in the toolkit for this book on the book series' website. Choose a few of the campaigns or resources to look into. How might you, your household, or your group (congregation, friend group, book club, circle of parents, neighborhood, etc.) engage with one of them? With whom could you collaborate in doing this? Consider your own finances. If you have savings, investments, or a checking account, where might you move that money so that it will help to build a more compassionate, equitable, and ecological world? Finally, consider the finances of your faith community, employer, or other institution with which you are connected. Is there a movement within it to "move the money"—perhaps to divest from fossil fuels? If so, how will you support it? If not, with whom might you collaborate to begin such a movement?

Now consider one of the following:
- How might this bring you joy?
- How might it align your life more fully with your real values?

- In what sense does it enable you to practice God's call to love neighbor as self or to care for creation?
- How would you feel five years down the road if you practiced this means of healing our economic life as individuals, a society, and a global community?

Resources for Digging Deeper

See the toolkit for this book on the series' website at: https://buildingamoraleconomy.org/.

CHAPTER TWELVE

Fingers on the Hands of Healing:
Resist the Wrong

[In the global economy] ... if the church is the ... body of Christ, this body of Christ is divided among active thieves, passive profiteers, and deprived victims.

—Peter Pero[1]

Evil asks little of the dominant caste, other than to sit back and do nothing. All that it needs from the bystanders is their silent complicity in the evil committed on their behalf.

—Isabel Wilkerson[2]

The Essence

Efforts that say no to exploitative or extractive economic and financial practices, policies, institutions, and larger systems.

Vignettes

From Central America:

Early in the morning, before dawn, a knock came at the door. It was a young woman from the village in which I lived and worked. I had agreed to join her, other campesinas and campesinos, and two Catholic priests in standing together to claim a piece of land near our village, land that had been taken over by a multinational corporation against the wishes and well-being of the people. They desperately needed that land for growing corn, beans, and vegetables to feed their children. I was aware of the need; working in a church-based health program, I saw firsthand the hunger and malnutrition that plagued the people when no land was available for growing food. These folks worked long and hard but could not feed their families adequately, because the land which their people had cultivated for generations had been taken from them.

We waited together, passing the time by laying palm branches on Earth in the protest area. Soldiers arrived. We did not know what would happen. Not far from our village, such protest had been met with violence and death at the hands of soldiers. Yet, on this sunbaked morning, the people stood firm. And the soldiers did not strike.

I honestly do not recall the entire sequence of events following that day. Much was unfolding that demanded attention. What I know is that the land ultimately was acquired collectively by the people. In this case, the effort to "resist the wrong" bore fruit. Had it not, had more barriers been raised, I now know that support from faith communities in the US who decided to "resist the wrong" by joining with us from a distance would have been invaluable and could have turned the tide. That support could have come in many forms: heralding the peoples' efforts in the press, lobbying the land-holding corporation's leadership, sending a few people to stand with us and making their presence highly visible to the soldiers.

* * *

From the United Nations:

September 23, 2002 slipped into history as a historic day. The president of Vanuatu called upon the nations of the world to establish a Fossil Fuel Non-proliferation Treaty to stop the expansion of all new fossil fuel projects, and manage a global just transition away from coal, oil and gas. EnviroNews Nigeria reported that "the President of Vanuatu, Nikenike Vurobaravu, made the historic call on the floor of the UN General Assembly."[3] In his speech, President Nikenike Vurobaravu said, "Every day we are experiencing more debilitating consequences of the climate crisis. Fundamental human rights are being violated, and we are measuring climate change not in degrees of Celsius or tons of carbon, but in human lives.... Our youth are terrified of the future world we are handing to them through expanding fossil fuel dependency, compromising intergenerational trust and equity. We call for the development of a Fossil Fuel Non-proliferation Treaty to phase down coal, oil and gas production in line with 1.5°C, and enable a global just transition for every worker, community and nation with fossil fuel dependence."[4]

Momentum toward this moment had been building since the 2015 Suva Declaration by Pacific Island Nations calling for an internationally binding moratorium on the extraction of fossil fuels.[5] As reported by Canada's National Observer, "Vulnerable Pacific island states have long been at the forefront of climate leadership. . . . The Fossil Fuel Non-proliferation Treaty Initiative . . . launched two years ago with support from civil society organizations . . . has grown quickly, and today is backed by more than 750 organizations; cities like Toronto, London and Los Angeles; thousands of scientists; academics and politicians, as well as over 100 Nobel laureates."[6] "The proposal has also been supported by the Vatican and the World Health Organization."[7]

Fuller Description

"Resist the wrong" is a many-splendored tool—legal action, public liturgies, boycotts, high visibility declarations, public protest and marches, civil disobedience, and other forms of nonviolent direct action are ways that people come together to cry out publicly for a halt to socially and environmentally damaging institutions, industries, businesses, and practices. Efforts to "resist the wrong" range from local to international. At times, international solidarity is key to local actions' success and may be a means of protecting activists or land protectors from violent repression.

The Club of Rome affirms,

> *Mass street protests . . . sustained over substantial periods of time, are essential to overcoming the major political obstacles we face. As movements such as Black Lives Matter, Occupy, and Extinction Rebellion all show, demonstrations are important both in bringing issues to public attention and in changing opinion. As a result of each of these movements, opinion polls showed substantial favorable shifts in public opinion, and there is a body of empirical research that shows that non-violent demonstrations are an effective way of shifting public opinion.*[8]

The US and the world are indebted to the Black Lives Matter movement for demonstrating the power of public protest as one means of resisting the wrong, particularly by awakening public awareness. Likewise, young climate justice leaders, joined by high level religious leaders in public protest are raising public awareness of the climate emergency and its roots in heedless economic activity. Indigenous communities around the world—including in the US—are known for courageous and creative protest against pipelines and drilling that will desecrate their lands and compromise their tribal structures. The Indigenous Environmental Network, in its "Indigenous Resistance against Carbon," documents some of that leadership and its impact.[9]

While visiting my son in Mexico, I met his boss, Angelica (name changed). She was leader of an organization dedicated to youth empowerment. Angelica described how her small town had organized successfully to block any multinational companies—from McDonald's to a golf course developer—from building in their town. The townspeople were vehement: "We do not want local business to be undone, our common lands despoiled, our water supplies used up."

Faith communities creatively cultivate public liturgies that speak the truth about wrongs that we are called to resist, and about the presence of the Sacred in those resistance actions. Some Christians view Jesus' turning over the tables in the temple (Matt 21:12–14) as form of public liturgy aimed at "resisting the wrong" in the name of the God of life. One faith community in Seattle designed a public ritual of table turning for the day after thanksgiving. They were encouraging people to "resist" the consumer mentality that drives so many people to the shopping malls on that day.[10] The courageous Palestinian leader and former bishop of the Lutheran church in Palestine, Yunan Munib, refers to such action as "evangelical defiance," meaning gospel-grounded defiance.

Public protest is not the only form of "resisting the wrong." Individuals, households, institutions, and governments "resist the wrong" also through boycotts, divestment (as discussed in chapter 11), and legal and legislative moves (as per chapter 10).

The Fossil-Fuel Non-proliferation Treaty in our vignette illustrates multiple means of resisting the wrong. This campaign uses advocacy with elected officials and governments (national and local) to "resist the wrong" of unrelenting fossil fuel extraction. The campaign also resists the wrong through education and consciousness-raising, public protest, activist art, and more.

Resisting the wrong may be risky, dangerous, even life-threatening. Some Indigenous people, for example, receive death threats and risk assassination for their work in protecting lands and waters.

An Indigenous woman from Panama sat beside me at the World Council of Churches (WCC) General Assembly 2022 in Germany. A report had just been read outlining the WCC's commitments to ecological and economic justice in the coming seven years until the next General Assembly. "What did you think of it, Jocabed?" I asked her, expecting a response similar to mine (that it was excellent). She looked at me with deep concern in her eyes: "It does not mention the Indigenous Earth protectors who are persecuted or killed for working against extractive industries." She was right. "How," I asked myself, "could I have failed to notice that?"

Her words held layers of meaning. They were a statement that the global communion of churches had a vital role to play in putting an end to these assassinations. If they go unnoted by the larger global community, they will continue. If, in sharp contrast, global solidarity steps in, then protections are raised; it is less likely that protestors of logging in the Amazon, oil drilling in the Niger Delta, internationally financed hydroelectric dam projects in India, for example, will be jailed, harassed, or killed if people the world over have made it clear that we stand at their sides and that such violations are completely unacceptable. Religious communities are crucial in making that stand visible.

That very afternoon my Indigenous colleague, Jocabed Solano, and a Venezuelan ecotheologian, Rev. Neddy Astudillo, led an effort to get this matter included in the report that had been read. They succeeded.[11] The statement now highlights the Escazú Agreement, a landmark legally binding international agreement signed by forty-six countries that can be used to protect the human rights of environmental defenders.

The legacy of public actions to "resist the wrong"—both legal and as civil disobedience—has a proud history in the US and worldwide. Its power is in its moral weight and in its making visible what people avoid seeing. Further power lies in the movement building that this form of action engenders. Some would say that the legacy goes back millennia to the Hebrew prophets and their fierce outcry against exploitative economies and oppressive political regimes.

"Seeing what is going on" (the first form of moral vision that we visited in chapter 4) is another form of resisting the wrong. Recognizing the suffering caused by systems that we may consider "just the way things are" or recognizing the oppression that goes unnoticed in the public eye is a step toward changing those systems. In many cases oppressive systems are designed so that people do not see them. The scholar and pastor Christopher Carter writes that industrial agricultural systems are designed to hide the exploitation that breeds their high profits. "We consumers are not supposed to think about where our food comes from."[12] A commitment to "see what is going on" resists such moral oblivion.

Life-Giving Links

"Resisting the wrong" through public demonstrations may pave the way for legislation that "changes the rules," as in the civil rights movement in the US, and may pave the way for building the new. For example, resisting by withdrawing money from Chase, Wells Fargo, and other banks that support fossil fuel extraction enables alternative banks to receive that money and thus to thrive. Moving the money by divesting may be seen as resisting the wrong. Solidarity with land and water protectors builds the bigger we. What other links do you see between resisting the wrong and the other fingers on the hands of healing change?

Sacred Journey Journal: Practicing This Healing Medicine

When and in what way have you, your family, or a group of which you are part (congregation, neighbors, friend group, book club, circle of parents, etc.) been involved in resisting the wrong? What was that experience like for you? How did you feel? How did others respond?

How might you or one of your groups engage in resisting the wrong in the near future? That is, how might you or this group take some kind of action to say "no more" to a practice or policy that is damaging to Earth or to people? The practice or policy may be of an institution (such as church, school, place of employment), government, business, or other entity.

How might that action lead to other benefits such as a changed law or zoning regulation, a retail store committing to responsible supply chains, reduced fossil fuel emissions, more people joining the cause, and so on?

Now consider one of the following:
- How might this act of resisting the wrong bring you joy?
- How might it align your life more fully with your real values?
- In what sense does it enable you to practice God's call to love neighbor as self or to care for creation?
- How would you feel five years down the road if you practiced this means of healing our economic life as individuals, a society, and a global community?

Resources for Digging Deeper

- See the toolkit for this book on the series' website at: https://buildingamoraleconomy.org/.

CHAPTER THIRTEEN

Fingers on the Hands of Healing:
Build the Bigger We

> Alone, I have seen many marvelous things, none of which is true.
> —African proverb

The Essence

Healing the economic life of individuals, institutions, and society, and moving from exploitative and extractive to life-giving economies by cultivating collaborative community at home and across the continents.

Vignette

She sat across a small lop-sided wooden table. A fan buzzed through humid air. Her eyes shone. A pastor, she had walked for two days with other women of a tribal village in Odisha, India, bearing the body of a person killed for organizing against the bauxite mines and aluminum refineries that were destroying their lands and driving them from their community. The mines and refineries were owned by global corporations. The tribal people continued in courageous resistance. They had lived on and cared for these lands for centuries. Now they were being cast aside and into urban destitution. They resisted and it was costly—harassment, arbitrary arrest, being charged as Maoists, even death. She was one of them.

"How," I thought, "could this people of a small tribal village in India possibly win against the power of those corporations? How could they withstand the risks to their lives?" Her response broke into my heart: "We are not alone." I learned that international supporters were calling on governments and other large investors to divest from the companies that owned these mines and refineries. Norway, it turns out, was the first. Norway's Government Pension Fund Global (GPFG), the world's largest state-owned investment fund, had divested from these companies because of their human rights violations and their dangerous environmental impacts.

Half way around the globe and two years later, I told this story to an audience of about 1500 people in Norway. Mountains, pines, and chirping birds surrounded us. The people were gathered in a biannual week-long camp of Korsvei, a Norwegian Christian organization with the fourfold aim of seeking justice, building community, living simply, and following Jesus. After the talk, a man came up to me. "I was the person who brought this to the Norwegian Pension Fund," he revealed in a quiet voice. We spent the evening talking around a fire in the cool Norwegian mountain air. I came to see that the tribal people with their courageous resistance and the people in Norway and elsewhere who supported them are part of a "bigger we." Imagine people of the US convincing our cities, states, universities, and faith communities to join in this bigger we. Imagine the tribal people safe on their lands, the bauxite mining stopped, remediation underway. Imagine this extending to mining operations in many lands.

Fuller Description

A tree grows near the street on which I lived.[1] The asphalt and concrete threaten to choke its roots. One small strand of root pushing up against the asphalt and the concrete stands no chance. It is as inconsequential as my individual divestment from the bauxite mining company or from large scale banking and investment firms. Yet, many strands of root *woven together* and persisting collectively in their struggle to nurture the life of that tree have pushed up large blocks of the concrete sidewalk and the asphalt street. So great is the disruption caused by those tenacious strands of root working *together* on behalf of life that trucks driving over the ridges in the road rattle. If each strand of root tried to do it alone or opted out, thinking it was too insignificant, their liberative power would go untapped. Let us learn from the communion of root strands.

I invite you to pause, to hold a holy moment. Honor the sacred reality of communion across the ages, continents, cultures, and ideological convictions—the cloud of witnesses, seeking to build a world that reflects their deepest values of compassion, justice, joy, equity, and Earth's integrity. These are ordinary-extraordinary human beings with a vision of economies for life, and the guts to live that vision into reality.

Cultivating Community across Time and Difference

Note the ancestors in this holy communion. We walk in their footsteps and may draw strength from being in community with them. For religious people, this may include forebearers in your faith tradition, such as the Hebrew prophets for Jews and Christians. What audacity they had, the ancient Hebrew people! What world-shaking nerve to claim this: the Sacred Mystery—the Source of the cosmos—created us human earthlings (made from dust and breath like all our creature kin) to be beloved by the Sacred Source, to serve and preserve the garden, and to "love neighbor as self." Ah, but their claim went further: with fierce prophetic tongue, they insisted that neighbor-love entails justice, that oppression was an abomination to the Holy One, and that humans could break free from oppressive ways to build communities of justice and compassion. This liberation from ways of oppression and exploitation would be enacting love for self, God, and neighbor, whomever one's life impacts. What a community in which to walk today!

Christians may draw strength also from ancestors such as early Jewish followers of Jesus who held all things in common, early church leaders such as St. Basil and St. Ambrose who excoriated the rich for depriving the poor, Reformation leaders such as Luther who decried the emerging capitalist economy (although that label did not yet exist) for its commercial and investment practices that damaged poor people, leaders of the Social Gospel movement, and Christian socialists in England.

The ancestral communion in the quest for a more just and compassionate world includes more recent forerunners. They are people such as early labor rights organizers who fought for laws against child labor, anti-apartheid activists in South Africa, those who stood against dictators in many lands, initiators of the movement to combat environmental racism, and early advocates of corporate social responsibility. Who would you add to this ancestral host?

Turn now to those companions alive today at this fulcrum point in the story of humankind—this time when we could carry on toward our extinction by climate change or could choose a different path toward life's flourishing. These companions are the movements and people the world over who have said no (or are moving toward saying no) to the outdated exploitative and fossil-fueled economy, and yes to a new economy that enables humans to live in balance with the rest of nature and that prioritizes well-being over maximizing profit. They are the youth climate leaders, the climate warriors of the Pacific Islands, the legislators pushing for living wage laws, the divestors from fossil fuels, the business leaders converting their companies to employee ownership, the daring small farmers building localized food systems from the ground up, the Poor People's campaign for moral budgets, and on and on!

This holy communion is underreported! Do many of us in the US know, for example, that the Indigenous Environmental Network, "formed by grassroots Indigenous peoples and individuals to address environmental and economic justice issues," has been at work since 1990 doing just that, and that its work includes all ten fingers on the hands of healing outlined in this book?[2] Are we aware that a network of Black farmers, organizers, and faith community leaders has been at work for years to build food sovereignty in Black communities? Do we realize that small island nations in the Pacific have been working toward a fossil-fuel nonproliferation treaty since 2015?

In 2007 Paul Hawken wrote *Blessed Unrest: How the Largest Movement in the World Came into Being and Why No One Saw It Coming*. It is a feast. Setting out to identify all of the organizations aimed at ecological sustainability, economic justice, and other forms of social justice, he was expecting to find some 100,000. But no, he finally concluded that there were at least 1 and possibly 2 million. They constitute the largest social movement in human history, Hawken concludes. The movement includes extremely impoverished people, wealthy people who do not want to continue making wealth at the cost of others, and folks in between.[3] It spans lines of race/ethnicity, age, and religion.

This movement, at times, builds community of shared purpose even across lines of ideological difference. Today, in the US, this is rare. However, it is possible. One friend, a gifted leader in faith-based community organizing, described her organizing work in Alaska. It brought together supporters of Donald Trump and supporters of Joe Biden to work collaboratively on measures to curtail economic exploitation in their community!

Cultivating community—"building the bigger we"—may be the single most important dynamic in the movement to build a moral economy. Cultivating community locally, across the nation, and around the globe also builds a sense of personal wholeness and belonging. For some, this may come quite easily, but for many of us it requires risk-taking, intentionality, and discomfort. It may mean facing one's blinders and opening one's eyes to experiences very different from one's own.

Cultivating Community at Home

"Build a team!" exhorted my cofacilitator of our course in Community Organizing as Spiritual Practice. "When you are faced with a challenging task, build a team." A year later, when I faced the challenge of creating a Certificate in Climate Justice and Faith at the seminary where I teach, I went back to my notes from that colleague's session in the course. But how, I mused, do I build a team? The notes went on, "Listen to people and discern whose values, purpose, and concerns cohere with mine." I had listened and I knew four people also committed to equipping people for faith-rooted climate justice work. After honest, probing conversations, all four were on board. We became a team, and gave birth to the Certificate in Climate Justice and Faith. The program now trains leaders from across the globe.

Melissa Reed, a pastor/community organizer from the interfaith world, spoke to another class. She maintained that nothing is more powerful for building a community of people committed to justice than daring to share the stories of our lives. Marshall Ganz says as much. Having developed and taught community organizing tools since his involvement in the civil rights movement in the 1960s and teaching now at Harvard, he has insisted for decades that sharing life stories is the place to begin. He calls this "the story of self."

If you are creating a team for building a moral economy, why not start with life stories? Why not share with one another such things as the following: What are your most ardent hopes and fears for your children, grandchildren, or other young folk? Why do you hunger for a more equitable, compassionate, and ecologically sane world? What keeps you awake at night? When in the last month have you felt joy? Why do you care about people who suffer from poverty? What people or events in your life have shaped you? What people or events have shaped your sense of yourself as beloved, or as inadequate and unworthy? What has shaped your sense of power or powerlessness for building a better world? What is one key challenge that you face in your life today, that may get in the way of your hopes and goals or well-being? What is one key opportunity?

Then you can move to what Ganz calls the "story of us." How do these experiences link us? What have we in common? What are our shared needs? What do they say about our community, and our needs as a community?

From the basis of shared life stories, your group might move on to discern the steps you will take to heal economic life in your households and in your community—which of the ten fingers on the hands of change you will enliven and how. Imagine your small community (congregation, neighborhood group, friend group . . .) as what Dietrich Bonhoeffer called "cells of prayer and righteous action." By this, he meant groups committed to acting rightly in the face of systemic injustice, and nurtured by their collective dependence on the Spirit.

Cultivating Community across the Continent and Continents

On the morning of April 24, 2013, Aanya kissed her mother goodbye as she left to work in the garment factory. By noon, her mother was dead. The nine-story Rana Plaza building in Bangladesh had collapsed, killing 1,138 workers and injuring more than 2,000. "The building had housed five garment factories, producing clothing for well-known Western brands, including Walmart, JCPenney, The Children's Place, Inditex (owner of Zara), Loblaw, Primark, and many others.

"Though it dwarfed other disasters with its scale, Rana Plaza was neither the first nor the last deadly accident in the Bangladesh garment industry." As we noted in chapter 9, "since 2005, more than 2,000 workers have been killed in factory fires and building collapses" in the Bangladesh garment industry.[4]

In Seattle, Sarah bought two shirts for her daughter made in that factory. Talking later that day with a friend, she exclaimed with a voice of accomplishment: "I got a terrific deal on these two shirts. Honestly, they were so cheap!"

Human rights abuses pervade global supply chains. Corporate Social Responsibility (CSR) has largely failed to rectify this ongoing human rights crisis. CSR does not include legally binding requirements to enforce standards. And monitoring frequently is done in-house.

This book reveals grim pictures of how our consumer products, our investments, and the complex economic structures and practices that shape our lives, damage people and Earth's life-systems. How, then, can we get food and clothing and meet daily needs without doing this harm? Perhaps by "building the bigger we" across the continent and across continents. Consider four manifestations of that move.

Worker-Driven Social Responsibility (WSR)[5]

Recall the Worker-Driven Social Responsibility movement introduced in chapter 9. WSR produced the Fair Food Program (FFP) that began with tomato growers in Florida. The FPP won Fair Food Agreements with more than a dozen of the world's largest food companies. It has expanded to cover crops in ten states and to include tomatoes, peonies, tulips, cantaloupes, sweet potatoes, peaches, lettuce, dill, mint, and squash.

Lives have been profoundly changed. Tomato pickers receive better wages and have decent working conditions and protection against sexual exploitation, wage theft, and other forms of harassment. Three short videos by the CNN Freedom Project "depict the dramatic genesis of dignity and respect in a place where unimaginable abuse had been the norm."[6] This required "building the bigger we," solidarity across the continent by people who use the products.

Build the Bigger We

The bigger we is growing even bigger. The fishing industry in the United Kingdom is exploring adapting the Fair Food Program model to the fishing industry.[7] In 2023, a news release from the US Department of Labor announced an initiative to "expand the successful Fair Food Program model with a pilot project to promote human and labor rights focused on cut flower farms in Chile, Mexico and South Africa.... The project will promote grassroots worker-driven social responsibility in agricultural supply chains."[8]

Only solidarity across the continent and the continents will wipe out the terrible abuses that now reign in global supply chains. This is a deeply meaningful part of "building the bigger we."

Divestment and Reinvestment

A second manifestation of "building the bigger we" across the continent and the continents is today's divestment movement (discussed in chapter 11 under "move the money"). This bigger we is delightfully diverse, with leadership from all walks of life, from youth to elders, in a veritable symphony of languages.[9] What would it mean to you and your companions to join the vibrant global community of people who are using divestment and reinvestment to usher out the age of fossil fuels and usher in the just transition to a world of renewable energy obtained by equitable means? Imagine your family, employer, faith community, and city divesting from what many call the weapons of mass destruction of our day—fossil fuels. Perhaps you already are a part of this movement.

Solidarity with Defenders of Water, Land, Forests, and Human Rights

> He approached me after class, a diligent young seminarian. Students milled about gathering computers, coffee mugs, backpacks. "Dr. Moe-Lobeda, may I have a minute?" "Of course," I responded instinctively. "I need to miss class two weeks from now," the young man declared. I raised my eyebrows, having a real distaste for students missing class. "I am going to Standing Rock to stand with the Indigenous water protectors. It will take two days of travel. I have begun the reading for that week and will turn in the paper ahead of time."

"Building the bigger we" takes a third form, glimpsed previously in chapter 12, "Resist the Wrong." It is solidarity in protecting Indigenous and other people who receive death threats or other harassment and risk assassination for their work in defending lands, waters, and forests against deforestation, mining, oil pipelines, or invasive industrial agriculture. Indigenous American theologian

Tink Tinker writes, "Our resistance must be matched with the resistance of our non-Indian relatives for there to be real and creative transformation in our world."[10] Those "non-Indian relatives" include many people who stood with the Indigenous at Standing Rock, and the people who shine the protective light of public awareness on Indigenous people who are being harassed or threatened for their work to stop the pipelines in Tanzania and Chad, the oil fields in the Niger Delta, the tar sands in Canada, and the mining operations in countries around the world.

This form of "building the bigger we" can be a matter of life and death. The Interfaith Rainforest Initiative (IRI) illustrates this reality. It is a global alliance enabling religious leaders to work with Indigenous peoples, governments, businesses, and civil society organizations to protect rainforests and Indigenous peoples who guard them. The director of the Indonesia branch of IRI explained in conversation with me, "Shining public light on these guardians makes it less likely that they will be killed."

Building the bigger in this way is life saving in yet another sense. All of our lives depend on the rainforests. All of our lives ultimately depend on curtailing carbon emissions. So, supporting initiatives to protect the forests and their defenders and to vastly reduce fossil fuel extraction is—in the long run—saving the lives of our children.

Reparations

I was stunned. My eyes bulged. Six or seven white men barged into the room and haughtily walked forth pointing at people, tables, bags, computers, declaring "mine," even grabbing some things. The four-hundred-plus people gathered for the opening meditation gawked, confused. They were assembled for the biannual conference of their region (Rocky Mountain Synod) of the Evangelical Lutheran Church in America. "What is going on?" the walls seemed to cry.

The synod's bishop and leadership council had spent months in thinking and prayer. "How," they pondered, "are we to raise up for our people the Doctrine of Discovery and the call to reparations as an act of faith?" This beginning for the assembly's opening session was one part of their response. It did not end there. The Synod (a word for a region of the Lutheran church) spent years of careful work with local Indigenous communities to discern how to engage in reparations. With careful listening and the courage to make mistakes, they are moving along in this uncharted terrain of being the church of Jesus Christ. This has included transferring to the Indigenous community the deed for property that had been used by the church for decades.

To me, because I have benefitted materially from unjust economic systems, reparation is a profound gift. It is a tool for enacting justice-seeking neighbor-love—a loom for weaving "right relationships" out of the torn and disgraced ruins of human injustice. Reparation is a spiritual practice of healing, a medicine in the medicine box of remedies to heal our diseased economic relationships and economies. And reparations are a magnificent means of "building the bigger we."

Yet, this, our fourth manifestation of building the intercontinental and cross-continental "bigger we" is also controversial. It is likely to raise eyebrows. And it is vexingly complex. So, we will give it a bit more attention here than we have given the first three.

Reparations is a necessary ingredient of building a moral economy in the United States. Why?

My life story sheds some light. My grandparents came to North Dakota from Norway in the mid-nineteenth century. I love and respect them so much. They were some of the finest people I have known. And, they built their lives on land that was taken from Lakota people who were banished to a reservation, their culture and livelihood decimated by this theft of their land. My grandma and grandpa struggled through drought, fierce winters, lost crops, tornados. They persisted. Their farm enabled my parents to receive college educations. My father then could access a salaried job. When I was a child, my parents may have received a loan to buy the home in which I grew up because redlining steered it to them rather than to a Black family. That home equity compounded, as did the wealth gained from my dad's salaried job, and I entered the world with this inherited economic base. It continues to give me benefits, such as home equity. This history and the advantages it provides mean that "simply existing where I am [and with what I have] is not a neutral act."[11] In short, people alive today are ensnared in what Ta-Nehisi Coates calls "compounding moral debts." Those debts are fierce, stupefying. "America will never be whole" until we reckon with them. Reparations are one pathway for beginning to do so.

Many Christian denominations and other institutions in the US and parts of Europe are grappling with the Doctrine of Discovery (DoD) promoted by the church beginning in the fifteenth century, and its legacy of horror. Many also are wrestling with the legacy of chattel slavery and the role of Christianity in it. Reparations is gaining attention as a valid and necessary, albeit partial, moral response to both legacies—the DoD and slavery.

The late Peter Pero, an African American theologian, shook me to the bones many years ago with his claim about the church in the contemporary world. "*In ecclesiological terms,*" he writes, "*if the church is the one universal body of Christ, this body of Christ is divided among active thieves, passive profiteers, and deprived victims.*"[12] (I would add, and courageous resisters.) If ever there was a call for reparations, it is this!

"How," I have asked, "might the passive profiteers become good neighbors, building right relationships out of the toxic soil of robberhood?" Again, reparations—understood as repair, repairing relationships—is one path.

Let us view a few illustrations.

Leaves whisper and little birds flutter as a small group of inquisitive seminarians traverses the grassy, graceful hillside. "So this is reparations?" queries one of them, brushing windblown hair from her eyes. "How did it happen?" Our leader, a member of the Oakland-based Movement Generation (MG), tells the story. This beautiful land—all forty-three beloved acres of it in the unceded Bay Miwok territory of the San Francisco East Bay Area—is now rematriated into Indigenous care. Movement Generation and the Sogorea Te' Land Trust, supported by a coalition of groups, saved the land from the speculative real estate market. Sogorea Te', an Indigenous women-led nonprofit that facilitates the return of Indigenous land to Indigenous people, now holds the deed.[13] "Returning land to Indigenous care is healing for us and healing for the land," says Corrina Gould, cofounder of Sogorea Te' Land Trust.[14] "I can imagine my congregation coming here to learn," mused one of the hikers, "especially the youth."

Land trust initiatives exist in many places. They enable non-Indigenous people to enact their commitment to justice by paying a voluntary land tax to Indigenous communities. For example, Pacific Lutheran Theological Seminary, where I teach, pays a land tax to Sogorea Te'.

Christian ethicist Sheryl Johnson illustrates the faith-based reparations movement:

> *In Canada, financial reparations from both the churches that operated Indigenous residential schools and the Canadian government, which instituted the system, have [been paid]. . . . Memorial Episcopal Church in Baltimore began paying reparations in 2021 because it was built with*

funds from a plantation where hundreds of people of African descent were enslaved. . . . United Parish in Brooklyn, Massachusetts launched the Negro Spiritual Royalties Project, through which the church pays voluntary royalties whenever spirituals who were written by people who were enslaved are sung in worship. . . . Reparations programs have also been initiated by several denominations and regional church bodies.

Another recent example of church-related reparations includes those paid by several religiously affiliate universities . . . in recognition that these schools actively participated in and financially benefitted from the slave trade.

To be sure, reparations take more forms than economic alone.[15] Yet reparations without an economic component are not reparations. The economic forms are not only monetary. They include people questioning where their money came from, who was wronged in the processes that brought them whatever wealth they may have. A "Faith and Reparations Toolkit," created by the Interfaith Movement for Human Integrity, offers a list of moves for enacting reparations for harms suffered by Black people as a result of slavery. The Toolkit provides also a history of reparations, spiritual resources, crucial background information, a "Reparationist Pledge of Accountability," and art.

Increasingly, the global interfaith community is proposing that one form of climate reparations should be releasing countries of the Global South from their debilitating external debt burdens.[16] This form of reparations fits beautifully with theologian Christopher Carter's sense: "Reparations means movement to heal toward right relationships on structural levels."[17]

Such was the message of Rev. Dr. Gordon Cowans, a Jamaican church leader, in his address to an international audience. Let's listen in on correspondence following that address. His presentation, entitled "Debt, Food, Energy and Climate Crisis," began with these words:

> Jamaica, like most of its Caribbean counterparts, lives in the shadow of its colonial past. As a former slavery colony, it knows what it is like to be an extractive economy. It has for centuries existed and produced for enrichment of others. It knows what it is like to be on the receiving end of the cost of exploitation of human and natural resources from which others benefit.

Cynthia (in an email conversation):

Rev. Cowans, thank you so much for your presentation!

You touched a raw nerve in my heart when you talked about the roots of the poverty that causes so much suffering in Caribbean countries—that it is rooted in centuries of exploitation by North American and European countries and corporations. That struck my heart because my life-long involvement in economic justice work was catalyzed by the exploitation of workers in the Caribbean in order to produce high profits for fruit and sugar corporations based in the US, and low costs for North American consumers.

You emphasized that the exploitation continues in new ways, such as small farms being destroyed to make room for sweatshops.[18] You also named another reason why so many people in Caribbean nations suffer from poverty—the international debt payments that drain money from impoverished countries into the industrialized world.[19] On top of all this, you noted that storms, intensified by climate change which Caribbean people did not cause, are making the poverty and hunger all the worse!

This is overwhelming. It just seems so unfair. My heart wants to scream, "Alright, alright! I hear you, BUT how can I possibly respond? It seems so far from the power of ordinary people like me. I have eaten cheap fruit from the Caribbean. The banks that process my paycheck gain from debt repayments by impoverished nations. My country produces more greenhouse gases per capita than almost any other country on Earth, and Caribbean people are ravaged by climate-related storms. 'Right relationships' that manifest neighbor-love seem impossible."

But then you went on to offer an opening, a path for some modicum of repair. You spoke of reparations. "Time has come for repair through reparatory justice.... Reparations is an opportunity for at least partially righting the wrong." You said that reparations are key to alleviating hunger! I think you mean reparations both for the centuries of extraction that left your people so drenched in poverty, and for the climate disaster caused by industrialized nations.

Your next words really blew my mind. "Churches," you declared, "have the potential for advancing the movement for reparations.... Churches can lead the way in acts of repentance and restitution that have the capacity in turn to influence" national governments.

So, I asked myself, What would reparations look like, and how can I be involved? Then, in re-reading my notes from your talk, I saw two forms that reparations could take.

One was working to cancel the debt of impoverished nations. My church could help by joining with Jubilee USA's advocacy for debt cancellation. The other was allocating resources for climate change adaptation and resilience in impoverished countries. This, you said, would provide "resources by which a grievously harmed people may recuperate." We could join in the campaigns pushing our government to step up to the plate in those ways.[20]

I would like to ask you more about this, Rev. Cowans. Could you possibly illustrate for us how reparations in the form of debt cancellation would reduce poverty and hunger? That is, if the global faith community and other civil society partners succeeded in getting finance institutions and wealthy nations to cancel the debt of highly impoverished nations, how would that translate to reducing poverty and hunger? How would it play out in the lives of particular people?

I realize that responding to this question is asking a lot of you, because your time is overfilled with more pressing things. But if you can squeeze time to do this, my readers and I would be most grateful. If not, then please don't worry about it and know that I am grateful for all that you already have illumined for me and others.

Response from Rev. Cowans:

Dear Cynthia,
   Warmest greetings.
   When a country is forced to prioritize repayment of external debt, precious little money remains to meet the country's pressing needs. Jamaica's debt to GDP ratio was consistently over 100 percent in 2000 to 2020.[21] The heavy burden of this falls to the ordinary citizen, many of whom live in conditions of generational poverty.
   For them, debt cancellation would signal hope of release from a cycle of need. Poverty alleviation programmes such as Jamaica's successful PATH programme could be capitalized to benefit so many more people than scarce funding now allows. PATH is an acronym for Programme of Advancement through Health and Education. Its effect is perhaps best seen in the nineteen-year-old eyes of Melissa, this year's high school graduate whose sojourn at one of the nation's most prestigious high schools has been sustained and bolstered by monthly payments to her single mother from the PATH programme. PATH also has provided her daily school lunch, often her only hot meal each day. Melissa has just heard of her acceptance at the nation's premiere university and will receive tuition support from PATH. We rejoice, and long for this to be the story of so many more young Jamaicans.
   Debt cancellation would free up the funds to make that happen. Melissa's trajectory could become common place if only the stranglehold of debt owed to the wealthy world was released. Such is the case for so many highly indebted nations.

Imagine a congregation or synagogue, a national faith body, or an interfaith network committing to reparations. Imagine their decision to use the Faith and Reparations Toolkit created by the Interfaith Movement for Human Integrity, or the Reparations Now Toolkit provided by M4BL.[22] Imagine them learning from and supporting the National African American Reparations Commission, the Caribbean Reparation Commission, or the Landback movement of Indigenous Americans.[23] These moves would invite painful learning. Yet, they also would be life giving and communion building. Reparations, then is our fourth manifestation of "building the bigger we" across the continents and the continent.

A moral economy in the US cannot be achieved without accounting for the historic reality of "active thieves, passive profiteers, and victims" (Peter Pero's words). The reasons are many. Consider four.

First, the trajectory of economic exploitation that began with the Doctrine of Discovery and chattel slavery did not stop. That exploitation has continued in varied forms. Anti-Black exploitation moved on through Jim Crow, racist hiring and compensation practices, housing policy including red-lining and exclusion from VA housing loans, exclusion of Black people from other New Deal opportunities such as VA college tuition, mass incarceration, and more. Likewise, the Doctrine of Discovery carries on in neocolonial extraction of minerals, forests, agricultural products, labor, and genetic material from Indigenous lands and peoples. And it undergirds some current legal decisions.

Second, a primary contemporary impact of the Doctrine of Discovery and the legacy of chattel slavery is the generationally compounding impoverishment of Indigenous peoples and of descendants of formerly enslaved Africans. The impacts of economic marginalization and violence in one era are felt generations down the road. The poverty of many Black Americans today stems from the anti-Black trajectory in economic policy. In Kelly Brown Douglas's words, "The past remains alive in the present."[24]

Volumes are published on this and here is not the place to elaborate but rather to illustrate. A white man received a home equity loan and college tuition under the New Deal. A Black man did not. A white woman was hired in a job qualifying for social security. A Black woman received no social security for her wages as a domestic worker. Consequently, the white offspring were raised in a family with home equity, which was used for college tuition and access to all that helps with entrance into a university. The Black children were not. The story goes on.

Third, the material gains also compound generationally. As we have seen, white people today are material beneficiaries of racist economic practices. Hearken back to me, my grandparents, and the Indigenous Lakota people displaced by my grandparents' and great aunts' and uncles' wheat farms.

For people of faith, the reason for taking seriously the history of exploitation runs even deeper, beyond these three reasons. We are aware of the sacred calling given to human beings. To receive, recognize, and relish the love of God, and then to live it into the world. Not only in interpersonal relations, but also in relationships that are shaped by systems, like economies. We are aware that life unfolds within a sacred story. In chapter 1 we called it the greatest love story ever told. Embodying neighbor-love, giving it societal form, means weaving right relationships from the savage webs of injustice. Reparations is one loom for that reweaving.

Disarming the Demon

Tremendous value lies not only in *"building* the bigger we,*"* but also in explicitly *recognizing* it—recognizing the community of which we are a part in efforts to build compassionate, just, and Earth-honoring economies. That recognition is gold, for it speaks to a demon that eats away at many of us who take seriously the daunting obstacles to structural change. It is the demon that murmurs, "What I do simply cannot make enough difference, so (and this part whispers under the radar of consciousness) I will just satisfy my hunger to help by doing kind and charitable service, and give up on trying to change the systems."

On the one hand it is true that what I do alone cannot build a moral economy. However, a far more empowering response to that reality is recognizing that while structural injustice transcends individual agency, it does *not* transcend collective agency; collective agency can overcome structural injustice, and collective agency requires individual agency. As "I" becomes "we," individuals' engagement bears rich fruit. For example? Citizens around the globe who took part in the Jubilee Campaign to cancel the debt of highly impoverished countries proved that people working together can influence some of the world's most powerful finance institutions in the name of justice.

Life-Giving Links

The links between "building the bigger we" and other fingers on the healing hands of change are so evident that I need not rehearse them here. Rather, I simply illustrate: In the dance of "building the bigger we," we have seen "live lightly" and "resist the wrong" appear in consumer support for initiatives of Worker-Driven Social Responsibility. We have seen "move the money" present in divestment movements. "Change the rules" came on board in reparations, worker protection laws, and more.

Sacred Journey Journal: Practicing This Healing Medicine

We have explored many dimensions of "building the bigger we" across time, in our own communities, and spanning the world. We have heard stories, seen images, encountered many people and networks. Briefly pass through the pages one more time. Choose one image, story, network, or person that catches your attention. Then sit for a moment with that image, story, person, or network. Allow yourself to imagine how it connects with your life, your people, your path. How might this open a door for you or your group to "build the bigger we" in your own path toward building more humane, just, and life-giving economies?

Then consider one of the following, choosing whichever speaks to you:
- How might this opening that door and exploring what is on the other side bring you joy?
- In what ways would it align your life more fully with your real values?
- In what sense would it be "loving your neighbor as yourself" with a love that seeks justice and liberation?
- How would you feel five years down the road if you practiced this means of healing our economic life and building a moral economy?

Resources for Digging Deeper

See the toolkit for this book on the series' website at: https://buildingamoraleconomy.org/.

CHAPTER FOURTEEN

Fingers on the Hands of Healing: *Practice Awe, Lament, Holy Anger, Gratitude*

> Our goal should be to live life in radical amazement... get up in the morning and look at the world in a way that takes nothing for granted. Everything is phenomenal; everything is incredible; never treat life casually. To be spiritual is to be amazed.
> —Rabbi Abraham Joshua Heschel

> If we learn anything from Joel [in the Jewish and Christian scripture] it is to know that the healing of brokenness and injustice the healing of social sin and degradation the healing of spiritual doubts and fears begins with an unrestrained lament one that starts at our toenails and is a shout by the time it gets to the ends of our strands of hair it's a lament of faith to the God of faith.
> —Emilie M. Townes[1]

> God invites us into a shared fury.... Anger is... the engine of hope.
> —Willie James Jennings[2]

> Gratitude for all the earth has given us lends us courage... to refuse to participate in an economy that destroys the beloved earth to line the pockets of the greedy, to demand an economy that is aligned with life, not stacked against it.
> —Robin Wall Kimmerer[3]

The Essence

Allowing ourselves to experience, share, and be moved by awe at the miracle of life; lament for the unnecessary suffering and all that has been lost; anger at what thwarts fullness of life; and gratitude for all that is good, life-giving, liberative, and healing.

Fuller Description

Awe

"To live life in radical amazement.... Everything is incredible.... To be spiritual is to be amazed." This is no blithe claim. It rises from the heart of one whose mother was murdered by Nazis and whose sisters died in a concentration camp, Rabbi Abraham Joshua Heschel.

We may be fed by awe. I am. Awe at what seems to be ordinary until I choose to remove the veil and see clearly. Awe at the magnificence of a leaf as it glitters in the breeze—the tendrils of light as they shimmer. Amazement that I awoke, alive on this Earth in human form, that my heart has continued for all of these years to beat and my lungs to breathe. Awe that the air molecules flowing into my body may have been "breathed out" by a tree in the Amazon forest, that the cells I shed today may biodegrade into a blackberry bush and be carried in a seed by a traveling bird to a town in Idaho where they enter the local water supply and are drunk by an ultraright neofascist leader, and thus a part of me becomes a part of his body. Amazement at the elegant dance of trillions of microorganisms collaborating to move my muscles and eyes so that I may type these words, and at the power of loving care to heal the wounded heart. Awe at the raw grit and strength of people who persist through harrowing struggle year after daunting year, and tenaciously build life and caring community in the midst of that struggle.

In some classes, I invite students to take an "awe bath." They are to sit with eyes closed outside, if possible in a place that has sounds of wind, or birds, or children, or something else that is lovely to hear. And it should be a place with something of beauty to greet the eyes—perhaps the sky, a leaf, or a stranger's face. Or they could choose to be inside, in a place with pleasant smells and something of beauty to see. While sitting for a moment with eyes closed, they are to ignore their senses. Then, in a flash they are to open eyes, ears, nose, all senses, and pretend that they are awakening here on Earth for the first time as if from another planet, a planet without color or sounds or smells or tastes, a planet on which they had no sense of touch and on which they could not perceive smiles or kindness on faces. They are to open eyes and allow themselves to gasp in wonder at what surrounds them, to drink in the "wild air, world-mothering air."[4] It is truly, in Rabbi Heschel's words "phenomenal," "incredible," "amazing."

Nearly fifteen hundred years past, Gregory the Great said as much: "Full of wonder then are all the things which [humans] never think to wonder at, because... they are by habit become dull to the consideration of them."[5] Like

Rabbi Heschel and Pope Gregory, Alice Walker's character Shug in *The Color Purple* knew something about awe. "I think it pisses God off when you walk by the colour purple in a field and don't notice it," she declares.[6]

To live with awe is to live with reverence. For some, it includes amazement that the great Source is "flowing and pouring through all things," "even the tiniest leaf."[7] But what has this to do with building a moral economy?

Could it be that awe at the miraculous wonder of being and of beauty feeds our love for this world, nourishes our strength to join in rescuing it from the jaws of destruction? Could it be that inattention or dullness to the splendor of life also dullens our courage and passion to fight for it? Awakening to awe quickens moral-spiritual power for the work of justice-seeking, Earth-honoring neighbor-love. And that is a wellspring of energy for economic transformation from economies of predation to economies for life. Yet psychology teaches us that feelings like awe may be stifled if we have stifled pain, grief, and anger.

Lament

It seems to me that we are—on a largely subconscious level—awash in grief. Grief at the massacres on public school campuses and shopping malls, grief that people are without homes and must live on the street, grief at the ominous climate future crashing into our present. Yet, if you are like me, you do not really feel it, at least in full force. I protect myself with a comforting cloak of numbness and denial. Denial and numbness are a birthplace of inaction, of doing nothing, of giving in to the way things are. We are lured into numbness that, at this moment, people are dying from climate change-related disasters that we are intensifying. We deny that maximized profit and cheap prices are covered with blood of innocent people.

Christian ethicist Christopher Carter casts light on this numbness. The colonial thinking undergirding Western culture, he contends, "socialize[s] us in ways that numb us to the everyday oppression of others."[8] Four decades earlier, Hebrew Bible scholar Walter Brueggemann said as much. Oppressive power structures, he argued "lead people to numbness, especially to numbness about death." Death in our world, he says, is "so daily, so pervasive, and so massive, and yet so unnoticed." "We deny it with numbness."[9] Both contend that this numbness blocks our power to challenge and change the death-dealing mechanisms of oppression. I agree.

Brueggemann insists that the prophetic task (which he sees as inherent in the life of faith) "is to cut through the numbness, to penetrate the self-deception." Cutting through the numbness, he maintains, begins with grief, with mourning that names the utter horror and magnitude of the loss, fear, and pain induced by social injustice, and crying out about it with anguished passion. This is the "language of lament," and, Brueggemann asserts, it cuts through the denial, the deadness to passion, the apathy. But most significant here, this embrace of lament unlocks sacred energy to imagine, express, and live toward an emancipated future, a future that has been heretofore unimaginable.

But does it? Cannot grief also block our power to challenge injustice? Cannot grief be as dispiriting as is numbness? What makes grief a source of hope and agency rather than a deadening rock weighing down our spirits?

A powerful sermon on the Hebrew Bible's book of Joel by womanist ethicist Emilie Townes responds. Townes claims *communal* lament is the precursor to social healing. Words from her sermon greeted us at the outset of this chapter. You might re-read them, slowly. Lament was integral to the ancient Hebrews' covenant relationship with God, suggests Townes, drawing on Brueggemann's work. A loss of lament meant "a loss of genuine covenant interaction with God." Communal lament, as Townes explains it, is the assembly crying out in distress to the God in whom it trusts. It is a cry of sorrow by the people gathered, a cry of repentance and a plea for help in the midst of social affliction. Deep and sincere "communal lament . . . names problems, seeks justice, and hopes for God's deliverance." Lament, as seen in the book of Joel, she says, forms people; it requires them to give name and words to suffering. "When Israel used lament as rite and worship on a regular basis, it kept the question of justice visible and legitimate."[10] You might pause for a moment to imagine lament in your faith community. What would it look like for your people to cry out in distress to the God in whom you trust, to grieve aloud together at the affliction and loss that eat away at people and our world?

Ugandan theologian Emmanuel Katongole sought to fathom how people ravished by horrific forms of violence and caught up "within a vortex of suffering" in Eastern Africa had transformed their suffering into hope and agency for nonviolent activism. After extensive listening to Christian activist communities of that area he concluded, "Lament is what sustains and carries forth Christian agency in the midst of suffering. . . . The practice of lament [is] the work of hope." Poring over "poems, songs, and artistic pieces from Eastern Congo and Northern Uganda that express the communities' lament," he found them to be "cultural moorings of hope."[11] Their communal expressions of lament were a form of wrestling with God and were an ongoing practice at the heart of their hope and agency.

As with the ancient Hebrews in the book of Joel, this was lament communally experienced and expressed. These people's agency for political engagement toward justice, he concluded, begins with a communal cry of lament. "Far from passively acquiescing to suffering . . . lament invites us into deeper political engagement."

While reeling from the murder of yet another Black person by the culture of racist police violence in the United States, the power of public lament came home to me. I received an email that had gone out to a large "public," the online readership of SojoMail, the regular emailing from *Sojourners Magazine*. The message was from Sojourners' executive director, Rev. Adam Russell Taylor. He cried out,

> *In painful moments like this, my impulse now is the same as when I first heard the news: I needed to talk to God. A prayer of lament is what I found on my lips and in my heart, and I offer one here in the hope that it might put into words some of the heartbreak, grief, outrage, trauma, and exhaustion you might also be feeling.*
>
> *The prayer begins with "Gracious and loving God, Sometimes our nation and world are so full of injustice, loss, and pain that words fail us and our spirit can find no rest. We don't even know what to say, how to pray, and where to begin to set right the many things that are so overwhelmingly wrong. The vicious murder of Tyre Nichols feels like one of those moments. We cry out to you." And it ends with, "Give us the strength, the resilience, and the hope to stay in this struggle for justice."*[12]

This was a public cry of lament, naming problems, seeking justice, hoping for deliverance. It was communal in a twenty-first-century internet form, and it flowed from trust that the lament would *give us the strength, the resilience, and the hope to stay in this struggle for justice.*

From the ancient Hebrew people to Eastern Africa to US society, evidence mounts that lament articulated collectively in the context of trusted community may render hope, resilience to stay in the struggle, and healing. Communal lament is a key to healing society, including diseased economies. Perhaps rituals that elicit grief and allow us to wail in the streets communally—about the suffering generated by climate change and a predatory economy, about all that our children and grandchildren will not have, about the damage we have done and cannot undo—will help to unlock hope and agency that we did not know we had. Let us hold this hope.

Anger

Numbness pertains not only to grief, but also to anger. What happens when we are numb to righteous anger at the unnecessary and excruciating suffering that rampages relentlessly in the midst of exploitative economic practices?

Hear the words of theologian Willie James Jennings. "Living the discipline of hope in this racial world, in this white supremacist-infested country ... requires anger ... because this God-bound anger, turns us toward the urgency of the moment, as Martin Luther King, Jr. said so eloquently, and the deep desire for a changed world." He speaks of anger also that life in this country is "now under the control of a merciless financial capitalism.... [We] need to change an entire structure built to enhance profit at the cost of a healthy common life."[13]

"So," Jennings asks, "what must be done?" His response points to the power for the good that may be found in anger: "Well, first, take hold of the anger.... Step into it and into God's own righteous indignation... knowing that God will also invite you to turn away from the hatred even as you enter the anger." "God invites us into a shared fury." Anger, Jennings insists, is "the engine of hope."

Anger "motivates the level of political involvement essential to striving for significant social change," concluded political theologian Jeffrey Stout. He distinguishes this from blind rage that can dissolve into scapegoating, unfocussed vitriol, and delusion. *The anger for positive change is concerned with "how broken and distorted relationships might be repaired."*[14]

Anger, however, is dangerous. Jennings and Stout share this warning. Claiming that God and I are angry at the same thing is especially dangerous. It is the fodder of holy wars and has justified killing, cruelty, and even death by torture. Jennings is explicit about this and clarifies that anger must not become hatred. We hear him again, "Take hold of the anger.... Step into it and into God's own righteous indignation.... Knowing that God will also invite you to turn away from the hatred even as you enter the anger."

Anger is dangerous also if it is denied, numbed, ignored, or repressed. As Brueggemann warned, the lack of pathos (*a-pathy*) becomes apathy, inertia in the face of social horrors. An "engine of hope" is lost.

In my experience the denial of anger is also dangerous for the person denying it. I recall vividly the day when I—as a young teenager—decided that I would never be angry again. Anger, I (so mistakenly) thought, was not Christian, not good; we should not be angry. Only after a time of therapy did I realize that anger denied becomes anger turned inward against oneself—in this case, me—in self-destructive behavior or turned outward in violence against others.

In truth, what freed me to be angry and to use anger as a force for the good was not only a good therapist. In 1981, Beverly Harrison, a mother of feminist Christian ethics and a beloved mentor to many, penned an essay that impacted untold lives, including mine. It was "The Power of Anger in the Work of Love." Harrison professed that anger at what is wrong in the world, anger at what thwarts God's gift of life in its fullness for all, is a vital force for social and personal transformation toward the good. I have met people from four continents whose lives were changed by that essay.

Yes, moral outrage—holy anger—is a vital ingredient of moral-spiritual power. Yet it will get us nowhere unless we have also the capacity to act on it. You, dear reader, are building that capacity as you journey through these chapters (and perhaps the subsequent volumes in the series), and as you engage in other means of honing your skills for building a moral economy.

Gratitude

The scientist and enrolled member of the Citizen Potawatomi Nation Robin Wall Kimmerer links gratitude to moral courage for transforming economic life. "Gratitude for all the earth has given us lends us courage to turn and face the Windigo that stalks us, to refuse to participate in an economy that destroys the beloved earth to line the pockets of the greedy, to demand an economy that is aligned with life, not stacked against it. It's easier to write that, harder to do."[15]

Kimmerer's *Braiding Sweetgrass* presents the mythical figure of the Windigo as "that within us which cares more for its own survival than for anything else," the part of ourselves that a capitalist society, she says, encourages to consume more and more without considering the consequences.[16] "The Windigo is the legendary monster of our Anishinaabe people," writes Kimmerer.

> *The Windigo is a human being who has become a cannibal monster.... The hideous stench of its carrion breath poisons the clean scent of snow as it pants behind us. Yellow fangs hang from its mouth that is raw where it has chewed off its lips from hunger.... The more a Windigo eats, the more ravenous it becomes.... Consumed by consumption, it lays waste to humankind ... in an eventual frenzy of uncontrolled consumption.*

While it originally was connected to the starvation conditions of a long winter, many contemporary Indigenous people also see Windigo thinking in today's market economy that commodifies the land and encourages constant consumption. Kimmerer states that the

> *Windigo mindset is even considered admirable in the modern world: "Indulgent self-interest that our people once held to be monstrous is now celebrated as success." "On a grander scale, too, we seem to be living in an era of Windigo economics of fabricated demand and compulsive overconsumption.... Multinational corporations have spawned a new breed of Windigo that insatiably devours Earth's resources 'not for need but for greed.'" "The footprints of the Windigo. They're everywhere you look. They stomp in the industrial sludge of Onondaga Lake. And over a savagely clear-cut slope in the Oregon Coast Range where Earth is slumping into the river. You can see them where the coal mines rip off mountaintops in West Virginia and in oil-slick footprints on the beaches of the Gulf of Mexico. A square mile of industrial soybeans. A diamond mine in Rwanda. A closet stuffed with clothes. Windigo footprints all, they are the tracks of insatiable consumption. So many have been bitten.*

> *You can see them walking the malls, eying your farm for a housing development, running for Congress." "What Native peoples once sought to rein in, we are now asked to unleash in a systematic policy of sanctioned greed."*
>
> *"Traditional upbringing was designed to strengthen self-discipline, to build resistance against the insidious germ of taking too much. The old teachings recognized that Windigo nature is in each of us, so the monster was created in stories, that we might learn why we should recoil from the greedy part of ourselves.... Do not feed it.... It is the Windigo way that tricks us into believing that belongings will fill our hunger, when it is belonging that we crave."*
>
> *"The fear for me... is far greater than just acknowledging the Windigo within. The fear for me is that the world has been turned inside out.... Indulgent self-interest that our people once held to be monstrous is now celebrated as success. We are asked to admire what our people once viewed as unforgiveable. The consumption-driven mind-set masquerades as 'quality of life' but eats us from within.... We have unleashed a monster."*

My main purpose in recounting Kimmerer's wisdom is to share her two antidotes to the Windigo mentality. "Defeating Windigo" is the title of her book's final chapter. There she lands on gratitude.

> *Gratitude is a powerful antidote to Windigo psychosis. A deep awareness of the gifts of the earth and of each other is medicine.... Each of us comes from people who were once indigenous. We can reclaim our membership in the cultures of gratitude that formed our old relationship with the living earth.... The practice of gratitude lets us hear the badgering of marketers as the stomach grumblings of a Windigo. It celebrates cultures of regenerative reciprocity, where wealth is understood to be having enough to share and riches are counted in mutual beneficial relationships. Besides, it makes us happy.... Gratitude for all the earth has given us lends us courage to turn and face the Windigo that stalks us, to refuse to participate in an economy that destroys the beloved earth to line the pockets of the greedy, to demand an economy that is aligned with life, not stacked against it. It's easier to write that, harder to do.*[17]

The other antidote, Kimmerer explains, also is "imperative." It pertains to "creating an alternative to destructive economic structures." It is to build "the economy of the commons, wherein resources fundamental to our well-being, like water and land and forests, are commonly held rather than commodified. Properly managed, the commons approach maintains abundance, not scarcity. These contemporary economic alternatives strongly echo an Indigenous world view in which Earth exists not as private property, but as a commons to be tended with respect and reciprocity for the benefit of all."[18]

Awe, Lament, Anger, and Gratitude—Held Together

Might it be that anger and lament at the devastation wrought by economic and ecological violence, awe at the beauty of what we hope to save, and gratitude, together, call forth yet another form of gratitude? It is gratitude for being alive at this pivotal point in human history when our decisions and actions matter so tremendously. While giving a public address in Norway, I painted the devastating picture of climate colonialism and the need for economic transformation in response to it. I ended by saying, "It is a good time to be alive." One listener approached me later in the day exclaiming how meaningful it had been to hear that last sentence! He noted how many people talk about what a terrible time this is to be alive, that some are even committing suicide at the thought of life under the climate catastrophe. "It is a very different story," he said, "to think of this as a *good* time to be alive." Gratitude for having been given life at this fateful point in history may well be another source of moral-spiritual power to engage the great work before us.

Long-standing religious and spiritual traditions are especially well poised to enable awe, communal lament, holy anger, and gratitude. As Kimmerer reveals, for example, some Indigenous spiritualities directly counsel gratitude as a counter to voracious collective overconsumption. Buddhism and other Dharma traditions beckon people to lives of gratitude and awe. Jewish traditions and Christian traditions building on them, are blessed with the Psalms that contain some of humankind's most poignant and soul-searing laments.

These psalms of lament are meant to be recited, sung, wailed communally. It may be that the depth of pain and grief to be unearthed by honest lament for all that we have destroyed can be sustained only in community, and only where hope also is offered. Here too religion is well poised. It offers communal rituals of lament linked with hope and gratitude. The Christian Eucharist is known as "the Great Thanksgiving," a service of gratitude. We touch further on these and other roles of religion in chapters 18 and 19.

Life-Giving Links

The past year has taught me that truth telling about "what is" calls for the courage to acknowledge that it is *both* too late and not too late. That is, we must face the magnitude of the catastrophe that at this point cannot be averted because "we are already too far down the road of destruction to be able to 'solve' climate change."[19] *At the same time, and this is crucial: it is* NOT *too late to make a monumental difference* in the degree of disaster. We can stave off vast amounts of suffering that will ensue if we allow climate change to go on relatively unmitigated. "A regenerative future is utterly possible."[20]

However—and here I speak from my heart and my commitment to tell the truth—since I drafted that paragraph at least a year ago, the reality of climate change is worsening. By the time you read this book, it may be that "a regenerative future" for the human species and countless other species is not "utterly possible." As Timothy Beal reminds us, more scientists are pointing to the very real possibility that—through climate change—we will extinguish human life that is recognizably human. It may be that my grandchildren will live on an Earth truly hostile to human survival. It may really be too late. What then of hope and action?

Now this is terribly important point for me, perhaps the most important point of this book: we could choose to give up, or we could choose to place our life in the ageless hope and calling—to live toward a world in which all people have the necessities for life with joy and justice, and Earth's astounding web of life may flourish. The choice is upon us. According to the Deuteronomic historians of ancient Israel, Moses declares, "I call heaven and earth to witness against you today that I have set before you life and death, blessings and curses. Choose life so that you and your descendants may live" (Deut 30:19).

To choose life where it seems that it is too late, requires lament, communal wrenching anguished lament. It calls for the anger to spur action. And it calls for gratitude and awe at all that is good and beautiful and redemptive.

However, if awe, lament, anger, and gratitude are to become medicine for healing our diseased economies, then they must be met with skills, tools, wisdom, and other resources developed in the other fingers on the hands of liberative change discussed in these chapters and in the book series which this book begins. Finally, this movement for economies of life calls for spiritual nurture. This we consider in the last finger on the hands of liberative change, "Drink the Spirit's Courage."

Sacred Journey Journal:
Practicing This Healing Medicine

First, I invite you take an "awe bath," as described above. Allow the sensual beauty that you behold to feed your soul. Relish it. Allow gratitude to fill you.

Now (or later when you may give at least twenty minutes for a journey of imagination):
- Please find a quiet place. Breathe deeply and slowly. Close your eyes. Allow the boundaries around your imagination to dissolve. See your imagination freely flowing. Imagine that you are held in the arms of an infinitely compassionate presence. Then, if you will, allow your grief to show its face—your grief about the suffering around you or about all that is endangered by climate

catastrophe, perhaps in your community or perhaps across the seas. Sit with that grief, even if only a tiny slice of it emerges. Know that the arms of compassionate Presence will not let you go.
- Then imagine a worshipping community or some other group in your life, practicing communal lament. Imagine that none are hindered by self-consciousness. What does it look like? What does it sound like? How do you feel? What does it feel like in your body? Whom do you touch?
- When you return from this imaginative space, allow yourself to sit quietly, to breathe deeply. Again, know that the arms of compassionate Presence continue to cradle you.

Resources for Digging Deeper

See the toolkit for this book on the series' website at: https://buildingamoraleconomy.org/.

CHAPTER FIFTEEN

Fingers on the Hands of Healing:
Listen and Amplify

The lands of the planet call to humankind ... for relief from the constant burden of exploitation.... Who will listen to the trees, the animals and the birds, the voices of the places of the land?

—Vine Deloria[1]

What is to be done about the extractive economy ... ? [In] extractive South American regions, there is already so much being done that what we require is a practice of listening and then amplifying.

—Macarena Gomez-Barris[2]

The Essence

Listening to the realities and wisdom of people and communities who are on the underside of the current economy or are highly impacted by climate change. Listening to people and communities who already are building the new economy. Listening to other-than-human parts of creation. Learning from these voices how to heal our diseased economic life. Then amplifying these voices so that others too may hear and learn from them. *This finger on the hands of change is especially relevant for people who are not on the underside of the current economy and are not part of communities most impacted by climate change.*

Vignette

"A radical act of resistance," she declared. "Listening across lines of difference and listening to people who suffer from unjust systems is a radical act of resistance. The powers-that-be would be thrilled if we did not get to know one another." Mary Lim was coteaching with me a course in community organizing for seminary students. She began the course teaching students to listen. That kind of listening is a threat to the powers that be; it reveals what needs to remain hidden.

I trusted this woman and her wisdom. I had seen the power for justice-oriented change that emerged from her practice of deep listening. I wanted her claims about listening to sink in with the students. "Mary," I said, "give us an example. When have you experienced listening as truly a radical act of resistance? Or when has listening really opened doors for power to challenge unjust economies?" Mary paused, tipping her head. Then, with a smile, she recounted the story of religious leaders listening to low-income youth of color in Oakland, listening to their struggles and needs. They learned that many kids did not show up to school because they lacked the money to buy a bus ticket to get there! Talk about economic injustice with consequences, I thought! As a result of that listening, Mary explained, those leaders, including youth leaders, organized in the community to initiate and ultimately pass Free Youth Bus Pass legislation for seven school districts benefitting some ten thousand youth. The program is spreading. It all began with listening.

Fuller Description

What do we mean by "the underside of the current economy"? The underside is people and communities whom the economy casts into poverty or leaves hovering on the brink of it, or harms by such things as dangerous working conditions or a toxic environment. This includes what many call the "sacrifice zones" discussed in previous chapters.[3] Examples of sacrifice zones are endless—people living in the wreckage of past extractive mining or in the violence caused by it; people whose water source has been privatized or whose rivers or soil have been toxified; people living in nuclear waste storage areas; people living beside oil-processing plants where particulate matter makes air dangerous; sweatshop workers; contingent hourly workers who receive no benefits; and so many more.

Perhaps the most remarkable claim of liberation theologies, which arose initially among oppressed peasant peoples of Latin America, is the "epistemological privilege" of people on the underside, or the margins, of power and privilege. Epistemology is a powerful word. It refers to how we come to know things.

Epistemological privilege of people on the underside means that they have particular insight into "what is going on" and what can be done to remedy it. This counters the common assumption that experts and educated people in positions of formal authority have the best analysis and solutions. In liberation theology, however, the epistemological privilege of people on the underside also means even more! People on the underside may have keener vision than others of where the liberating power of the Holy Spirit is at work in situations of oppression and exploitation. Liberation theologies hold that Jesus honored the epistemological privilege of people on the margins or the underside of power and privilege. The message is clarion: "Listen and listen keenly to these voices."

Listen for what? If you are not suffering from economic poverty or vulnerability, then listen first to learn something of the reality of life for people who are. Lawrence Foy of the Interfaith Movement for Human Integrity writes, "There are still two Americas: one America that affords opportunity and access to goods and services . . . and the other America which is fraught with poverty and disenfranchisement." People in the former frequently know nothing about daily life for the latter. What is it like for a mother to get her young children to school when she has no car, is forced to work two part-time jobs with one shift beginning at dawn, cannot miss work for fear of losing her job, has no money for childcare, and is ill from lack of health benefits? How do you get showered and clothed for a job interview if you live on the streets because your wages are too low to afford rent?

Listen also for solutions, for paths forward. Community groups of economically impoverished people may hold the key to what they need to overcome poverty. Recall the Beloved Community Incubator in Washington D.C. Their network of cooperatives has changed people's lives. *"In 2016 the congregation launched a listening campaign. The goal was to listen to neighbors, with a focus on the most marginalized, in order to build community and learn what they might undertake together. At listening sessions with immigrant neighbors, they heard stories about the totality of their lives—dreams for their families, their workplaces, and their community. The listeners learned of the low wages, wage theft, and desire for work that did not abuse them."*[4] This listening campaign planted the seeds of cooperative strength. The fruits have been safe housing, good employment, food security, and deep community.

Listen for what? Listen for worldviews that existed before the onslaught of colonialism and that were negated or subjugated by it, but that have survived in the lives and consciousness of Indigenous people and peoples around the world.[5] Those worldviews contain wisdoms that humankind may need in order to escape from the extractive worldviews undergirding Western civilization, worldviews that have justified exploitation, extraction, and domination as though they were necessary, natural, or even God's will. Encounter and learn from worldviews and epistemologies that "invert" or "refuse" the extractive view.[6] For instance, the dominant worldview sees land as a commodity. Perceiving land as living kin—as do some Indigenous peoples—inverts that worldview. Indigenous theologian Tink Tinker says this beautifully: "Our White relatives must begin to learn from indigenous peoples worldwide the importance of respecting all their own relatives in the created world, including trees and rivers, animals and flying things. It is this worldview of the interrelatedness of all on the earth, including the earth itself, that gives us a chance to imagine genuine justice and an authentic peace in the world around us."[7]

This is not to imply that Indigenous wisdoms are alike; that would be false. They are as highly varied as are Indigenous peoples. Nor is it to imply that Indigenous people are always wise. No, they too are fallible and finite as are all people. But it is to suggest that vital—by which I mean both necessary and life-giving—knowledge for building mutually beneficial relationships between humans and the rest of the Earth community may reside in the wisdom of many Indigenous peoples.

Listen for what? Listen for surprising alternatives to economic life as we know it. To illustrate, creative Indigenous groups are developing alternative economies that do not center on private ownership of land, but rather on communal ownership. Macarena Gomez-Barris, in her recent book *The Extractive Zone,* notes that in the process of living with and learning from Indigenous communities of South America, her "perspective on how to challenge extractive capitalism has shifted." She argues that learning from Indigenous ways of knowing might help non-Indigenous people to "move beyond coloniality and extinction."[8]

Some Indigenous communities are offering their knowledge to the world. *Escucha Winka!,* written collaboratively in 2006 by a group of Mapuche scholar-activists, illustrates. This set of four essays is directed to non-Indigenous people (*winka* means "foreigner," "invader," or "colonizer").[9] It is an appeal to "listen up" (*escucha*).[10] It offers a way for settler peoples "to think differently about our relations to social and ecological worlds."[11] (Thinking differently is part of the terrain explored in the next chapter.) Across the Pacific, in an initiative begun by the Pacific Theological College, Indigenous people of the Pacific islands are carefully identifying and documenting Indigenous climate science in order to use it for themselves and to offer it to the global community seeking to respond to the climate crisis.

Listen for what? Listen for what is possible. Many of us seem to assume that low wages and living on the borders of poverty are *inevitable* for some people in our society. That is just "the way things are." Not so at all, however, cry countless people who know the horrors of poverty through their own experience or their solidarity with people suffering it. Martin Luther King Jr. in his *Where Do We Go from Here?* exemplifies:

> There is nothing but a lack of social vision to prevent us from paying an adequate wage to every American citizen whether he be a hospital worker, laundry worker, maid or day laborer. There is nothing except shortsightedness to prevent us from guaranteeing an annual minimum—and livable—income to every American family. There is nothing, except a

tragic death wish, to prevent us from reordering our priorities![12] *He goes on: True compassion is more than flinging a coin to a beggar; it understands that an edifice which produces beggars needs restructuring.*[13]

King's sense of the possible is reflected in today's movements to build a moral economy.

A question looms. Is listening to and learning from subjugated peoples just another manifestation of "extraction"—extracting vital knowledge? What modes of listening and relationship can prevent that dynamic? The question is vital. I have no definitive response. However, listening has provided me with a few clues.

One is that listening to peoples who have been marginalized in the extractive global economy must be done with respect. By this I mean both the respect that is due to every human being, and the respect that is due to people who must struggle to survive—respect for the courage and fortitude to maintain that struggle. Second, such listening will be accompanied by a commitment to amplify these voices, doing so in ways that are suggested or approved by them. Many people and peoples on the underside of neoliberal capitalism and climate change have been "muffled."[14] Amplifying is unmuffling. A third clue is that listening to and learning from people who have been brutalized by the colonial systems that have enabled my life—if the listening is not to perpetuate colonization—should be not only for my own growth. It should be also in order to

- hear their historical and contemporary life realities;
- acknowledge the depth of their suffering and of the injustice wrought upon them;
- perceive the "untruths that have been systematically constructed about" Indigenous and other subjugated peoples;[15] and
- gain and practice insight for dismantling those untruths and the on-going systems of injustice.

Pause for a moment to consider more closely this call to "hear the historical and contemporary life realities" of people whose lives have been on the underside of colonization. Whew! I have learned through painful experience that this can be done with integrity only if I realize that the pain, trauma, and horror caused by colonization and its attendant white supremacy are greater than one not suffering from them can fathom. So too are the pain, trauma, and horror of climate displacement and of extreme poverty. This I have learned through the pedagogy of friendship—in this case, friendships with Indigenous and Afro-descended people who had the courage and generosity to allow the depth of their anguish to be glimpsed. Pain carried intergenerationally is real. The terror of one's child being hunted and shot for walking in a white neighborhood while Black or driving while Brown is beyond what I can imagine. The ongoing microaggressions of well-intended white people are searing. Being forced from one's land by climate change may be exile from one's very life in ways that are incomprehensible to me, for whom one land is not my life. Such listening is not for the purpose of feeling shame or blame. Those feelings can immobilize, paralyze.[16] No, this kind of listening is for the purpose of building authentic relationship and for participating in truly liberative and healing response.

Where do people who are not on the underside economically begin such a listening shift? Perhaps with a sense of gratitude that it is possible to seek out and listen to people whose lives and realities are not my own. From there, you, dear reader and your reading companions, may call on your creative insights. The response depends on context. What I know is that the most meaningful listening for me has been where I am walking or working alongside people. I know also that liberative listening is both local and global. It means listening to people in our very specific localities, and people in the broader world. For the latter, why not regularly search the websites of the Indigenous Environmental Network, the NDN Collective, and the Climate Justice Alliance? The first conveys Indigenous voices from around the world who are addressing the nexus of economy and ecology, while the second expresses Indigenous voices here on Turtle Island, and the last centers on a wide variety of frontline communities in the climate crisis.

Listening in these intentional ways to people who are suffering at the hands of the current economy is a spiritual practice because it opens doors to healed relationships. It is a step along the way toward economic lives in which people are "good medicine" to one another. In this sense liberative listening is a blessing.

Listening for the sake of healing our economic life means not only listening to other humans, but also to the wisdom of our other-than-human kin in the weave of creation. We noted in "changing the story" the invitation from Indigenous communities to heed other animals and the plants as "elders" and as "teachers."

> *Plants were here first and have had a long time to figure things out. They live both above and below ground and hold the earth in place.... Plants know how to make food and medicine from light and water.... Not only do they feed themselves, but they make enough to sustain the lives of all the rest of us. Plants are providers for the rest of the community and exemplify the virtue of generosity, always offering food. What if Western scientists saw plants as their teachers rather than their subjects?[17]*

Perhaps if Western people (and not only Western scientists) practice listening to the plants we will learn sweet wisdom about how to cultivate economies "in which people and land are good medicine for each other."[18] Fr. Thomas Berry, one of the first people to declare that the Earth crisis is also a spiritual crisis, and one of the twentieth century's most influential thinkers about the relationship of humankind to the cosmos, said as much: "Humans," he writes, "are talking only to ourselves. We are not talking to the rivers, we are not listening to the wind and stars. We have broken the great conversation.... The disasters that are happening now are a consequence of that." He insisted, "The universe is a communion of subjects, not a collection of objects."[19] Berry prescribed relearning to listen to our other than human kin. What a world-healing, economy-healing medicine.

Life-Giving Links

Listening to people who are damaged by the way things are is "radical act of resistance." Yes, listening and amplifying is a way to "resist the wrong." And such listening is crucial in discerning what policy initiatives are needed ("change the rules"), where community-based finance could bear good fruit ("move the money"). It inherently "builds the bigger we" and is crucial to "changing the story."

Sacred Journey Journal: Practicing This Healing Medicine

Recall a time in your life when you have listened to other-than-human parts of Earth community, or to a person suffering from economic violence in ways that you have not experienced. Perhaps during the COVID crisis, while isolated from humans, you became much closer to a plant in your house or to a scraggly weed emerging from the cracks in the sidewalk. Perhaps you began to "see" the lifeforce pulsating through an old tree in a vacant lot. Or perhaps as a youth, in some volunteer work, you actually heard the life-story of a person who was hungry and without a home. Recall your feelings, your heart. What did you hear that you may have run from taking in? Or what might you hear if you were to listen more closely?

Now, imagine one way that you could take on listening to and amplifying the voice of someone or some group on the margins of power and privilege. Take this on as a spiritual practice in your life. (Reviewing this chapter or chapters 8–14 might give you ideas.) Practice doing this for a few weeks, and observe what happens with you. Pay close attention to your feelings, your body. No judgement is called for here. Just see what may emerge from this practice.

Resources for Digging Deeper

See the toolkit for this book on the series' website at: https://buildingamoraleconomy.org/.

CHAPTER SIXTEEN

Fingers on the Hands of Healing:
Change the Story

To get our future right, we must get our economics right. To get our economics right, we must get our story right.

—David Korten

Nations and People are largely the stories they feed themselves. If they tell themselves stories that are lies, they will suffer the future consequences of those lies. If they tell themselves stories that face their own truths, they will free their histories for future flowerings.

—Ben Okri[1]

If you want a different ethic, tell a different story.

—Christina Roberts[2]

Just as our bodies are made of blood and flesh, our identities are made of narratives. . . . Just as we tell ourselves stories about the world we live in, stories also tell us how to live.

—Center for Story-Based Strategy[3]

The Essence

Recognizing and assessing the overarching narratives that shape economic life in U.S. society; rejecting those that are damaging the Earth community; and reclaiming more life-giving narratives.

Vignette

She traveled from village to village in the mountains of Guatemala. The villagers were Indigenous people who had been subject for centuries to the colonizers' story of their inferiority. Upon entering a village, she could tell, without exchanging a word, whether it had been visited regularly by *promotoras de la palabra* (young people who traveled into the countryside and distant villages to lead "base Christian communities"). These young people taught villagers to read by reading the Bible. In these villages people walked differently, she said. They walked with dignity and self-respect.

What, she mused, was going on? Why did they walk with self-respect and dignity? It was, she finally realized, because, in reading the Bible for the first time, the people had learned and internalized the story of God's "preferential option for the poor," Jesus's solidarity with oppressed people, and their infinite dignity and worth. They had learned a different story of who they were.

Fuller Description

Story. The power of story. We humans are a story-weaving animal. We are unique among Earth's creatures in our capacity to collectively write epic narratives of our origins, nature, purpose, destiny, and place in the cosmos, and then to spread among huge numbers of people the assumption that this story is a worthy guide for life. This capacity, argues Yuval Harari, may be *Homo sapiens*'s evolutionary strength. Harari's account of the power of shared narratives is striking.[4] Guiding narratives "become the lens through which we see our world. They help us define the values and institutions that moor our relationships with one another and the earth."[5] They explain who we are and what our purpose is, how we ought to live our lives and order our life together.

While exploring narrative imagination in chapter 3, we considered the need to recognize and assess the societal narratives that shape our lives, as individuals and as societies. Assessing narratives that lead us into damaging relationships with one another and with Earth is essential to gaining freedom from their control and constructing more life-giving narratives.

Then, in chapter 5, we noted that major social change entails change in three arenas of human life: behaviors or practices, social structures, and mindset. And we noted the growing sense in many fields that the third of these—the mindset or assumptions that shape our lives—function as narratives, and that human beings construct narratives and then order life so as to be players in them. They provide meaning and guidance, instructing us unconsciously in what to value, who is worthy, who is not, what constitutes a good life, what is normal, what to own, how to spend our time, and more. We heard the Canadian biologist David Suzuki explaining that the human "brain creates a narrative. . . . The brain selects and discards information to be used in the narrative, constructing

Change the Story

connections and relationships that create a web of meaning.... When the mind selects and orders incoming information into meaning, it is telling itself a story."[6]

Here we take those ideas about the role of story in human life to the next steps, by (1) exploring further the power of narrative, (2) tracing the development of the narrative shaping economic life, (3) noting key storylines in that narrative and the consequences of continuing with them, and finally, (4) daring to "change the story."

To be honest, I tried to delete a great deal from the second and third of these steps in writing this chapter. They are discouraging. But I could not. That is because understanding "what is going on" (recall chapter 4) is crucial for changing it. *We must understand the dangerous story shaping our lives and how it came to have a hold on us, if we are to adopt life-supporting alternatives.*

If moving through these steps becomes discouraging for you, then you might move temporarily into the chapter's nearly final section ("Life-Giving Links: How Are We to Change the Story?"). That might lighten this foray into the role of false narratives in economic life.

The Power of Narrative to Shape Life

Guiding stories—myths—operate on individual and societal levels. The two are often related; my individual consciousness is shaped in large part by the consciousness around me. I think of the narrative in my own life that convinced me I was worthy only if I achieved exceptionally and was better than other people. That narrative/myth was shaped by the culture around me, and it influenced my decisions, actions, and relationships, even though I was unaware of it. It commanded behavior that, in the long run, did not lead to the life I wanted. I had to rewrite that story, adopt different assumptions, and then embody them to become free from that false narrative regarding my worth.

Consider the seductive and destructive narrative that convinces young girls that they must look sexy, and convinces women that their worth depends on a certain version of beauty. A friend and colleague, Sonora Jha, presents a chilling account of the beauty industry's strategic marketing to shape what women desire and how women understand their self-worth. She described the cosmetic and plastic surgery industries convincing countless women in India that they must try to lighten their skin or alter their face's shape in order to look more Western.

These illustrations reveal again links between guiding stories on the individual level and on the collective or cultural level. Society's story of what a woman should be shapes individual girls' and women's stories of what they should be. Being socialized in a society that measures worth by individual achievement impacted my story of my own worth.

Michael Pollan, working with studies in neuro- and cognitive sciences, emphasizes the power of such narratives to run our individual lives. The human brain, he says, develops a story, organizes its perceptions to confirm that story, and then demands that we live according to its "truth."[7]

One of my mentors in faith is the second-century theologian Irenaeus of Lyons. Irenaeus knew how difficult it was to follow the way of Jesus rather than the way of empire when the cost of doing so might be death by torture at the hands of Rome. He was the leader of a community that scholars think was martyred by imperial Rome because the people refused to swear allegiance to Rome; their allegiance was to the God of Jesus. Irenaeus's teacher, Polycarp, had been burned to death by Rome for refusing allegiance to it. When early Christians were debating what books would go into the Christian Bible, many argued that it should not contain the Hebrew Scriptures (what Christians now call the First or Old Testament). Irenaeus, in contrast, was vehement that the Christian Scriptures must include the Hebrew Bible. Why? Because, Irenaeus insisted, followers of Jesus *would gain identity and courage by locating themselves in the epic story* that began with creation, carried on with the Hebrew prophets and the life of Jesus, and culminated in communion with God. By seeing themselves primarily as players in *that* story *rather than* in the dominant narrative of imperial Rome, people would be able to withstand the pressure to live in allegiance to the emperor and instead give their allegiance to the God of life. Being players in one story led to a very different set of values, choices, and lifeways than being players in the other.

Lisa Laskow Lahey and Robert Kegan in their groundbreaking book, *Immunity to Change*, probe why human beings tend to resist change even if we know that failure to change could kill us.[8] What, they asked, is at the root of this immense gap between knowledge that change is necessary and acting on that knowledge? In their quest they uncovered a dynamic they call "immunity to change." It "actively prevents us from changing because of its devotion to preserving our existing way of making meaning."[9] Immunity to change, they found, is rooted in a set of "big assumptions" that are core to our identity and our sense of what gives our lives meaning and worth. They call them "big assumptions" because people do not perceive them as assumptions. Rather, we simply hold them as true.[10] These assumptions form a "mindset," a meaning-making story of the way we need to be in the world, and they bind us to live within that story.[11] We act in obedience to these assumptions, they argue, because doing so protects us from the anxiety that would plague us should we transgress our identity or our internal convictions about what makes us worthy.

I find their research fascinating and invaluable. I believe that it may describe not only individuals' and organizations' "immunity to change," but also the reticence of societal or collective mindsets to change. This includes mindsets about what is normal or good in economic life, mindsets about fossil fuel use, and so much more.

Most captivating to me is their insistence that we can overcome the immunity to change. We do so, they teach, by recognizing the unacknowledged big assumptions (and accompanying commitments) that guide us to resist change, recognizing the cost of continuing to live by them, and then choosing to act according to other assumptions and commitments that better reflect our true values. The awareness alone, they aver, is not sufficient; *we need to practice or act out the different mindset in order for it to actually to reshape how we live.*[12] Their findings support the import of "changing the story" and then living according to the new story as one key strategy for building the new economy.

The Center for Story-Based Strategy says as much:

> *Power creates narratives that validate its legitimacy. . . . These stories can become invisible as they are passed from generation to generation—carrying assumptions that become "conventional wisdom." Many of our current social and ecological problems have their roots in the silent consensus of assumptions that shape the dominant culture: Humans can dominate and outsmart nature. Women are worth less than men. Racism and war are part of human nature. U.S. foreign policy benevolently spreads democracy and liberation around the world. . . . To make real and lasting social change . . . these stories must change.*[13]

For our purposes here, we are considering the stories and mindsets that govern economic life. Countless voices now argue that the constellation of narratives (or taken-for-granted "truths") undergirding economic life as we know it—explaining *who we are, how the world operates, what is right and good, and the purpose and nature of economic life*—has gotten us into the mess of climate catastrophe and grotesque wealth inequities. These narratives lock us into economic systems that shape diseased relationships with other people and Earth.

The Development of the Narrative Shaping Economic Life

How did we get the narrative shaping contemporary economic life? Embark with me on a swift trip through history. (No, I must correct my Euro-centric self. This is not a whirlwind tour through "history," but rather through the history of one part of humankind—the part shaped by Western worldviews.) Recall our purpose in this tour—to understand the worldviews or guiding narratives that shape our economic life and to understand how they resist change, so that we may assess and transform them. In short, we heed Vaclav Havel's prescient warning:

> *Today the most important thing, in my view, is to study the reasons why humankind does nothing to avert the threats about which it knows so*

much, and why it allows itself to be carried onward by some kind of perpetual motion. . . . It cannot suffice to invent new machines, new regulations, new institutions. It is necessary to change and improve our understanding of the true purpose of what we are and what we do in the world. Only such a new understanding will allow us to develop new models of behavior.[14]

Prevailing interpretations of the biblical creation stories, in partnership with Neoplatonic thought, elevated the human creature over other life-forms, and rendered the human not a *creature* at all. Moreover, some humans were above others (e.g. men above women), and the world of reason and spirit was above the material world. This understanding became known as the "great chain of being."

Already here were sown the two great fallacies that have shaped Earth-human relations and human relations: human exceptionalism, and a hierarchy that elevated some people over others. Said differently, the groundwork was laid for the story that elevated Western Europeans over all others, wealthy people over impoverished people, and men over women. Hand-in-hand with this hierarchical understanding of human groups was the story that human beings are set *apart from* rather than *a part of* Earth's larger economy of life. *Thus, our human economies need not be restricted by the limits of Earth (Earth's economy), for we are above it, not part of it.*

The impact of both fallacies has been deadly. "As long as we erroneously see ourselves as outside and above the rest of the living world, we will continue to contribute to its destruction."[15]

The two fallacies were linked in a single economic story. Human exceptionalism included the human right to dominion over "nature," and white European wealthy men's higher place in the human order gave them the right to dominion over all others. Early capitalism was launched with the twin engines of extraction from lands and exploitation of the people who lived in them. According to the story, those lands and peoples had no value other than to serve the colonizers' needs and wants.

Colonization of the Americas enacted and reinscribed this story, and demonstrated its savage consequences, including genocide and chattel slavery. Thus, colonization in its historical and contemporary forms reveals the power of an undergirding story to render brutal realities as normal, natural, inevitable, or God's will.[16]

Modernity and the Enlightenment filled in the details. Francis Bacon, reinforcing the dominant understanding of Genesis's first creation story, averred that God ordained humans to have dominion over "nature."[17] With Descartes, the human capacity to think makes humans superior to all other life and elevates our cognitive capacities over our bodies and emotions. This set the table for "science"—including economic thought—to reign over other forms of knowing.[18]

Change the Story

Isaac Newton convinced the Western world that the universe is a predictable, knowable, manageable machine. We can understand it by knowing its parts. Discouraged was any notion that the whole might be an organism, more fully known by recognizing the synergy among parts.

Meanwhile, classical economic liberalism narrowly defined human freedom as freedom for individual choice and individual rights, especially the right to do as one pleases with one's property (which at that time included one's wife).[19] This was a crucial chapter in the story. It linked freedom to "free" markets.[20]

The groundwork was set for contemporary neoliberalism, in which individual "freedom" to do as one wanted with investments and capital, regardless of the cost to other people, vulnerable nations, and Earth, became enshrined and unassailable. (Ah, but we get ahead of ourselves. Step back again in time.)

Classical economic theory, modified by neoclassical economic theory, played a key role in this world-shaping narrative. It posited the human being as primarily *homo economicus* (economic man), driven primarily by self-interest measured in economic gain. In line with this understanding of human being, some versions of evolutionary theory, driven by a shallow understanding of Darwin's survival of the fittest theories, painted the human as primarily competitive.

Reordering of the global economy following World War II presupposed growth to be unlimited and morally good. Postwar economic thought also defined this "economic man" as "the consumer,"[21] and saw wealth maximizing as a virtue. This line in our story was key. Put it in bold and striking highlights. The purpose of the economy and of business becomes maximizing growth in the production and consumption of goods and services for the sake of maximizing wealth accumulation. In 1959, Raymond J. Saulnier, chairman of the President's Council of Economic Advisers, declared in testimony to the Joint Economic Committee of Congress, "I understand an economy, its ultimate purpose is to produce more consumer goods. This is the goal. This is the object of everything that we are working at."[22]

Consumption, then, takes on myriad purposes beyond meeting human needs.[23] Keeping the economy growing and maximizing wealth accumulation are foremost among them, but also included are identity formation and sense of self-worth. Unbounded consumption became the path to happiness, and wealth-maximizing became a virtue. The economist Victor Lebow wrote in 1955,

> *Our enormously productive economy demands that we make consumption our way of life, that we convert the buying and use of goods into rituals, that we seek our spiritual satisfactions, our ego satisfactions, in consumption.*

Lebow goes on to declare the vital importance of advertising to stoke the flames of consumer desire:

> *Television achieves three results to an extent no other advertising medium has ever approached. First, it creates a captive audience. Second, it submits that audience to the most intensive indoctrination. Third, it operates on the entire family.*[24]

These concepts spread. "Wealth maximizing behavior became a powerful dimension not only of Western economics, but of Western culture and is being exported around the world."[25] And wealth accrued especially to people with capital, the people who had ownership of financial resources as well as productive resources.

The next chapter in this developing narrative was neoliberalism. In this stage of the story, starting in the late 1970s, maximizing short-term profit—not just making a profit over the long haul—became more urgent. This is in part because the finance industry and its speculative trade in money for short-term gain surpassed trade in goods and services, taking precedence over investment in long-term, production-oriented, economic activity. That is, money became a commodity, and trade in money far outstripped trade in goods and services. Many speak of this era—our era—as financialized capitalism. To maximize short-term profit, neoliberalism sought to eliminate as much as possible the regulations established to protect workers, consumers, and the environment. Multilateral trade agreements included clauses that stripped regulations, liberalized markets, favored large corporations over small local business, and protected corporations from legal interference with anything that would enable maximizing profit.[26]

The World Trade Organization reinforced these moves, making it nearly impossible for nations and cities to counter them. Corporate actions aimed at maximizing shareholder returns gained moral, as well as legal, sanction. Marjorie Kelly says it well: "The notion that shareholder returns must be maximized" came to be "a myth with the force of law. We might call it our secular version of the divine right of kings." It was "considered unchallengeable."[27]

Not long ago, a college student spoke with me after an address I had given on her campus. "My generation has lived our entire lives in the worldview and lifeways established by neoliberal capitalism," she lamented. This young woman decided to dedicate her studies to understanding the implications of this and how to respond to it. She provoked me to face more deeply the colonization of consciousness and material life by the mindsets and accompanying norms, desires, and lifeways of neoliberal capitalism. Unwittingly, our desires, economic actions, many other daily activities, and relationships are shaped by its precepts, serve its purposes, and reinforce its power alignments.

As we have noted, the elevation of human creatures over all others is central in this narrative. People were considered *not* to be creatures.[28] Human superiority was linked inseparably with white superiority and wealth superiority; further, the elevation of white people and people with money over other people is at the

Change the Story

heart of the economic narrative. Theologian Kelly Brown Douglas brilliantly traces the development of white supremacy from the first-century Roman historian Tacitus through its pervasive presence in contemporary US society. White people, and especially white Americans (the myth says), have the God-given and legally codified right to make a profit through the exploitation of others (without calling it that). Moreover, this exploitation is considered economically savvy.

This, then, is a brief history of the narrative shaping the economy as we know it—the outdated economy, racialized capitalism. Little wonder that we have arrived at an economy grounded in exploitation and extraction. Formative narratives orient us, morally form and malform us, without our being aware of that influence.

Key Lines in the Narrative Shaping Economic Life Today, and Consequences of Continuing with Them

Shortly, we begin to explore the life-giving work of rewriting the story that undergirds our extractive and exploitative economy. But first, plunge with me more deeply into the quagmire of its compelling myths and the consequences of our society continuing to be guided by them. Doing this—unpleasant as it may be—is crucial. *Transforming an economy for an ecological equitable civilization means recognizing not only the history of its undergirding narrative, but also the key assumptions that the narrative instills in people today,* and the consequences of continuing in that story.

What are those key assumptions? As you read this litany, consider where you see it operative in the world around you, perhaps on a subconscious, yet influential, level.

- Capitalism and democracy inherently go together.
- Capitalism is natural, or normal, or inevitable, or God's will.
- Economic growth is inherently good; the greater the growth, the better off we are.
- The more we buy, the more we are supporting the economy and thus the common good.
- An economy should maximize profit and growth.
- Business corporations and the finance industry should maximize profit; it is their obligation.
- Human freedom includes the right to accumulate as much wealth as possible, and to do as we wish with our possessions as long as we stay within the law.
- An unregulated market is a mark of freedom.
- Getting a "good deal" (a lower price) in a purchase is a good accomplishment.
- Poverty is largely due to deficiencies in poor people.
- Earth and its plentitude are primarily here to meet human needs, material and aesthetic.

- White people in general have more natural right to (or need for) material comforts than have Black, Brown, or Indigenous people; Black, Brown, and Indigenous people are more naturally poor.

The tricky thing is that on a conscious level, we may distinctly *disbelieve* some of these claims. We may in fact work against them. Yet they still influence our society and to a certain extent infiltrate our own individual psyches. The myth of white superiority is a good example. Isabel Wilkerson in her landmark book *Caste* describes the lurking influence of assumed white superiority. Labeling US society as a caste system with white the highest caste and Black the lowest, she writes,

> *A caste system centers the dominant caste as the sun around which all other castes revolve and defines it as the default-setting standard of normalcy, of intellect, of beauty, against which all others are measured, ranked in descending order by the physiological proximity to the dominant caste. They are surrounded by images of themselves from cereal commercials, to sitcoms, as deserving, hardworking, and superior in most aspects of American life, and it would be the rare person who would not absorb the constructed centrality of the dominant group.... Those accustomed to being the measure of all that is human can come to depend on the reassurance that, while they may have troubles in their lives, at least they are not at the bottom.*[29]

What are the consequences of continuing according to the dominant economic narrative? Maximizing profit and consumption will illustrate the dangers, as will the story line that some people are more worthy than others. (Note that this critique of *maximizing* profit is NOT a critique of *making* profit.)

Maximizing shareholder returns is built into corporate charters in the United States and into the US American psyche. It is part of our economic story. It is behind the practice of moving industrial production to wherever the labor protections, wages, and environmental regulations are lowest. Lawrence Summers's declaration as chief economist of the World Bank, and subsequently Harvard University president, is chilling:

> *I think the economic logic behind dumping a load of toxic waste in the lowest-wage country is impeccable and we should face up to that.... Just between you and me, shouldn't the World Bank be encouraging more migration of the dirty industries to the less developed countries?*[30]

Maximizing profit is behind paying workers wages too low for some to afford housing, and employing many people part-time in order to avoid paying healthcare benefits. Maximizing profit leads to the commodification of water, airspace, genetic material, and more.[31]

Change the Story

Maximizing profit, and thus shareholder returns, is also behind charging too much for life-saving drugs. CBS News reported the following story:

When the CEO of Turing Pharmaceuticals acquired rights to Daraprim, a life-saving antiparasitic medication, he quickly raised the drug's price from $13.50/pill to $750/pill. Asked by an audience member at a healthcare summit hosted by Forbes ... what he'd do differently if he could go back in time to before his highly criticized decision to raise the price of a 62-year-old drug, he replied:

> *"I probably would have raised prices higher, is probably what I should have done. I could have raised it higher and made more profits for our shareholders. Which is my primary duty. . . . No one wants to say it, no one's proud of it, but this is a capitalist society, capitalist system and capitalist rules, and my investors expect me to maximize profits, not to minimize them, or go half, or go 70 percent, but to go to 100 percent of the profit curve that we're all taught in MBA class."*[32]

What are the consequences? What is the impact on the human psyche of identifying human beings as consumers and of assuming that our purpose in economic life is to maximize profit, growth, and consumption? What are the consequences for a sense of identity and worth? Maximizing consumption leads to a voracious marketing industry. The average American child is said to watch about forty thousand commercials on TV each year. How is that child formed to understand who she is and what gives her joy and worth? I tremble at the impact this could have on my grandchildren.

What are the consequences for our viability as a species, given the "planetary boundaries" and Earth's limited capacity to process toxic waste, garbage, and "novel entities" such as plastics?[33] Maximizing consumption means producing products that will wear out and need to be replaced. Without adding accountability for environmental damage into corporate charters and the bottom line, maximizing profit and consumption also means increasing toxic waste and carbon emissions. The fashion and textile industries, for example, have "an enormous carbon footprint ... and as we increase our consumption of fast fashion, the related emissions are set to grow rapidly."[34]

The economic story began with the great chain of being that elevated some people over others, giving some people more worth, proximity to God, and rights than other people. What are the consequences for a nation if economic practices and policies tacitly reinforce that story line—even if consciously we deny it? Essentially, by living according to the current economy and its undergirding story we are embodying or practicing a fundamental value that most of us would resoundingly deny. It is that people with substantial monetary wealth (who are disproportionately white people) have rights that other people do not have—rights such as a livable wage, healthcare, and a safe working environment.

As players in this story, we violate a value that we claim is dear to us: that all people are equal.

Changing the Story

The economic narrative is beginning to unravel. Its falsehoods are being exposed.

We are capable of rewriting our stories, of replacing narratives that lead to a dead end with life-giving stories. We can do this as individuals and as a society. We can reorient ourselves away from the assumption that extraction and exploitation are normal or necessary. We can resituate ourselves as a part of Earth's economy of life. We can reframe the nature of human being and of freedom, and the purpose of economic life to reflect our deepest values rather than betray them.

The poet, novelist, and playwright Ben Okri notes the power of narrative change. "Nations and People are largely the stories they feed themselves. If they tell themselves stories that are lies, they will suffer the future consequences of those lies. If they tell themselves stories that face their own truths, they will free their histories for future flowerings."[35] Reflecting on this, Maori scholar Moana Jackson notes, "Stories for and about transformation rely on honesty about the misremembered stories and the foresight to see where different stories might lead."[36]

The solarpunk movement affirms that reshaping story aids in reshaping society. Solarpunk, writes Sarah Lazarovic, "is a movement in speculative fiction, art, fashion, and activism that seeks to answer and embody the question, 'what does a sustainable civilization look like, and how can we get there?' ... The point of solarpunk is to start telling that new, creative story. Illustrating a world where humans don't live in opposition to nature."[37]

Changing the economic story undergirding extractive capitalism can lead to a life-giving economy. Alternative economic stories are available. The New Economy Coalition writes, "What if we saw our economy as a fabric of relationships? From the fibers of worker co-ops, community land trusts, electric cooperatives, and countless other threads, we're weaving a solidarity economy." How strikingly resonant that assertion is with the biblical perspective that economic life is primarily a matter of relationships with neighbors and thus is guided by the commandment and invitation to "love your neighbor as yourself." The NEC and the biblical witness tell a story of the purpose of economic life, a story very different from the one that shapes contemporary capitalism. Christiana Figueres, former executive of the United Nations Convention on Climate Change and a chief negotiator for the UN at the Paris Agreement, proposes as one of ten major actions to avoid the worst of climate disaster: "See yourself as a citizen, not a consumer."[38] She is rewriting the story of who we are.

Cautions are in order. For white people of economic privilege who have benefited materially from the dominant story, rewriting has a necessary companion. We must continue to learn and face more fully the damage and ferocious suffering rendered by the narratives of white exceptionalism, manifest destiny, and their links to economic life. Without a commitment to that knowing, the quest for a new narrative may become a whitewashing of truth. Such whitewashing will not bring forth enduring good.

Let us look more closely at rewriting six components in this matrix of stories that normalize economic life as we live it. May you enjoy this venture into soil for the new economy, the economy for a more life-giving future.

Change the Story: You Are a "We"

Until quite recently, I thought that I was a *human* being. Did you? What a surprise to find that I am not primarily human at all! Less than half of the cells in human body are "human."[39] The rest are a wild menagerie of organisms, dancing and prancing around in our tear ducts and guts, on our skin and hair follicles, between our toes and in our ears. You could not breathe for a moment without this micro-zoo, this biome more symbiotic and collaborative than any system designed by human beings. Take a moment to give thanks for this marvelous and mysterious "we," this communion that composes you, enabling your eyes to read and your brain cells to race as you ponder this page.

And what of the community across time that gives us life? Let us honor and give thanks for the elemental ancestors—the carbon and other elements that burst forth some 13.5 billion years ago in the "Big Bang." Without these ancient cosmic forebearers, there is no you. And they are not only past; they compose the collaboratory of our bodies today. There you are, a dance of carbon, oxygen, hydrogen, nitrogen, calcium, and phosphorus with a wee bit of sulfur, potassium, sodium, chlorine, and magnesium as support staff.

Ah, and consider our kin throughout the biosphere, hydrosphere, and geosphere without whom we would not live for a moment. The trees of the Amazon who serve as our external lungs, the 4 trillion organisms in a square foot of soil that produced the breakfast that we enjoyed today. Biologist David Haskell writes, "Wild biological relationships permeate every being.... We're all—trees, humans, insects, birds, bacteria—pluralities.... We are part of the community of life composed of relationships with 'others,' so the human/nature duality that lives near the heart of many philosophies is, from a biological perspective, illusory."[40] Who are we if not part of a wild and highly fruitful creative collaborative communion of being? A magnificent mysterious web of matter and energy that renders this raucous and resplendent orgy of life in garden Earth.

"Jesus was a mammal," I entitled a talk one year at a local university. I was trying to get across that we humans are mammals; we are part of Earth's creaturely menagerie. Later in another effort to do the same, my email to a large group of neighbors began with, "Hello, Fellow earthlings, descendants of stardust, eaters of sunlight converted to delectable edibles." It was an effort to say,

"We are not who we think we are." We are Earth creatures, earthlings, stardust assembled in human form, *humus* rendered as human.

What we choose and what we do depends upon who we assume that we are. On top of the false notion that we are not a part of nature, modernity produced another set of misguided assumptions or "guiding" narratives about who the human being is. Note core features of the theory of the human that accompanied the colonial enterprise and the rise of industrial capitalism. We are essentially autonomous individuals. We are fundamentally competitive. In economic life, we are by nature motivated primarily by the quest for personal financial gain and material acquisition. We have the right to acquire as much as possible and to do as we wish with our possessions within the limits of the law. Human worth is in relationship to buying power; those who own much are more worthy than those who own little or nothing. And finally, harnessing Earth's resources for personal convenience or gain is a moral good.[41]

Even if we don't individually hold these claims to be true, they form a mindset in which we are socialized. They influence our psyches, decisions, and behaviors, and our social structures such as the economy.[42]

Many are the voices decrying the dangers of this notion of the human. To illustrate, a global interreligious consultation on finance, held in Bangkok, declared this understanding of the human to be

> *a delusional narrative of the self as an isolated entity that is rightfully obsessed with its individual interests. Such a fragmented and fictitious understanding undermines and destroys an interrelational narrative of the self which is at the heart of our faith traditions. . . . Constructing a new international financial architecture for an economy of life requires a counter-narrative based on inter-connectedness and ethics of reciprocity. This is at the core of our spirituality.*[43]

Others also highlight the dangers and falsehoods in this dominant concept of the human and argue that it has been constructed rather than being a reflection of reality.[44] The notion that we are by nature essentially "greedy, selfish, competitive" is, they assert, the product of an economic system that rewards greedy, selfish, competitive behavior.[45]

In fact, though the nature of the human is studied in fields from biology to religion, we do not definitively know "who we are." However, ample empirical evidence in multiple fields challenges the *homo economicus* notion of the human, suggesting that it prevails only when social systems are set up to reward it. That is the case in the neoliberal economy. We are rewarded for maximizing profit, consumption, and material wealth. Evolutionary biologist David Sloan Wilson suggests that our species' evolutionary success is—to the contrary—based on our capacity to cooperate as groups. Evolution favored highly cooperative groups.[46]

The stakes could not be higher. A future for humankind with any degree of humanity will require us to be a species that collaborates and recognizes our dependence on other species and on Earth's life-support systems. This means collaboration in many forms, not least of which are collaboration in the face of disaster and collaboration in knowledge-building among fields of human inquiry.[47]

How fortunate, then, that biological sciences, physical sciences, behavioral sciences, and theology are joining ancient mystics and other ancient religious wisdoms in recognizing quite a different story of who we are as a species. This story challenges both the assumption that humans are independent of "nature," and that we are the *homo economicus* constructed by colonial modernity. This alternative story says that we exist only in relationship to others (human and not); you are a we. And your highest form of being is your being in communion. Moreover, you and your fellow humans evolved more as a result of your symbiotic nature than your competitive nature. To top it all off, you are utterly at every moment dependent on other beings and elements, human and other.

Recall chapter 1's discussion of the claim found now in physics, biology, and theology that we are—along with the entire cosmos—"wired for communion." Life—including human life—is oriented around connection and symbiosis. We are swimming in a vast communion that we tend not to see.[48] In the words of Dietrich Bonhoeffer, we are created and called into "life together." We heard theologian Willie James Jennings asserting that communion is God's intent for human beings; second-century theologian Irenaeus of Lyon saying that communion is the destiny of all creation; and the Eastern Orthodox conviction that the truth of human existence is communion.[49]

Some hold that God already has given this communion and that humans are called to recognize it and then actualize it in relationships, both personal and structural.[50] I am struck by suggestions, even from outside of theological discourse, that this communion has been provided for us to recognize and embody. Einstein said as much. "A human being is part of a whole, called by us the universe.... He experiences himself, his thoughts, and feelings, as something separate from the rest, a kind of optical delusion of his consciousness." Canadian biologist David Suzuki writes of a "vast story of cooperation and quest for communion that enabled life to emerge on earth and then to evolve into more complex forms."[51] Feminist physicist Karen Barad, as we noted previously, suggests that the cosmos is wired for communion.[52] Humans may have evolved out of the capacity for highly sophisticated communion.[53] *These accounts of nature's cooperation and quest for communion resonate with my claim that the purpose of economic life includes cultivating that communion, not thwarting it.*

Recall, too, the insidious story line that our self-worth lies in what we earn and own, and that wealthy people have more rights to a comfortable life than do economically poor people. This is baked into our psyches, and it is diametrically opposed to core religious teachings. Changing the story of who we are is a beautiful invitation to resist that narrative and to build the opposite. Unhoused people have as much right to a cozy bed and a retirement plan as do I. Rich people and others who can pay for it do not have a stronger right to good education, or to health care and adequate compensation for their work. What could we do to bake that counternarrative into our psyches, and into the minds of our children? How might you codify it in your organization's wage and benefits structure, and in local and state laws? A first step is recognizing wealth privilege in our subtle inner voices and in our laws.

Likewise, biblical studies have punched holes in the narrative, grounded in interpretations of the Genesis creation stories, that we are separate from nature and are here to dominate, use, or improve it. Countless scholars point out that better translations of the Hebrew words in the biblical creation stories suggest that humans truly are Earth creatures and that we are here to "serve" Earth. In the text commonly translated as "God formed man from the dust of the ground" (Gen 2:7) the word for human is *ha'adam,* a generic word meaning neither male nor female. The word translated as ground is *ha'adamah.* Literally, *ha'adam* is from *ha'adamah,* the human is Earth creature made from Earth. We are human made from humus. The text, famously and consequentially translated as "God took the man and put him in the garden of Eden to till and keep it" (Gen 2:15), is more accurately translated as "to serve and preserve it." The Hebrew words are *abad* and *shamar.* Elsewhere in the biblical texts, *abad* "most commonly means 'serve' (as in serving God, other gods, or another superior). Perhaps that was unthinkable to the translators of the King James Version and many other Bibles, who took it figuratively to mean something more like tilling and working the land."[54] Who we are is just one storyline in the narrative that undergirds economic life today. We could spend an entire book—indeed multiple books—on the exciting and creative foray into rewriting a truer and more life-giving story of who we are. What will be your part in that creative adventure? It is joined by another—the story of what Earth is.

Change the Story: What or Who Earth Is

Trees talking, mountains shouting, plants sending emergency alerts, and birds singing while they make babies, while God is "flowing and pouring through all things," "even the tiniest leaf."[55] What planet are we on?

The dominant economic story holds that Earth is essentially a resource. Earth and all that we commonly call "nature" are not subjects with agency. That is, Earth does not have intrinsic worth, relationships, and the power to respond, to do, to communicate, to act. Earth is an "it," not a "thou."[56] (I use "Earth" from this point on to indicate all that is frequently called "nature" or the "natural world.")

Quite a ride it is to enter into rewriting that strain in the story! I suspect you have begun to do so. Here again, Indigenous wisdoms, re-readings of Christian

Change the Story

and Jewish Scriptures, and many people's experience come together, leading in one wildly evocative direction. Earth, it turns out, is not just an object and a resource. Rather, it is an active "agent," an entity with intricate complex relationships and actions. Even plants have agency.

Earth sciences now agree with what many Indigenous peoples have long taught. Earth's creatures and elements are kin to us ("all our relations"). Every bug, stone, terrestrial walker (including humans), flying or swimming creature, particle of sand, flower, and water molecule on Earth is descendent of a common ancestor—the ninety-four elements blasted forth in the Big Bang some 13 and a half billion years ago. The Potawatomi elder and scientist Robin Wall Kimmerer notes that her language uses personal pronouns not only for people, but for other living and nonliving members of the Earth community.[57] Indigenous peoples of Ecuador have pushed for constitutional provisions that extend rights to Earth.

Moreover, according to many Indigenous wisdoms, the other-than-human parts of this Earth community are considered elders and "teachers" for the human "younger brothers of creation." Teachers! "We say that humans have the least experience with how to live and thus the most to learn—we must look to our teachers among the other species for guidance. They teach us by example.... Plants know how to make food and medicine from light and water, and then they give it away."[58] Indigenous elder Vine Deloria Jr. too demonstrates that in his people's understanding, humans must listen to the other animals if people are to live rightly.[59]

Biologists are showing the complex communications networks among plants and fungi. Robert Macfarlane of the *New Yorker* describes the "research revolution" that

> is changing the way we think about forests.... Individual plants are joined to one another by an underground [fungal] network: a dazzlingly complex and collaborative structure that has become known as the Wood Wide Web. The relationship between these mycorrhizal fungi and the plants they connect is... largely one of mutualism—a subset of symbiosis in which both organisms benefit from their association....
>
> The implications of the Wood Wide Web far exceed this basic exchange of goods between plant and fungi, however. The fungal network also allows plants to distribute resources—sugar, nitrogen, and phosphorus—between one another. A dying tree might divest itself of its resources to the benefit of the community, for example, or a young seedling in a heavily shaded understory might be supported with extra resources by its stronger neighbors. Even more remarkably, the network also allows plants to send one another warnings. A plant under attack from aphids can indicate to a nearby plant that it should raise its defensive response before the aphids

reach it. It has been known for some time that plants communicate above ground in comparable ways, by means of airborne hormones. But such warnings are more precise in terms of source and recipient when sent by means of the myco-net.

The revelation of the Wood Wide Web's existence, and the increased understanding of its functions, raises big questions... about what trading, sharing, or even friendship might mean among plants. "Whenever I need to explain my research to someone quickly, I just tell them I work on the social networks of plants," [Merlin] Sheldrake told me.[60]

Philosophers and social theorists likewise attest that agency is not only the province of humans, but also of other animate beings and inanimate matter. According to the chair of Political Science at Johns Hopkins University, Jane Bennett, a "vital force" pervades the material world, and humans exist in a cosmic web of vibrant matter. Our actions are influenced by the agency of other-than-human material entities.[61]

Biblical scholarship has discovered (rediscovered) that biblical texts are full of testimonies to Earth's agency. Earth's creatures and elements collaborate with God in creation (Genesis), witness (Deut 30:19), embody God's love (Ps 33:5),[62] fear God (Ps 33:8), reveal God (Rom 1:20), praise God (Ps 148:3–13; 150:6), see and understand God (Rom 1:20), proclaim God's work (Ps 19:1), teach (Job 12:7–8), lament (Hosea 4:3), and even fulfill God's commands (Ps 149:8). Other texts too portray Earth's agency in these and other senses. As Timothy Beal notes, "The biblical texts show God interacting not only with humans but also with nonhuman creatures and things.... Mountains shout. The sea roars. The land rests, and grieves, and might at any moment spit us humans out if we don't start behaving."[63]

The inhabitants of a modern Western worldview do not customarily think of such agency in creatures and elements other than human. We commonly assume that a unique characteristic of humankind is our capacity for hearing, heeding, and teaching who God is. These texts suggest otherwise.

The plot (in the reclaimed story of Earth's agency) thickens. Not only does Earth *act*; theologians throughout time have claimed that Earth is a dwelling place of God—that *other-than-human creatures and elements are full of God's creative, saving, revelatory, empowering presence*. Many of these theological voices have been ignored, leaving Christians to worship a God who is only above and beyond them or perhaps within them, but surely not within the other creatures and elements. I, for example, spent four decades as a Lutheran before encountering Martin Luther's insistence that the created world is a dwelling place of God! God, he taught, "is flowing and pouring through all things."[64] God "is in and through all creatures, in all their parts and places."[65] "The power of God... must be essentially present in all places even in the tiniest leaf."[66] How tragic

Change the Story

that Lutherans, in general, have tended to ignore this world-shaking faith claim until very recently.

God's Spirit of boundless justice-seeking love at play within and with otherkind may nurture humans' power to embody that love. We are well advised to learn from the other-than-human languages of this Earth. It is uncharted terrain—creation as abode and servant of divine and indefatigable love.

This does not mean that "nature" models morality. One predator devouring the mother or offspring of another, the tormented faces of tsunami survivors, the fierce onslaught of disease, or slow and agonizing death dispel that notion. What is natural is not necessarily moral any more than humans are necessarily moral. The point is not to hold up nature as a blueprint for morality.

Rather, the point is to cultivate receptivity to hearing the "voices" of other-than-human parts of nature, listening for the voice of God in them, and learning from them. In this way, God's Spirit at play in creation may nourish us. That holy nourishment may feed hope and power for the journey toward economies in which humankind is not toxic to our planetary home and in which none amass wealth or power at the cost of others' impoverishment or degradation.

Change the Story: Freedom

"Freedom requires unbounded market freedom" is a central story line in the dominant economic narrative.[67]

Imagine rewriting that story line. First, we would identify the assumptions linking human freedom to private property and market "freedom,"[68] and linking market freedom to public well-being. They are seductive:

- The "freedom" to accumulate wealth and consume without limits, to use one's wealth as one chooses, and to have vast consumer choice is integral to human freedom. It is a necessary condition for human freedom to flourish.
- Freedom is threatened by taxation and regulation, for these constrain people's freedom to use wealth and possessions as they choose.
- Market "freedom," as seen in capitalism is a necessary condition for democracy.
- Market forces "free" from regulation inevitably will serve the well-being of a society that plays by "free" market rules. The more "free" the markets are and the more "free" people are to accumulate wealth, the more prosperous the society is.
- The human species is "free" to use Earth's resources for the sake of profit. (That freedom effectively pertains particularly to those humans who can buy access to Earth's resources.)

This notion of freedom is integral to the narrative that makes our form of economy seem morally good. Attaching the word *free* to markets implies that market freedom is a grounding of human freedom. Labeling deregulated commerce as "free"—that is, with the terminology of unalienable moral rights—associates it with freedom of the human spirit, political freedom, moral freedom, and democracy.[69] This notion of freedom is not only implicit but also explicit in much "free" market discourse.[70]

Adam Smith is hailed as the father of capitalism. Justifications of contemporary capitalism often appeal to him. Yet contemporary capitalism ignores and contradicts his trenchant warnings! He cautioned *against* making laws based on the interests of people who live by investment profits (the main source of profit for today's wealthiest people). While neoliberal capitalism claims that individuals' freedom to accumulate wealth will lead to a more prosperous society, Smith overtly contradicts this claim. In his *Wealth of Nations* (a kind of holy scripture for capitalist economies), Smith warns that the interests of

> "those who live by ... the profit of stocks" are not connected to "the general interests of the society." They are more knowledgeable, he says, of "their own interest" than of the "publick interest." In fact, he goes on, their interest "is always in some respects different from, and even opposite to, that of the publick." For this reason, he warns, "The proposal of any new law or regulation of commerce which comes from this order (those who live by profit of stocks), ought always to be listened to with great precaution, and ought never to be adopted" unless it has been "long and carefully examined ... with the most suspicious attention. It comes from an order of men ... who have generally an interest to deceive and even to oppress the publick, and who accordingly have, upon many occasions, both deceived and oppressed it."[71]

Smith's warning resounds for us today. May we bring his prescient admonition to the halls of legislation and policy.

In short, a principle of contemporary capitalism is the freedom to do as one pleases—within the limits of the law—in the marketplace. What are the results? International mining companies have the freedom to extract wealth and leave devastated and toxic landscapes with little or no benefits to the majority of local people impacted. Individuals had the freedom to reap vast profit from the COVID pandemic.[72] Fossil fuel companies have the freedom to persist in relentless drilling and refining despite the devastating impact on Earth's life-sustaining climate range. Corporate executives and boards have the freedom to keep labor cost cheap: move plants to countries where environmental and worker protection standards are low, pay miserable wages and no health care benefits, ignore dangerous and toxic working conditions.[73]

People are rewriting the story of freedom. The rewrites are varied and contextual. But many revolve around freedom as the opportunity to flourish as beings-in-community, using one's gifts not only toward the well-being of self and loved ones, but also toward the well-being of the larger human communities and yet larger community-of-life that enables us to exist.[74]

Change the Story: Purpose of Economic Life and Purpose of Business

Imagine a terrible worldwide pandemic. Countless people lose their jobs or livelihoods and do not have adequate money for food. Yet US billionaires add over $2 trillion to their wealth.[75] Let it sink in. Something is terribly wrong with the purpose of a system that allows this to happen. It is diseased.

Maximizing wealth for a few, and maximizing growth where doing so imperils Earth's life-support systems and impoverishes others, is a purpose unworthy of decent people. It warrants not our allegiance.

As declared in the "World Scientists' Warning of a Climate Emergency," endorsed by over 14,000 scientists from 158 countries, the purpose of economic life must shift from maximizing "GDP growth and the pursuit of affluence toward sustaining ecosystems and improving human well-being by prioritizing basic needs and reducing inequality," from providing "maximum returns to short-term investors" to "long term benefits to society."[76]

Economics has long claimed to be a value-free, morally neutral science. We now know otherwise. Economic life, and ideas about it, are a terrain of morality and ethics because they shape relationships with others and with Earth. "Budgets are moral documents. They reveal priorities and values, and as a society, they are the primary way that we care for one another, especially for the vulnerable."[77] (I would change this to "a," not "the," "primary way that we care for one another.") The Poor People's Campaign said as much when it created A Poor People's Moral Budget.[78]

A strong movement has arisen to change the story about the purpose of economic life and of business. Marjorie Kelly writes, "What is emerging—or reemerging—in our time is a democratic economic principle: corporations must serve the public good, or at least must not harm it."[79] In 1993 the successful businessman Paul Hawken called upon business to transform its purpose from maximizing profit, or continue in its path of "destroying the world."[80] With strong confidence in the potential of business to change, he declares,

> We need a system of commerce and production where each and every act is inherently sustainable and restorative." "We have the capacity and the ability to create a remarkably different economy, one that can restore ecosystems and protect the environment while bringing forth innovation, prosperity, meaningful work, and true security.

In other words, the purpose of economic life and of business as a part of it becomes not only a reasonable profit, but also ecological restoration and social well-being that centers the well-being of marginalized people and groups.

Impossible? No, this shift is possible precisely because human beings constructed the exploitative extractive economy and, therefore, we can reconstruct it. One key to doing so is changing the narrative regarding the purpose of business.

Change the Story: Inevitable[81]

A key piece in the assemblage of myths underlying the economy as we know it, is the assumption that it is inevitable. As Margaret Thatcher so infamously asserted, "There is no alternative." According to this myth, advanced global capitalism is a form of manifest destiny. In the words of Francis Fukuyama, "The logic of modern natural science would seem to dictate a universal evolution in the direction of capitalism."[82] Modern liberal democracy and capitalism are "the final form of human government, and as such ... the end of history.[83]

That myth is changing.[84] You—as a reader of this book—are a part of that sea change. Many of the organizations, movements, and people highlighted in this volume and in the series to come are midwives of the change. The rules and practices that shape the outdated current economy are not "forces of nature beyond our control, but have been designed by people.... They have been designed in favor of the market rather than people and planet. In little more than a decade, we must redesign them again."[85] You have heard me say it before: what is constructed by human beings can be dismantled and replaced—transformed. This includes economies.

Change the Story: White Superiority

As we have discussed, the myth that white people have more worth and deserve more rights and comfort than other people permeates our society. It is in laws, history, health care, the criminal (in)justice system, education, employment policy, and so much more. This myth works in a way more dangerous than explicit claims; it functions, for many, *below* conscious awareness. That is, it shapes social life while hiding. Unacknowledged, it can be ignored and denied. As we have seen, this myth is integral to capitalism in the United States. Without this myth, our economy could not have developed as it has, for the slavery and genocide that established our economy required this myth. So too, the subsequent centuries of economic exploitation against Black, Brown, Indigenous, and other people of color (here in the US and around the world) has needed this myth to give that exploitation a veneer of "acceptability."

The point here is simply to recognize that changing the narrative undergirding the predatory economy includes exposing and then refuting the myth of white superiority. We have begun to do so by exposing some roots of this myth, the links between human exceptionalism and white exceptionalism, and the connections to distorted notions of freedom. While this challenge is vast, it also is encouraging, for it signals that by working to dismantle white superiority and white racism, we also are building a firm foundation for a new and moral economy.

Change the Story: Growth

"Myth matters. Every culture, every society, clings to a myth by which it lives. Ours is the myth of growth. For as long as the economy continues to expand, we are assured that life is getting better." "The myth of growth has dominated our cultural story for a century or more." It is "coded into the guidance manual of the modern economy."[86]

In essence the growth myth claims that economic growth as measured by gross domestic product (GDP) produces economic well-being for all, is an accurate indicator of that well-being, and is necessary for that well-being to be achieved. Moreover, as noted by British economist Tim Jackson, GDP is seen as indicator not only of economic well-being but of well-being as a whole.

Why is it so dangerous? To see the dangers, we must see why it is invalid. The myth that growth in GDP is a legitimate indicator of economic well-being is invalid today for at least four reasons.[87]

- First, growth as measured by GDP counts destructive activity as a gain.[88] Children buying cigarettes, sale of pornography, collisions on the freeway, electrocutions, all contribute to growth. The more a household buys, throws away, and replaces, the more good it is doing, for consumption adds to growth. Ignored is the danger that overconsumption presents to the ecosystems upon which life depends.
- Second, growth theory does not account for distribution of wealth and income. According to a United Nations report, in many nations, while GDP has grown, income distribution has worsened and poverty has increased.[89]
- Next, growth, as measured by GDP, is an inadequate measure of economic well-being because GDP attributes to a host country profits which are never seen by that country's people. Corporate profit that leaves with the corporation is counted as growth *for the host country*. Recall the riveting story of Lenora, the African woman fighting for tax justice.
- And finally, the goal of unlimited growth is invalid because it fails to recognize Earth's natural limits. Thus, for example, "We continue to pursue economic growth through the unbridled extraction and burning of fossil fuels, with a fatal impact."[90]

Since the 1972 publication of *Limits to Growth*, critiques of economic growth as a measure of well-being are plentiful. They come from many fronts—from grassroots activists to international policy institutes to climate scientists.

But what are the alternatives to the GDP? "A global 'beyond GDP' movement has generated far better indicators to use to guide public budgets.... One metric extensively vetted by economists—the Genuine Progress Indicator (GPI)—is gaining traction worldwide."[91] In 2021 federal legislation was introduced to move the GPI into US economic policy making.[92]

A final point is important. The role of growth in economic well-being is contextual. Economies of many impoverished nations *do* need to grow. In these contexts, growth—if it is pro-poor, pro-jobs, pro-environment, and distributed rather than concentrated in a wealthy sector—is vitally important; it adds to well-being.[93] Arguments against the validity of growth as indicator of well-being must recognize also that not all growth is the same. For example, growth due to production of goods that meet essential needs and are produced without ecological or social harm is qualitatively different from growth due to production of luxury items produced in ecologically or socially destructive ways.

We have said that "changing the guiding stories" is crucial for building a moral economy. Therefore, let us be honest. It is not likely that a society (e.g., our society) can say no to GDP as primary indicator of economic well-being without also saying no to other related myths. The growth myth is driven in part by the desire to maximize profit and wealth, and the assumption that doing so is normal and is a measure of human worth and success. We land again in the challenge of *how*. *How* are we to change consciousness or the fundamental narratives that shape our assumptions and actions? To that question we now move.

Life-Giving Links: How Do We Change the Story?

Some fifteen years ago, an undergraduate student at Seattle University—wise beyond her twenty years—called for "divesting from the exploitative, extractive narrative" and "investing in a more life-giving story."[94] The New Economy Coalition writes on its website, "We amplify stories, tools, and analysis, weaving a collective new economy narrative that can build shared identity, shift culture and policy, and promote a clear vision of the next system." Clearly, I agree that changing the story is key to building a moral economy.

But allow me to play the "devil's advocate." Does changing the story *really* matter? Does changing what we hold to be true matter? We theologians involved in ethics vehemently hold that it does matter. Beliefs shape how we live. Ideas about what is good, right, normal, God's will, or reality are the basis of life choices. But, is this really the case? If, for example, I change my belief about who we humans are—if I come to understand that I am a we, a collectivity within my own body and a matrix of relationships spanning time, species, and continents—does this change how I live? If I change the story to believe that getting a good deal on what I buy (maximizing profit) is not as important as supporting a new worker-owned business where goods cost a bit more because

Change the Story

they do not use cheap labor and pollute rivers, does it change how I live? Does it change society?

Perhaps a new narrative changes how I live and changes our society ONLY IF *I actually practice or enact the new story.* Only if I switch from being a *player* in the old narrative and *materially enter* the new one. Changing the story changes how I live only if I shift my practice intentionally to cohere with the new story. And, this changes society only if I (we) do these things publicly, if we act publicly and consistently as players in the new story.

We revisit now our friends Lisa Laskow Lahey and Robert Kegan, whom we met earlier in this chapter. Awareness of the life-shaping "big assumptions"— mindset or stories—is not sufficient to enable change, they say. We need to acknowledge the cost of continuing to abide by them, *and then practice or act out the different mindset in order for it to actually to reshape how we live.*[95]

The philosopher Michael Foucault struggled to understand how it would "be possible to think differently, instead of legitimating what one already knows." (He uses "thinking differently" much as we are using "changing the story.") He too concludes that thinking differently is not simply a cognitive matter, but rather entails deep commitment to inner work including "*the practices we must undertake* to transform ourselves, the necessary work of ourselves on ourselves, in order for us to have access to truth."[96] This inner transformation and the practices that enable it are what he calls spirituality. Practices! After all of these pages of exposing the false economic narrative, its historical development, its component myths, and the consequences of remaining in the thrall of that story, we face a final but crucial question: *What "practices" would enact the changed story?* What behaviors would enable the changed story to become real, to overturn the false story? What practices of personal life and what practices as public action?

In my experience a *first step of practice* in gaining freedom from a destructive story is to recognize its voice (inside of me or in society) and the habits that reinforce it, rather than letting these remain unnoticed. Doing this helps us to realize that this story is a *construct*, not an objective truth. To illustrate: for many of us, the myth of white superiority (central to the economic narrative) is unconscious; we don't believe it on a conscious level. Nevertheless, it influences us. What habits reinforce it and normalize it? Think of worship in many Christian churches. We sing of being washed white as snow from sin. Angels often are painted in white, while demons are black. Baptismal gowns are white. Although images of Jesus are changing in many churches, many of us were raised with a Jesus who looks like he came from Norway, a Mary with blue eyes, and angels with curly golden hair. To change the story of white superiority requires an initial step of recognizing it and the habits that reinforce it.

A *second step of practice* is to recognize the consequences—material and spiritual—of continuing to live according to the old stories. This includes acknowledging who gains and who loses from the stories' influence. If you are a white person, you might pause to list the many ways in which you have gained materially from the unconscious societal assumption that white people are better.[97]

A *third step of practice* is intentionally to tell the truer story (the "changed" story) and enact it. How can we enact refuting the story of white superiority? The question is worth gold. What is your response? I share one. In the church context noted above, surely refuting the story of white superiority and telling the truer story would include featuring not a white Jesus, but images of Jesus and Mary showing their actual brown skin and brown eyes. Telling and practicing a truer story would include getting rid of language that equates white with good and black with evil. It would include depicting angels with Black skin, Brown skin, Indigenous features, or Asian features.

This third step of practice is rooted deeply in ethical theory since Aristotle. Ethics claims that practices (or habits) form our dispositions and ultimately our character and behaviors, as individuals and societies. I would argue that practices both form and malform us, and practices may re-form us. Moreover, practices made public or done collectively also may form, malform, and reform groups, institutions, and societies. The seminary at which I teach was buying a book for each student in a new January course. Guided by the story line of "it is important and good to get the best deal you can for your money," I was all set to buy the books for these twenty-five students from Amazon. My colleague stepped in and said, "Listen, why don't you buy them from the local Black-owned independent bookstore?" I did. Moreover, we made this public; we put a flyer from the store inside each book, and informed the students and other colleagues how to access the store online for future use.

My colleague had led me and others to refute the story line that we needed to get things at the lowest price, the story line that the financial bottom line is all that matters. She helped me to practice a changed story line that says, "The impact that buying things has on human well-being and on shaping economic life also matters." Had I taken the time to make this more public, in the local consortium of institutions of which mine is a part, think of the impact!

Being public in changing practices is key to changing the story on a societal level. I will never forget a global gathering of some sixty leaders in ecumenical networks. Suddenly, in the midst of the discussion, one rather quiet woman (we will call her Natalie) rose up and uttered in a resounding voice: "ch ch ch ch ch." Startled, we jumped. It took a moment, but soon we got it. Someone (we will call her Amanda) had said something in which "black" indirectly was equated with bad. Natalie had interrupted that language publicly, calling attention to it, signaling that it was dangerous, and inviting us all to rethink how we used words connoting blackness. Her brief words following the silence dislodged any attribution of shame to Amanda; Natalie clarified that the tendency to equate "blackness" with evil is in us all. I have practiced Natalie's interruption and shared that experience over the years, probably with over five hundred people. If the other sixty people present have done the same, then her three-to-four minute practice has helped some thirty thousand people to change the story of white superiority.

The stories undergirding a predatory economy are insidious because they go unnoticed. I awaken most mornings with a simple prayer and centering time. Often, I begin with gratitude and then move into those three steps of story-changing practice that we just noted. I call into my awareness at least one false story that I am likely to tell myself (or that the world around me is likely to tell me) unconsciously that day. This morning, to illustrate, I called to awareness the story that "I am not good enough; I am deficient." Next (step two), I glanced at the consequences of living as a player in that story, the consequences for me and for the world around me. I would not, for example, have the confidence to finish writing this book or engaging other authors to write the subsequent books in the series if I let myself live according to the story of my inadequacy. Then (step three) I remind myself of a different story—one that I claim as true and into which I want to live as a player. In this case, it was the story that I am a precious and beloved child of the living God who pours the light of Love upon me and calls me to relish it and live it into the world as justice-making neighbor-love. Living my day as a player in that story makes for a much different day. It shapes significant decisions. I mold my behavior to match the new story. In this case, that means carrying on with writing as though I truly believed that I am not deficient, unworthy, or not good enough, and that God calls me to this work.

Let us make two leaps from that illustration. The first is the leap to the market myths we have been unearthing. One was the myth that some people—especially white people with money—are more worthy than other people. How might the three-step sequence of practices play out in changing that story? Years ago, I began to look in myself for where I—on a very subconscious level—allowed myself to hold that (for example) the woman cleaning the floor in front of the hotel elevator was less important than my colleague entering the elevator, and to note the consequences of believing that. I began explicitly to refute that lie, reminding myself, "No, they are of equal worth." I enacted that changed story, in part by greeting them both with eye contact, a sincere smile, and warmth. This behavior reinforced the changed story about human worth.

The second leap is from personal inner story/consciousness (as in the illustration) to public story/consciousness and social structural change. How could I address the public myth that the janitor is less worthy? Perhaps I could look for "language" in the public discourse that reinforces that false narrative. By language I mean not only verbal language but also the languages of other symbols and of policy and rules. In the hotel, there is a separate entrance for the housekeeping and janitorial staff. It is bleak and grubby. What if I were to point out to the management that this seemed to me to be degrading and discriminatory, and that I would be looking for a hotel in which janitorial staff and guests used the same entrance? Better yet, what if I asked management whether janitorial staff at this hotel were prevented from unionizing and what they were paid, and suggested that the organization sponsoring the annual meeting I was attending would—in the future—only use hotels in which janitorial staff were permitted to unionize and were paid a living wage with good benefits.[98] I would be helping to "change the story" of who holds worth and has rights, on a more public or social systemic level.

This link between inner personal "story" and societal "story" is important. We are subject not only to our inner stories; we are assailed also by titanic social forces seducing us to remain true to the narrative that underwrites the old economy. The advertising industry feeds my granddaughter the story that she will be happier if she owns a shirt with a Disney character on the front. We are subject to public discourse that refers to speculative money traders whose moves have just raised food costs in hungry countries as "good investors." We are bombarded with language that blithely heralds growth as a good without acknowledging the damages that the growth may have done. Intensive corporate investment in marketing sucks us like a magnet into the old story.

Therefore, and here is the beauty: in "changing the story" we are utterly dependent on our being as a "we," not an "I." I alone cannot change the story for myself, my grandchildren, or my society. Changing the story is a collective communal dance of the we. It draws upon a rich array of gifts and talents. Let us touch on a few of them.

Artists—musicians, poets, visual artists, creative writers, performing artists on the streets and in performance halls—are key in telling a new economic story. Street muralists show the strength and goodness of the janitor in my illustration above. A creative writer speaks of "the resplendent blackness we call night."[99] The climate justice organization, 350.org writes, "As we envision [the] future, art plays a vital role in reshaping our collective imagination."[100] Describing a number of networks through which art is changing the narrative and bringing new social structures into being, the sociologist Barbara Adams writes,

> *Creativity and imagination are essential and active capacities in world- and future-making.... Through deconstructing and reconstructing the dominant narrative, these artworks explore how we might imagine more expansive alternatives and possibilities.... Artistic practice ... makes room for things in the public imagination that would otherwise seem too remote or amorphous. This anticipatory quality proposes a way of prototyping, of bringing new social and political forms into being.*[101]

Librarians, teachers, and religious leaders are powerful story changers. Children's picture books may defy the myth of white superiority and enable children to see and internalize racial equity. Theologians and worship leaders design Earth-honoring worship and lead sacred rituals to protest exploitation of workers

Change the Story

and of rivers. Recall the story of Guatemalan villagers who believed a new story about themselves and their worth after learning to read by reading the Gospels.

CEOs and boards of directors who decide to level the pay scales are publicly rewriting the story that some people are worth more than others. While visiting a seminary in India over ten years ago, I was thrilled to learn that they paid everyone (from janitors to president) the same salary.

Public institutions changing their purchasing practices can change the economic story. (Recall the "building the new" and the call for government purchasing to use local worker-owned business.) Wealthy people who publicly work toward higher taxes for wealthy people are shifting the narrative that says one should accumulate as much wealth as possible. (My elderly father once shouted into the phone in response to a political caller who had said "Support this candidate because she will lower your taxes." My father, fed up with the narrative behind that appeal, barked into the phone, "Listen, I will support him if he works to install an income tax in this state!") Changing the story is many splendored and hope giving. This has been but a tiny glimpse of the possible.

Notice now the links between various fingers on the hands of change. Changing the story enables and is enabled by personal lifestyle changes ("live lightly"). When my student, for her project, moved her small savings from a large mainstream investment firm to socially and ecologically responsible funds ("live lightly" and "move the money"), she took a step in disbelieving the story that the purpose of money was only to make more money. She inhabited the story that her money also had the purpose of building a better world. When she made that move public through letters to her congregation and denomination, she spread that changed story. And that lifestyle change contributed to "building the new" in the form of alternative finance.

Fruitful indeed is the overlap between "changing the story," "changing the rules," and "building the bigger we." Imagine you and your companions organizing parents, teachers, and students to convince the school board to "change the rules" about acquisition of food for the school cafeteria. The new policy might call for buying locally or regionally grown produce, and using supply chains that do not exploit farmworkers. In this move, you begin publicly to "change the story" of the purpose of economic activity. And you have "built the bigger we" and "resisted the wrong" in the process.

Sacred Journey Journal:
Practicing This Healing Medicine

We have trekked through dense terrain, exploring the power of narrative to shape how we live, the historical development of the mainstream economic narrative, key story lines in it, and changing that story.

Briefly review these pages, noting things that you find particularly (1) jarring or disturbing, (2) resonant with your experience, and (3) hope-giving or energizing. Sit for some minutes with what you have identified. Why did it disturb you? In what sense did it resonate with your experience? What about it enlivened hope or energy?

Then choose one part of the overall economic story that you would like to practice changing. It might be one of the thirteen "key lines in the narrative shaping economic life today," or one of the five assumptions regarding freedom. It might be something else. Over the next week, practice the three steps identified above that are entailed in "changing the story."

> Step 1: Where do you see this assumption or story line at play, consciously or not, in you or in others?
> Step 2: What damage does it do?
> Step 3: What could you DO to enact a different story? Now actually do one of these things! How do you feel? What risks does it require you to take? Is there someone you could enlist to support you in this step?

Finally, congratulate yourself for this effort! Regardless of how it goes, honor your courage to take on changing the story.

Resources for Digging Deeper

See the toolkit for this book on the series' website at: https://buildingamoraleconomy.org/.

CHAPTER SEVENTEEN

Fingers on the Hands of Healing:
Drink the Spirit's Courage

> The Hebrew word for Spirit might well be translated as "bold undaunted courage."
> —Martin Luther[1]

> Our vision nurtures our cultures, souls and spirits through song and ceremony, through practice and play.
> —Movement Generation[2]

The Essence

Receiving and sharing food for the journey—spiritual sustenance that cultivates moral-spiritual power, courage, hope, and imagination for the journey toward life-giving economies.

Fuller Description

The most potent configuration of forces ever convened in human history is lined up against the transition to truly equitable, ecological, and democratic economies. These forces include the speculative finance industry and its commitment to maximizing short-term profit despite the costs, fossil fuel industries bent on unfettered extraction and transport of fossil fuels, related high-carbon emitting industries such as plastics and industrial meat production, the myths of white supremacy and American exceptionalism, and the captivity of democratic political processes to big money. A formidable array of forces!

To stand up to these forces we must be well fed with moral, spiritual, and material sustenance. To learn to think and live differently, to rewrite our formative stories, to resist the wrong, to rewire our brains, to change the rules and build new forms of business, finance, energy, and agriculture—for this, we ordinary people who live in extraordinary times, are called to be ordinary but extraordinary heroes/sheroes. As adults and young adults alive at this momentous moment in history, we are called to a reorientation of life that will save life, and that leads through both perils and joys. Wherein lies the courage that we need? Not without reason have we referred to economic life as spiritual practice. Moral-spiritual power for crafting life-giving economies may be fed by the Spirit.

Ancient wisdom claims that human earthlings may be nourished by the sacred Source of all that is, the intimate Mystery whom some call God or Spirit. Some wisdom traditions hold that this Spirit is flowing and pouring through all things, that it infuses us with its life-sustaining power if only we will receive it. Moreover, this Energy or indwelling Spirit fosters in humans the capacity to love with a love that seeks justice and honors Earth.

Peoples and people throughout time have named and understood this Spirit differently. Gandhi referred to it as

> *an indefinable mysterious power that pervades everything, I feel it though I do not see it. It is this unseen power which makes itself felt and yet defies all proof. . . . There is . . . a living power that is changeless, that holds all together, that creates, dissolves and recreates. That informing power of spirit is God. . . . I see [this power] as purely benevolent, for I can see that in the midst of death life persists, in the midst of untruth truth persists, in the midst of darkness light persists. Hence I gather that God is life, truth, light . . . is love.*

Gandhi held that God's presence made ahimsa [the power of nonviolent love] possible.[3]

The ancient Hebrews called this Spirit the *ruach* of God. The Hebrew Bible is rife with witness to the *ruach* as a force emanating from God or the force of Godself. It reaches into the depths of people and awakens power (or *is* power) for crafting relationships that cohere with God's purpose of life in its fullness for all. These relationships may be interpersonal, societal, between humans and Earth, or between God and God's creation.[4] Sixteenth-century reformer Martin Luther once said that the Hebrew word for Spirit might well be translated as "bold undaunted courage."[5] Many throughout the ages attest to this Spirit and its courage-building power.

In the work of building more equitable, compassionate, and Earth-honoring ways of living together in this planetary garden, we work in partnership with, in Gandhi's words, a "mysterious power that pervades everything." We are offered courage, hope, and strength—and spiritual power—by the Sacred Spirit that is coursing throughout the created world. We not only are *beckoned* to join with this Spirit in its healing and liberating movement, but also are *nourished* by it for that very purpose.

Drink the Spirit's Courage

But how? How do twenty-first-century people receive Sacred Spirit as "bold undaunted courage" and moral agency? How especially are we to receive it in the face of ecological and economic devastation that is unprecedented in history—a moral crisis that dashes hope, courage, and moral-spiritual agency with torrential force?

People and peoples hear and are fed by the Spirit coming to them/us in an array of channels. Art, including music, visual arts, poetry and other literary arts, and performing arts, is one such channel. So too are the other-than-human things of Earth—the mountains, rivers, trees, winds, flora, and fauna—media of Spirit. Yet another channel is the great religious traditions and their scriptures, moral teachings, rituals, prescribed lifeways, and prayer or contemplative practices that bring people into awareness of the ever-present Spirit and then toss them back into the world to live according to that Spirit. Some people receive or hear the Spirit through relationships with other human beings. Of course, these four channels overlap. For example, religion at its best includes art, encounter with Earth, and relationships with other people. Yet they also may remain distinct. All four of these channels of the Spirit are present in my life, and are deeply present in the tradition that nurtured me—Christianity rooted in Judaism.

My strong hunch is that we will heal our diseased economy—our malformed relationships with Earth and one another—only if we drink deeply from varied spiritual sources of courage and wisdom, allowing them to deepen and enliven the knowledge that each source would bring alone. Robin Wall Kimmerer in *Braiding Sweetgrass* demonstrates this, as she brings together "Indigenous wisdom, scientific knowledge, and the teachings of plants." Let us glimpse the four sources or channels that we have named: art, human relationships, Earth's other-than-human creatures and elements, and religious traditions.

Art

The Argentine singer Mercedes Sosa, known also as *La Negra*, was loved by many throughout Latin America and elsewhere for expressing people's struggles for dignity, hope, and freedom during years of brutal military regimes in her country and others. The dictatorship and its supporters feared, arrested, and imprisoned her, menaced her with death threats, and banned her from her country. Why was she beloved by people and feared by the repressive regime? Why would the regime arrest her and her entire audience of students at a performance in 1979? "Poets and artists are silenced," writes Hebrew Bible scholar Walter Brueggemann, "because they reveal too much of what must remain hidden."[6] Known as "voice of the voiceless ones," Sosa's art revealed to the world what the regime needed to hide: the horror and suffering of repression, and the reality of people's courageous resistance. This is a spiritual power of art.

Brueggemann gives a second insight into spiritual power within art. Regarding "poets and artists," he writes, "The ones who minister to the imagination, who enable people to see the world differently and to live now in the world they see are fatally dangerous to the establishment."[7] Sosa enabled people to see life emerging from death (resurrection) where that life was not apparent, to see love for life where life was terrifyingly bleak, to see resilient resistance where death squads sought to quell it with terror and torture.

And yes, this power of art is so threatening to oppressive forces that art may be "a dangerous occupation."[8] Some, such as Chile's Victor Jara, another singer of that time who also "inspired opponents of South America's brutal military regimes," was tortured and finally shot to death by Pinochet's soldiers after the 1973 military coup (supported by the US) in Chile. Others, poet Pablo Neruda among them, were exiled. The Ukrainian poet Irina Ratushinskaya was sentenced to seven years in a Soviet labor camp, including one in solitary confinement in an unheated cell during the Soviet winter, for writing and circulating her poems. She was convicted for "agitation carried on for the purpose of subverting or weakening the Soviet regime." *"Crime: poet" was written in the prison's record of her.*[9] Her "subversive" poems had centered on Christian theology, love, and artistic creation.

At a meeting of a small team called together to advise the World Council of Churches and other ecumenical organizations regarding their advocacy toward a New International Financial and Economic Architecture, Cuban theologian Dora Arce-Valentin ended her morning meditation with these words: "Part of our resilience as Latin American countries comes from the ways in which we have collected and hold our historical memories through art, music, poetry, literature." The year was 2022, thirteen years after Sosa's death. Valentine went on to play Sosa's powerful rendition of the resistance song "As the Cicada," calling it a prayer, a hymn in "our secular hymnbook full of laments and hope," and "a song of resurrection, a testimony to life in the face of death." A portion of this "hymn's" words are these:

So many times they killed me,
so many times I died
however I'm here
resurrecting...
and I kept singing.
So many times they erased me
so many disappeared...
and I kept on singing
Singing in the sun like the cicada
after a year underground.

The Spirit may speak to us bringing "bold undaunted courage," hope, insight, wisdom, and potent imagination through art. The sociologist Barbara Adams argues that *"our capacity to imagine, act, and create a world that is different from the one in which we are located, can be nurtured through artistic means."* Artists, she explains, may "play a principal role in the ability of society to inaugurate new forms of itself."[10] Adams could be describing one central role of God's Spirit according to biblical texts!

Could it be that the Spirit uses art and artists to help human creatures imagine and live into "new social and political forms into being," including the building blocks of the new economy?[11] Might it be that music can "utter in notes"[12] what we need to perceive in order to reorient our lives? Here we have glimpsed the role of artists in social transformation, and the invitation to receive insight, hope, wisdom, and courage through music, poetry, and other forms of art.

Human Relationships

Mercedes Sosa goes on to sing,

> *So many nights you will spend*
> *desperate*
> *at the time of the shipwreck*
> *and the darkness . . .*
> *someone will rescue you*
> *to keep on singing.*

"Someone will rescue you to keep on singing." In my experience, the Spirit bolsters hope, confidence, joy, and courage through trusted relationships with other people. The means are infinite. Note just one: for me, a powerful spiritual practice is attuning myself to the subtle but virulent inner voice that can sabotage my commitment to work for societal healing. I speak here of internal voices that lure me off course, sucking me toward giving up. They whisper in my ear, hovering just below my consciousness. I am painfully aware of two such voices. One murmurs, "The changes required are too complex to grasp and therefore too complex to address." The second chimes in, "What I do cannot really make a difference in changing the economy; it is entrenched and I have too little power. On a societal level, things will go on as they are despite whatever I try to do, so I will restrict my efforts to the micro level where I can make a difference—by providing direct aid to people who are suffering."

Many—perhaps most of us—hear these or similar voices. Their impact is cruel and evil. They seduce people to continue living in ways (that is, enacting economic principles, policies, and practices) that kill people around the globe and destroy Earth's life systems. Not only cruel and evil, the impact also is tragic, for living in such ways violates the dearest and deepest values of many people who, nevertheless, continue in these lifeways—values such as compassion for the suffering and enabling one's children to have a future.

However, "confessing" these voices to trusted companions helps me to refute them. Brené Brown in her work on shame resilience says as much. Knowing that we are not doing what we should do can be paralyzing. However, she explains, talking about this in trustworthy relationships helps to free us from that paralysis. This is just one of countless ways in which relationships with trusted others may nourish moral-spiritual power. In your life experience, how have relationships helped your moral-spiritual power to grow?

Earth and Its Creatures and Elements

I emerged onto the street bleak, defeated, sapped of spirit. And then... birdsong. The pure lilt of a tiny creature entered my ear, sped to my heart, and awakened my spirit, lifting it from the pit where it had lodged. I laughed.

How is it that the simple song of a bird, the brush of breeze on skin, the sight of bud emerging from winter's stark stem may so restore one's spirit? How is it that people have turned to the small wild plants in a deserted urban lot, the rivers, the tree on the corner or in the forest to renew their spirits?

Is it because we, it turns out, are built of water, Earth, and air? The molecules that construct us are the molecules that also construct the soil, wind, and waters. When we see, touch, smell, hear, or taste the elements and creatures of Earth, we are present with our kin. Is this a part of why attuning to their presence and beauty feeds our souls?

Or is it because, as we glimpsed in "changing the story," the elements and creatures are beings, have agency, and the Spirit speaks through them? We recall the wisdom of some Indigenous peoples of Turtle Island (named North America by its colonizers) who are taught, "land and all its elements have agency by virtue of their very life energy in a way that they do not in Western culture."[13] The poet, activist, and biblical scholar Anne Elvey suggests that Earth may be "enacting a kind of neighbour love to humans and other animals" by sustaining our lives.[14] Does that love move our hearts in ways that we do not recognize?

Or is it Earth's resilience that inspires us? Tiny shoots break through concrete. Spring appears, despite the fiercest winter. Mt. St. Helens's catastrophic eruption in 1980 "destroyed all organic matter and living organisms as it moved through forested areas."[15] Triggering the "largest subaerial (on-land) landslide in Earth's recorded history," the blast sent the mountain's north face sliding away.[16] I recall hearing that forests might never return to that volcanic wasteland. Yet, that once lifeless landscape now is home to young red alder, Douglas fir, hemlock, and all sorts of green living things. It turns out that wind played a vital role; spiders,

Drink the Spirit's Courage

insects, and seeds rode its waves into the blast zone. Resurrection seems to be Earth's song. Does living with that unfailing melody build courage for resilience into our blood and bones?

Or is it simply the power of beauty to restore the weary soul? How is it that Earth may be allowing you to drink the Spirit's courage?

Religion/Faith

Religion and faith are the focus of the final chapters. In them we probe this source of spiritual sustenance for reshaping economic life. Here, let us note simply that while religion has wielded vast power for terror and brutality throughout history, religion also has provided boundless moral and spiritual energy for history's most liberative and noble movements. It lies with people of religious traditions to recognize and reckon with both, what I call the graced and disgraced aspects of religions. We move momentarily to do so in chapters 18 and 19, focusing on the role that religious faith may have in nourishing the great transition from economies that eat away at life to economies that nourish it. The beautiful challenge for people within a religious tradition is to plumb its depths for the spiritual and moral fire that will energize and encourage people for this work, and then offer these resources to the broader public.

Fascinating questions will arise as we explore this role of religion: "How," in the words of Paul Tillich, "does spiritual power work, how is it related to physical and psychological power?"[17] How is it related to liberation from economic systems that abuse some people to enrich others? How is it that religion can feed and water efforts to build more compassionate and just communities when doing this is fraught with apparently insurmountable obstacles? What are the particular gifts that religion brings to economic-ecological transformation? How might religious wisdoms collaborate with other forms of wisdom such as the natural sciences, the arts, the social sciences, other-than-human voices of Earth, and more?

May this brief foray into four sources of moral-spiritual courage and power—art, human relationships, Earth, and religion/faith—entice you to explore them further. More importantly, may you and your companions in the healing journey dig around to cultivate where you experience the Spirit nurturing your power for healing economic life.

Life-Giving Links

This finger on the hands of healing change—drinking the Spirit's courage—becomes nourishment for enacting the other nine. And they may bring with them the experience of spiritual nurture through art, relationships, Earth, or religion. "Changing the story," for instance, may involve *art* or *religious* rituals that, in turn, feed the spirit. "Building the new" or "changing the rules" may generate human *relationships* that feed the spirit. Heading to the seacoast to "resist the wrong" in a protest to prevent its sale to a hotel chain may bring spiritual sustenance from sound and sight of the waves (*Earth*).

Sacred Journey Journal: Practicing This Healing Medicine

Allow yourself to sit or to walk slowly in a quiet place. If you choose to sit and if you are one whose reflection is aided by using your hands, then feel free to do so in ways that fit for you—perhaps by doodling, coloring, knitting, molding clay. You might allow your eyes to close. Reflect back on your life. What is one time in which you received courage or other spiritual nurture from an art form? From Earth? Through religious practice? Through a relationship? Dwell with one of these. What insight do you gain that might guide you for the future?

Resources for Digging Deeper

See the toolkit for this book on the series' website at: https://buildingamoraleconomy.org/.

IV

Religious Roots
of a Moral Economy

CHAPTER EIGHTEEN

Religious Roots of a Moral Economy

Jesus, a Brown-skinned Jew who led a moral revolution ... constantly was disrupting systems of empire.

—Rev. Terri Hord Owens[1]

Religion may be a seedbed of a new economy.

—Marjorie Kelly[2]

The day will come when humanity, after harnessing the energies of space, winds, water, and gravity, will harness the energies of love—and on that day humans, for the second time in the history of the world, will have discovered fire.

—Pierre Teilhard de Chardin[3]

Climate change is fundamentally a religious and spiritual issue. Religion therefore has a vital role to play.

—Ecumenical Patriarch Bartholomew[4]

The lack of thinking in economic terms is fatal to a sense of reality, and every Christian is under orders to learn how to think in these terms.

—Vida Scudder[5]

To believe in God is to believe in the possibility of possibilities, that the world can be fundamentally different, that the world can be transformed, that we can be part of that transformation.

—Rabbi Michael Lerner[6]

A young woman pastor moves from island to island, from community to community, in a province of more than one thousand islands. She is strong, courageous, tenacious, creative. Pastor Hana (name changed) works with Indigenous people. They are fighting for human rights amid exploitative mining practices and the pernicious onslaught of palm oil plantations that destroy traditional food sources. Her maternal grandmother was a member of the Eri—one of Indonesia's Indigenous Peoples. "Do you fear retaliation from the powers that be who want the mining and plantations to continue?" I asked. She looked at me, paused, and responded, "Sometimes."

* * *

Late one night, a motley crowd circled in a dancing spiral, faces aglow, a few tiny children, a number of elders, a rabbi in their midst, his face filled with joy and awe. It was Yom Kippur. The haunting beauty of the cello's Kol Nidre echoed yet in our hearts. The ritual of repentance had called us to realign our lives, to return to the God of justice and compassion, to turn away from the structural sin woven into our lives that causes untold suffering.

* * *

A Muslim student—a bright finance major in his senior year—was offered several lucrative positions in banks and investment firms. He used his moral deliberation paper in my religious ethics course to discern whether he could accept these positions, given that his faith held that usury was morally unacceptable. The student concluded that he could not! This decision was grounded specifically in his Muslim faith. He graduated and became a leader of an interfaith movement focused on issues of social well-being.

* * *

The depth of winter in the Midwest. Cold. You could see your breath. A class of seminary students clustered around a large snag (a dead log) in the woods, eyes trained on a student's face peering out from within the log. He was preaching! Yes, this was a course in worship leadership. The professor was helping these students reclaim an ancient Christian teaching (long obscured by many parts of the church) that God speaks from within the winds, waters, trees, and creatures. The "first book of revelation" was not the Bible; it was creation. How would we treat this Earth, Professor Dahill challenged the students, if we truly believed that God dwells within (but not only within) Earth?

* * *

His eyes looked older than his face as he spoke of the tribal people's courage and years of perseverance in trying to save their homes and culture. Bauxite mines in southern Orissa, one of the poorest regions of India, were forcing tribal people off the lands that had sustained them for centuries and into urban destitution.[7] People by the thousands were losing their homes, villages, sacred lands, communities, livelihoods, and culture. For some, these losses were worse than death. Their resistance was tenacious, courageous. Some had been killed by the repression that met their efforts to organize opposition to the mining operations.

This Indian church leader spoke too of allies in the Global North, "swimming upstream" to counter this injustice, guided by their contacts among the Indian tribal people. Together with several organizations, he was assisting the people in their appeals to churches in the mining companies' home countries. The hope was that these churches would urge the companies to cease the mining operations and urge their governments to divest from those companies. The church of Norway and the Norwegian government were the first to respond. Following an extensive study by its ethics council, Norway's pension fund (the world's second-largest sovereign wealth fund) sold $13.2 million US dollars' worth of shares in Vedanta Resources, a British mining company working in Orissa, due to the "systematic" environmental and human rights failures including "forced relocation" of indigenous tribes.

Bauxite is used to make aluminum. As I listened to his story, my mind crept to my home and the many products in it that are made with aluminum—food and beverage cans, construction materials, electronics, car parts. Did that bauxite come from Orissa? Which of India's urban poor had been forced into the city by mines that provide the aluminum in my life? Could I move my church (on a national level) to divest—"move the money"—from supporting that mining?

* * *

"Nuns and nones? What on earth is that?" I wondered, having spent much of my life in the "none zone," the part of the US where most people, when asked about their religious identity, reply "none." One of the nuns explained: a group of nuns and nones—sisters and seekers— came together in 2016 to explore their hunger for community and belonging, justice and spirituality, and ways to respond to the world's raging needs. Community groups were born, a national network took shape, and a shared commitment to the long-term work of spiritually rooted repair and renewal emerged. A scant six years later, the Nuns & Nones collective launched the Land Justice Project and began to incubate an experimental, multireligious, multiracial community, the Covenantal Community. "What," I asked, "do you mean by land justice?" The nun paused and then went on. Land justice, I learned, is a way to address centuries of racial injustice in land ownership and use. Land justice moves lands into Indigenous land trusts, Black food sovereignty efforts, regenerative farming cooperatives, habitat restoration, affordable housing solutions, and more. "Religious communities," say the Nones and Nuns, "can be the much-needed catalyst... for these possibilities to flourish."[8]

* * *

One Day in 1982—during the reign of terror in Guatemala led by General Efraín Ríos Montt—a small market town north of Chichicastenango, Guatemala, was taken over by the army. The villagers were assembled and told that five of their community leaders were "subversives" whom their relatives must kill that very night or the army would raze the village and its neighboring villages.

The army withdrew, and the villagers discussed the brutal choice, unanimously concluding "we don't do it." The community leaders (catechists, health workers, cooperative organizers) were loved and valued for their work, for the instruction they had given to promote cooperatives, and for their instruction on the Bible. But such consciousness raising was subversive in the military's view because it helped to awaken the Indigenous masses, who are a majority of Guatemala's population. Teaching Indigenous communities to read and write could be punishable by death, as demonstrated by the murders of fifteen priests and a nun who were involved in literacy and leadership training programs for Mayans. *The Bible was, of all books, the most subversive because it taught that everyone was equal in the sight of God—hence the ferocious persecution of the catechists who traveled from village to village, leading people in Bible study and theological reflection, often teaching literacy by reading the Bible.* Health books were also subversive because they gave people a way to claim their own destiny and be less dependent. Promoting cooperatives was subversive because it taught people to work together for the good of the community.

The villagers had refused to do the deed, but the five community leaders insisted that they must: "It is better for us to die than for thousands to die." At 4:00 a.m. a weeping procession, led by the community leaders, arrived at the cemetery. Graves were dug, the people formed a circle around the kneeling men, and relatives of the five drew their machetes. Many could not watch the scene; some fainted as the blades fell, and the executioners' tears mingled with the blood of their leaders. The bodies were wrapped in plastic and buried. The villagers returned home in silence.

The next day the army captain was informed that his orders had been carried out. Another "source of subversion" had been eliminated. Or had it? The army's policy failed to work in that village and elsewhere in the Quiché area of Guatemala because the people honored such martyrdom."[9]

For these people and communities, religious faith was key to transformative action in the world.

I left the church years ago. Stories of faith like these had not been present in my life. Forefront in my mind was Christianity's role in atrocities—colonization and the genocide of Indigenous peoples, the enslavement of African people, Nazism, homophobia, US imperialism, and so much more. I was outraged at the church's role in these. That a religion born to tell the story of a loving God could underwrite such cruelty seemed unthinkably wrong. I must, I thought, either deny these realities or leave the church. I left.

A sequence of experiences and people brought me back. There is, I realized, another option instead of denial or departure from religion. That option is a different lens through which to view religion and its role in the world.

It may be that you—like me at that point—see in religion primarily the evil that it has done. Or, perhaps, you see religion as singularly a force for good. You may, on the other hand, dismiss religion as irrelevant, outdated, or too ambiguous. Or perchance you see it as only a matter of personal enlightenment or salvation, not pertinent to social and ecological realities. If any of these describes you, then I invite you to try a different way of viewing religion.

Imagine that there truly is a Sacred Mystery, a force of profound goodness, beauty, truth, healing, liberation, life abundant. It flows and pours through all things and is above, below, and beyond all things. A force that continuously creates and seeks to mend the world, an energy that is beyond human words, but that words attempt to name, calling it God, *Allah*, *Elohim*, YHWH, the Spirit, the Sacred, the Divine, a Higher Power, Ultimate Reality, the Light, the "Transformative Power of the Universe."[10] It is both intimately present and a vast Mystery. It imbues all and embraces all. We human creatures can only glimpse the fullness and radiant goodness of this Force and can only begin to describe it. Within the limited schema of human language, perhaps "love" in the fullest sense of love's intimate mystery comes closest.

I understand this Sacred Love as present with and for us (and all of creation) regardless of what we say, do, think, feel, experience, or fail to do. It will not leave us, regardless of any failure on our part or evil that we do. This Sacred Force ultimately will bring all to fullness of life in its beauty and goodness. Finally, this Reality hungers for human creatures (and perhaps all of creation) to awaken to its Presence, rejoice in it, give thanks for it, trust it, swim in its flow, be fed by it, and allow it to work in us to shape us, to heal, and to liberate the world. These convictions reflect my understanding of the heart of Christianity and Judaism.[11] They are present also in other religious/spiritual traditions.

Let us further imagine that the world's long-standing religious traditions arose, in part, from human longing to know, experience, listen to, understand, be in relationship with, and be guided by this Sacred Force. Religious thirst seeks to align life with the ways of this Love. Religious faith traditions are—in a sense—different wells that draw energy from an ever-flowing River. They are varied wells to this great Source of Life, the Sacred Mystery. Each religion is incomplete. Each brings different gifts. Religious and spiritual traditions at their best enable people to grasp, experience, pass on, and align their lives with this Sacred Reality.

Yet these efforts are human and, therefore, inevitably fallible and incomplete. Religious and spiritual traditions are led astray, sidetracked. At times they even distort and betray the very good they seek to know and pass on. In many instances, that betrayal is more heinous than words can describe. The persecution of Jews by Christians and the role of the church in justifying and enabling the enslavement of African people and the genocide of Indigenous people around the world reveal how religious belief can lead to human atrocity. Accounting for that heritage of betrayal—the "dis-graced" aspects of a religion—is vitally important. Ignoring it invites repetition and precludes reparations. Being faithful to a religious tradition necessarily includes being critical of where it has gone wrong. I have done so in countless publications, presentations, and teaching, and will continue to do so. That is not the purpose in this chapter, however.

Religion's betrayal of the good is only half of the story. I did not realize that reality when I left religion behind in my youth. There is another truth, the "graced" aspects of a religion, and they include the roles that religious traditions have played in movements to resist social atrocities and to liberate and heal the Earth community from all that thwarts well-being.[12] Religions—in their graced aspects—equip us to drink from the ultimate Source of compassion and communion. They enable us to embody and enact the great Spirit. In the current context, spirituality and religion may be a fountain of power from which we can forge life-giving economies, power for transforming predatory economic life.

Just as it would be deadly and dangerous to ignore the horrors that religion has rendered, it would be equally devastating to forego the other half of the story. Why? If religious traditions can evoke and nourish our liberating and healing capacities, to ignore religion as such would be to reject life-saving power that we desperately need.

This is crucial: *If religions can cultivate moral-spiritual power for the good, then it is up to people within them to plumb their depths for the wisdom and courage to reverse our deadly dash into climate disaster and further economic violence.* This is a matter of life and death.

This chapter lays the groundwork for that sacred work. How might spirituality or religious faith foment moral-spiritual power to reverse the torrential forces of economic violence and climate crisis unleashed by extractive, exploitative economic life? We are seeking moral-spiritual power in alignment with and in-spired (breathed into) by the Sacred Force that many call God. First, a word about the word *religion* is needed.

Religion—a Confusing Term[13]

Religion is a problematic word! It is used for and means many different things. Religion may signify the institutionally sanctioned doctrines, ways of worshipping, rules, and boundaries that humans have constructed to define a particular religious quest (e.g., Judaism, Christianity, Islam, Buddhism, or Hinduism). That definition is not the one we use to talk about religion in this book and this series.

Rather, by religion, I reference the life-giving streams that orient (and reorient) us into closer alignment with the Spirit. Religious practices in this sense help enable us to hear and heed that Sacred Source. They sustain us through pain, loss, grief, and confusion. Religions are dynamic living traditions with historically rooted "communities" (many of which span continents, cultures, and centuries), grounding stories, *evolving* beliefs and practices, and institutional structures. They include Judaism, Christianity, Islam, Buddhism, Hinduism, and others.

The word *communities* in this understanding of religion is key. One Latin root of "religion," *religare*, means to "reconnect." Religion reconnects us to communities that span time, space, and culture. Religion situates human beings among ancient and evolving communities of communities. Religious tradition puts Jews, for example, into community with the enslaved Hebrew people liberated by God from the Pharaoh and into community with the ancient Hebrew prophets. Christianity places Christian-identified people into community with these same Hebrew ancestors and with our predecessors from the first and second centuries. We may ask them for their wisdom. I have asked these ancestors, "What gave you the courage to risk death in order to be faithful to God?" "How did baptism enable you to shift your allegiance from the emperor to God, especially knowing it could mean torture and death?"

Another word in this description of religion is crucial. We said *evolving* beliefs and practices. "Religion" is rooted also in the Latin *relegere* (to reread). Religion, in its truest sense, is not about repeating and accepting beliefs and practices as if they were cast in concrete. It is about "creatively reinterpreting and remaking inherited traditions—scriptures, ideas, beliefs, practices, and institutions—in light of new" situations.[14] What a difference that makes, as we will see!

Finally, many people, especially Christians, see religion primarily as a set of beliefs: one must believe certain things to be saved. That understanding is a distortion of the concept of religion, including Christianity. Religions are primarily practiced relationships of trust and love—relationships among people, between people and the Ultimate, and with all of creation.[15] The Jesus movement, for example, was led by a faithful Jew calling people into a trusting relationship with the living God and calling people to live in ways that practiced the reign of that God on Earth. Judaism, Islam, the Dharmic traditions, and Indigenous traditions likewise call people to practice certain ways of life. If you have seen religious faith primarily as a matter of believing what is correct or true, I invite you to consider this broader understanding and its potential power for the good.

In this book, we use the terms *religions, religious traditions, faith traditions*, and *spiritual traditions* interchangeably. Of course, they can also be used distinctly. But for our purposes, they similarly reflect the meaning described above.[16]

In describing religions in this way, I make two critical assumptions. First, I do not elevate one religious or spiritual tradition over the others. Earth's varied faith traditions have distinct and often overlapping gifts. All are needed. It is impossible in the span of one chapter to cover the unique gifts offered by each religious or spiritual framework for building a moral economy. I primarily use Christianity to illustrate religion's roles because it is the only tradition that I know well. I hope that readers situated in other religious traditions will explore the powers and gifts offered by your own.

Second, I presuppose that religion's offerings bear full fruit only when religion is held in close dialogue and collaboration with secular bodies of knowledge, including the natural sciences, the behavioral sciences, agricultural wisdom, communications expertise, social theory, legal expertise, philosophy, educational theory, health care knowledge, and the arts. The time has come for religious and secular wisdoms to sing together!

A Return to the Love Story

It would be wise to reread "An Astounding Love Story," the section at the end of chapter 1 and the "Religion for Now" section toward the end of chapter 3. This current chapter builds on those foundations.

Here we pursue more fully the questions of where we find the strength, vision, courage, raw grit, and humor to challenge fiercely powerful forces lined up to keep predatory economies in place.[17] Where do we—everyday people—find moral and spiritual resources to transform them into economies for life, a transition "as awesome as the transitions from hunting and gathering to agriculture eleven thousand years ago and from agriculture to industry a few hundred years ago"?[18] How shall we hold steady to visions of the good that seem unattainable? How dare we stare into the abyss—the horrors of climate crisis and the ravaging of lives on the underside of our economies—and not be consumed?

As human beings, we have this heroic capacity. The Spirit nourishes it in us, and that nourishment comes in many ways. In chapter 17, we considered four sources: art, community, Earth, religion. This chapter focuses on the last of these—the world's living religious traditions.

To Accept Love's Offer

The Sacred Mystery offers us ways of living that build life in its fullness for all, ways of structuring life together that heal. Ours is to hear and heed the offering, accepting the invitation. Let us see this as accepting "Love's offer."[19]

The people you met at this chapter's outset—the Muslim finance major, the Guatemalan *celebradores de la palabra*, the Indonesian pastor, the Nuns and Nones, and the others—were accepting Love's offer. Not perfectly of course, nor completely, but in humanly imperfect ways.

Accepting Love's offer includes accepting ourselves as beloved. In Christian traditions, this means trusting the utterly unstoppable love of the reality we call God, and it means coming authentically to love ourselves. This too we will not do fully or perfectly, but we can grow in this direction.

Never before in human history have the stakes been so high in accepting Love's offer. If religious traditions exist to understand, even slightly, how to live together in ways that cohere with the Spirit, and to empower people to follow those ways, then never before has it mattered so much for people within religious traditions (and people who do not identify as religious, but are moved by the values of religious traditions) to plumb their depths.

Will we accept Love's offer? Let us say yes.

How? If Love's offer includes the moral-spiritual wisdom, courage, and sacred community to forge life-giving economic lives, how do we go about accepting this offer? In the coming pages, we will explore that question together and grow in capacity to accept Love's offer.

Be assured: my aim is not to convince you to adopt any particular religion or spirituality. Rather, I ask you to recognize that all of Earth's wisdom traditions—including the sciences, the healing arts, religion, and more—must bring their gifts to the table for the great work of building economies that enable life to flourish. Religions have many treasures to offer. Let the exploration begin.

What Can Religious Faith and Spirituality Bring to Building a Moral Economy?

What roles can religion play in building a moral economy? What do human beings—as spiritual beings—bring to this movement?

Karen Armstrong in *The Great Transformation* argues that the enduring faiths that emerged between 900 and 200 BCE—Hinduism, Buddhism, Confucianism, Judaism—as well as Judaism's offsprings, Christianity and Islam, arose to reshape what it meant to be human and to reorient human life towards the empathy, compassion, justice, sacred presence, and generosity enabled by surrendering the ego:

> *Their objective was to create an entirely different kind of human being. All the sages preached a spirituality of empathy and compassion; they insisted that people must abandon their egotism and greed, their violence and unkindness.... As far as the Axial sages were concerned, respect for the sacred rights of all beings—not orthodox belief—was religion. If people behaved with kindness and generosity to their fellows, they could save the world.*[20]

Walter Brueggemann, one of the most significant Hebrew Bible scholars of the twentieth and early twenty-first centuries, demonstrates similarly that the God revealed in the Bible directed people to organize their societies in ways that built economic justice. Heeding this God today, he says, "requires advocacy for polity and practice that are pro-neighbor, anti-predation, and anti-accumulation."[21] To separate the God of the Bible from practices of equity is "a key distortion of biblical faith."[22]

Rabbi Michael Lerner, in the same vein, writes that Judaism inaugurated a world-shaking religious claim. It was that God was not simply a divine power, but also "a moral force that rejected the inevitability of oppression and that demanded and made possible world transformation."[23]

These three renowned scholars—Armstrong, Brueggemann, and Lerner—all similarly conclude that these initial roots point to religion as a possible seedbed of resistance to predatory economies, and a source of nourishment for building life-giving alternatives.[24]

This fascinating understanding of religions' profound relevance for today is voiced also by others. Theologians Ulrich Duchrow and Franz Hinkelammert argue convincingly that the "prophecy of Ancient Israel and Torah, Buddhism, the Jesus movement and the early ... church" arose to protest the exploitative political economies emerging just before and during the Axial Age.[25] Like the resistance movements needed today, these religious streams rejected political economies based on accumulating wealth for a few and dispossessing others of their lands. They sought change both in oppressive structures and in the accompanying "thoughts, feelings, and behaviors of persons."[26]

The point is that, with these roots, these religions (along with Islam, which Duchrow and Hinkelammert describe as a renewal of Axial Age spirituality) may provide spiritual strength today to confront exploitative economies and the thoughts, feelings, and behaviors that accompany them. I believe that these scholars are correct about the potential within these living religious traditions for countering the exploitative economies of our day. Religious traditions are goldmines of moral-spiritual power.

In essence, a primary function of religions is to teach ways of structuring life together along the lines of justice, compassion, and Earth's well-being and to link us, deeply and tangibly, to the power for embodying or practicing those lifeways. The Hebrew prophets, and their ardent outcries against economic violence in the first millennia BCE, are emblematic of that calling.

Since that time, some strains of religious traditions indeed have denounced economic oppression and resisted exploitation of the poor. Scriptures heralding justice as God's call are read aloud in synagogues, masjids, and churches. Religious groups—local and international—have taken up the work of economic justice.

Yet, more strains of these religious traditions have ignored and even betrayed their world-shaking and liberative roots. Our tendency has been to leave those roots behind. Instead, we adopt religious practices and beliefs that comply with exploitative and extractive economies.[27] We tend, for example, to privatize the call to love neighbor as self, as though it pertains only to interpersonal relationships, rather than applying it to social structures.[28] Or we perform acts of charity and call them acts of justice. Or we may ignore altogether the aspects of religious faith and spirituality that challenge the status quo.

Let us, therefore, reclaim the life-giving, justice-making power of faith. Let us assume that religion or spirituality can nourish our power for living rightly, for building life-giving economies, for turning away from (repenting of) economies that devastate life for multitudes of species and hurl so many people into the jaws of poverty.

We ask of religion, spirituality, and faith, "What, then, do you offer to enable us on that sacred path? We are mere human beings! How on Earth can you equip us to counter the fierce forces of predatory economic life? If the Loving Mystery calls us to such a path, then surely this Sacred Source must provide the gifts needed to walk it. What are they?"

(Partial) Freedom from Selves Curved in on Selves

The time is the near future. A heatwave has killed millions in India. The Ministry for the Future—a global department established with UN funding to advocate for future generations—struggles to find ways to counter climate change. The incoming director of the Ministry speaks earnestly to its current director: "I think we need a new religion.... Well, maybe it's not a new religion. An old religion. Maybe the oldest religion. But back among us, big time. Because I think we need it.... We're going to bring it back. We need it."[29]

Religion offers far too many gifts to address in a single chapter. We will focus on one. It may be the core of religion and the heart of why we need it now. Religious practice, at its best, has the capacity to draw us out of captivity to "selves curved in on self" and to see and serve a greater good instead, a good oriented around inclusive and widespread justice and compassion. By "selves curved in on self," I refer to the human propensity to serve self and one's tribe alone regardless of cost to others. The term comes from Martin Luther.

Said differently, religion or spirituality may enable a degree of freedom from self-absorption and, therefore, freedom *for* aligning with one's real values and understandings of the ultimate good. Religion may open the door to an identity different from "I am what I own or what I achieve" or "I am how I look to others." Karenna Gore says it well: religion "calls people to a sense of purpose bigger than self."[30] Baraka Lenga, Tanzanian climate scientist and activist, echoes this sentiment: "Religious groups, no matter the faith, have the power to tame the society's greedy and save lives."[31]

Recall the Muslim student who turned down lucrative, high-status job offers. His religious faith offered him freedom from serving himself alone and from needing others to see him as "Mr. Success." What of the *celebradores de la palabra* and the freedom they had for serving the good of the people, even though it cost them their lives? It was a freedom rooted in their religious faith and practice. So too with the villagers of Le Cambon who risked life to save Jewish people during the Holocaust. This is precisely Karen Armstrong's assertion about the rise of religion in human society: the great religions arose "to reorient human life along the lines of empathy, compassion, justice, sacred presence, and generosity enabled by surrendering... egotism and greed."

Let us look more closely at these claims considering today's crises of economic violence and climate injustice rooted in extractive economies.

I follow here the leads of the renowned literary figure Amitav Ghosh and of theologian Martin Luther. Ghosh, speaking *not* as a religious person, lays out the horrors of climate change and humankind's apparent inability to deal with it. He notes, however, a few "signs of hope," continuing that "the most promising" of these "is the increasing involvement of religious groups and leaders in the politics of climate change."[32] This potential of religion, Ghosh suggests, lies partly in its capacity to move people beyond the compulsion to serve primarily "the interests of a particular group of people"—oneself and one's group—be it a nation, a corporation, or other. He also sees the potential of religion in its already existing networks and communities capable of mobilizing large numbers of people.

Five hundred years earlier, Martin Luther said as much—that religion (in his case, faith in Christ) can free us from lives as "self curved in on self," and for lives that serve the well-being of our neighbors, especially our neighbors in need. One Lutheran preacher, building on Luther's teachings, claims that the freedom we have in faith includes freedom "from giving in to all of the pressures of the world ... freedom from indulging in our pride and conceit and from doing whatever we might darn well please no matter how harmful to another human being or to any of God's creation, freedom to be all that we have been created to be as lovers of self, neighbor, and God."[33]

Let's also be honest. We are human, and therefore we are (in Luther's words) God's *rusty* tools, not God's bright, shiny, perfect tools. This side of death, we will never be *fully* freed from selves curved in on self. Yet we can become partially free, and religion is one path to that freedom.

If religious faith offers a degree of freedom from "selves curved in on self"— freedom to live according to a higher calling and to serve a higher good—*then religious faith, authentically practiced, offers some degree of freedom from the norms and demands of an extractive economy and its magnetic pull toward maximizing personal gain over all else. It offers, instead, freedom to orient economic life in more life-giving ways.*

Hear that claim again: *religious faith, practiced authentically, offers some degree of freedom from the norms and demands of an extractive economy and its magnetic pull toward maximizing personal gain over all else. It offers, instead, freedom to orient economic life in more life-giving ways.*

Religion has a unique set of gifts for that purpose. We will explore them momentarily. But first, a word about the profound significance of this claim.

Significance beyond Measure

This claim overflows with import. Why?

Financialized capitalism is so dangerous and destructive precisely because it sucks people into elevating personal gain over the well-being of others and Earth, even when that behavior on a collective level has terrible consequences. The current economy, as a way of life, snares people into the chains of "selves curved in on self," as individuals and as societies. To illustrate, in 1992 just before the Earth Summit in Rio de Janeiro and after the United States had been criticized for its dangerously high and unsustainable consumption of the world's resources and its high emissions of greenhouse gases, then President Bush infamously declared, "The American way of life is not up for negotiation. Period." He was revealing a society "curved in on self" regardless of the cost to others.

Indeed, one widespread critique of contemporary capitalism is of the way it distorts not only our actions, but also our perceptions of ourselves, of our worth, of our purpose, of what constitutes success, and of others' worth. This form of economy (including the culture that supports it) draws people into behaviors that benefit self while hurting others so that we can meet the demands laid on us by economic and financial systems. And it morally mal-forms society in such a way that these behaviors become normal and acceptable.

This impact includes fanning the flame of endless desire for stuff. Vincent Miller argues that "advanced capitalist societies are marked by some of the most sophisticated systems for forming and inciting desire that the world has ever seen." From infancy, he goes on, we are trained "to never cease desiring" the advertised delights.[34]

Theologian Kathryn Tanner reveals how this moral malformation happens. The "spirit of finance-dominated capitalism," she asserts, has "deforming effects on the way people understand themselves and their relations with others."[35] By this "spirit," she means "beliefs, values, and norms that . . . get people to do willingly what capitalism requires of them by encouraging them to see what they are doing—what they *must* do to get ahead—as meaningful, valuable, or simply inevitable," despite the dangerous impacts.[36]

Of course, personal, institutional, corporate, and societal examples are endless. A Washington state apple grower once said to me with sorrow and admirable honesty, "To pay my workers a decent wage, I would have to raise the prices of my apples. That means losing customers who will buy cheaper apples. I am stuck paying rotten wages because if I lose my business, my kids will suffer." A university in Southern California may continue to invest in banks that finance the fossil fuel industry even while wildfires induced by climate change threaten its campus. A young middle-class family may buy a home in a gentrifying neighborhood despite knowing that their entry is part of booting out the neighborhood's lower-income residents because buying the house gives this family the equity they need to secure a future under predatory capitalism. The "spirit of finance-dominated capitalism" has "deforming effects."

The emotional, social, and structural incentives to maximize profit despite the cost—if not adequately checked—will kill us as a species through climate change, taking much of God's good creation with us.

What can possibly begin to free us from the magnetic grip of this force?

In this context, the significance of a force that has some power to counter the suck toward "selves curved in on self" cannot be overstated. This is a particular calling of religion now at this crucible point in history. Indeed, Tanner goes on to assert that while *"capitalism may now have the power to shape people in its own image,"* as *"one of the few alternative outlooks on life with a capacity to shape life conduct to a comparable degree, religion might remain a critical force against it"* (italics mine). She asserts that some "historically significant strands of Christianity . . . may have radically transformative effects" in countering "what contemporary capitalism demands of people in the effort to align their behavior with its own mechanism for profit generation."[37]

Recall the conclusions of Armstrong, Brueggemann, Lerner, Duchrow, and Hinkelammert. The enduring faiths that emerged in the Axial Age, and their offspring of Christianity and Islam, arose to reorient human life along the lines of empathy, compassion, justice, sacred presence, and generosity. As declared by

Armstrong, the leaders of these religions "preached a spirituality of empathy and compassion; they insisted that people must abandon their egotism and greed.... If people behaved with kindness and generosity to their fellows, they could save the world."[38]

Countless others have come to similar conclusions. Scholar of Hinduism Rita Sherma, for example, insists that power exists within religions "to move, heal, and inspire individuals and communities towards the pursuit of the common good and a higher purpose in life."[39] Rico Palaca Ponce, academic director of the Institute of Spirituality in Asia, writes, "Transformative spirituality is a 'life-energy.' It is a breath of fire.... It calls the person to go beyond oneself to concern for, and relationships with, the others."[40]

Many questions arise from these assertions. If religion has this power, then what on earth is going on—why has religion not assumed this role more fully and evidently? *In what sense is religion equipped to offer a degree of freedom from the demands of an extractive economy and freedom for reorienting economic life in more life-giving ways?*

CHAPTER NINETEEN

Ingredients of Freedom

> As scientists... we understand that what is regarded as sacred is more likely to be treated with care and respect. Our planetary home should be so regarded. Efforts to safeguard and cherish the environment need to be infused with a vision of the sacred.
>
> —The Union of Concerned Scientists[1]

> Bleak though the terrain of climate change may be, there are a few... signs of hope.... The most promising... is the increasing involvement of religious groups and leaders in the politics of climate change.... If religious groupings around the world can join hands with popular movements, they may well be able to provide the momentum that is needed for the world to move forward on drastically reducing emissions without sacrificing considerations of equity.
>
> —Amitav Ghosh[2]

> At its most authentic, religious faith builds moral muscles that push the human species to become more generous and just and guard against it backsliding into barbarity. While shallow religion shapes people for instinctive compliance to authority... a deep faith tradition trains for moral discernment and formation of conscience and provides a narrative for how to resist immoral actions.
>
> —Rose Marie Berger[3]

THIS CHAPTER PURSUES the second question posed at the close of chapter 18: *What elements within religious faith could help us break free from the demands of an extractive economy and the "selves curved in on self" that it breeds? What within religious faith could enable freedom for the urgently needed movement into ecological and equitable ways of structuring economic life?*

We will unearth ten elements of religious and spiritual faith that may nourish this freedom struggle: (1) a heritage of faith-rooted resistance; (2) resources for kindling our hunger for communion/community; (3) ethical teachings and values; (4) connection with a higher power that is both within us and transcends us; (5) resources for combining inner work with outer work; (6) courage;

(7) hope; (8) grounding stories; (9) identity as beloved; and (10) internal critique. After examining these elements, we will explore two practices—ritual and inter-religious engagement—whereby faith-based communities might mix these ten ingredients to create transformative presence and action.

Let us be clear: we are walking in the shifting borderland of religion as it *could* be practiced and religion as it *is* practiced. Sometimes the two are the same; religious communities do practice their liberative elements. However, that is not always the case. More often than not, they/we fall short of embodying the healing and liberating riches within faith traditions. I do not pretend otherwise. May walking this borderland inspire readers involved in religious and spiritual traditions to hold them up to their incredible potential to help free us from death-dealing economic ways and build life-giving economies.

Freedom from Selves Curved in on Self: Ingredients Offered by Religious Faiths

The fact that religious traditions offer these liberative elements does not assure that religions will step up to the plate. The momentum towards continuing with spirituality and religion as we now live them is mighty; it drags us along like the force of gravity, invisible in its compelling allure. *If religions are to help avert our mad dash into the worst of climate disaster and economic violence, then people who identify in some way with religious and spiritual practices must take hold of these liberative ingredients and stir them up with the explicit intention of concocting more equitable and ecological forms of economic life.* Yes, this is a matter of life and death. It is also a beautiful calling.

Heritages of Resistance

Nazi forces occupy the small rural village in Vichy France. A woman walks from small farm to small farm quietly arranging with the peasants to house Jewish children who will be smuggled out of the occupied territories to safety. These humble villagers are risking their lives, but led by their pastor and Protestant school teacher, they would smuggle four thousand Jews out from under the noses of Nazi officials.

"What gave these simple villagers that moral courage?" I ask students in my ethics course. As they review the film of this rescue operation, the role of ancestors becomes clear. These people identified themselves as living within a living heritage of resistance to systemic wrong. They are Huguenots, whose ancestors resisted persecution by the Catholic church of France. A sketch in the hymnal (songbook) that they used in worship speaks far more powerfully than words. It depicts one of their foremothers imprisoned for thirty-six years in a tower. In the drawing, she scratches into the concrete with her knitting needle: *résistez* (resist).

Weapons of the Spirit

Song and ritual reinforced the villagers' will to embody their forebearers' courage and pass it on to their own children.[4] In the film we hear them sing,

> Hail, beloved mountains,
> Sacred land of our ancestors.
> Your green summits are sown
> With their glorious memory.
> May the spirit that gave them life
> Inspire their children
> To follow their example.[5]

Ancestors matter. We who abide in religious traditions—or honor them—are descendants in a long heritage of resisters, people who risked imprisonment, torture, and even death in order to practice the ways of compassion, justice, and community to which the Spirit called them.

For Christians, this community is at least three thousand years old. Imagine that "cloud of witnesses." They include the bold midwives who saved baby Moses from death at the Pharaoh's hands, the Hebrew prophets who decried the exploitative economies and rulers of their day, Jesus and early Christian martyrs who defied the ways of imperial Rome, Hadewich of Brabant and other medieval mystic women who resisted the church hierarchy to claim their leadership and truth (some of whom were burned at the stake for it), the early Reformation leaders who resisted the demands of a church gone astray, the enslaved Africans whose underground worship strengthened them for survival and freedom struggle, the abolitionists crying out against chattel slavery, Christians who defied Hitler's forces and risked concentration camps or death to save Jews, the civil rights leaders, and Witness for Peace and Peace Brigades who have stood firm against brutalizing armies. What a holy body of forebearers!

Imagine walking in their footsteps, with this heritage in your DNA. Heritage travels not only back in time, but also forward. The Huguenot villagers taught their children that they were living in the footsteps of resisters *and* that they were to pass on this heritage. Imagine the moral formation toward resistance and courage that would ensue if we taught our children that they walk in the footsteps of people who resisted systemic injustice and that they are to pass on that heritage. Pastor Anne did just that:

> *She rose to preach. The new pastor for children and youth in our church was a gentle woman who exuded a deep and authentic love for people. I had known and respected her for some time. Little did the congregation know the kind of history and power that this woman held! I wondered what would happen when they learned.*
>
> *Never will I forget one of her first children's sermons. It concerned a biblical text describing the apostle Paul's experiences in prison for his allegiance to Jesus and the gospel. "I could relate to Paul in solitary confinement," she said with a smile while the children gathered before her at the front of the church. "Because the last time I was in jail, I too was in solitary confinement." I glanced around, wondering, "What were the parents in the congregation thinking?" Pastor Anne went on to describe in simple terms that this had been her twenty-seventh time in jail for her resistance to war and to the nuclear submarines passing through the waters of Puget Sound. In the years to come, youth from the congregation joined her in acts of resistance.*

Kindling Our Yearning for Communion . . . Forming Us for Communion

An ancient faith claim whispers through the ages, "We are created and destined for communion—with one another, with the Creator, with all of creation."[6] Voices in physics, biology, social theory, and other fields have joined that quiet chorus. Communion or community, they say, may be life's destiny.[7] In chapter 3, we listened in on some of those voices.

Howard Thurman, one of America's great spiritual leaders, said as much. Thurman, an African American theologian, was acutely aware of the brutality

Ingredients of Freedom

inherent in human life. Yet he knew God's presence to be still more powerful. His words are riveting. In seeking a clue to God's purposes in humankind's "collective or social life on the planet," Thurman asserts,[8]

> It cannot be denied that a part of the face of human society is the will to destroy, to lay waste, to spend.... And yet always, against this, something struggles.... Always there is some voice that rises up against what is destructive, calling attention to an alternative, another way... the intent to community as the purpose of life.... [These voices] are not tolerated; they are taken out of circulation so that their spirit may not be contagious; but they always appear and reappear.... The moving finger of God in human history points.... There must be community. [This is the] fundamental intent of life.[9]

Thurman goes on to illustrate with Gandhi who, he says, embodied this purpose, including its call to subvert exploitative economic systems.

We have seen that predatory capitalism thwarts communion with one another. It drives us apart by enabling and encouraging some to exploit others and Earth. In this context, an infinitely powerful role of religion is to remind us of our calling and destiny—community or communion—and to equip us for it. The reminder insists that the Great Spirit hungers for our healing, that we be restored on a path toward communion.[10] Healing includes restructuring economic life to foster not exploitation but togetherness and belonging. That is a direct challenge to the economy as we know it.

Reviewing the previous chapter's opening stories and other stories in this volume through a lens of communion/community reveals the communion-building that dances through the new economy movement. The young Indonesian pastor was building an inter-island community of resistance. A seminary class listening for God in the winds and trees was heeding the community of creation. Unlikely conversation partners exploring their hunger for community gave birth to the Nuns and Nones Land Justice Project.

The network of small farming cooperatives in New Mexico that we met in "Setting the Stage" illumines the power for economic transformation that flows from a splendid array of communions—communion with indigenous Spirit ancestors;[11] communion of cooperation among the farm co-ops; and communion of intercultural listening among Euro-descended Quakers, Indigenous communities, Latino communities, and more.[12] In that story, young Stefano found joy and motivation from belonging and being included in the community's effort and celebration. The story in fuller form includes a prayer at planting time: "This seed is for myself and my family, this seed is for my neighbor, this seed is for the animals, and this seed is for the thief" (knowing that the thief might very well be a person in great need).[13] What a communion-fostering prayer.

Perhaps communion or connection is the music that shapes the cosmos. *Perhaps a role of religion and spirituality is to help us to hear and sing it.* How might worship and other practices of your church, synagogue, mosque or other locus of spiritual gathering help to form people for deep communion that extends to economic life?

Ethical Values and Teachings

Religion at its best is a rich source of ethical wisdom that guides people to live rightly. Buddhism, for example, holds up compassion for self, others, and all sentient beings. Judaism brought the call to justice into religion. Christianity—along with Judaism and Islam—claims that life is to be guided by God's commandment, heard first in the Hebrew Scriptures, to "love your neighbor as yourself" (Lev 19:18), with heavy emphasis on neighbors who are suffering under poverty or other forms of marginalization.

Three startling and powerful gifts emerge from biblical teachings about neighbour-love. First, neighbour-love, like compassion in Buddhist teaching, explicitly extends beyond the in-group (or one's own people) to *outsiders*. This is vital, especially considering recent findings in psychology and evolutionary biology that humans may have a species-specific capacity for cooperation across large numbers of people *within* one's own group, while continuing to commit atrocities against outsiders.[14] The biologist E. O. Wilson refers to this as tribalism and sees the tendency to cooperate within groups and defend against outsiders as an "absolute universal" of human nature.[15] *"The emergence of ethical behaviour that extends love, compassion, or help to outsiders is not favoured by our evolutionary heritage."*[16] If the "tendency that we inherit is for cooperative and altruistic behaviour toward insiders ... as the evolutionary biologist Ernst Mayr says, real ethical behaviour requires a transformation of our evolutionary inheritance, 'a redirecting of our inborn cultural tendencies toward a new target: outsiders.'"[17] Wow! An ethical mandate explicitly calling for loving treatment of the "other" is a game changer if implemented. *Many religions bear that moral mandate, that gift to humankind!* It is at the heart of Jewish and Christian teaching to love neighbor and at the heart of Buddhist compassion.[18]

Secondly, neighbour-love is not an emotion, but a lived commitment to the well-being of others. Thirdly, it pertains not only to interpersonal relationships but to social-structural relations.[19] Thus, neighbor-love, as a religious calling and teaching, includes transforming unjust systems that bring suffering to our neighbors.

On these grounds, religious communities can insist that economic and financial systems are moral and spiritual matters. These systems sharply influence whether my daily life will serve the well-being of vulnerable neighbors or damage them. Economic systems may determine who will have water, food, and health care. They may cause terrible suffering or prevent it.

Insisting on life-enhancing economic systems is a powerful role of religion. For example, Bahá'í teaching explains that inequality between rich and poor is a "source of acute suffering" and that—for this reason—economic systems should "foster economic justice." According to Bahá'í teaching, fostering justice includes "avoid[ing] privatization . . . whereby only those with means can afford things like quality education and healthcare." And it "requires strong institutional arrangements that prevent people from over-accumulating at the top and under-accumulating at the bottom." Fostering justice entails policies aimed at "redistribution—for example, a steeply progressive tax not just on income but on wealth, and effective corporate taxation strategies to curb tax avoidance . . . as well as labor market regulations that do not allow for extreme wage dispersion."[20] The geographer Paul Cloke highlights the "potential for religion and for [faith-based organizations] to fundamentally challenge, from a multiplicity of theological and political standpoints, the way that contemporary society operates, to confront and alter values that drive it."[21] Indeed, several global religious networks vehemently critique the neoliberal global economy and seek to support people in building alternatives.[22]

We noted earlier the tendency to leave behind the liberative roots of religious traditions, to ignore the elements in them that challenge unjust social structures. Neighbor-love, as a biblical calling, is a glaring example. It has been sorely commodified, domesticated, truncated, tamed, and squished by the entwined assumptions that it is primarily about feelings and that it pertains singularly to interpersonal relationships. These are false interpretations of Scripture. The Hebrew Scriptures are clear that love (the English translation of two Hebrew words, *hesed* and *aheb*) is conditioned by justice (English translation of *tzedakah* and *mishpat*). All four words are rich and multilayered. This is not the place to fully unfold their connotations, but central among them is a steadfast commitment to the well-being of neighbors through "right relationships." Right relationships include enabling people who had been marginalized to flourish. Moreover, from a biblical perspective, these standards apply not only on the interpersonal level, but on the *level of systems, especially economic systems*. The Hebrew prophets are among humankind's most poignant and passionate denouncers of systems that exploit some for the gain of others. Jesus's call to love neighbor assumes and iterates that tradition. Yet, upon hearing the word *love*, most of us do not assume these liberative implications.

Martin Luther King, Jr. asserted that "our responsibility as Christians is to discover the meaning of this command [to love neighbor] and seek passionately to live it out in our daily lives."[23] Just imagine what might ensue if your faith community committed to "discover[ing] the meaning of this command" and how "to live it out" in the context of contemporary economic life?

Ethical teachings, of course, are not sufficient for changing economic life. Teachings have power only when people enact them. Christianity, for example, is replete with teachings that Christians must eschew exploitative economic

practices as not compatible with Christian faith. Such has been the message of many highly respected and influential Christian leaders for nearly two millennia:
- St. Basil (329–379): "The rich ... preoccupy common goods, they take these goods as their own. If each one would take that which is sufficient for his needs, leaving what is superfluous to those in distress, no one would be rich, no one poor.... The rich man is a thief."[24]
- St. Ambrose (340–397): "How far, O rich, do you extend your senseless avarice? Do you intend to be the sole inhabitants of the earth? Why do you drive out the fellow sharers of nature and claim it all for yourselves? The earth was made for all.... Why do you rich claim it as your exclusive right? The pagans hold earth as property. They do blaspheme God."[25]
- Martin Luther vehemently denounced acquiring wealth in ways that burden or oppress the poor, calling it egregious theft.[26] He condemned the emerging financialized trade economy because it enabled some to line their coffers through market practices that impoverished others, and he beseeched German political leaders to regulate against such practices.[27] He condemned, for example, the practice of buying up an essential commodity at a low price and selling it high, because so doing would hurt the poor who could not then afford the commodity. (Buying low and selling high is the practice undergirding today's economy.) "Everyone," he rails, "uses the market according to his caprice, and is even defiant and brags as though it were his fair privilege and right to sell his goods for as high a price as he please, and no one had a right to say a word against it."[28]

Such teachings, however, have not kept Christians from engaging in and complying with exploitative economic practices and economies. To enact ethical teachings that counter the torrential force of maximizing profit requires, among other things, spiritual strength and the inner work to cultivate it. We consider these next.

Linking Us to the Sacred within Us

Ethical teachings alone will not change ways of living or the structure of society. Change comes when something moves the human heart. Joy, grief, anger, pain, compassion, beauty, and love—these can move the heart. The Spirit can move the human heart. Awareness of the God-presence within us and beyond us, connection with the Intimate Mystery that some call God—these can move the human heart.

Religious faith and practice and spiritual attentiveness are doorways to these movers of our hearts. They may open our eyes and hearts to the Sacred present in every moment, in everything. They may clear away the fog so that we know the presence of the Sacred within our very beings and see the invisible string connecting our spirit to the Great Spirit. "The true purpose of all spiritual disciplines is to clear away whatever may block our awareness of that which is God in us."[29]

Awareness of a holy, liberating, and healing Sacred Source within us calls forth a response. It beckons us to be that presence in the world.

Combining Inner Work with Outer Work

Injustices are spiritual diseases.
—Imam Omar Suleiman[30]

... and my roots are digging deep to living waters.
—Song of a faith-based activist

Nuns & Nones is an intergenerational, spiritual community dedicated to care, contemplation, and courageous action in service of life and liberation.
—Nuns & Nones website[31]

The force of a torrential river is fierce. One cannot swim upstream without strength.

No less fierce are the forces of extraction and exploitation. Turning the world away from these forces requires inner strength. People do not have the strength for that long haul without deep inner resources—resources of spiritual fortitude, courage, hope, joy, and capacity to resist the demands of influential others. Religions at their best integrate internal spiritual strengthening with the external work of societal change.

But how does this work? I posed this question to two colleagues who are wise and seasoned in the arts of wedding inner work with justice-building. Let's listen in:

"Juan Carlos, how do you experience inner spiritual strength integrated with external work of social change?" In response, Juan Carlos sent me the story of his life and his profound learning that friendship is a spiritual practice of great worth. By friendship, he meant trusted relationships that included sharing vulnerabilities, especially the wounds, broken places, and inner longings of one's life. He intentionally practiced cultivating such friendships, in particular with people that society had ignored or oppressed. Truly hearing and honoring them and sharing life space with them led him to join their struggles for basic human rights and justice. Such friendship and hospitality he wrote, "rouse us from our silence and lack of imagination ... create new paths of communion." They enable "collective wisdom and hope ... acts of resistance and resilience in support of dignity, of Life and of Mother Earth." Before opening himself to vulnerability in this way, Juan Carlos said, "I had been deaf."[32]

"Anne, how do you experience inner spiritual strength integrated with external work of social change?" "Throughout my life," she responded, "worshipping in community with others has empowered me to resist the American empire that spends trillions on weapons and war while the world's children go hungry. Circles of prayer with other followers of Jesus have given me faith, hope and strength to work toward the realization of God's beloved community of justice and peace."[33] (Anne is a Baptist and Lutheran pastor who has been arrested nearly thirty times for her acts of peaceful civil disobedience to protest war and other human rights violations.)

No one describes the integration of inner and outer work better than the womanist ethicist Emilie Townes. The heart of religiously rooted neighbor-love, she teaches, is to love, respect, affirm, and honor self so deeply that one may—together with others—challenge oppressive social structures including economies. Townes writes,

Liberation has spiritual and social dimensions.... The spiritual dimension of liberation concentrates on the acquisition of power that enables each person to be who she or he is. This power is not one that dominates and subordinates. Rather it fosters the security to give the self to others.... This does not mean that a person participates in self-abnegation.... One gives through love but not at the expense of self. A delicate balancing act achieves spiritual liberation, for one must give through the God-presence in each of us and not solely through the fully human parts of oneself. Social liberation is participation in the world.... Social liberation and spiritual liberation are tremendous challenges and awesome gifts....[34] *[Their goal is] transformation of the person and also the oppressive structures of this society and our churches.*[35]

A moral economy is built on the transformation of unjust systems. It is built also on the transformation of individuals—our worldviews, allegiances, senses of self-worth and identity, capacities for love and compassion. Religious faith is a home of this inner work toward spiritual and social liberation. We see this in exemplary figures of social liberation such as the Hebrew prophets, Julia A. J. Foote, Gandhi, Vida Scudder, Howard Thurman, and Martin Luther King Jr.

Ingredients of Freedom

Today many religious communities are bringing their resources for inner development into the work of building a more equitable economy. Examples are endless. The stories at this chapter's outset illustrate. Networks such as CreatureKind, JewishVeg, and the Vegan Muslim Initiative all bring spiritual resources to challenging industrial meat production, its cruelty to animals, and its massive emissions of greenhouse gasses.[36] The Black Church Food Security Network and its Soil to Sanctuary program bring miniature farmers markets to churches on their day of worship. Greenfaith—an interfaith organization fighting climate change—notes that thousands of congregations in the United States identify as green churches, synagogues, masjids, or temples.[37] Vibrant faith communities such as Detroit's Grace in Action, Redeemer Lutheran Church in Minneapolis, and St. Luke's Lutheran Church of Logan Square in Chicago combine worship with community organizing for justice.

This is as it should be. Religion, as we have seen, was born, in part, to bring spirituality into the service of creating a more compassionate world. Great spiritual leaders throughout history have embodied and taught this truth. Religious communities today are challenged to reclaim and practice it.

Courage

The Hebrew word for Spirit [Ruach] might well be translated as "bold undaunted courage."

—Martin Luther[38]

A bishop once said to me, "I would like to live out my faith more fully in the work of justice." "What would it take for you to do that?" I asked him. He paused. Then, with admirable honesty, he replied, "Courage."

It requires courage to read this book and to contemplate working toward a more just economy when many people see that as impossible or threatening. Reversing the fossil fuel orgy calls for courage. Courage is needed to face the anguish of a climate-tormented future and one's role in causing it. Moral courage, spiritual courage.

Courage sustained the people we met at this chapter's outset. The Indian church leader and his companions drank from springs of courage in their life-endangering work to resist corporate exploitation. So too, the young Indonesian pastor and the church workers in the Guatemalan village.

Throughout history, religions have supplied courage to do what is right even when risky or dangerous. Luther's words (above) reveal much. All of Earth's great religious and spiritual traditions claim the presence of a Spirit in some form, a Spirit that transcends the material world and also lives within it. That Spirit, if we learn to heed it, brings courage.

Hope

To believe in God is to believe in the possibility of possibility, that the world can be fundamentally different, that the world can be transformed, that we can be part of that transformation.

—Rabbi Michael Lerner[39]

One evening a dear friend laid before me the depth of her fear and despair related to climate change and the seemingly unstoppable jaws of injustice eating away at life. We talked into the night. Early the next morning, I awoke with a sinking feeling. I realized I had failed my friend. I had not shared with her the real source of my hope—a hope that withstands and endures beyond my despair. I did not share it with her because I feared seeming too "religious." It was a mistake. I vowed never to make it again. So here I share with you where my hope lies, and then we will dig more into religion as a seedbed of hope.

My hope is fed by the astounding movement of movements, now afoot around the world, to build more compassionate and Earth-honoring ways of structuring our life together. However, this is not the foundation of my hope. The unshakable foundation is a faith claim that will stand even if these movements fail. This faith claim is that God brings life and love out of the most excruciating, devastating, tortuous, and deadly circumstances. For me that is the meaning of the story of Jesus's resurrection after being tortured and executed by imperial Rome. Death and destruction are not the last word. In some way that we do not understand, the Sacred Force that some call God raises en-spirited life out of the worst that human cruelty and ignorance can do. Even in the deepest abyss of human depravity, suffering, and sin, the God of life is present and—in some way that we simply cannot fathom—will bring healing and liberation. Ultimately the power of Sacred Love will reign.

I do not believe that this guarantees the survival of our species. Nor do I believe that this promise absolves us from our call to work toward a more just and compassionate world. I do know, however, that whatever befalls, the Sacred Lover will hold each of us and all of creation in loving embrace and Spirit-filled life. That knowing strengthens the call to work for change because this Spirit works through us. It is our calling and blessing to allow this Spirit to flow through us, bringing fullness of life from the wastelands.

Studies show that hopelessness related to climate change is widespread, though it often is hidden "underneath the mask of apathy," silence, and denial.[40] That sense of hopelessness often breeds denial and moral inertia; it cuts off our ability to act. Hopelessness is dangerous, not only for the person experiencing it, but also for the societal loss of that person's sense of power to make a difference.

Religious communities are well equipped to "frame climate change" in ways that enable "hope in the midst of tragedy."[41] Hope in the midst of climate tragedy cannot be blithe religious appeals to hope for the afterlife with disregard for life in this world. That would be blasphemy. Nor can it be the hope in God's providence easily expressed by people of climate privilege who can disregard the magnitude and anguish of the losses that have taken place and will take place for climate vulnerable people.

What is it about religious faith that can foster *authentic* hope while acknowledging the horrors of climate change and economic violence? Let us consider three fountains of hope that flow from religion.

The first is the healing power of communal lament, grief that is shared and expressed. Recall Ugandan theologian Emmanual Katongole (chapter 14) and his quest to understand how people writhing in "a vortex of suffering" had transformed their suffering into hope and agency.[42] After working closely with Christian activist communities of eastern Africa (especially eastern Congo and northern Uganda), he concluded that "lament is what sustains and carries forth Christian agency in the midst of suffering.... The practice of lament [is] the work of hope." He found the poetry, music, and other art from Eastern Congo and Northern Uganda that expresses communities' lament to be "cultural moorings of hope." Communally expressed lament was at the heart of people's hope and agency. The communal cry of lament led people into active political engagement toward healing.

The Hebrew and Christian Scriptures—especially the prophets of ancient Israel—teach and offer the hope-instilling reality of raw lament. Theologian Timothy Beal says it well when he avers that hope "requires grief." Hebrew biblical tradition "offers a deep imaginative pool of language to help us give voice" to grief that may give rise to authentic hope.[43] Beal writes,

> *[The Hebrew Prophets] give voice to the reality of loss that their own people whom they love and for whom they grieve refuse to face.... The prophet Amos (Amos 6:1, 3–7), lamenting the deep denial that was driving the most prosperous among his people ... describes the ill-gotten prosperity of the nation's elite who bask in their wealth and security, putting calamity out of their minds.... They lounge on expensive furniture. They stretch out. They eat fancy foods like lamb and veal. They sing and play with expensive instruments. They drink fine wine from bowls. They anoint themselves with opulence. Then, very abruptly ... Amos cries out in horror for those who recline in denial and do not grieve the ruin that is outside their high walls and doors.... Amos expresses grief over their imminent demise, about which they are in complete and total denial.... The prophet confronts this denial ... with grief and invitation to deep sadness over what has been irreparably lost. Then and only then is it even possible for the prophet to confront the despair of an empire in ruins with hope for the possibility of healing and restoration.[44]*

Amos could be describing today's realities of climate change and excruciating poverty in the midst of opulent wealth. He bids us to lament, and Scripture offers stunning language for doing so. Perhaps we should be wailing communally in the streets, grieving what has been irreparably lost, lamenting the suffering induced by climate change and poverty that flow from the extractive economy. That communal lament could be a seedbed of hope.

But lament can be terrifying. It means facing realities that we would rather deny as did Amos' people. How can we dare to enter the pain of authentic lament?

Second, religions are beautifully equipped to make space for communal lament precisely because they offer visions and promises of more just and compassionate Earth communities—visions and promises that lead beyond the probable. Each religious tradition is unique and each holds diverse interpretations of its own promises and visions. I have shared with you my understanding of Christianity's hope-giving promise. People in other religious traditions can probe for the hope-instilling promises that they offer. Visions and promises of a better and possible future—here in this world—are a second fountain of hope flowing from religious traditions.

Third, religions may invite us to live with hope-giving paradox. Life may be brutal, but it also is imbued with the sacred and with beauty. Holding this paradox has been lifesaving for me. Theologians Rita Nakashima Brock and Rebecca Ann Parker express it well. After acknowledging that we are faced with "legacies of injustice and current forces of evil," they write,

> *However, it is also true that we already live on holy ground, in the presence of God, with bodies and souls sanctified by the Spirit's anointing, surrounded by the communion of saints. Our spiritual challenge is to embrace this reality: histories of harm are all around us, forces of evil operate within and among us, and yet everywhere bushes are on fire, the risen Christ is with us on the road, the Spirit rises in the wind, the rivers of paradise circle the earth, and the fountain of wisdom springs up from the earth we tread, from this holy ground.*[45]

Hope is a practice, not merely a feeling. "If someone had tapped David on his way to fight Goliath and asked, 'David, are you hopeful?' David would have pushed him out of the way and said, 'I've got a job to do.'" With these words about a figure in the Hebrew Bible, Rabbi Mordechai Liebling describes what he learned from the Buddhist teacher Joanna Macy.[46]

Hope is fed by the practices of communal lament, acting toward a vision of the world as it should and could be, and embracing paradox. How, then, might your worshipping community build communal lament into its worship practice? How might you build action toward a more life-affirming economy into your lives together? What practices, perhaps rituals, will remind you of the paradox? These practices may be leaven that gives rise to hope.

Reforming Grounding Stories

We get outcomes based on the stories we are telling ourselves and our children.

—Peniel Joseph[47]

As human beings, we've always told stories: stories about who we are, where we come from, and where we're going. Now imagine that one of those stories is taking over the others, narrowing our diversity and creating a monoculture.... In these early days of the twenty-first century, the master story is economic.... Economic beliefs, values and assumptions are shaping how we think, feel, and act ... because how you think shapes how you act; the monoculture isn't just changing your mind — it's changing your life."

—F. S. Michaels[48]

In chapter 16, we traced the development of the "master" economic story. We uncovered dangerous aspects of it and explored ways of changing them. One aspect is the story of who we humans are and another is the story of what Earth is.

If the dominant story of economic life is dangerous and destructive, then generating a different story is crucial. Religious traditions and the spiritualities within them provide grounding stories for life—the stories of who we are, what the world is, where we come from and are going, what makes life worth living.[49] *Religion, then, has the power to reteach us who we are.*

The reigning economic story subtly fabricates two myths about who we are: that humans are outside the circle of nature's economy and that some humans are inherently more worthy than others. These fallacies shape how we treat ourselves, others, and the world. Rereading the biblical creation stories in Hebrew, the language in which they were written, reveals treasures.[50] We find that we humans (*ha'adam*) are soil (*ha'adamah*) into which God has breathed God's life breath, allowing us to become a *nefesh hayah*[51] (meaning "breathing life" or "living creature"), as are the other land animals! The story of Noah refers to every creature as a *nefesh hayah* (Gen 9:15).[52] In short, we are of Earth, and we are kin with the other animals. Likewise, the Qu'ran emphasizes "the profound human-soil connection" by describing humans as "a mixture of clay and Allah's creative power (*Sura* 23:12–14)."[53]

Religious traditions are also uniquely situated to change the story of what Earth is. The reigning economic story sees Earth as a wealth of resources to be used and enjoyed at best, and exploited for maximum profit, at worst. In stark contrast, some streams within religious traditions understand Earth as sacred; as able to rejoice, grieve, and serve God; as source of wisdom for humankind; as revealing God; and even as a dwelling place of God.[54]

The Hebrew Scriptures are replete with Earth's agency and sacred nature. Psalm 96:11–12, for example, declares,

> *Let the heavens be glad, and let the earth rejoice;*
> *Let the sea roar and all that fills it;*
> *Let the field exult and everything in it.*
> *Then shall all the trees of the forest sing for joy.*

According to the third-century church leader Athanasius, the word of God "fills all things everywhere." Martin Luther and many others have declared as much. Hildegard of Bingen, a twelfth century Benedictine abbess, composer, healer, and poet taught that Earth is imbued with *Viriditas*, the divine Force of nature, the greening power of the Divine (or divine healing power of green).[55]

Islamic sacred literature reminds us that Earth itself "is rightly seen as a *mosque*, a sacred space in which all humanity and all life forms dwell."[56] Traditional Hawaiian spirituality views "the entire world as being alive . . . and as family."[57] Jewish teaching holds that the created world is "a commentary on Torah."[58]

Whether we manage to change the operative story from "Earth as resource to be exploited" to "Earth as sacred" may determine whether we save or destroy Earth as habitable by humans.

Finally, religions may help change the story of what is possible. The British anthropologist Maurice Bloch argues that the core of religion is "the capacity to imagine other worlds."[59] The "imagining of possibilities" is crucial to achieving a livable future, insists Amitav Ghosh. "If there is one thing that global warming has made perfectly clear," he writes, "it is that to think about the world only as it is amounts to a formula for collective suicide."[60]

Seeing Self as Beloved and Fully Worthy

The reigning economic story is particularly virulent in convincing people that our worth depends upon what we own and how we look. Economist Tim Jackson argues that in consumer society, consumer goods establish social position. Companies maximize profit, he says, by promoting the story that one can be fully worthy and maintain one's social standing only by consuming certain things. I suspect that he is right. A gnawing but unacknowledged fear of our own unworthiness foments the excessive consumption that a profit-maximizing economy requires. "If I have this device or clothing, or look this way, then other people will respect me, like me, or defer to me," filters through our psyches beneath the radar of awareness.

Jackson calls for a strong "counter narrative" that offers other definitions of worth, well-being, and social value. Making these changes, he writes, "may well be the biggest challenge ever faced by human society."[61]

Religious traditions may be one force on Earth capable of providing that strong counter narrative. Some religious faiths proclaim that each of us—as well as all of creation—is beloved in the eyes of God, and that this identity is primary and irrevocable. We cannot lose it. In chapter 1, I described this as part of "the greatest love story ever told." It is—I believe—the core of Christianity at its truest. Seeing self through the eyes of God—seeing what God sees—reveals a human creature loved beyond all comprehension. This is an "I" who cannot become more worthy or important by owing things, achieving wealth, or looking right.

The power of receiving this identity and trusting it is beyond full human knowing. But I suspect that it is one ingredient of freedom from continuing in patterns of consumption that will destroy Earth's life systems and that damage so many people.[62]

Internal Critique

Some religious traditions, as we have said, helped to construct the dominant economic narrative. The story of human dominion over Earth is rooted in interpretations of the Bible's creation stories. Some forms of Christianity claimed that Earth was the polar opposite of the sacred. Some religious beliefs have justified or supported exploitative economic practices. Among religious traditions, Christianity arguably has had the most consequential set of alignments with oppressive powers. From Constantine in the fourth century through colonialism and on to advanced global capitalism, different Christianities have supported economic oppression. The literature on this abounds. Images of God have been made in the image of exploitative powers in order to justify them.[63]

Christianity, thus, can model the game-changing tool of religious self-criticism. This is the healing and liberating practice of acknowledging where we (as religious traditions) have gone wrong.

Critique is part of a "triple lens" for living within a faith tradition. That trio is critique, reclamation, and rebuilding. This means that religious traditions will (1) expose where their beliefs and practices have undergirded oppression and Earth's exploitation; (2) retrieve healing and liberative dimensions of our traditions that may have been ignored or repressed; and (3) rebuild Earth-honoring and justice-seeking beliefs and practices grounded in the critique and retrieval.

Critique leads to processes of repair. Churches entering into reparations may influence other institutions in that direction, as Rev. Dr. Gordon Cowans of Jamaica (whom we met in chapter 13) insists. After declaring the need for reparations, he goes on to say that "churches can lead the way."

> *Time has come for repair through reparatory justice. Time has come for the just cause of redress for centuries of deprivation of black and brown people, originating in the trans-Atlantic trade and enslavement of African*

> *people, to resonate in centers of power everywhere in the world. . . . The Church has a significant role to play. Time has come for churches and faith-based organizations to awaken to the truth of their complicity in the tragedy of enslavement and commit to practical actions and redress among current and future generations of descendants. . . . Churches can lead the way in acts of repentance and restitution which have the capacity in turn to influence governmental parties for good.*[64]

Healing power emerges when religion critiques itself and seeks reparation for where it has betrayed the good.

Ingredients of Freedom—in Sum

This chapter has asked, *What elements deep within religious faith could help us break free from the demands of predatory capitalism and the "selves curved in on self" that it breeds? What within religions could enable freedom for the urgently needed movement towards ecological and equitable ways of structuring economic life?* (Our quest, of course, is always for partial—not perfect—freedom, as we humans are imperfect creatures.) We noted ten ingredients of such freedom that are offered by religion, spirituality, and faith.

How are we to activate these vital resources?

Two Transformative Practices: One Ancient and One Dawning

Faith traditions are a treasure house of practices for activating these tools for freedom. Here we consider just two practices. One is the ancient practice of ritual. The other—which has emerged powerfully in recent decades—is interreligious engagement.

Ritual

> *Powered by transformative liturgy, religion can be the spark plug that animates communities to provide effective responses to the challenge of climate change.*
>
> —Ezra Chitando[65]

> *Our elders say that ceremony is the way we can remember to remember. . . . Remember that the earth is a gift that we must pass on . . . and more than anything, I want to hear a great song of thanks rise to on the wind. I think that song might save us.*
>
> —Robin Wall Kimmerer[66]

Ingredients of Freedom

> *Much of what I learned about spiritual grounding for sacred activism came to life in 2017 when I spent nearly a week at the Standing Rock encampment.... Standing Rock embodied what it looks like to act for justice and sustainability in the wake of genocide while being guided by the Spirit.... When we entered the area where the pipeline was being built and knew that the police were going to confront and order us to leave, we were instructed by the [Native American] Elders to behave as though we were engaged in sacred ceremony. There would be no violence, no angry words or disrespect.*
>
> —Rabbi Mordechai Liebling[67]

"Sacred ceremony." "Transformative liturgy." What is it about the ancient practice of ritual that cultivates moral-spiritual power to build a better world? Viewing a few snapshots across time and space might shed light on this question. Then we will look more closely at the Christian ritual of Eucharist (also called holy communion) as a "school for seeing."

In Chile, during the torturing and terrorizing Pinochet regime, the Eucharist formed "the church into a body capable of resisting oppression."[68]

* * *

Decades later, Ezra Chitando, a professor of religion in Zimbabwe who is deeply engaged in justice struggles, insists that "liturgy has the capacity to influence action ... prophetic action.... Developing and embracing liturgy that reinforces a theology of enough [for example], particularly in the Global North, is an urgent undertaking."[69]

* * *

His little nose is cold, but his eyes sparkle. The wind buffets his small but colorful banner. It bears a five-year-old's scrawling letters: "Families belong Together!" The ritual is one of prayer and protest outside a detention center holding immigrants from Central America, some of whom have children being held in cages at the border between the United States and Mexico. Led by the Interfaith Movement for Human Integrity (IM4HI), the people who are gathered write letters and sign petitions. My little grandson, with his banner, and my infant granddaughter are among them.

* * *

A few years later the same IM4HI leads a Christmas Eve ritual of prayer for a ceasefire in Israel's war on Palestinians in Gaza. The ritual is mirrored around the nation. New Year's Eve sees rituals blessing "Love Demands Ceasefire Now" banners being unfurled at two Oakland churches. Again, the IM4HI draws people of many faith traditions to share in ritual of prayer and protest.

* * *

Nikkeya, a seminary student in 2018, outraged by the killing of Black people by police, creates a Black Lives Matter liturgy for a class in "Faith-Based Social Transformation." Now an ordained Lutheran pastor, she says, "The process of thinking this liturgy through and writing it has shaped the ways I preach. . . . My ministry has been inspired by it. . . . I believe in the power of the words we hear in worship and those we say together to transform our hearts and move us towards action."

* * *

Recall the stories at this chapter's outset: the young boy Stefano's excited voice exclaiming, "I saw Fidel and his friends dancing to bless the land"; the dancing spiral of elders, youth, and rabbi, engaged in the ritual of repentance for structural sin; the seminary students preaching in the dead of midwestern winter from a snow-laden tree trunk.

Two thousand years ago, in many early Christian communities, the Eucharist was intimately linked with action to ameliorate suffering, while the ritual of baptism strengthened people for the subversive act of switching allegiance from imperial Rome to Christ and—as a consequence—risking death by torture. "Acts of generosity and justice were inseparable from the Eucharist. Christians received the body of Christ to become the life-giving presence of God in the world and to recognize it in Creation." As a result, for example, one fourth-century church in Antioch "reported that it fed three thousand widows, orphans, disabled, and poor people every day. Augustine's congregation in Hippo raised money to buy people out of slavery. [A] church in Edessa created hospitals for an entire city during a yearlong famine."[70]

What is the connection between the ritual of Eucharist and transformative action in the world?[71] Since at least the second century, the Eucharist has been known by some as a school for seeing and, thus, for living.[72] Cyril of Jerusalem admonishes participants to "hallow your eyes by the touch of the sacred Body."[73] Thirteen centuries later, Martin Luther insisted that vision of who we are and

Ingredients of Freedom

how we are to live is obscured when sacramental practice is ignored or distorted.[74] The sacraments are a "way of God in getting through to us, in opening our eyes to face reality."[75] In the Eucharist, we experience that the Creator and Liberator of all is *within* the elements of Earth—in grain and wine—not only within humans or above and beyond it all.[76]

It is no wonder that sharing in the body and blood of Jesus Christ would enable seeing. Jesus constantly opened peoples' eyes, pushing and prodding them to see the world around them differently ("what is"), to see how to live ("what could be"), and to see God present. In first-century Palestine, according to the authors of the Gospel of Mark, Jesus queried his disciples, "Are your hearts hardened? Do you have eyes, and fail to see?" (Mark 8:17–18). Today Jesus asks his followers the same.

To what will the sacrament open our eyes if, through it, God enables people to see differently so that they may live differently, reoriented toward the healing of the world? What kind of vision will evoke the wisdom and courage to struggle toward economic life reshaped along contours of compassion, justice, and Earth's health? Perhaps it is the forms of seeing discussed in chapter 4—what is, what could be, the great Spirit within creation, and beauty.

Rita Nakashima Brock and Rebecca Parker, after years of studying eucharistic ritual in early Christian communities, argue that ritual's power lies in opening our eyes to see "the Spirit of God" filling all things and the beauty that radiates in that divine presence.[77] The "key purpose of the Eucharist" in the early church, they write, was rekindling perception so that people could perceive the divine presence in the world and, thereby, could love neighbor as self.[78] To this day the Eastern church holds that "ritual initiates people into this life-changing knowledge [that] the whole world [is] illumined by the brilliance of divine presence."[79] That knowledge, Brock and Parker explain, cultivates our power to respond to the holy, liberating, and healing Presence in the world.[80] This makes sense—when we are highly attuned to God's presence, we are drawn to respond.[81]

By attuning us to the Spirit's power within us and flowing through all things, religious ritual also may enable truth-telling and the lament that truth may evoke. Ritual can remind us that we can bear to recognize the horrors entwined in our lives without drowning in despair because we are not alone and can find hope. Ritual can reveal that a healing Presence is at work within and among us. That saving Presence—according to Jewish, Christian, Islamic, and many other traditions—is incarnate; it "abides in" the earthy and earthly. Christian Eucharist reveals that this saving power flows instinctively to life's broken places, nurturing power to reshape society in the contours of God's will that all may have life in its fullness.

Filipino theologian Fr. Randy Calo Odchigue takes this concept a step further.[82] If the Eucharist opens eyes both to the Living Presence and to the horrors of injustice, it can also evoke the question of why. If God is present and longing for all to have fullness of life, and if people's lives are broken by systems that cause climate change and terrible poverty, then what is going on? The Eucharist becomes "an event of interrogation as to why some of God's children have large portions of their daily bread while others languish in deprivation.... It is an event of enquiry why there is a hellish division between the 'haves' and the 'have nots' ... why the body of God's creation ... is exploited and made to serve the caprice of the few." In this sense, according to Odchigue, the Eucharist has the "potential to be an event of resistance of the unjust setup of the present."[83]

Yet, religious ritual—including the Christian Eucharist—may also reinforce compliance with the way things are and may even encourage turning away from suffering and its causes. What makes the difference? One factor may be intentionality. If we intend for the Eucharist to connect us to the healing, liberating power of God in our midst, then perhaps that is more likely to happen.

I vividly recall witnessing the power of intentionality:

> Ministerial students in one seminary class had the task of designing a worship and education plan that included tracing the ecological and social justice impacts of everything used in celebration of the Eucharist—grapes that produced the wine, ingredients in the bread, textiles on the altar, the altar itself, the chalice and plate, even the production and transportation of these items. The students were asked to design a way to engage the congregation—both youth and adults—in this inquiry. Second, they were asked to redesign the community's eucharistic practice so that it had, to the extent possible, no negative social or ecological impacts—and instead might even have positive impacts such as supporting the well-being of vulnerable people and of Earth. Upon revealing the negative impacts, eyes were opened; shock jolted the community. Emotions rang out. Some weeks later, the youth and adults in that congregation set out on pathways of courage. They were pathways toward loving neighbors whom they had never considered, neighbors impacted by the congregation's Eucharistic ritual. Engaging this ritual with the intentionality of allowing it to feed their power for Christ-like neighbor-love began to reform the congregation's economic life.

As this story reveals, ritual can help us see both the ways things are and the ways things could be. It can guide us to align our lives with the current of healing and liberation flowing through all things. By enabling us to see the Presence within us, among us, and flowing through all things, ritual can build a bridge between us and that Presence.

Rituals, Brock and Parker insist, are core to a community's life. "They are our most significant form of communication, more powerful than words.... Rituals guide us through the storm-tossed seas of the world—its principalities

Ingredients of Freedom

and powers and its addictive demons." Rituals enable us to "express and survive pain, anger, lamentation, and despair, while being held by others."[84] The familiarity, structure, and rhythm of rituals create a container that can hold the conflicts and tragedies that touch every life and every community.

Interfaith Communion Building

The great trees in forests feed us with oxygen and beauty. They do not work this magic alone; they nourish, support, and complement each other. Where a birch lacks some nutrient, a nearby fir will ferry that element over to her neighbor through a marvelous network of subterranean fungal connectors linked to the trees' roots!

So it is with the world's great faith traditions. When the going gets tough, each has more power for nourishing life when complemented by others. If spirituality and religious faiths have the power to move people toward the good, to free people from captivity to "selves curved in on self," then imagine the power unleashed when religious traditions join efforts, supporting and complementing one another like trees in the forest.

This is already happening in the movement to build life-giving economies.

My hope is fed by the amazing network of religiously rooted groups that is emerging globally, tenaciously committed to building a world where people do not suffer from poverty and injustice and Earth's ecosystems are able to flourish. They have inspired me, challenged me to the core, and taught me. I want to share that inspiration with you. These faithful folks are Indigenous people and settler-colonial people, elders and youth. They include people with no schooling and people with PhDs. They range from "climate warriors" to government policy advocates. They hail from all continents. The beauty of deep listening, respect, and collaboration infuses this fluid and porous network.

This interfaith body of people and organizations working towards economic justice, climate justice, or both is largely invisible to the public eye. Their work includes calls to action, teachings about the role of justice seeking and creation care in the life of faith, resources for public policy advocacy, partnerships with secular organizations, testimonies to policy-making bodies such as the World Bank and the International Monetary Fund, participation in marches and civil disobedience, and more. Their work incorporates theological education, prayer, rituals and other practices, and reinterpretations of scriptures from Earth perspectives.

Ecological crises, especially climate change, are catalyzing interfaith collaboration. Jews, Muslims, Christians, Buddhists, Bahá'ís, Hindus, Indigenous communities, and others have forged alliances across theological and cultural boundaries to bring healing and hope.

My fervent hope is that you will see yourself and your local communities as part of this greater global community of people deeply moved by their faith and spirituality. That you will find yourself called to throw passion, time, and other resources into the sacred work of building a flourishing and equitable Earth community in accord with your highest values and sense of the Sacred. Here we glimpse a sampling of that feast. Then, I invite you to go further and explore the networks listed here and in the online toolkit that accompanies this book. What local interfaith networks are at work in your city or state? Is there a local or state chapter of GreenFaith, Interfaith Power and Light, or another interfaith group noted here? What would it look like for you or your community to link forces with them?

Let us savor a small sampling!

- Baháʼí, Buddhist, Christian, Hindu, Islamic, Jewish, and Rastafarian folks gather in an Interfaith consultation on Just Finance and Reparations. Their purpose? To "dialogue with and learn from diverse faith perspectives and to deepen interfaith cooperation on economic justice."[85] They produce a joint statement entitled "Just Economics for Liberation and Life: Interfaith Message on Just Finance, Debt, and Reparations." It "identifies common ground and calls for urgent action to tackle the debt crisis and to build more just, reparative, and restorative financial and economic structures."[86] The plea emphasizes releasing countries in the Global South from their damaging external debt burdens.
- The Inter-religious Climate and Ecology Network (ICE) emerged from an interreligious conference in Sri Lanka. ICE is a pan-Asian organization based in South Korea. Its purpose is "to bring the wisdom of religious traditions and the influence of religious leaders and institutions into dialogue and action around climate change... to address the root causes of climate change and respond to its emerging effects."[87] In 2022, the ICE Network brought together 35,000 people in Seoul to march in the fourth Global Climate Strike. Their "2022 Statement for Climate Justice by the Global South,"[88] signed by sixty-three interfaith organizations, drew attention to the impact of climate change on Global South countries. Members of the ICE Network have brought this statement to the embassies of every G8 country.
- The Muslim Council of Elders, New York Board of Rabbis, World Council of Churches (WCC), and United Nations Environment Programme jointly signed a landmark appeal, "Climate-Responsible Finance: A Moral Imperative and Responsibility to All Children and the Living World."[89] The 2022 launch of the appeal featured the UN Secretary-General, who supported the call.[90]
- The World Council of Churches was one of the first organizations to link economic exploitation with climate change. For decades, the WCC has called Christian communities to advocate for justice in the global economy and to seek justice for climate-vulnerable communities. From the beginning, this work has been in collaboration with other ecumenical and interfaith

organizations as well as with secular organizations such as several United Nations' programs.
- The Interfaith Rainforest Initiative, GreenFaith, Temple of Understanding, Interfaith Power and Light, La Foie et le Bien Commun (Faith and the Common Good), and the Jubilee Campaign are other examples of interfaith initiatives working towards climate justice, economic justice, or both.[91]

May the impetus for interreligious communion-building thrive and rise above the barriers that humans have constructed between religions. May religious traditions, once known for enmity, rise together to nourish one another's power—like the trees in the forest—to help forge moral economies at this crucible point in history.

In Sum

Advanced global capitalism—as a culture and as an economic system—sucks individuals and societies into absorption with self, including accumulating wealth, escalating consumption, and ignoring the consequences of these on others and Earth. The collective impact of that trajectory has become deadly. Religious traditions are uniquely situated to help individuals and communities gain a degree of freedom from that self-absorption and freedom for serving a good that includes self and others—a good characterized by compassion, social justice, and Earth's well-being.

We explored the understanding that the world's long-standing faith traditions arose to orient people around that greater good. We then noted ten elements within religious faiths that could make them a life-giving force of freedom from "selves curved in on self" in the current context, freedom for the urgently needed movement towards more ecological and equitable economies. Finally, we noted two practices of religious traditions—one ancient and one dawning—that could help equip people who draw from religious traditions to play this life-saving role.

The verb *could* appears twice in what you just read. It matters. These ingredients and practices do not assure that religions will come to our aid. That depends upon people working with one another, with Earth, and with the great Spirit—people who will dig into these elements and practices of religion, honing them intentionally to bring forth their riches in this time of dire need. Yes, this is a matter of life and death. And it is a beautiful calling.

May people who have been fed by spiritual and religious leanings bring the gifts of religions and spiritualities to the great moral-spiritual challenge of our time—forging forms of economic life that this glorious planet can sustain and that cultivate fullness of life for all.

Moving On
Pathways for People of Courage

> I go and look at a stonecutter hammering away at his rock, perhaps a hundred times without as much as a crack showing in it. Yet at the hundred and first blow it will split in two, and I know it was not that last blow that did it, but all that had gone before.
>
> —Jacob August Riis

> Oh Great Spirit, "you have called your servants to ventures of which we cannot see the ending, by paths as yet untrodden, through perils unknown. Give us faith to go out with good courage, not knowing where we go, but only that your hand is leading us and your love supporting us."
>
> —Holden Village Prayer[1]

WHEN MY GRANDCHILDREN were wee babes, I watched their fierce determination to push up on their little legs to stand. They tumbled and struggled up again, to stand and to walk. They fell, scraped, cried in frustration, allowed themselves to be comforted, and then those tenacious little spirits pushed up yet again to stand and to venture forth. They could not be held back. With courage they faced unknown perils on the paths before them.

Together with companions the world over, you venture forth. With tenacity, with courage. The pathways lead to ways of living together on this planet that enable garden Earth to sing its song of life, ways of living that reverse the mad rampage toward climate catastrophe and instead cultivate well-being for all. I cannot pretend to have absolute certainty that we will succeed. But I am certain that we are blessed and called to move forward embodying hope in strategic, collaborative action.

Throughout we have recognized this journey as one of healing—healing ourselves, our loved ones, our communities, and our society from a diseased form of economic life to an "economy for life." Healing our relationships with neighbors far and near. We have dared to see economic life as a spiritual practice.

Savor the vision: economic life as a web of relationships in which people and Earth are good medicine for each other, and people are good medicine for one another. Ah, but it is more than vision alone. It is reality in the making. The sacred healing journey is underway and has spread among cultures and continents.

Bear in mind the five vital links introduced in "Setting the Stage." They build power for healing economic life. They are bridges in the journey toward a more compassionate, just, and ecologically sane future. They are the interplay

- among ten fingers on the healing hands of change (or forms of action);
- among local, national, and global efforts;
- among behavioral, structural, and consciousness change;
- between resistance and rebuilding;
- between small practical steps and larger systemic change.

Why is it so vital to recognize and amplify these connections? Our efforts, when seen as isolated, can seem so small. "Perhaps," we muse, "they make a difference on a small scale, but surely they will not subvert capitalism as we know it, transforming it like a caterpillar into a different kind of creature!" *However, when we intentionally notice how our efforts are or could be linked in these five ways, then our role in building a new economy emerges into view.* You might try diagramming how these links exist already in your life or in the work of your faith community or other network. Then, with another color, diagram how you could augment these connections.

Living into these connections enables us to address the crucial question that confronts all who hunger for more equitable economic lives, for economic systems that enable life to flourish: How are we to bring about change in huge systems such as the economy? No question could be more important in the current crucible of economic ways that are hurdling us into disaster. Yet a practical realistic response is elusive. Many people abandon the quest because it seems unattainable. *Herein lies the value and power of the links noted above. They reveal paths into systemic change. These are pathways for people of courage.*

In walking these paths, you will find yourself in a community of communities that transcends cultures, continents, and time. You will find yourself in a creative, tenacious, fallible and faulty, but sacred host of holy friends.

Do you recall the metaphor of the chrysalis offered by Emily Kawano in chapter 8?

> *"When a caterpillar spins its chrysalis, its body starts to break down into this nutrient rich group, and within that nutrient-rich group are what are called imaginal cells. And those cells have an imagination of what it could be that's different from the caterpillar.... They find each other and they begin to clump.... As they clump and come together and recognize*

each other, they start to specialize into a wing and an antenna, an eye and a leg until they emerge as a butterfly, a transformed creature." This is metaphor for building a moral economy.[2]

Previously we saw this metaphor revealing connections between various efforts to "build the new" (the first finger on the hands of healing change). Yet, the metaphor illumines also the interaction among the ten fingers on the hands of change, and the interplay afoot in all of the vital links that we have noted in the movement to build a moral economy. The movement itself is a bit like a caterpillar transforming into a butterfly. The various fingers on the hands of healing are like imaginal cells. Some orient around policy change. Others become new forms of business, agriculture, or finance. Still others lead direct acts of resistance, while yet others focus on moving money from extractive industries to just and renewable ones. Other cells change the story through resistance art, theology and liturgy, or other means. Some work their magic locally and others in global networks. None of the butterfly parts (the wings, antennae ...) could function alone. Yet, together they are shedding the violence of economies based on exploitation and extraction. They are birthing life-giving forms of economic life, in which people are good medicine for each other and Earth—economies without sacrifice zones, economic life that honors our deepest values of human dignity, justice, compassion, and Earth-care.

This book is followed by five others. They, unlike this one, are "small books," about one hundred pages. The books focus on
- climate justice and climate hope
- food and food justice for all
- water and water justice for all
- housing and housing justice for all
- religion as a source of hope and power for building moral economies

Each of them (including this one) has a carefully curated online toolkit. These toolkits overflow with resources. In them you may find companions from around the world in this healing journey, hear their stories, receive hope and wisdom from them. You may listen to the books' authors to learn more of their hopes, fears, and sources of moral-spiritual power. You will find film, art, music, more readings, exercises, and other tools for the journey toward an equitable and ecologically sane future.

The books and toolkits are not comprehensive, but rather illustrative in carefully planned ways that point to a more comprehensive picture of economic transformation. You will find information on them at this series' website: https://buildingamoraleconomy.org/. I invite you to have a look, and enjoy the feast.

Parts of you are older than Earth. Our bodies are over 50 percent water. Some of those water molecules, scientists suggest, may have landed on Earth in meteors that came from planets in other solar systems that predate ours. Those water molecules in your body, then, are older than Earth. There is wisdom in we humans, wisdom of the ages. Earth now needs us to use it. So do our neighbors.

Let us use our wisdom to forge pathways into a future where we, our descendants, and our other-than-human kin in this garden Earth may flourish. These are pathways for people of courage.

NOTES

INVITATION

1. Occasionally I refer to humans as "creatures" or "earthlings" in order to reinforce our awareness that we are indeed "animals" and as such are a part of, rather than separate from, Earth's economy of life—water, air, soil, and living things made of the elements that burst forth 13.5 billion years ago in the "Big Bang." This we discuss more fully in chapter 16.
2. The "we" here is Earth's high-consuming people.
3. Scientists vary in estimating the number of years remaining in which we may radically reduce greenhouse gas emissions before it is too late to avert the full extent of climate disaster. Some say the time is past, while others insist that we still have a few more years.
4. William J. Ripple, Christopher Wolf, Thomas M. Newsome, Mauro Galetti, Mohammed Alamgir, Eileen Crist, Mahmoud I. Mahmoud, and William F. Laurance. "World Scientists' Warning to Humanity: A Second Notice." *BioScience* 67, no. 12 (2017): 1026–28. https://doi.org/10.1093/biosci/bix125. See also https://www.earth4all.life/.
5. I talked recently at a party with a young woman who had completed an enormously challenging physical feat that stretched over many hours. "How did you manage to do it?" I asked. "The support of my companions," she said with a grin.
6. Psychotherapist Nancy Ulmer says, "You might call it intentionally making 'social justice' friends, soul friends, whatever. If there is a spiritual base, all the better."
7. We build on these efforts by
   - making them visible to people not yet aware that they exist on such a broad scale;
   - distinguishing three arenas of change—behavioral change, systems change, and worldview change—and demonstrating the mutually empowering links between them;
   - building capacity for engaging in this movement of movements;
   - conceptually organizing the multiple forms of action into the framework developed in part 3;
   - making global-local connections;
   - indicating the invaluable role of religious/spiritual traditions in this movement;
   - demonstrating the joy and even delight to be found in aligning our lives with the "arc of the universe bending toward justice."
8. Marti Stortz, "Address to the ELCA Cabinet of Executives," unpublished paper, December 17, 2002.
9. See chapter 18.

CHAPTER ONE

1. Justice Louis D. Brandeis (1856–1941).
2. Coral Davenport, "Major Climate Report Describes a Strong Risk of Crisis as Early as 2040," *New York Times*, October 8, 2018, https://tinyurl.com/ysb868ft. The article cites a report issued in 2018 by the Intergovernmental Panel on Climate Change (IPCC). See https://www.ipcc.ch/sr15/.
3. Naomi Klein. "Foreword," in *The Making of a Democratic Economy*, by Marjorie Kelly and Ted Howard (Oakland, CA: Berrett-Koehler Publishers, 2019), ix–x.
4. This is the introductory volume for a series of books on building a moral economy. The books will be published between fall 2024 and fall 2026. All are accompanied by a set of online resources. See this book's "Moving On" for further information on the series.
5. The Sustainable Economies Law Center says it well: "Neither our communities nor our ecosystems are well served by an economic system that incentivizes perpetual growth, wealth concentration, and the exploitation of land and people. Communities everywhere are responding to these converging economic and ecological crises with a grassroots transformation of our economy that is rapidly re-localizing production, reducing resource consumption, and rebuilding the relationships that make our communities thrive" (https://www.theselc.org/mission).
6. According to the website www.inequality.org, one man—Elon Musk—owns more wealth than the bottom 40 percent of (US) Americans (https://tinyurl.com/24tw2bdz). According to the *New York Times Magazine*, in one minute Jeff Bezos adds more to his wealth (about $30,000) than some people make in a year of full-time labor (https://tinyurl.com/4vka78pk). But, according to *Forbes*, virtually none of that wealth growth—the main source of billionaire income—may ever be taxed (https://tinyurl.com/38mwfh63). During the pandemic, billionaires like Bezos and Musk got 70 percent richer while millions of US Americans lost their incomes. (https://tinyurl.com/4377ykum). These sources were provided by former Secretary of Labor Robert Reich in an email from his organization, Inequality Media, on April 18, 2022.
7. Thomas Berry, *The Great Work: Our Way into the Future* (New York: Bell Tower, 2000).
8. See n2. In a similar tone, earth4All notes, "The next ten years must see the fastest economic transformation in history." See https://www.earth4all.life/. Accessed February 10, 2024. earth4All is a network of leading economic thinkers, scientists, policy leaders, and advocates, convened by the Club of Rome, the Potsdam Institute for Climate Impact Research, the Stockholm Resilience Centre and the Norwegian Business School.
9. Robin Wall Kimmerer, *Braiding Sweetgrass: Indigenous Wisdom, Scientific Knowledge, and the Teachings of Plants* (Minneapolis: Milkweed Editions, 2013), x.
10. See https://fairfoodprogram.org/. Accessed February 10, 2024.
11. See Mike Davis, *Late Victorian Holocausts: El Nino Famines and the Making of the Third World* (London: Verso, 2001).
12. Food deserts are geographic regions in which people have few or no options for convenient access to affordable and healthy food, especially fresh vegetables and fruits.

Notes

13. To illustrate: Jewish and Christian Scriptures are utterly clear that love for God and love for neighbor are inextricably related. See, for example, Matt 22:36-40 and Lev 19:18.
14. Rabbi Mordechai Liebling, "Living in the Four Worlds," in *Rooted and Rising: Voices of Courage in a Time of Climate Crisis*, ed. Leah D. Schade and Margaret Bullitt-Jonas (Lanham, MD: Rowman & Littlefield Publishers, 2019), 5.
15. See Tracy Matsue Loeffelholz, "Divesting Money from Fossil Fuels," *Yes Magazine*, December 27, 2022, https://tinyurl.com/498y58z2.
16. When I say "their lands," I mean that to include their forests, minerals, waters, and more.
17. Hadewijch of Brabant, *The Complete Works of Hadewijch*, trans. Mother Columba Hart (New York: Paulist Press, 1980). Hadewijch was a thirteenth-century mystic woman of the Beguine community.
18. "Mud creatures" is close to the Greek word used by second-century theologian Irenaeus of Lyons to translate the Hebrew *a-dam*. See Denis Minns, *Ireneaus* (Washington, DC: Georgetown University Press, 1994).
19. In chapter 3 we will explore the notion of communion.
20. See an excellent discussion in Paul Tillich, *The Courage to Be* (New Haven, CT: Yale University Press, 1952), 3, 23–24, and 32.
21. Fr. Jon Sobrino, conversation with the author at University of Central America, San Salvador.
22. World Inequality Lab, "World Inequality Report 2022," World Inequality Report, https://wir2022.wid.world/. Accessed February 10, 2024.
23. Daniel C. Maquire, *The Moral Core of Judaism and Christianity* (Minneapolis: Fortress Press, 1993), 10.
24. See n2.

CHAPTER TWO

1. Speaking in conversation to a delegation that I co-led for the Center for Global Education (CGE) of Augsburg College.
2. Speaking to a delegation of US religious leaders that I co-led for the CGE of Augsburg College.
3. From a speech at the UN Summit on Climate Change, Copenhagen, September 22, 2009.
4. Factory farming of cattle for meat production produces dangerous amounts a methane, a greenhouse gas that remains in the atmosphere even longer than CO_2.
5. William J. Ripple et al., Christopher Wolf, Thomas M. Newsome, Mauro Galetti, Mohammed Alamgir, Eileen Crist, Mahmoud I. Mahmoud, William F. Laurance, and 15,364 scientist signatories from 184 countries, "World Scientists' Warning to Humanity: A Second Warning," *BioScience* I 67, no. 12 (December 2017). See also an Oxfam report documenting extreme carbon inequity (Oxfam, "Extreme Carbon Inequality," Oxfam Media Briefing December 2, 2015).
6. John Paul II, *Solicitudo Rei Sociales* [The Social Concern], Encyclical Letter on the Concern of the Church for the Social Order, December 30, 1987. https://tinyurl.com/yckkbxy9.

7. Lim Mah-Hui and Michael Heng Siam-Heng, *COVID-19 and the Structural Crises of Our Time* (Singapore: ISEAS-Yusof Ishak Institute, 2021), 9.
8. For example, see Vincent Gallagher, *The True Cost of Low Prices* (Maryknoll, NY: Orbis Books, 2006).
9. Sarah Anderson and Sam Pizzigati, "Executive Excess 2022" (Washington DC: Institute for Policy Studies, June 2022), 4. https://tinyurl.com/mwwa2bvp. The study examined three hundred publicly held US corporations that had the lowest median wages in 2020.
10. For example: "At $171,000, the net worth of a typical white family is nearly ten times greater than that of a Black family ($17,150) in 2016." In Kriston McIntosh et al., "Examining the Black-White Wealth Gap," *Brookings Institute Commentary* (blog), February 27, 2020, https://tinyurl.com/bdfzpd52.
11. See David Callahan, "How the GI Bill Left Out African Americans," *Demos Blog* (blog), November 11, 2013, https://tinyurl.com/4xtwa4z9; Eileen Boris and Michael Honey, "Gender, Race, and the Policies of the Labor Department," *Monthly Labor Review*, February 1988, https://tinyurl.com/bdf9knnp; Michael Harriot, "The Great White Heist," *Yes Magazine*, August 26, 2020, https://tinyurl.com/579ydced; Leah Douglas, "US Black Farmers Lost $326 Billion Worth of Land in 20th Century—Study," *Reuters*, May 2, 2022, sec. United States, https://tinyurl.com/4dpav5un; Darrick Hamilton and Naomi Zewde, "Truth and Redistribution," *Yes Magazine*, August 26, 2020, https://tinyurl.com/3jpk9e7w; and an excellent library of resources from Duke's World Food Policy Center on Black Land Loss at https://tinyurl.com/u9z3mtrv.
12. Vincent Miller, *Consuming Religion: Christian Faith and Practice in a Consumer Culture* (New York: Continuum, 2005), 107 and 110, cited in Erika Katske, "St. Augustine and Economic Desire," unpublished paper, 2022.
13. In 1929, to illustrate, the Committee on Recent Economic Change, established by President Hoover, found that the nation needed a robust advertising industry to create "new wants that will make way for endlessly newer wants as fast as they are satisfied." Al Gore, *The Future: Six Drivers of Climate Change* (New York: Random House, 2013), 159.
14. Significant parts of this paragraph are taken from Cynthia Moe-Lobeda, *Resisting Structural Evil: Love as Ecological-Economic Vocation* (Minneapolis: Fortress Press, 2013), 99–100.
15. John C. Stauber and Sheldon Rampton, *Toxic Sludge Is Good for You: Lies, Damn Lies, and the Public Relations Industry* (Monroe, ME: Common Courage Press, 1995), 17–24.
16. "Advertising aimed at women works by lowering our self-esteem," writes Naomi Wolf, author of *The Beauty Myth*. Betty Friedan's *The Feminine Mystique* traces some of the origins of advertising to American housewives in the 1950's that began manipulating insecurities into dollars. A marketing service report at that time instructed advertisers to capitalize on "guilt over hidden dirt" and to stress the "therapeutic value of baking." Identify your products with "spiritual rewards," almost a "religious belief," the report advised. Today focus has shifted from household goods to clothes, cosmetics, and the body itself. Betty Friedan as cited in Naomi Wolf, *The Beauty Myth: How Images of Beauty Are Used against Women* (New York: W. Morrow, 1991), 66–67.

17. See for example Richard G Wilkinson and Kate Pickett, *The Spirit Level: Why Greater Equality Makes Societies Stronger* (New York: Bloomsbury, 2010) and Richard Wilkinson and Kate Pickett, *The Inner Level: How More Equal Societies Reduce Stress, Restore Sanity and Improve Everybody's Wellbeing* (New York: Allen Lane, 2018).
18. "The Science of Inequality," *Scientific American*, November 1, 2018, https://tinyurl.com/yc4fz6u4.
19. Richard Wilkinson and Kate Pickett, "From Inequality to Sustainability" (Geneva, Switzerland: earth4All, a Project of the Club of Rome, April 2022), https://tinyurl.com/2e36v4xr. It is interesting to note that the authors are professors of social epidemiology and epidemiology respectively. They note that "across all income groups, people in more unequal societies feel more anxiety about status and how others judge their status. . . . Inequality increases what might be called the 'pressure to consume.' As a result, debt and bankruptcies are higher in more unequal societies as people try to maintain appearances of affluence and respectability." The authors draw on Robert Frank, *Falling Behind: How Rising Inequality Harms the Middle Class*, vol. 4 (Berkeley: University of California Press, 2013); R. Layte and C. T. Whelan, "Who Feels Inferior? A Test of the Status Anxiety Hypothesis of Social Inequalities in Health," *European Sociological Review* 30, no. 4 (June 4, 2014): 525–35, https://doi.org/10.1093/esr/jcu057; and Lukasz Walasek and Gordon D. A. Brown, "Income Inequality, Income, and Internet Searches for Status Goods: A Cross-National Study of the Association between Inequality and Well-Being," *Social Indicators Research* 129, no. 3 (November 2, 2015): 1001–14, https://doi.org/10.1007/s11205-015-1158-4.
20. Wilkinson and Pickett, "From Inequality to Sustainability." The authors cite studies published in *Journal of Adolescent Health*, *European Journal of Public Health*, *Research in Social Stratification and Mobility*, and *Public Health*.
21. Deanna Thompson, unpublished paper on sin and shame (presentation, Annual Meeting of the American Academy of Religion, Denver, November, 2022).
22. This form of economic life is variously known as neoliberalism, corporate- or finance-driven globalization, advanced global capitalism, and financialized capitalism.
23. Earth cannot continue to provide for what this form of economy requires:
    - Unlimited growth.
    - Unlimited "earth services" (required for unlimited growth) such as "soil formation and erosion control, pollination, climate and atmosphere regulation, [and] biological control of pests and diseases." (See Janet Abramovitz, "Putting a Value on Nature's 'Free' Services," *World Watch Magazine*, January 1998, 14–15.)
    - Unlimited "resources" (required for unlimited growth) such as oil, timber, minerals, breathable air, cultivable soil, oceans with a balanced pH factor, the ocean's food chain, and potable water.
    - An unregulated market in which the most powerful players are economic entities that have:
        - Mandates to maximize profit
        - The legal and civil rights of a person
        - Limited liability
        - No accountability to political bodies, be they cities, states, nations, or other
        - The right to privatize, own, and sell goods long considered public

- Freedom of individuals to do as they please with economic assets (including unlimited carbon emissions and speculative investment that results in the economies of nations crashing).
24. This reality is documented in countless studies. For example: Lawrence Mishel and Jori Kandra, "CEO Pay Has Skyrocketed 1,322% since 1978," Economic Policy Institute, August 10, 2021, https://tinyurl.com/bdh99567; Sarah Hansen, "Richest Americans—Including Bezos, Musk and Buffett—Paid Federal Income Taxes Equaling Just 3.4% of $401 Billion in New Wealth, Bombshell Report Shows," *Forbes*, June 8, 2021, https://tinyurl.com/47p5ucb7; Barbara Kollmeyer, "The World's Richest 10 Men Doubled Their Fortunes to $1.5 Trillion during the Pandemic, Says Oxfam," *MarketWatch*, January 17, 2022, https://tinyurl.com/5bdrztm5.
25. "If our most powerful elites are now essentially beyond the reach of accountability, as they increasingly seem to be, then why suppose that our polity qualifies as a *democratic republic* at all? It appears to function, rather, as a plutocracy, a system in which the fortunate few dominate the rest.... The question of democratic hope boils down to whether the basic concepts of our political heritage apply to the world in which we now live." Jeffrey Stout, *Blessed Are the Organized* (Princeton, NJ: Princeton University Press, 2020), xv. Also see chapter 3 in Cynthia Moe-Lobeda, *Healing a Broken World: Globalization and God* (Minneapolis: Fortress Press, 2003).
26. "Kindom" of God is used by many people instead of "kingdom" of God to avoid the connotation that God is male and a king.
27. This calling may be situated theologically in various ways in Christian traditions:
- As a framework for heeding God's two great economic rules—to serve and preserve God's garden earth (Gen 2:15) and to love thy neighbor as thyself (Lev 19:18 and Matt 22:39).
- As a framework for living the resurrection.
- As a mode of discipleship.
- As embodying the biblical call to justice.
28. These voices arise from varying locations politically. See for example Drew Hansen, "Unless It Changes, Capitalism Will Starve Humanity by 2050," *Forbes*, February 9, 2016, https://tinyurl.com/msefnucv.
29. Just Capital, "Survey: What Americans Want from Corporate America during the Response, Reopening, and Reset Phases of the Coronavirus Crisis," June 8, 2020, https://tinyurl.com/4ryfjhce.
30. Matthew Beaumont, "Imagining the End Times: Ideology, the Contemporary Disaster Movie, *Contagion*," in *Žižek and Media Studies*, ed. Matthew Flisfeder and Louis-Paul Willis (New York: Palgrave Macmillan, 2014) and citing Fredric Jameson, "Future City," *New Left Review* 21 (May–June 2003): 76.
31. Eric Liu, *You're More Powerful Than You Think: A Citizen's Guide to Making Change Happen* (New York: Hachette, 2018), 201.
32. See https://www.mondragon-corporation.com. Accessed February 10, 2024.
33. The FFP began with tomato growers in Florida and has expanded to large tomato growers in seven states and is moving into other crops in other states. See https://tinyurl.com/4e68rhv9.
34. https://fairfoodprogram.org/ and https://ciw-online.org/about/. Accessed February 10, 2024.

Notes

35. https://fairfoodprogram.org/. Accessed February 10, 2024.
36. Circular economies are based on three principles: eliminating waste and pollution, circulating products and materials, and regeneration of nature. The European Parliament defines a circular economy as "a model of production and consumption, which involves sharing, leasing, reusing, repairing, refurbishing and recycling existing materials and products as long as possible." From European Parliament, "Circular Economy: Definition, Importance and Benefits," European Parliament, May 24, 2023, https://tinyurl.com/4x5ay39u.
37. https://tinyurl.com/4hz9j38t. Accessed February 10, 2024.
38. C40 Cities, "Amsterdam's Circular Economy Roadmap: Lessons Learned and Tools for Upscaling," C40 Cities, November 2018, https://tinyurl.com/ywyxy5v2.

CHAPTER THREE

1. Kate Raworth, *Doughnut Economics* (White River Junction, VT: Chelsea Green Publishing, 2017), 243.
2. Chabad.org, "What Is Tikkun Olam?," June 12, 2017, https://www.chabad.org/library/article_cdo/aid/3700275/jewish/What-Is-Tikkun-Olam.htm. The article goes on to say, "Tikkun Olam is a profound Jewish concept, the place where mysticism meets activism."
3. For further discussion of indirect violence in relationship to economic and ecological injustice and the initial theorist behind this concept, John Galtung, see Moe-Lobeda, *Resisting Structural Evil*, chapter 3.
4. I am not alone in understanding our economic lives as diseased. Imam Omar Suleiman, founder and resident of Yaqeen Institute for Islamic Research, identifies historic injustices as "spiritual diseases" (See "Moral Revolution: An Interfaith Response to the Coronavirus Pandemic," April 9, 2020. https://fb.watch/qNKIZPt8qj/). In addition Jesuit priest Ignacio Ellacuría, in his last speech given ten days before his assassination in 1989 by US trained elite forces of the Salvadoran Army, averred "This civilization is gravely ill—sick unto death. . . . To avoid an ominous, fatal outcome, the civilization must be changed. . . . We have to turn history around, subvert it, and send it in a new direction" (quoted in Jon Sobrino, *No Salvation Outside the Poor* [Maryknoll, NY: Orbis Books, 2015]). Likewise, the contemporary Poor People's Campaign, in its Jubilee Platform, speaks of "a society sick with the interlocking injustices . . . of systemic racism, poverty, ecological devastation, militarism, and the war economy."
5. The assumption that it is part of God's plan is an element of the doctrine of Manifest Destiny, which has theological roots. For example, theologian Willie James Jennings documents the late sixteenth-century Jesuit priest Jose de Acosta Porres's argument that God had endowed the Americas with mineral abundance for the purpose of creating colonial desire so that the Europeans would "seek out and possess those lands" and, in the process, bring Christianity and "worship of the true God to men who did not know it." Willie James Jennings, *The Christian Imagination: Theology and the Origins of Race* (New Haven, CT: Yale University Press, 2010), 92, citing Jose de Acosta Porres, *Historia* IV:2.
6. See, for example, David Suzuki and Amanda McConnell, *The Sacred Balance: A Vision of Life on earth* (Vancouver: Greystone Books, 1997), 131; and Karen Barad,

"What Flashes Up," in *Entangled Worlds*, ed. Catherine Keller and Mary-Jane Rubenstein (New York: Fordham University Press, 2017), 21–88.
7. A significant portion of this paragraph and the next are taken from Moe-Lobeda, "Method in Eco-Theology: A Perspective from the Belly of the Beast," in *An Earthed Faith*, vol. 2, *How Would We Know What God Is Up To?*, ed. Cynthia Moe-Lobeda and Ernst Conradie (Eugene, OR: Pickwick, 2023).
8. Willie James Jennings, *After Whiteness: An Education in Belonging* (Grand Rapids, MI: William B. Eerdmans Publishing Company, 2020), 10 and 152. Howard Thurman also argues that "community . . . is the fundamental intent of life" in *Disciplines of the Spirit* (Richmond, IN: Friends United Press, 2003), 94–95.
9. Bartholomew I, Ecumenical Patriarch of Constantinople, and John Chryssavgis, *Cosmic Grace, Humble Prayer: The Ecological Vision of the Green Patriarch Bartholomew* (Grand Rapids, MI: W.B. Eerdmans, 2009), 28, 218, 315.
10. See https://tinyurl.com/4em27tbz.
11. A Buddhist maxim.
12. Yuval Noah Harari, *Sapiens: A Brief History of Humankind* (New York: Harper, 2015), 24–39.
13. For more details about racism in housing and zoning policy in the US since the 1920s, see Richard Rothstein, *The Color of Law: A Forgotten History of How Our Government Segregated America* (New York: Liveright Publishing Corporation, 2017).
14. As taught by the anthropologist Levi-Strauss.
15. Parker J. Palmer, *The Courage to Teach: Exploring the Inner Landscape of a Teacher's Life* (San Francisco: John Wiley & Sons, 2007), 26.
16. The term, "tragic gap" comes from Parker Palmer. See https://tinyurl.com/mspcfj8z. Accessed February 10, 2024.
17. Stay tuned for more regarding employee-owned business in chapter 8.
18. Palmer, *The Courage to Teach*, 74.
19. A gift of Lutheran theological tendencies (the tradition in which I am critically situated) is to recognize that the two are deeply intertwined.
20. To illustrate:
    - Religious traditions both pass on and betray the heart of their message.
    - While I am a "beneficiary" and perpetuator of racism, economic exploitation, and climate violence, I also am damaged by these systemic evils and strive to dismantle them.
21. Michael Simire, "Vanuatu Makes Historic Call for Treaty to End Fossil Fuel Era," *EnviroNews Nigeria*, September 23, 2022, https://tinyurl.com/yvafd42e.
22. Simire, "Vanuatu Makes Historic Call."
23. https://fossilfueltreaty.org/history. Accessed February 10, 2024.
24. They go on to say that "Vanuatu's call builds on years of diplomatic efforts to curb fossil fuel production. Eight years ago, 14 Pacific Island nations met in the Solomon Islands to consider a treaty that would ban new fossil fuel development for signatories and commit them to renewable energy targets. At the UN climate conference in 2017, Fiji underscored the importance of managing the phaseout of fossil fuels, and at COP26 in Glasgow last year, Tuvalu was at the forefront of pushing for reparations for damage caused by climate change."

25. Simire, "Vanuatu Makes Historic Call."
26. The Sustainable Economies Law Center says it well: "Neither our communities nor our ecosystems are well served by an economic system that incentivizes perpetual growth, wealth concentration, and the exploitation of land and people. Communities everywhere are responding to these converging economic and ecological crises with a grassroots transformation of our economy that is rapidly re-localizing production, reducing resource consumption, and rebuilding the relationships that make our communities thrive" (see https://www.theselc.org/mission).
27. "Economy for life" is the term used by, among others, the Indigenous Environmental Network, the Uniting Church of Australia (see https://tinyurl.com/ffpjf4kc) and Movement Generation's Justice and Ecology Project (see "From Banks and Tanks to Cooperation and Caring," page 2; https://tinyurl.com/2kw6hs5z). "Economy of life" is also used by the Council for World Mission and by the World Council of Churches, which also uses the term "new international financial and economic architecture." The Solidarity Economy Networks use the term "solidarity economy." "New Economy" is used by the New Economy Coalition, among others. "Moral Economy" is a term made popular in recent years by the Poor People's Campaign. "The new restoration economy" is used in Phoebe Barnard et al., "World Scientists' Warnings into Action, Local to Global," *Science Progress* 104, no. 4 (October 2021), https://doi.org/10.1177/00368504211056290. The Center for Economic Democracy uses the terms "economic democracy" and "new democracy movement." "Wellbeing economy" is a term used by the Club of Rome and by some national governments including Iceland, New Zealand, Finland, Wales, and Scotland (see https://weall.org/wego). For a description of solidarity economy, see Emily Kawano and Julie Matthaei, "System Change: A Basic Primer to the Solidarity Economy," *Nonprofit News* (NPQ, July 8, 2020), https://tinyurl.com/yysr2x7u. They explain that solidarity economy is "a post-capitalist framework that emerged in Latin America and Europe in the 1990s. It rejects state-dominated authoritarian forms of socialism, instead affirming a core commitment to participatory democracy. Furthermore, it is explicitly feminist, anti-racist, and ecological, and advocates for economic transformation that transcends *all* of forms of oppression, not just class." Solidarity Economy embraces "many co-existing visions . . . of democratic post capitalist economic systems."
28. For example, the (disproportionately white) investing classes in the US profit financially through enterprises that exploit Black and Brown lives. Those enterprises include privatized prisons that use prisoners (disproportionately Black) for cheap labor and require monetary payments from them upon leaving prison; weapons manufacturing and sales that kill people of color around the globe; companies using contingent labor and paying unliveable wages; and more. In discussing the financialization of the US economy and its racialized nature in recent decades, sociologist Matthew Desmond argues, "As it's usually narrated, the story of the ascendancy of American finance tends to begin in 1980, with the gutting of Glass-Steagall, or in 1944 with Bretton Woods, or perhaps in the reckless speculation of the 1920s. But in reality, the story begins during slavery. During slavery, 'Americans built a culture of speculation unique in its abandon,' writes the historian Joshua Rothman in his 2012 book, *Flush Times and Fever Dreams*. That culture would drive cotton production until the Civil War, and it

has been a defining characteristic of American capitalism ever since. It is the culture of growth and wealth acquisition regardless of the cost to others, and of abusing the powerless. It is the culture that brought us the Panic of 1837, the stock-market crash of 1929, and the recession of 2008. It is the culture that has produced staggering inequality and undignified working conditions. If today America promotes a particular kind of low-road capitalism — a union-busting capitalism of poverty wages, gig jobs and normalized insecurity; a winner-take-all capitalism of stunning disparities not only permitting but awarding financial rule-bending; a racist capitalism that ignores the fact that slavery didn't just deny black freedom but built white fortunes, originating the black-white wealth gap that annually grows wider — one reason is that American capitalism was founded on the lowest road there is" (Matthew Desmond, "American Capitalism Is Brutal. You Can Trace That to the Plantation," *New York Times*, August 14, 2019, https://tinyurl.com/2hyfn9rj).

29. See chapter 7 for more on climate justice.
30. As discussed in chapter 7, the "just transition" emphasis within the climate justice movement specifies that transition to renewable energy economies must include explicit provision for the employment and well-being of economically vulnerable people who could be hurt by the transition away from fossil fuels. Likewise, just transition demands that the move to renewable energy sources not sacrifice the well-being of people who stand to be decimated by extraction of minerals used in renewable energy production. Thus, climate justice links economy and ecology. (It is no wonder that the two words come from the same Greek root, *oikos*.)
31. Both quotations are from the Doughnut Economics Action Lab (https://doughnuteconomics.org/). Hubs of new economic thinking include the Doughnut Economics Action Lab, the Next System Project, the Club of Rome, the US Solidarity Economy Network, and the Schumacher Center for a New Economics.
32. Michel Foucault, *The Order of Things: An Archaeology of the Human Sciences* (New York: Vintage Books, 1994), 168.
33. Consider, for example, the forces that lined up to convince the world that smoking cigarettes was not dangerous to human health. Some of those same brilliant minds are behind the propagation of climate denial in the US. See Naomi Oreskes and Erik Conway, *Merchants of Doubt: How a Handful of Scientists Obscured the Truth on Issues from Tobacco Smoke to Global Warming* (London: Bloomsbury, 2010). See also the 2014 film *Merchants of Doubt*, directed by Robert Kenner. And consider the efforts of the fossil fuel industry to obscure the perilous climate impacts of fossil fuels and to maintain legal rights to fracking, continue oil extraction and transport, and limit regulations on coalmining.
34. To illustrate, the Union of Concerned Scientists declared, "As scientists ... we understand that what is regarded as sacred is more likely to be treated with care and respect. Our planetary home should be so regarded. Efforts to safeguard and cherish the environment need to be infused with a vision of the sacred." (Union of Concerned Scientists, "Preserving and Cherishing the Earth: An Appeal for Joint Commitment in Science and Religion.") The United Nations Environmental Programme (UNEP) launched a Faith for earth Initiative to "encourage, empower and engage with faith-based organizations as partners" in addressing environmental issues (https://tinyurl

Notes

.com/46bmzuk8). The Initiative's 2019 assembly brought together 135 faith leaders from twelve different religions to discuss using faith to address environmental matters (https://tinyurl.com/35zt2xfn). In 2020 the UNEP and the Parliament of World's Religions jointly released a book entitled *Faith for Earth: A Call to Action* (see https://tinyurl.com/3htcvy4x).

35. Examples include GreenFaith, Interfaith Power and Light, the Laudato Si Movement, and the Catholic Climate Covenant. Many more can be seen on the website of the Yale Forum on Religion and Ecology (https://fore.yale.edu/).
36. Examples include the World Council of Churches, the Council for World Mission, the World Communion of Reformed Churches, the Lutheran World Federation.
37. See first section of this chapter.
38. Max Liboiron, *Pollution Is Colonialism* (Durham, NC: Duke University Press, 2021), 1.

CHAPTER FOUR

1. Iris Murdoch, *Existentialists and Mystics* (New York: Penguin, 1997), 375, 329.
2. This section draws heavily on Moe-Lobeda, *Resisting Structural Evil*.
3. Amitav Ghosh, *The Great Derangement* (Chicago: University of Chicago Press, 2016), 11.
4. Christiana Figueres and Tom Rivett-Carnac, *The Future We Choose: Surviving the Climate Crisis* (New York: Alfred A. Knopf, 2020), 107.
5. This citation of Baldwin is by Eddie Glaude, scholar of African American Studies, in podcast called *The Lie at the Heart of America*, January 18, 2021. https://tinyurl.com/23vv9efd. Accessed December 14, 2023.
6. Mordecai Cohen Ettinger, "Coming Home: The New Economy and Honoring the Inherent Sacredness of All Life," *Tikkun* 33, no. 3 (2018): 18–23 (quote on 21).
7. John Prendergast, "Can You Hear Congo Now? Cell Phones, Conflict Minerals, and the Worst Sexual Violence in the World," April 1, 2009, on website of Enough: The Project to End Genocide and Crimes against Humanity. See https://tinyurl.com/y6nusmy7. Accessed December 9, 2023. See also https://tinyurl.com/4ae6fwus. The Enough Project, Global Witness, UN reports, and others have documented extraordinary human rights abuses associated with the lucrative mining industry in the Congo. "The general use of violence against communities includes forced labor, torture, recruitment of child soldiers, extortion, and killings by armed groups to oppress and control civilians," reports the Enough Project. In the context of a Congolese war in which warlords use terror as an essential weapon to ensure control of regions where international companies mine for valuable metals, sexual violence is especially horrendous. "Competing militias rape in order either to drive communities out of contested areas or else as a means of controlling or subjugating those living in the areas they control." The impact of coltan mining on biodiversity, soil, and water quality is also devastating.
8. Another example of art exposing "what is going on" below the surface of our food and other daily practices shaped by predatory economies is a book of elegant poetry by Paul Hlava Ceballos, called *Bananas*. Paul Hlava Ceballos, *Bananas* (Pittsburgh: University of Pittsburgh Press, 2022).

9. Jayati Ghosh et al., "A Just Transition: How Can We Fairly Assign Climate Responsibility?," Deep Dive Paper 06 (Geneva, Switzerland: earth4All, July 2022), 2, https://tinyurl.com/3256k4rb.
10. CDP, "The Carbon Majors Database: CDP Carbon Majors Report 2017" at https://tinyurl.com/2s3meeyy. For coverage of the Report, see https://tinyurl.com/yuttn4jw. In his address to the addresses the opening of seventy-seventh session of the UN General Assembly Debate, UN Secretary-General António Guterres calls out the role of fossil fuel companies in the climate emergency: "The fossil fuel industry is feasting on hundreds of billions of dollars in subsidies and windfall profits, while households' budgets shrink and our planet burns. Excellencies, let's tell it like it is: our world is addicted to fossil fuels, and it's time for an intervention. We need to hold fossil fuel companies and their enablers to account." UN Department of Social and Economic Affairs, https://tinyurl.com/4wr3ukvr.
11. William J Ripple et al., "World Scientists' Warning of a Climate Emergency," *BioScience* 70, no. 1 (November 5, 2019): 8–12, https://doi.org/10.1093/biosci/biz088.
12. World Inequality Lab, "World Inequality Report," World Inequality Report 2022, https://wir2022.wid.world/. The report goes on to note the even higher inequity related to the very rich: "The richest decile in North America are the most extravagant carbon emitters in the world with an average of . . . 73 times the per capital emission of the poorest half of the population of South and Southeast Asia." An Oxfam report, "Extreme Carbon Inequality," comparing the lifestyle consumption emissions of very rich people and poor people indicates that the world's richest 1 percent were responsible for more than twice the greenhouse gas emissions of the poorest half of humankind. Oxfam, "Extreme Carbon Inequality: Why the Paris Climate Deal Must Put the Poorest, Lowest Emitting and Most Vulnerable People First," Media Briefing (Oxfam America, December 2, 2015), 1, https://tinyurl.com/cf75ddek. The report goes on to show that "comparing the average lifestyle consumption footprints of richer and poorer citizens in a range of countries helps show that while some 'emerging economies' like China, India, Brazil, and South Africa have high and rapidly rising emissions, the lifestyle consumption emissions of even their richest citizens remain some way behind that of their counterparts in rich OECD countries, even though this is changing and will continue to do so without urgent climate action. The lifestyle emissions of the hundreds of millions of their poorest citizens, meanwhile, remain significantly lower than even the poorest people in the OECD countries" (2). More recent research shows that "millionaires alone are on track to burn 72% of the remaining carbon budget for 1.5°C. This is an egregious assault on humanity and the living world. . . . It is dangerous to continue supporting an over-consuming elite in the middle of a climate emergency" (Jason Hickel, professor at the Institute for Environmental Science and Technology at the Universitat Autonomo de Barcelona and Fellow of the Royal Society of Arts, discussing a study by scholars in Norway, Sweden, and Germany). See https://tinyurl.com/dbwxyway. Accessed December 9, 2023. The study goes on to say that "continued growth in emissions at the top makes a low-carbon transition less likely, as the acceleration of energy consumption by the wealthiest is likely beyond the system's capacity to decarbonize." Hickel's quote appears in Kenny Stancil, "140+ Experts to Rich Nations:

Notes

Redirect Trillions in Public Money to Curb Climate, Inequality Crises," *Common Dreams*, June 19, 2023, https://tinyurl.com/5v68kw5b.

13. Ghosh et al., "A Just Transition," 5. While the national emissions of rising middle income (measured by GDP) countries like China, India, and Brazil have risen to rival those of the US, "the United States showed 8 times the per capital carbon emissions of India in production terms in 2015, and this difference increases to 12 times once final demand emissions are calculated" (11). The inequity, however, is more complex when we combine the cross-country comparisons with comparisons of individual emissions. The difference in per capita carbon emissions across countries does not reveal the full extent of inequality in carbon emissions. According to data in the 2021 World Inequality Report, "global carbon inequalities are now mainly due to inequalities *within* countries.... There are globally high emitters in low-and middle-income countries and globally low emitters in rich countries."

14. Many documents and books articulate these links. See for example: Amitav Ghosh, "The Colonial Roots of Present Crises," *Green European Journal*, October 19, 2022, https://tinyurl.com/46f98524.

15. John A. Powell and Stephen Menendian, "The Debate over Ending Structural Racism: A Way Forward for the Biden Administration," *Othering & Belonging Institute Blog* (March 24, 2021), 5, http://lawcat.berkeley.edu/record/1202378.

16. As we have seen, the climate catastrophe illustrates the economy-ecology link. Economically impoverished people (who are also disproportionately people of color and Indigenous people) are—in general—most devastated by the ravaging impacts of climate change, which is caused predominantly by wealthier people. This is documented in countless texts and reports. See for example the United Nations Department of Economic and Social Affairs statement on the impact of climate change on Indigenous people at https://tinyurl.com/4krm3xk8. Accessed January 15, 2024. This differential makes climate reparations a priority of the climate justice movement.

17. Ivone Gebara, *Out of the Depths: Womens' Experience of Suffering and Evil* (Minneapolis: Fortress Press, 2002), 2–3 and 58.

18. Amitav Ghosh, *The Great Derangement* (Chicago: University of Chicago Press, 2016), 11.

19. The Blue Planet Prize Laureates, "Environment and Development Challenges: The Imperative to Act," UNEP Presentation (Nairobi: The Asahi Glass Foundation, February 20, 2012), 5, 11, https://tinyurl.com/mt2ecjjy.

20. Ghosh, *The Great Derangement*, 128–29.

21. Jeremy Lent, "What Does an Ecological Civilization Look Like?," *Yes! Magazine*, Spring 2021, 20.

22. Pew Research Center, "Little Change in Public's Response to 'Capitalism,' 'Socialism,'" (Dec. 28, 2011). https://tinyurl.com/y9zdkb3w. Likewise, in Britain, speaking of millennials in Britain, Owen Jones writes, "According to a report published in July [2021] by the rightwing think tank the Institute for Economic Affairs...nearly 80% blame capitalism for the housing crisis, while 75% believe the climate emergency is 'specifically a capitalist problem' and 72% back sweeping nationalisation. All in all, 67% want to live under a socialist economic system." Owen Jones, "Eat the Rich! Why Millennials and Generation Z Have Turned Their Backs on Capitalism," *Guardian*, September 20, 2021.

23. Stef W. Kight, "Exclusive Poll: Young Americans Are Embracing Socialism," *Axios*, March 10, 2019, sec. Politics & Policy, https://tinyurl.com/2nyss935. This report *preceded* the coronavirus pandemic. The pandemic's ghastly exposure of the deep inequities existing within and among societies, the racial lines of economic inequity, and the treachery in profit-maximizing corporate behavior has led to wider questioning of unbridled capitalism.

24. David Callahan, "The Biggest Problem with Capitalism That Nobody Talks About," *Demos* (blog), January 31, 2014, https://tinyurl.com/3h3r5vbs.

25. David Brooks, "Biden's Move to the Left May Have Consequences," *San Francisco Chronicle*, March 30, 2021.

26. Sandrine Dixson-Declève, "Presentation to the 5th Meeting of the Ecumenical Panel for a New International Financial and Economic Architecture (NIFEA)" Bali, Indonesia, October 14, 2022.

27. Marc Benioff, "We Need a New Capitalism," *New York Times*, October 14, 2019, https://tinyurl.com/28uk982c.

28. Moe-Lobeda, *Resisting Structural Evil*, 272. The text goes on to discuss six such gateways.

29. See, for example, https://tinyurl.com/4ndvtyjt. Accessed February 11, 2024.

30. Sharp critique of capitalism in its current form comes also from within mainstream economics. Joseph Stiglitz, Columbia University professor of economics and winner of the Nobel Prize in Economics, is perhaps the most influential mainstream economist who is critical of neoliberal capitalism, especially for generating the mounting gap between rich and poor.

31. Carmen Lansdowne, paper respondent, Religion and Economy Unit Session (American Academy of Religion Annual Meeting, Denver, 2022).

32. United Nations Research Institute for Social Development (UNRISD), "Overcoming Inequalities: Towards a New Eco-social Contract (UNRISD Strategy 2021–2025)" (UNRISD, 2021), https://tinyurl.com/4kkcywj2. One example is the theory of doughnut economics, originated by economist Kate Raworth. It is gaining traction in municipal public policy around the globe.

33. Think, for example, of the decision by the United Kingdom during World War II to tax the wealthiest people at a rate of 99.25 percent, and President Roosevelt's decision to halt production of civilian automobiles for two years during WWII so that the automobile industry could focus on equipment to support the war.

34. A model for building wealth in deprived urban areas, the Cleveland Model develops a group of employee-own co-op businesses that provide goods and services for "anchor institutions," like universities and hospital systems. The co-ops provide reliable well-paid employment for economically marginalized local residents. These are jobs in which workers, as owners, have a say in decisions. The model began in Cleveland with the Evergreen Cooperative Initiative including a commercial laundry service (used by the local hospital system and hotels), a produce company with a hydroponic greenhouse producing year-round pesticide-free produce, and and an energy company. "The success and impact that a simple model has had on Cleveland—and the dignity it has restored to local communities—is truly inspiring. And other cities are taking note, replicating and adapting this innovative approach to economic development, green job creation and neighbourhood stabilization. It's

Notes

being exported around the world," including to England and Scotland. Atlas of the Future website: https://tinyurl.com/mupkxnff. Accessed February 11, 2024. See also this book's chapter 8.

35. The reference is to a network of small cooperative farms in New Mexico that enables small-scale local agriculture to thrive and thirty thousand school children to have organic produce for lunch. The network began through the work of a Quaker organization. The state funds school districts to buy from these local farms. See this book's "Setting the Stage" and chapter 10.

36. In addition to those noted in the text, see, for example, Pope Francis, *Laudato Si': On Care For Our Common Home* (Huntington, IN: Our Sunday Visitor Pub, 2015); the Wendland-Cook Program in Religion and Justice's focus on Climate Change and Capitalism (https://tinyurl.com/yc6yy8fv); the Coalition on the Environment and Jewish Life (https://www.coejl.org/), and the Care for Creation and Climate Justice initiative of the World Council of Churches (https://tinyurl.com/2fu4djyf), to name a few efforts. All accessed February 11, 2024.

37. In 1998, the WCC launched a process called AGAPE, which began with an in-dept study of neoliberal economic globalization. The study found neoliberal globalization to be fraught with economic injustice that caused terrible suffering. Eight years later, the AGAPE process issued a call to work against the economic injustice inherent in the neoliberal economy. Rogate R. Mshana and Athena Peralta, eds., *Economy of Life: Linking Poverty, Wealth and Ecology* (Geneva, Switzerland: World Council of Churches Publications, 2013). This report linked the wealth gap and the ecological crisis to corporate- and finance-driven capitalism. This conclusion was reached by the study's processes on poverty, wealth, and ecology, which involved more than five hundred participants (including women, youth, Indigenous People, and theologians others) organized from 2007 to 2013 by the WCC Poverty, Wealth, and Ecology (PWE) project.

38. The three other networks are the Lutheran World Federation (LWF), the World Communion of Reformed Churches (WCRC), and the Council for World Mission (CWM). They have been joined more recently (2022) by the World Methodist Council (WMC), and the global Mennonite network is poised to join soon. The NIFEA initiative is guided by a team of about fifteen individuals representing an impressive range of knowledge: Indigenous People from India, the Pacific Islands, and Turtle Island; church leaders from Africa and Latin America with decades of experience in economic justice work; theologians and economists; and more. The initiative has developed many materials and projects. One, the Gem School, prepares young adults for leadership in economic justice. Another the Zacchaeus Tax (ZacTax) and its toolkit help people fight tax evasion by mining corporations who are draining mineral resources—as well as monetary resources—from countries in Africa. NIFEA was first imagined in an historic Global Ecumenical Conference on a New International Financial and Economic Architecture organized by the WCRC, the WCC, and the CWM in 2012 in São Paulo, Brazil. Together these organizations, joined also by the LWF, made a commitment to work collaboratively toward an economy that would bring humanity and creation closer to fullness of life. They called for "a global ecumenically instituted commission . . . to link with other faith communities, civil society organizations, interested governments, institutions and other relevant stakeholders" to develop a proposal for

transformative engagement of churches and other likeminded public partners to work toward a more humane and ecologically sound global economic and financial architecture—an "Economy of Life." For information on the Zach Tax see https://tinyurl.com/yc3z4de6. For information on the Gem School, see https://tinyurl.com/ymzfthnj; for the initial NIFEA paper see https://tinyurl.com/yhfpkvpb. All accessed February 11, 2024.

39. See for example the analysis and guide compiled by the Climate Justice Alliance (https://tinyurl.com/ca4ktnnh); curricula and training manual offered by Movement Generation's Just Transition initiative (https://tinyurl.com/wp8t2bec); and the New Economy Coalition's resources at https://tinyurl.com/4ftzc2ej. All accessed February 11, 2024.

40. See for example http://usfoodsovereigntyalliance.org/ (United States–based) and https://viacampesina.org/en/ (global). Regarding Black Food sovereignty, see Black Food Sovereignty Coalition at https://blackfoodnw.org/; Black Church Food Security Network at https://blackchurchfoodsecurity.net/. All accessed January 12, 2024. For more information, see Frontline Solutions and NPQ, "Black Food Sovereignty: Stories from the Field," *NPQ*, January 19, 2024, https://tinyurl.com/bdfrrec6; and Christopher Carter, *The Spirit of Soul Food: Race, Faith and Food Justice* (Urbana: University of Illinois Press, 2021).

41. To illustrate, C40 is an international network of cities dedicated to reducing emissions through innovation. The Thriving Cities Initiative aims to demonstrate how cities can cocreate regenerative systems and powerful narratives to inspire collective behavioral change and mainstream 1.5° C living. For insight into three cities see Chris Winters, "Three Cities Switching to Life-Affirming Economies," *Yes! Magazine*, February 16, 2021, https://tinyurl.com/y9cd2anj.

42. See the UN Research Institute for Social Development, the UN Environment Programme, and other UN agencies.

43. The prospectus for this initative notes that "our own economic activity is often at the root of unsustainability.... The ideas, institutions and actions that gave credibility to the modern ideal of economic development have been called into question.... Once positioned on the radical fringe or considered not to have systemic or structural significance, alternative ways of thinking, living, and organizing—including alternative economies, such as the social and solidarity economy—are attracting more attention within mainstream knowledge and policy circles." See the prospectus published by the United Nations Research Institute for Social Development's publication: https://tinyurl.com/4kkcywj2. Accessed February 11, 2024.

44. Two prominent examples are 350.org on international and local levels, and Extinction Rebellion.

45. Kate Raworth, *Donut Economics: Seven Ways to Think Like a 21st-Century Economist* (White River Junction, VT: Chelsea Green, 2017), 2–3.

46. Sallie McFague, *The Body of God: An Ecological Theology* (Minneapolis: Fortress Press, 1993).

47. David Suzuki, Adrienne Mason, and Amanda McConnell, *The Sacred Balance: Rediscovering Our Place in Nature* (Vancouver: Greystone Books, 1997, 2007), 270.

48. In theological terms, this Spirit is both immanent and transcendent.

Notes

49. Cited in Rita Nakashima Brock and Rebecca Ann Parker, *Saving Paradise: How Christianity Traded Love of This World for Crucifixion and Empire* (Boston: Beacon Press, 2008), 144.
50. Suzuki, et.al., *Sacred Balance*, 270.
51. Martin Luther, "Sermon for the Sixteenth Sunday after Trinity," in *Sermons of Martin Luther*, ed. John Nicholas Lenker, vol. 8 (Grand Rapids, MI: Baker Books, 1983), 275.
52. Brock and Parker, *Saving Paradise*, 145.
53. Brock and Parker, *Saving Paradise*, 155.
54. Brock and Parker, *Saving Paradise*, 155.
55. Fyodor Dostoyevsky, *The Idiot* (London; New York: Penguin Books, 2004).

CHAPTER FIVE

1. Larry L. Rasmussen, *The Planet You Inherit: Letters to My Grandchildren When Uncertainty's a Sure Thing* (Minneapolis: Broadleaf Books, 2022), 6.
2. While in the fields of sociology, the terms *systems* and *strucutures* are used differently, in the common public discourse, and for our purposes here, they are used interchangeably.
3. For our purposes here, the word *institutions* refers to business and financial firms, governmental entities, and institutions of civil society such as religious organizations and schools. According to Thad Williamson, systemic or structural change "typically means changes in multiple institutional structures over time," from Thad Williamson, *The New Systems Reader Guide: A Supplement to The New Systems Reader: Alternatives to a Failed Economy* (Washington DC: The Democracy Collaborative, 2020), 8, https://tinyurl.com/25mtmnjh.
4. While these four terms may have different connotations, for our purposes we use them interchangeably to capture the depth of what we mean by this terrain of human existence.
5. For a clear argument that the movement for significantly changed lifestyles to counter the "business as usual economy" contributes to more systemic transformations, see Juliet Schor and Craig J. Thompson, "Cooperative Networks, Decentralized Markets, and Rhizomatic Resistance: Situating Plentitude within Contemporary Political Economy Debates," in *Sustainable Lifestyles and the Quest for Plenitude: Case Studies of the New Economy*, ed. Juliet Schor and Craig J. Thompson (New Haven, CT: Yale University Press, 2014), 233–49. For a clear counterargument, see Douglas B. Holt, "Why the Sustainable Economy Movement Hasn't Scaled: Toward a Strategy That Empowers Mainstreet," in Schor and Thompson, *Sustainable Lifestyles*, 202–32.
6. These policies would provide bike lanes on all arterials, create low-cost bike acquisition programs for low-income people, and close many streets to all but bikes, scooters, and buses.
7. Speculation on food for example drives up food costs on the global market and leaves many very poor people to starve; it is a a significant causal factor in famine. Speculation can make vulnerable economies collapse suddenly, bringing investors

profit but leaving many people devastated. These are two of many examples of the damages wrought by speculation.

8. Although a "triple bottom line" is common practice in many European contexts, in the United States it is still emerging and entails a tremendous shift in worldview. The joy, of course, is that a significant movement in the world of business and finance has made or is making this move. See for example the B-Corporation movement and the business schools that teach about the triple bottom line. (For example, this article appears on the Harvard Business School's blog, "Business Insights": https://tinyurl.com/yc7fmyb9). Accessed February 11, 2024.

9. For example, Christiana Figueres (former executive of the United Nations Framework Convention on Climate Change) and Tom Rivett-Carnac, in *The Future We Choose*, identify ten action areas necessary to avoid the worst of climate disaster. The ten include all three of these terrains. "We have discussed the mindset everyone needs to cultivate in order to meet the global challenge of the climate crisis, but on its own, this is not enough. For change to become transformational, our change in mindset must manifest in actions." They go on to frame actions both in "your lifestyle" (behavioral change) and in "political engagement by everyone" (structural change) to achieve "a fairer economic system." Christiana Figueres and Tom Rivett-Carnac, *The Future We Choose: Surviving the Climate Crisis* (New York: Alfred A. Knopf, 2020), 84, 86. Likewise, the group of world scientists who wrote the 2019 "World Scientists' Warning of a Climate Emergency" issued a follow-up paper that illustrates the interplay of these three terrains. While they focus on social structural change, they close by adding that "each of us can also work to change the culture within society. . . . And each of us can make changes in our own behavior." Phoebe Barnard et al., "World Scientists' Warnings into Action, Local to Global," *Science Progress* 104, no. 4 (October 2021): 21.

10. Maina Talia, "Am I Not Your (Tu)Akoi—Neighbour?" (Discernment and Radical Engagement—DARE, virtual conference: Council for World Mission, 2022), 4.

11. Andrea Brower, "What to Say When People Say 'It's Impossible,'" *Yes! Magazine*, June 14, 2013, https://tinyurl.com/3x6ebxf2.

12. Martin Lukacs, "Neoliberalism Has Conned Us into Fighting Climate Change as Individuals," *Guardian* (July 17, 2017).

13. Brower, "What to Say When People Say 'It's Impossible.'"

14. Mark Kaufman, "The Devious Fossil Fuel Propaganda We All Use," Mashable, July 13, 2020, hhttps://tinyurl.com/4muhay4t, cited in Rebecca Solnit, "Big Oil Coined 'Carbon Footprints' to Blame Us for Their Greed. Keep Them on the Hook," *The Guardian*, August 23, 2021, https://tinyurl.com/3n336r6v.

15. Sociologists calls this *socialization*; anthropologists tend to use the term *enculturation*.

16. As Elaine Pagels writes in a *New Yorker* article, "Much of what seems to be wittten into nature itself is a matter of cultural patterning." (David Remnick, "Tragedy Led the Religion Scholar Elaine Pagels to Ask: What Is Satan?," *The New Yorker*, March 26, 1995, https://tinyurl.com/2u7pfu3k).

17. Stephen Brookfield, *The Power of Critical Theory: Liberating Adult Learning and Teaching* (San Francisco: Jossey-Bass, 2005).

18. Brookfield, *The Power of Critical Theory*, 102.

Notes

19. Suzuki et al., *Sacred Balance*, 21.
20. Yuval Noah Harari, *Sapiens: A Brief History of Humankind* (New York: Harper, 2015), 24–39.
21. Carter, *The Spirit of Soul Food*, 159.
22. This line is a paraphrase of a sentence in Kendra Ward, "How to Awaken Our Ecological Psyche," *Yes! Magazine*, February 16, 2021, https://tinyurl.com/92j4mcry.
23. Gandhi describes *satyagraha* in M. K. Gandhi, *Non-violent Resistance (Satyagraha)* (Mineola, NY: Dover, 2001).
24. For Gandhi, "noncooperation with evil" translated into the refusal to obey laws, travel restrictions, and other unjust measures (sometimes the word *satyagraha* is used to refer only to this kind of refusal). "Cooperation with good" took forms such as education and political empowerment in Indian communities, community living, local farming, simplicity, the elimination of untouchability, boycotting foreign cloth, uplifting women, and more. All were considered part of the principle of *svadeshi* or localism. See Michael N. Nagler, *The Search for a Nonviolent Future: A Promise of Peace for Ourselves, Our Families, and Our World* (Novato, CA: New World Library, 2004).
25. To read more about the International Alliance for Localization (IAL), see https://tinyurl.com/2s3v7ke. Accessed January 12, 2024.
26. Figueres and Rivett-Carnac, *The Future We Choose*, 152–53. Extinction Rebellion is an organization using nonviolent direct action to persuade governments and businesses to act on the climate emergency. For more on Extinction Rebellion, see https://rebellion.global/. Accessed January 12, 2024.

CHAPTER SIX

1. Pathways to a People's Economy, "Our Vision," Pathways to a People's Economy, accessed January 21, 2024, https://tinyurl.com/2b3v9apt.
2. Robin Wall Kimmerer, *Braiding Sweetgrass: Indigenous Wisdom, Scientific Knowledge and the Teachings of Plants* (Minneapolis: Milkweed Editions, 2013), x.
3. For more information about the program, see https://tinyurl.com/4r3afh6k.
4. See Marjorie Kelly and Ted Howard, *The Making of a Democratic Economy: Building Prosperity for the Many, Not Just the Few* (Oakland, CA: Berrett-Koehler Publishers, Inc., 2019), 1–3. Also, see Mariana Mazzucato, *Mission Economy: A Moonshot Guide to Changing Capitalism* (New York: Harper Business, 2021), who emphasizes the potential of government procurement as a significant source of support for local businesses that build wealth in low-income communities.
5. Foundation for the Economics of Sustainability et al., "Community Wealth Building and the Next Economic System: Interview with Sarah McKinley," Bridging the Gaps Podcast, February 28, 2023, https://tinyurl.com/5n7ch7fj.
6. Quote from Ronn Richard, former Evergreen Cooperatives Board chair..
7. Tim Jackson, *Post Growth: Life after Capitalism* (Cambridge: Polity Press, 2021), xv.
8. This and the following six paragraphs are taken, with very slight revision, from Moe-Lobeda, *Resisting Structural Evil*, 245–46.
9. "A Greener Bush; Energy and the Environment," *The Economist*, February 15, 2003, https://tinyurl.com/yc67d93a.

10. Union of Concerned Scientists, "1992 World Scientists' Warning to Humanity," www.ucsusa.org, July 16, 1992, https://tinyurl.com/5awphrvy.
11. They refer to this as the "New Democracy Movement."
12. https://climatejusticealliance.org/.
13. https://neweconomy.net/.
14. New International Financial and Economic Architecture (NIFEA), "Just Economics for Liberation and Life: Interfaith Message on Just Finance, Debt and Reparations" (Council for World Mission, October 16, 2020), https://tinyurl.com/yc3rsv4s.
15. See the New Economy Coalition website: https://neweconomy.net/.
16. The first two guideposts express the two biblical rules for economic life—creation care and neighbor-love. The third guidepost coheres with the Bible's frequent warning against the tendency to accumulate power and wealth and to dominate others.
17. Theoretical or intellectual homes of this movement toward a new economy grounded in these three principles are varied. They include circular economics, doughnut economics (led by economist Kate Raworth), the new economics (including economists Juliet Schor and David Korten and political economist and historian Gar Alperovitz), and ecological economics (initiated in large part by Herman Daly and Richard Norgaard). The term *new economics* is also used by some theorists to describe a broader movement to challenge conventional economic theory.
18. Stan Cox, *The Green New Deal and Beyond: Ending the Climate Emergency While We Still Can* (San Francisco: City Lights Books, 2020), 2.
19. Kimmerer, *Braiding Sweetgrass*, 6.
20. Some cities are developing policies and public awareness with this very aim in mind. The Carbon Neutral Cities Alliance (CNCA), for example, is a collaboration of cities around the world working to achieve carbon neutrality in the next 10–20 years. Amsterdam's goal is a 95 percent reduction of emissions by 2050. Copenhagen intends to be the first carbon neutral capital in 2025. Glasgow is committed to becoming a Net Zero Carbon City by 2030. See: https://carbonneutralcities.org/.
21. The cultural historian and priest Thomas Berry, said it vividly: "Humans must situate our economic activity *within* earth's 'great economy,' rather than *separate from* it." Thomas Berry, *The Great Work: Our Way into the Future* (New York: Crown, 2013). To the contrary, both capitalist economies and centralized socialist economies (and the theories behind them) have treated human economies as entirely *separate from* earth's economy. This promotes the false assumption that human economic activity is not contingent upon the earth's physical limits. (What a deadly myth this has proven to be!) The bottom line in corporate activity does not account for the ecological and social costs of that activity. Those costs are "externalized"; they are not paid by the corporation that creates the degradation and benefits financially. The costs are left to be paid by society or by future generations or are borne by the people suffering from the degradation. The horrendous ecological and social costs of mining (toxic water, loss of homes, valleys filled with discarded rock and waste, deforestation, and flooding) illustrate. The mining corporations (especially in countries with fewer regulations such as in Africa and Latin America) take the profit but leave the costs to be paid by the society or people impacted.
22. Cox, *The Green New Deal*, xxiv.

Notes

23. A 2019 UN Environment Programme report is clear: "We are on course for 3.2 degrees Celsius temperature rise," which would be catastrophic almost beyond imagining. To keep to a 1.5 degree increase requires that greenhouse gas emissions turn around now and start falling at a high rate of 7.6 percent per year annually. See *The Emissions Gap Report 2019* (Nairobi, Kenya: United Nations Environment Programme, 2019), https://tinyurl.com/3jf4a3md.
24. Cox, *The Green New Deal*, xxiv–xxvi. Cox goes on to outline how this might be accomplished on pages 83–111.
25. Sacrifice zones are people, communities, and lands that are damaged in the process of obtaining resources for producing renewables. (See chapter 7's discussions of sacrifice zones, just transition, net-zero emissions, and green and blue colonialism.) Moreover, some fossil fuel uses cannot be replaced by renewable sources. See Kenneth M. Sayre, *Unearthed: The Economic Roots of Our Environmental Crisis* (Notre Dame, IN: University of Notre Dame Press, 2022), 152–55.
26. Morally loaded, international controversy accompanies this claim. Many in the Global South insist that wealthy countries must reduce emissions by higher percentages than impoverished countries in which large numbers of people still do not have electricity or adequate consumption. In international climate negotiations, the US has opposed this, saying that all should reduce equally. We citizens can call upon our elected officials to adopt higher emissions reductions goals.
27. A report by the International Monetary Fund (IMF) indicates that in 2015, cutting out those subsidies would have eliminated over a quarter of global carbon emissions and nearly half of deaths related to fossil fuel air pollution, while also significantly increasing government revenue. The largest subsidizers in 2015 were China ($1.4 trillion), United States ($649 billion), Russia ($551 billion), European Union ($289 billion), and India ($209 billion). See David Coady et al., *Global Fossil Fuel Subsidies Remain Large: An Update Based on Country-Level Estimates* (Washington, D.C.: International Monetary Fund, 2019), https://tinyurl.com/3wp5wn6p. Accessed February 11, 2014.
28. The World Council of Churches, at its 11th Assembly in 2022, included a directive to "challenge government subsidies to the fossil fuel sector." See World Council of Churches 11th Assembly, "The Living Planet: Seeking a Just and Sustainable Global Community" (World Council of Churches Publications, September 2022), https://tinyurl.com/2pdfdxdp. Accessed February 11, 2024.
29. According to the Wikipedia entry on methane emissions, "though methane causes far more heat to be trapped than the same mass of carbon dioxide, less than half of the emitted CH_4 remains in the atmosphere after a decade. . . . The global warming potential (GWP) is a way of comparing the warming due to other gases to that from carbon dioxide, over a given time period. Methane's GWP_{20} of 85 means that a ton of CH_4 emitted into the atmosphere creates approximately 85 times the atmospheric warming as a ton of CO_2 over a period of 20 years. On a 100-year timescale, methane's GWP_{100} is in the range of 28–34." See "Methane Emissions," Wikipedia (Wikimedia Foundation, December 17, 2019), https://tinyurl.com/3ducvj3m. Accessed February 11, 2024.
30. For example, a factory would include in the bottom line the cost of keeping water clean, replacing cropland, and maintaining carbon neutrality.

31. This does not preclude all economic growth as a good. Some forms of growth are critically needed in impoverished nations. However, growth as a measure of economic well-being must be accompanied by other measures and must be qualified. That is, growth-producing policies and practices must (1) be ecologically sustainable; (2) reduce the wealth gap; (3) produce long-term, adequately compensated jobs open to unionization; and (4) bolster rather than undermine local communities and cultures. See Cynthia Moe-Lobeda and Daniel Spencer, "Free Trade Agreements and the Neo-liberal Economic Paradigm: Economic, Ecological, and Moral Consequences," *Political Theology* 10, no. 4 (December 11, 2009): 685–716, https://doi.org/10.1558/poth.v10i4.685.

32. From a World Bank internal memo, December 12, 1991. See John Bellamy Foster, "'Let Them Eat Pollution': Capitalism and the World Environment," *Monthly Review* 44, no. 8 (January 2, 1993): 10, https://doi.org/10.14452/MR-044-08-1993-01_2.

33. From M. K. Gandhi, "The Great Sentinel," *Young India*, October 13, 1921, 672.

34. Raworth, *Doughnut Economics*, 23.

35. A Certified Benefit Corporation (B Corporation) is a for-profit entity committed to making a positive social and environmental impact. Companies can receive certification through B Lab Global, an international nonprofit that rates applicants on a broad scale of environmental, governance, worker equity, and transparency standards. According to B Lab Global's website, "B Corp Certification is a designation that a business is meeting high standards of verified performance, accountability, and transparency on factors from employee benefits and charitable giving to supply chain practices and input materials. In order to achieve certification, a company must: 1) demonstrate high social and environmental performance by achieving a B Impact Assessment score of 80 or above and passing our risk review; multinational corporations must also meet baseline requirement standards; 2) make a legal commitment by changing their corporate governance structure to be accountable to all stakeholders, not just shareholders, and achieve benefit corporation status if available in their jurisdiction; and 3) exhibit transparency by allowing information about their performance measured against B Lab's standards to be publicly available on their B Corp profile on B Lab's website." To read more, see https://tinyurl.com/4jce83j3.

36. Theological ethicist Christopher Carter documents the insidious ways in which "our food systems can be described as structurally racist" (75). The corporate-controlled food system—in the US and globally—emerging in the 1980s, was shaped by interests of transnational agrofood corporations to produce cheap food (for Europeans and US Americans) and high corporate profits. This came at tremendous cost to Black and Brown farmworkers in the US and Black, Brown, and Asian subsistence farmers around the world. See Christopher Carter, *The Spirit of Soul Food: Race, Faith, and Food Justice* (Urbana: University of Illinois Press, 2021). In many countries, agribusiness seed companies, petrochemical companies, and governments collude to coopt small farmers into such terrible debt that farmer suicide rates skyrocketed. See Carter, *The Spirit of Soul Food,* 57–74. See also Cynthia Moe-Lobeda, *Healing a Broken World: Globalization and God* (Minneapolis: Fortress Press, 2002). Moreover food systems in the US, as Carter demonstrates, are organized to give Black, Indigenous, and other people of color "less access to food, and the food they can access is likely less nutritious. . . . Just as our economy has become starkly

Notes

stratified with wealth concentrated at the top, it is increasing clear that we live in a two-tiered food system in which the wealthy tend to eat well and are rewarded with better health, while the poor tend to eat low-quality diets, causing their health to suffer" (75). Food deserts—areas with little or no access to quality food—and the proliferation of fast food joints are major causal factors. See also Kristin Wartman, "Why Food Belongs in Our Discussions of Race," *Huffpost* (blog), September 8, 2016, https://tinyurl.com/y2anf7xa. A report by the Johns Hopkins Center for a Livable Future found that "34 percent of African Americans live in food deserts, compared to only 8 percent of white residents." See Natalie Wood-Wright and Barbara Benham, "Report: One in Four Baltimore Residents Lives in a Food Desert," The Hub (John Hopkins University, June 10, 2015), https://tinyurl.com/yc6m98md.

37. "By 'inequality' we mean the material inequalities of income and wealth that divide the rich from the poor, both within and between societies." Richard Wilkinson and Kate Pickett, "From Inequality to Sustainability" (Switzerland: earth4All, a Project of the Club of Rome, April 2022), 1, https://tinyurl.com/2e36v4xr. Accessed February 11, 2024. For research on the negative impacts of inequality on society as a whole, see the studies cited in that report.
38. Wilkinson and Picket, "From Inequality to Sustainability," 1. This report outlines six ways in which inequity blocks attempts to deal with environmental crises.
39. Cited in Chuck Collins and Felice Yeskel, *Economic Apartheid in America: A Primer on Economic Inequality & Insecurity* (New York: New Press, 2005), 13.
40. Abraham Lincoln, cited in Harvey Wasserman, *America Born & Reborn* (New York: Collier Books, 1983), 89–90.
41. Delivered as part of a speech to the Southern Christian Leadership Conference Board on March 30, 1967.
42. Abraham Lincoln, cited in Wasserman, *America Born and Reborn*, 89–90.
43. Joseph E. Stiglitz, *People, Power, and Profits: Progressive Capitalism for an Age of Discontent* (New York: W. W. Norton & Company, 2019), xvii.
44. Many organizations aimed at building the new economy explicitly articulate these three principles as their basis. The widely respected New Economy Foundation in England, for example, is "guided by three missions": (1) a new social settlement ensuring that "people are paid well, have more time off to spend with their families, and have access to the things we all need for a decent life;" (2) a Green New Deal, which for them means a "plan for government-led investment to reduce the carbon we emit and massively boost nature, while creating a new generation of jobs;" and (3) a democratic economy to "transform ownership of the economy to give us all an equal stake in the places where we live and work." For more information, see https://neweconomics.org/.
45. See especially the sections on "climate injustice," "green and blue colonialism," "low-emissions economy," and "just transition."
46. Peter Hall and David Soskice distinguish two forms: liberal market economies (such as the UK and the US) and coordinated market economies (such as Germany and Denmark). The former are more grounded in liberalized, deregulated markets, and the later are more grounded in stronger social institutions and strategic, mutually beneficial relationships between firms—as opposed to competitive relationships. See Peter A. Hall and David W. Soskice, eds., *Varieties of Capitalism: The Institutional*

Foundations of Comparative Advantage (Oxford: Oxford University Press, 2004). See also William J. Baumol, Robert E. Litan, and Carl J. Schramm, *Good Capitalism, Bad Capitalism, and the Economics of Growth and Prosperity* (New Haven, CT: Yale University Press, 2007), which delineates four kinds of capitalism.

47. Joerg Rieger uses both terms in one page. See Joerg Rieger, *Theology in the Capitalocene: Ecology, Identity, Class, and Solidarity* (Minneapolis: Fortress Press, 2022).

48. Kim Stanley Robinson, *The Ministry for the Future* (New York, NY: Orbit, 2020), 273. Robinson is describing the policies that guide Mondragon, a collective of cooperatives in the Basque region of Spain that employs more than 80,000 people (as of 2019).

CHAPTER SEVEN

1. Pierre Bourdieu, *Language and Symbolic Power* (Cambridge: Harvard University Press, 1991), 236.
2. In fact, the term *climate injustice*" is more complex than this brief note indicates. I invite you to learn more through any of the following resources: https://tinyurl.com/ycx6c2p5, https://tinyurl.com/zfmc4nay, https://tinyurl.com/5bjh3rnp. For a more academic treatment, see https://tinyurl.com/5fjjvuts. All accessed February 11, 2024.
3. Maima Va'ai is a youth climate justice leader from Samoa. A member of the Methodist Church in Samoa, she was an ecumenical enabler for the Ecological Stewardship and Climate Justice Desk at the Pacific Conference of Churches.
4. Maima Va'ai, speaking at the end of the World Ocean Day march, June 8, 2023.
5. As early as 2001, the Third Annual Report of the IPCC alerts that "the impacts of climate change will fall disproportionately upon developing countries and the poor persons within all countries, and thereby exacerbate inequities in health status and access to adequate food, clean water, and other resources." R. T. Watson, Daniel L. Albritton, and Intergovernmental Panel on Climate Change, eds., *Climate Change 2001: Synthesis Report* (New York: Cambridge University Press, 2001), https://tinyurl.com/2p8xm956.
6. One report shows that "global warming amplifies nearly all existing inequalities" (1). African Americans, it demonstrates, are more adversely impacted by climate change than their white counterparts and some approaches to reducing greenhouse gas emissions have disproportionately adverse impacts on African Americans. See Nia Robinson and J. Andrew Hoerner, "A Climate of Change: African Americans, Global Warming, and a Just Climate Policy for the US" (Oakland, CA: Environmental Justice and Climate Change Initiative, July 2008), https://tinyurl.com/3da6j7b9. Accessed February 11, 2024.
7. Seth B. Shonkoff et al., "The Climate Gap: Inequalities in How Climate Change Hurts Americans and How to Close the Gap" (Los Angeles: USC Equity Research Institute, May 2009), 5, https://tinyurl.com/2un4w59b. See also Douglas Fischer, "Climate Change Hits Poor Hardest in US," *Scientific American*, May 29, 2009, https://tinyurl.com/5899f23w.
8. *Climate vulnerable* refers to nations and sectors that are particularly at risk of impacts of climate change including drought, fierce storms, rising sea levels, disease, food

Notes

shortage, and more. As defined by the IPCC, *vulnerability* refers to "the degree to which a system is susceptible to, or unable to cope with, adverse effects of climate change." See James J. McCarthy and Intergovernmental Panel on Climate Change, eds., *Climate Change 2001: Impacts, Adaptation, and Vulnerability: Contribution of Working Group II to the Third Assessment Report of the Intergovernmental Panel on Climate Change* (New York: Cambridge University Press, 2001). I use *climate privilege* to indicate nations and sectors most able to adapt to or prevent those impacts, or to be less vulnerable to them.

9. A team of Indian scholars points out that "poor and marginalized communities in the developing countries often suffer more from ... climate mitigation schemes than from the impacts of actual physical changes in the climate." Soumya Dutta et al., *Climate Change and India: Analysis of Political Economy and Impact* (Delhi: New Delhi: Daanish Books, 2013), 12, https://tinyurl.com/tc7y385c. This study notes that climate change has "two sets of impacts" on vulnerable sectors. One is the actual impact of climate change. The "second set of impacts originates from actions that our governments and corporate/industrial bodies undertake in the name of mitigating climate change. This includes large-scale agro-fuel and energy plantations in the name of green fuel ... extremely risky genetically modified plants (in the name of both mitigation and adaptation to climate change), more big dams for 'carbon-free' electricity," and more (12).

10. *CJ4A Short Film 2 - Climate Induced Relocation in Fiji* (Climate Justice for All, 2021), https://tinyurl.com/mr429s2e. Accessed February 11, 2024. The last line in this attribution is the voice of Maima Va'ai.

11. Only with COP 27 in 2022 was progress made in officially acknowledging that industrialized nations do owe something to the world's so-called developing nations.

12. Inter-religious Climate and Ecology Network, "2022 Statement for Climate Justice by the Global South," September 23, 2022, https://tinyurl.com/msejeyth.

13. Mayra Rivera, "What Is the Role of the Study of Religion in Times of Catastrophe?," *Journal of the American Academy of Religion* 91, no. 1 (December 11, 2023): 1–8, https://doi.org/10.1093/jaarel/lfad063.

14. Susanne Normann, "Green Colonialism in the Nordic Context: Exploring Southern Saami Representations of Wind Energy Development," *Journal of Community Psychology* 49, no. 1 (January 2021): 77–94 (quotes from 78–80), https://doi.org/10.1002/jcop.22422.

15. The Pacific Blue Line, "Protect Our Ocean Statement," Pacific Blue Line, n.d., https://tinyurl.com/4yzn8ne8. Accessed February 11, 2024.

16. While the permit was issued by the Papua New Guinea (PNG) government, the Pacific Parliamentarians' Alliance on Deep Sea Mining (PPADSM) and sister organizations, in meeting with people, found that nearly 100 percent opposed deep-sea mining. "The National Council of Women, National Council of Chiefs, National Council of Youth all have come out clearly to say we do not want deep-sea mining now or in the future," explained PNG parliamentarian Ralph Regevanu. (*Ecological Racism and Deep-Sea Mining in the Pacific*, G20 Interfaith Forum Webinar, 2022, https://tinyurl.com/3ryf7f49.) In an August 2016 statement, the Federation of Catholic Bishops Conferences of Oceania voiced their opposition to deep-sea mining (see https://tinyurl.com/ru9exebt). Likewise, in a 2021 interview with Aljazeera, Rev.

James Bhagwan, general secretary of the Pacific Conference of Churches, articulated the call for a ban on deep-sea mining. Cardinal John Ribat, archbishop of Papua, New Guinea, explains that DSM would devastate the seabed leading to destruction of the ecosystem, and the destruction of species that are key to the food chain. Moreover, the mining operations could disrupt the ocean's carbon storage capacities and could hit methane sinks in the ocean floor. All accessed February 11, 2024.

17. Pacific Blue Line, "Protect Our Ocean Statement."
18. Pacific Blue Line, "Protect Our Ocean Statement."
19. Normann, "Green Colonialism in the Nordic Context," 78–80.
20. Pennelys Droz and Julian Brave Noisecat, "Mobilizing an Indigenous Green New Deal," Position Paper (Rapid City, SD: NDN Collective, September 2019), https://tinyurl.com/2suj74ka. Accessed February 11, 2024.
21. "Global South" and "Global North" are terminological shortcuts to designate a complex reality. While they often are seen as designating Africa, Asia, the Pacific nations, and Latin America/Caribbean on the one hand and Europe and North America on the other, they are not actually geographic in that people of the Global South live in the lands often designated as the Global North. Moreover, often Indigenous peoples and highly impoverished people who have always lived in Europe or North America are still considered a part of the Global South.
22. For further information, see the organizations, publications, and website in the endnotes in this section.
23. "Theory of Change" (Center for Story Based Strategy, n.d.), https://tinyurl.com/f3bfzh76. Accessed February 11, 2024.
24. Senate Bill 5141: The Healthy Environment for All (HEAL) Act: https://tinyurl.com/yc7zb8yp. Accessed February 11, 2024.
25. Front and Centered, "Healthy Environment for All (HEAL) Act," Front and Centered, November 9, 2022, https://frontandcentered.org/heal-act/.
26. Movement Generation and the Climate Justice Alliance have articulated a widely used framework for Just Transition. "Just transition" has a dynamic and international history. In the US context, some trace it back to a 1970s labor leader who proposed a "Superfund for Workers" to support them as they transitioned out of toxic industries. Others locate the origins with environmental justice advocates concerned about the environmental racism that leaves communities of color and low-income communities disproportionately impacted by toxic wastes and industrial practices. Thus, just transition has roots also in the civil rights movement that helped give rise to environmental justice. Grounded in these histories, the just transition movement in the United States includes a wide range of strategies to build healthy economies that provide "dignified, productive, and ecologically sustainable livelihoods, democratic governance, and ecological resilience. . . . Core to a just transition is deep democracy in which workers and communities have control over the decisions that affect their daily lives." See https://tinyurl.com/4szyssr8. Accessed February 11, 2024.
27. Another example is Washington state's Clean Energy Transformation Act of 2019 (CETA). It "requires that the state's transition to a 100% renewable or non-emitting electric grid includes the equitable distribution of clean energy benefits and reduction of burdens to communities highly impacted by climate change." From "Chapter A: Equity—Build an Equitable, Inclusive, Resilient Clean Energy Economy,"

Washington 2021 State Energy Strategy (Washington State Department of Commerce, 2021), https://tinyurl.com/4z6dpfsa. Accessed February 11, 2024.

28. Tamara Krawchenko, "Managing a Just Transition in Denmark," Canadian Climate Institute, July 18, 2022, https://tinyurl.com/3x7xsfm9.

29. Quote from Hadrian Mertins-Kirkwood, Senior Researcher, Canadian Centre for Policy Alternatives, in UNRISD, "Just Transition(s) to a Low-Carbon World: Just Transitions, Power and Politics," Webinar (Just Transition Research Collaborative, December 9, 2020), https://tinyurl.com/tna35zrd.

30. As stated by the Just Transition Alliance, the process of building an ecologically sound economy and world "should be a fair one that should not cost workers or community residents their health, environment, jobs, or economic assets." The people who may be damaged by the transition "should be in the leadership of crafting policy solutions." (Just Transition Alliance, "Just Transition Principles," Just Transition Alliance, n.d., https://tinyurl.com/mwus54zw. Accessed February 11, 2024.)

31. The Democratic Republic of Congo, for example, is rich in coltan, and its mining industry is built on appalling exploitation of children. See Oluwale Ojewale, "Child Miners: The Dark Side of the DRC's Coltan Wealth," *ISS Today, Institute for Security Studies*, October 18, 2021, https://tinyurl.com/bdh76vyz. Argentina, Bolivia, and Chile are rich in lithium, and New Calcedonia is known as "the land of nickel."

32. A paper by four economists from University of Massachusetts states that "today's rich countries are responsible for nearly 80% of all human-related carbon emissions from 1850-2011.... This historical accumulation of greenhouse gas emissions is the major contributor to the cimate impacts the world is facing today.... More than 50% of these historial emissions occurred in the last 30 years." See Jayati Ghosh et al., "A Just Transition: How Can We Fairly Assign Climate Responsibility?," Deep Dive Paper 06 (Geneva, Switzerland: earth4All, July 2022), 5, https://tinyurl.com/jmr5ne5a. This paper does an excellent job of mapping the complexities inherent in assigning climate change responsibility, especially since emissions include "extreme and growing inequities in carbon use *within* countries" (italics mine), 12.

33. These are ways to address the climate debt that have featured so heavily in the demands for climate justice arising from the Global South and Indigenous communities. As stated by three economists from University of Massachusetts, "concerns about existing climate debt ... need to be addressed in any conception of a 'just transition.'" Ghosh, "A Just Transition," 5.

34. For example, according to Carbon Brief, "Indigenous peoples have been forcibly removed from their land because of carbon-offsetting in the Republic of the Congo and Democratic Republic of the Congo (DRC), the Brazilian, Colombian and Peruvian Amazon, Kenya, Malaysia and Indonesia." See https://tinyurl.com/vs8ndsed. Accessed February 11, 2024.

35. Indigenous Environmental Network, "Just Transition Guide," 2019, https://tinyurl.com/472sdjpn. Accessed February 11, 2024.

36. The statement notes, "Just Transition is a framework for a fair shift to an economy that is ecologically sustainable, equitable and just. After centuries of global plunder, the profit-driven, growth-dependent, industrial economy is severely undermining the life support systems of Mother earth. An economy based on extracting from a finite system faster than the capacity of the earth to regenerate will eventually come to an

end. Our Indigenous Nations must be ready. A Just Transition requires us to build an economy for life in a way that is very different than the economy we are in now. This calls for strategies that democratize, decentralize and diversify economic activity while we damper down consumption, and redistribute resources and power.... As Just Transition is becoming popular with different theories, practices and approaches, the Indigenous Environmental Network felt the need to compile a set of Indigenous-based principles of what Just Transition means to Indigenous peoples in North America-Turtle Island.... The following Indigenous Principles of Just Transition is a result of this process.... These principles are... the foundation upon which Tribes and their communities can build localized, living economies for the next seven generations and beyond."

37. See https://tinyurl.com/4szyssr8; https://tinyurl.com/55xjv534; or https://tinyurl.com/bddde2ns. The Oakland-based Movement Generation spent years developing resources to guide just transition work. Their "just transition" website provides an overview, brief history, an illustrated just transition zine, and links to adaptations of that zine by Indigenous Alaskans and South African activists.

38. The Climate Justice Alliance proposes five questions to help in that assessment: who tells the story? (frontline communities must have the authority and platform for explaining impacts and their proposed solutions); who makes the decisions?; who benefits and how? what else will this impact?; how will this build or shift power? See https://tinyurl.com/yy8tvm8p.

39. Stan Cox, *The Path to a Livable Future: A New Politics to Fight Climate Change, Racism, and the Next Pandemic* (San Francisco: City Lights Books, 2021).

40. The company markets lead as part of the solution to the transition to renewable energy and slowing climate change. See https://tinyurl.com/bdfwrz3b. Accessed February 11, 2024.

41. See for example Damian Carrington, "The World's Most Toxic Town: The Terrible Legacy of Zambia's Lead Mines," *Guardian*, May 28, 2017, https://tinyurl.com/3yn9xnv9.

42. Kimmerer, *Braiding Sweetgrass*, 375.

43. M. K. Gandhi, "Wardha Letter Third Class: Result of Exploitation," *Young India*, December 13, 1928, 997.

44. Speaking at the World Council of Churches General Assembly, Germany, 2022, as part of a tax justice workshop.

45. Benjamin Hitchcock Auciello, "A Just(Ice) Transition Is a Post-extractive Transition: Centering the Extractive Frontier in Climate Justice" (London, UK: War on Want and London Mining Network, September 2019), https://tinyurl.com/22a3782s.

46. First quotation: William J Ripple et al., "World Scientists' Warning of a Climate Emergency," *BioScience* 70, no. 1 (November 5, 2019): 8–12, https://doi.org/10.1093/biosci/biz088. Second quotation: Phoebe Barnard et al., "World Scientists' Warnings into Action, Local to Global," *Science Progress* 104, no. 4 (October 2021), 18, https://doi.org/10.1177/00368504211056290.

47. Theodore Roosevelt, "Outlook," November 18, 1914, Mem. Ed. XIV, 220; Nat. Ed. XII, 237. Cited by Tom Wheeler, "Who Makes the Rules in the New Guilded Age?" Brookings Institution, December 12, 2018, https://www.brookings.edu/articles/who-makes-the-rules-in-the-new-gilded-age/

48. Marjorie Kelly, *The Divine Right of Capital: Dethroning the Corporate Aristocracy* (San Francisco: Berrett-Koehler Publishers, 2003), ix–x (foreword by William Greider).
49. Arguably, capitalism and democracy derive from opposing principles and are therefore inherently antagonistic. In sum, the capitalist principle of capital concentration works against the democratic norm of relatively equal political power, and the capitalist principle of excluding economic power from democratic accountability works against the democratic norm of accountable power. This argument is articulated by Harry Ward and Ellen Meiskins Wood. They argue historically that the notion of capitalist democracy, which developed in the United States, gave formal political powers to all, but retained the power of rule or control through capital in the hands of the propertied elite. Formal democracy could co-exist with inequality and hence worked against rule by the people. (I would add, however, that the democratizing of government has been only partial and highly limited by race, class, and gender.) Harry F. Ward, *Democracy and Social Change* (New York: Modern Age Books, 1940). See also Naomi Klein's foreword in Marjorie Kelly and Ted Howard, *The Making of Democratic Economy* (Oakland, CA: Berrett-Koehler Publishers, 2019), ix-x; and Cynthia Moe-Lobeda, *Healing a Broken World: Globalization and God* (Minneapolis: Fortress Press, 2002), chapter 2.
50. For example, the 2010 Supreme Court case *Citizens United vs. Federal Election Commission* freed corporations to spend unlimited amounts on communication to help or defeat a candidate. According to a 2015 paper from Harvard Law School, *Citizens United* was the latest in a series of cases to expand corporate rights to "free speech." See John C. Coates, IV, "Corporate Speech and the First Amendment: History, Data, and Implications," *SSRN Electronic Journal*, 2015, https://doi.org/10.2139/ssrn.2566785.
51. For an excellent account of this process, see Marjorie Kelly, *Wealth Supremacy: How the Extractive Economy and the Biased Rules of Capitalism Drive Today's Crises* (Oakland, CA: Berrett-Koehler Publishers, Inc, 2023).
52. Quinn Slobodian writes that "the neoliberal project focused on ... inoculat[ing] capitalism against the threat of democracy" (2); "the real focus of neoliberal proposals is ... on redesigning states, laws, and other institutions to protect the market" (6). Their project "offered a set of proposals designed to defend the world economy from a democracy that became global only in the twentieth century" (4). The "confrontation with mass democracy was also at the heart of the Century for neoliberals" (14). For them, the world must be "kept safe from mass demands for social justice and redistributive equality" (16). Quinn Slobodian, *Globalists: The End of Empire and the Birth of Neoliberalism* (Cambridge, MA: Harvard University Press, 2018).
53. Exploring the historical conflict in the United States between democracy and property rights, Robert Dahl argues that "from the beginning of our nation's existence, and indeed earlier, the question of the relative priority of democracy and property has received two fundamentally conflicting answers.... On the one side, supporters of property held that political equality must finally yield to property rights.... Those who supported the goal of democracy insisted, on the contrary, that a person's right to self-government, and thus to political equality, was more fundamental than the

right to property." He suggests that modern democracy, while it provided political liberty (e.g., the right to vote), has not provided political equality (e.g., equality of power). That shortfall he attributes in significant part to the ideology of freeing property (including finance) from democratic control (52–83). Robert Alan Dahl, *A Preface to Economic Democracy* (Berkeley: University of California Press, 1985).

54. See Allen L. White, "Transforming the Corporation," GTI Paper Series: Frontiers of a Great Transition (Boston: Great Transition Initiative and Tellus Institute, 2006), https://tinyurl.com/3edtwaee, 16–20, for an example of three quite diverse forms of economy all characterized as "economic democracy." Accessed February 11, 2024.

55. Following are a few sources reporting the increase in billionaire wealth during the pandemic: Juliana Kaplan and Andy Kiersz, "American Billionaires Added $2.1 Trillion to Their Fortunes during the Pandemic," *Business Insider*, October 18, 2021, https://tinyurl.com/yc7y39p3; Jack Kelly, "The Rich Are Getting Richer during the Pandemic," *Forbes*, July 22, 2020, https://tinyurl.com/ykc94eup; Chuck Collins, "Updates: Billionaire Wealth, US Job Losses, and Pandemic Profiteers," *Inequality.Org: Blogging Our Great Divide* (blog), November 21, 2022, https://tinyurl.com/2awkpy43; Barbara Kollmeyer, "The World's Richest 10 Men Doubled Their Fortunes to $1.5 Trillion during the Pandemic, Says Oxfam," *MarketWatch*, January 17, 2022, https://tinyurl.com/ptmakcce; US Senate Committee on Finance, "Wyden Unveils Billionaires Income Tax," www.finance.senate.gov, October 27, 2021, https://tinyurl.com/3x8u58uh.

56. Economic democracy refers less to an endpoint than to a process of piece-by-piece conversion from centralized economic power (centralized in corporate management and the largest shareholders) to shared and publicly accountable economic institutions and practices. It refers also to the values and public policies that support that conversion.

57. Kelly, *Wealth Supremacy*, xiv.

58. Atlas of the Future, "Cities Copy Cleveland's Prosperity Model," Atlas of the Future, October 2, 2019, https://tinyurl.com/2wemjhc8.

59. Mayor's Office of Equity and Racial Justice and CWB Advisory Council, "City of Chicago: Community Wealth Building Initiative" (Chicago, IL: Community Wealth Building Initiative, 2023), https://tinyurl.com/575fm285. Accessed February 11, 2024.

60. Rieger, *Theology in the Capitalocene*, 48–9.

61. See https://tinyurl.com/2eb5z4te.

62. See https://neweconomy.net/ and https://tinyurl.com/mw2k6arm.

63. Gary Dorrien, *Economy, Difference, Empire: Social Ethics for Social Justice* (New York: Columbia University Press, 2010), 168.

64. *David M. Richardson v. Christian H. Euhl and Russel A. Alger* (Michigan Supreme Court November 15, 1889). See https://cite.case.law/mich/77/632/.

65. Law professor Michael Klarman, as described by law professor Amna Akbar, writes that "wealthy Americans and interest groups have disproportionate political influence and that such a political system 'is not a democracy.'" Amna A. Akbar, "Demands for a Democratic Political Economy (Responding to Michael J. Klarman, 'The Degradation of American Democracy—and the Court')," *Harvard Law Review* 134, no. 1 (December 2020), https://tinyurl.com/3s6fdsp8.

Notes

66. The theoretical genealogy of this perspective is situated in at least four historical debates. I explain them in Moe-Lobeda, *Healing a Broken World*, chapter 3.
67. Both classical and contemporary theorists of participatory democracy argue that substantive economic inequity works against democratic political participation. For example, Jean-Jacques Rousseau considered that a degree of economic equality was necessary for effective political participation. "Liberty cannot exist without [equality].... No citizen shall ever be wealthy enough to buy another, and none poor enough to be forced to sell himself." Jean-Jacques Rousseau, *The Social Contract and Discourses*, bk. II, ch. 11 (London: Everyman, 1973), 225. According to Carole Pateman, Rousseau's theory does not require absolute equality as is often implied, but rather requires that economic inequity not be large enough to result in political inequality. Carole Pateman, *Participation and Democratic Theory* (Cambridge: Cambridge University Press, 1975), 22.
68. Dorrien, *Economy, Difference, Empire*, 142.
69. Maxine Burkett, "Climate Reparations," *Melbourne Journal of International Law* 10 (2009): 2.
70. COP stands for Conference of Parties. It is the annual climate summit held by the United Nations and attended by the nations who signed the United Nations Framework Convention on Climate Change. This includes most nations on earth. The number following COP stands for the year of the summit.
71. "Loss and damage" has varied connotations but most refer to the loss of and damage to livelihoods, communities, lands, and lives caused directly or indirectly by climate change. For more on the impact of climate change on Indigenous peoples and the role of Indigenous communities in addressing climate change, see: UN Department of Economic and Social Affairs, "The Effects of Climate Change on Indigenous Peoples," https://tinyurl.com/2aujvzdx. Accessed February 11, 2024.
72. The case for climate reparations is made by political philosopher Olúfẹ́mi O. Táíwò, who argues that "a politically serious reparations project must focus on climate change." Olúfẹ́mi O. Táíwò, "The Fight for Reparations Cannot Ignore Climate Change: Racial Redress Should Be Modeled on the Global Anticolonial Tradition of Worldbuilding," *Boston Review*, January 10, 2022, https://tinyurl.com/89af4ark.
73. Saleemul Huq, director of the Bangladesh-based International Centre for Climate Change and Development, spoke for many in insisting that "loss and damage [funding] is by far the most important issue that needs to be discussed" at COP27. See Sam Meredith, "A Showdown over Climate Reparations Is Brewing—and It Will Determine the Success of the COP27 Summit," CNBC, November 4, 2022, https://tinyurl.com/27xppzvv.
74. Climate reparations as some form of "payment of what is due to them because of what has been done to them" is complicated by the meaning of "what has been done to them." For many colonized peoples, this includes the forced removal from their land (for peoples to whom land was life, both spiritually and materially) or despoilment of their lands that left people sorely vulnerable to the ravages of climate change. As an example, writing about the devastating August 2022 floods in Pakistan that displaced 50 million people and killed more than 15,000, Amitav Ghosh points out that "one of the reasons why so many people were displaced in these floods is because, going back to colonial times, many nomads who moved with the rhythms

of the river were forced to settle by river banks." (Ghosh, "The Colonial Roots of Present Crises.") This theme is key, and it is enormously controversial because it points to land repatriation/rematriation and accountability. This is one reason why repatriation of land, land reform, land repossession and redistribution, and reparations for removal from lands are central for many people in the Global South and Indigenous people discussing climate justice. See also Sifiso Mpofu, "A Theology of the Land and Its Covenant Responsibility" and Garnett Roper, "Empire 2.0: Land Matters in Jamaica and the Caribbean," in *People and Land: Decolonizing Theologies*, ed. Jione Havea (Lanham, MD: Lexington Books/Fortress Academic, 2020), 77–90 and 101–12.

75. Talia, "Am I not your *(Tu)akoi*—neighbour?"
76. In addition to the resources in the endnotes for ths section, see Isabelle Gerretsen, "Who Will Pay for the Damage Caused by Climate Change?," BBC, December 13, 2021, https://tinyurl.com/mtjfdm4h.
77. The earlier stories of green and blue colonialism and sacrifice zones illustrate.
78. La Via Campesina, "COP26: Adopt Peasant Agroecology to Achieve Climate Justice and Keep Carbon Markets out of the Paris Agreement," La Via Campesina—EN, November 5, 2021, https://tinyurl.com/22fu38ex. (Bold is in the original.)
79. Rev. Gordon Cowans in an address to the World Council of Churches NIFEA team meeting in Indonesia, October 2022: "It is time for the world to act towards the cancellation of debt of these struggling economies and the allocation of resources to them for development, recognizing the unique role that colonialism and enslavement played in stultifying economic progress in so many African and African descendant societies, leaving them more vulnerable to climate change damage."
80. Grants were "provided by the Bipartisan Infrastructure Law and Inflation Reduction Act," said UN Secretary General António Guterres as he opened the global summit of the Convention on Biological Diversity in Montreal, December 2022.
81. Farooq Tariq, "After the Floods, Pakistan Needs Reparations, Not Charity," New Internationalist, September 5, 2022, https://tinyurl.com/3zk82vwz. Tariq is the general secretary of the Pakistan Kissan Rabita Committee, a network of twenty-six peasant organizations and a coalition member of La Via Campesina.
82. David Wallace-Wells, "Climate Reparations: A Trillion Tons of Carbon Hangs in the Air, Put There by the World's Rich, an Existential Threat to Its Poor. Can We Remove It?," *New York Magazine*, November 1, 2021, https://tinyurl.com/3z5cvrh3.

SETTING THE STAGE

1. adrienne maree brown, *Emergent Strategy: Shaping Change, Changing Worlds* (Chico, CA: AK Press, 2017), 19.
2. I have adopted those six strategies and added to them. I am indebted to the CJA for its clear articulation of these means of change and I refer you the reader to them. https://climatejusticealliance.org/. I have drawn also on frameworks provided by the New Economy Coalition in their "Pathways to a People's Economy," and by the Sustainable Economies Law Center's strategies toward sustainable economies."
3. Pamela Haines, "Feeding Children, Communities, and Souls," *Tikkun Magazine*, Summer 2018, 45. This entire story comes from that article.

Notes

4. The quotations in this paragraph are from: Haines, "Feeding Children, Communities, and Souls," 46, 49, 46.
5. The quotations in this paragraph are from: Haines, "Feeding Children, Communities, and Souls," 46, 47, 48.
6. Haines, "Feeding Children, Communities, and Souls," 48.
7. Haines, "Feeding Children, Communities, and Souls," 46–47.
8. Haines, "Feeding Children, Communities, and Souls," 46.
9. Kelly Marciales, in coteaching a course at Pacific Lutheran Theological Seminary.

CHAPTER EIGHT

1. William Greider, "Foreword," in Marjorie Kelly, *The Divine Right of Capital* (San Francisco: Berrett-Koehler, 2001), xi.
2. Naomi Klein, "Foreword," in Marjorie Kelly and Ted Howard, *The Making of a Democratic Economy* (Oakland, CA: Berrett-Koehler Publishers, 2019), ix–x.
3. Klein, "Foreword," xiii.
4. "Worker cooperatives are businesses owned, operated, and democratically controlled by their workers who share in the profits of their labor and practice solidarity. Control is exercised on the premise of 'one worker, one vote.' Workers own the majority of the equity in the business and control the voting shares. They decide what is produced or what service is rendered and how this is done, how to the distribute the profit, and they put worker and community benefit at the core of their purpose. These typically small businesses can be found in every sector and industry, from engineering and manufacturing to retail and service." Rosemarie Henkel-Rieger, "Deep Solidarity: A Pre-requisite to Resisting and Building Economic Democracy," unpublished paper presented at DARE (Discernment and Radical Engagement) conference, 2020, 16.
5. Democratizing ownership and control are the central feature of such business. That may mean employee-owned cooperatives that are fully owned by employees who have equal ownership stake, or employee stock ownership plan companies (ESOPs) in which employee ownership may be either full or partial. Many begin as employee owned but others begin as traditional businesses and convert to employee ownership.
6. It is supported by organizations such as the Southeast Center for Cooperative Development and the Sustainable Economies Law Center that provide supportive legal infrastructure, training and other capacity building.
7. This is the focus, for example, of Wellspring Cooperative Corporation in Springfield Massachusetts and of the Democracy Collaborative, which pioneered the Cleveland Model encountered in chapters 6 and 7.
8. https://tinyurl.com/4s963txd. "The study, which the authors describe as the most comprehensive integrated assessment of Detroit urban agriculture to be published in a peer-reviewed academic journal, appeared online March 25 in the journal *Cities*." https://tinyurl.com/2tu5wazr.
9. See for example, the Agrarian Trust. https://www.agrariantrust.org/.
10. https://tinyurl.com/448bpvej.
11. https://tinyurl.com/3xsj533x.
12. The Democracy Collaborative, a leader in community wealth building, for example, sees its local initiatives as helping to build "a new economic system where shared

ownership and control creates more equitable and inclusive outcomes, fosters ecological sustainability, and promotes flourishing democratic and community life." Website of the Democracy Collaborative. See https://democracycollaborative.org/. As noted by Aaron Tanaka, founding director of the Center for Economic Democracy and founder of Boston's Ujima Project, such models not only demonstrate that democratic, equitable business is possible; they also "leverage grassroots political and cultural power to win policy solutions that support" the new economy.
13. Simon Mont, "Introduction to the Next Economy," *Tikkun Magazine*, 2018, 16.
14. The movement includes a number of national networks providing training and support, especially for low-income people to create and sustain worker-owned cooperatives that build wealth in communities exploited and abandoned by traditional business models. Examples of national and regional support networks include The Democracy at Work Institute, the U.S. Federation of Worker Cooperatives, and the Southeast Center for Cooperative Development. See https://institute.coop/, https://www.usworker.coop/en/, and https://www.co-opsnow.org/.
15. Henkel-Rieger, "Deep Solidarity," 17.
16. See https://tinyurl.com/yc6t7vzd.
17. Decolonizing Economics: Third Annual Post-Capitalism Conference, April 21–23, 2022.
18. Emily Kawano, presentation, at Decolonizing Economics Conference, 2022.
19. To illustrate: Creating and sustaining worker co-ops requires public policy that enables co-op development and financing. An example is the Limited Cooperative Association Act of 2019 or 2020 in Illinois—HB 3663.
20. Karen Baker-Fletcher, *Sisters of Dust, Sisters of Spirit: Womanist Wordings on God and Creation* (Minneapolis: Fortress Press, 1998).
21. Robin Broad and John Cavanagh, "It's the New Economy, Stupid," *Nation*, November 28, 2012. https://tinyurl.com/bdcz7seb.

CHAPTER NINE

1. Jess Rimington, "The Means Are the Ends," in *The New Possible*, ed. Philip Clayton et.al. (Eugene, OR: Cascade Books, 2021), 123–31, quote on 129–30.
2. Stated while teaching in Faith-Based Community Organizing course at Pacific Lutheran Theological Seminary. Used with permission.
3. Martin Luther King Jr., "A Christmas Sermon on Peace," sermon preached at Ebenezer Baptist Church, December 24, 1967.
4. Eric Schlosser, in the documentary *Food Chains*.
5. In her Union Day address, "The Future of Union, the Union of the Future," at Union Theological Seminary, 2001.
6. Vincent A. Gallagher, *The True Cost of Low Prices* (Maryknoll, NY: Orbis Books, 2008).
7. https://dayenu.org/.
8. It is true also that in the US many people are too strained by the relentless and exhausting demands that poverty exacts on time, energy, creativity, and coping mechanisms, to make such lifestyle changes. Those of us in such circumstances may not be called to enact lifestyle changes toward more equitable and ecological

Notes

economies unless those changes also make life safer and more secure for the vulnerable self and dependents.

9. James Poling, *Deliver Us from Evil* (Minneapolis: Fortress, 1996), 121.
10. Poling, *Deliver Us from Evil*, 121.
11. "For generations, farmworkers have suffered from levels of poverty and abuse unparalleled in the US labor market. Well-documented abuses in the workplace have included physical and verbal abuse, rape and widespread sexual harassment, discrimination, and high fatal and nonfatal injury rates. Farmworkers have also faced endemic wage theft, resulting in widespread violation of minimum wage laws. In the extreme, farmworkers have faced situations of forced labor. In these instances, workers have been held against their will, with the threat or actual use of violence, and forced to work for little or no pay." Several of these cases, some involving hundreds of workers, have been successfully prosecuted by the US Department of Justice over the past two decades. The Coalition of Immokalee Workers (CIW), a farmworker organization based in Florida, has worked on the investigation and prosecution of nine such cases with federal law enforcement agencies since 1997 alone. This paragraph is from https://tinyurl.com/yx5e4juf. Accessed February 17, 2024.
12. Over a fifteen-year period, "9 major investigations and federal prosecutions have freed over 1,200 Florida farmworkers from captivity and forced labor, leading one U.S. attorney to call these fields "ground zero for modern slavery." https://ciw-online.org/about/ and https://ciw-online.org/slavery/. Accessed February 17, 2024.
13. "The history of farm labor in the United States is a history of exploitation. Most people have no idea that they're connected to this system every time they buy fresh fruits and vegetables." Eric Schlosser, *Food Chains*.
14. International Accord for Health and Safety in the Textile and Garment Industry, https://tinyurl.com/5n74pu3b.
15. International Accord for Health and Safety in the Textile and Garment Industry.
16. International Accord for Health and Safety in the Textile and Garment Industry.
17. Accord on Fire and Building Safety in Bangladesh. See https://bangladeshaccord.org/about.
18. https://fairfoodprogram.org/ and https://ciw-online.org/about/.
19. https://fairfoodprogram.org/.
20. For example: the program received the Presidential Medal for Extraordinary Efforts in Combatting Modern-Day Slavery at a White House ceremony in 2015. Seven years later the American Bar Association awarded the CIW the Frances Perkins Public Service Award for its human rights achievements. Kevin Jones, "Spotlight on Coalition of Immokalee Workers," American Bar Association, February 23, 2023.
21. See https://tinyurl.com/mcxmv4nb.
22. https://tinyurl.com/37cmkxhs.
23. See also chapter 13.
24. https://www.sfalliance.org/. CIW also had helped to form two other organizations—Interfaith Action of Southwest Florida, which brought in spiritual resources and the moral weight of faith-based voices, and Just Harvest USA, building on the consumer movement for justice in food production.
25. Significant parts of this section come from Moe-Lobeda, *Resisting Structural Evil*, chap. 9.

26. Juliet Schor and Craig Thompson describe this movement as "plenitude practitioners." Their description highlights the links between building the new and living lightly. Juliet B. Schor and Craig J. Thomson, "Introduction," in *Sustainable Lifestyles and the Quest for Plenitude*, ed. Juliet B. Schor and Craig J. Thompson (New Haven, CT: Yale University Press, 2014), 3.
27. Schor and Thomson, "Introduction," and "Cooperative Networks, Decentralized Markets, and Rhizomatic Resistance: Situating Plentitude within Contemporary Political Economy Debates," in Schor and Thompson, *Sustainable Lifestyles and the Quest for Plenitude*, 1–25 and 233–49.

CHAPTER TEN

1. Dylan Matthews, "The Big Drop in American Poverty during the Pandemic," *Vox*, August 11, 2021, https://tinyurl.com/4vf2n6d4.
2. Joseph Stiglitz, *People, Power, and Profits: Progressive Capitalism for an Age of Discontent* (New York: W.W. Norton and Company, 2019), xvii.
3. New Economy Coalition at https://peopleseconomy.org/about-the-toolkit/.
4. https://tinyurl.com/44csejvw.
5. https://tinyurl.com/3v2922pp. https://tinyurl.com/5b423e5e.
6. Pennsylvania was one, with its $100 million program for historically disadvantaged small business. Ayana Jones, "Grant Program Established to Assist Minority-Owned Businesses Impacted by COVID-19," *Philadelphia Tribune*, June 11, 2020.
7. Sustainable Economies Law Center and Shareable, "Policies for Sharable Cities: A Sharing Economy Policy Primer for Urban Leaders" (2013), 4, 16. In 2013, the Sustainable Economies Law Center (SELC) partnered with Sharable (a non-profit dedicated to building sharable economies) to publish this 39-page policy primer. It provides policy recommendations regarding four "pocket-book issues" for cities—transportation, food, housing, and jobs. It illustrates the power of public policy to move toward ecological, equitable, and democratic economies on the local level. The social theorist Pierre Bourdieu argues that rules or laws established by recognized authorities (in this case by a local, state, or national legislative or policy making body) have the power to "bring into existence what they decree." Pierre Bourdieu, *Language and Symbolic Power* (Cambridge, MA: Harvard University Press, 1991), 222.
8. Recall chapter 3's discussion of the large (28%) reduction in global carbon emissions that could be achieved by public policy that eliminated fossil fuel subsidies by governments. See https://tinyurl.com/3wp5wn6p.
9. Imam Omar Suleiman, founder and president of Yaqeen Institute for Islamic Research, in "Moral Revolution: An Interfaith Response to the Coronavirus Pandemic," a webinar on April 9, 2020.
10. A circular economy means that the city will have no waste due to aggressive recycling, reusing, and other measures.
11. Regarding doughnut economics see Kate Raworth, *Doughnut Economics* (White River Junction, VT: Chelsea Green Publishing, 2017).
12. "Eco-Actions," *Green American* magazine, Summer 2023, 5.
13. Webinar, Rise Up for Justice, June 8, 2022.

Notes

14. See Marjorie Kelly, *The Divine Right of Capital* (San Francisco: Berrett-Koehler, 2001), 127–44, 198–99.
15. Marjorie Kelly lays out a spectrum of legal moves that could reign in the power of corporations and lay the legal infrastructure for economic democracy, and in particular for the shift to worker- or employee-owned business as a default mode of business. *The Divine Right of Capital*, chapters 7–11.
16. In their report "Environment and Development Challenges: The Imperative to Act" presented at the 2012 meeting of the UNEP.
17. Website of United for a Fair Economy. https://www.faireconomy.org/. Accessed February 17, 2024.
18. United for a Fair Economy.
19. See for example the Limited Cooperative Association Act of Illinois—HB 3663 (2019). https://tinyurl.com/2p99urya.
20. The NEC notes that this work was inspired by the Black Lives Matter policy demands and the "just transition principles" of the Climate Justice Alliance.

CHAPTER ELEVEN

1. Bill McKibben, "Money Is the Oxygen on Which the Fire of Global Warming Burns," *New Yorker*, September 17, 2019.
2. Kelly, *The Divine Right of Capital*, 196.
3. Every year Jewish people celebrate the Passover by telling the story of how their ancestors gained their freedom from the Egyptian pharaohs. This happens in the seder meal. The street seders and other Passover actions in 2022 were coordinated by "Dayenu—a Jewish Call to Climate Action" in collaboration with the Jewish Youth Climate Movement, the Shalom Center, the Exodus Alliance, Interfaith Power and Light, and other ally organizations. https://dayenu.org/.
4. The All Our Might Campaign draws its name from the *Sh'ma* prayer.
5. Vignette told by Pamela Haines, a Philadelphia Quaker.
6. "Climate activists on Trial over Credit Suisse Tennis Stunt," Swissinfo.ch, 8 January 2020, https://tinyurl.com/4x9unrd3.
7. The letter states that "while low income households around the world have been pushed further into poverty over the last few years, oil and gas companies made record profits and wealthy countries continued to heavily subsidize them. This does not just defy economic justice, but climate science too.... Ending fossil fuel handouts in high-income G20 countries alone would raise about USD $500 billion a year."
8. Regarding this debt, the letter declares, "The last few years of global crises have compounded already untenable debts in many developing countries, draining public funds that are critically needed to deliver both vital social services and climate action. These debts are also unfair, having been incurred through our neo-colonial global financial system or in many cases during colonization."
9. The letter also explains that "unlocking and redistributing public trillions is of course only part of what is needed—our international monetary, trade, tax, and debt rules are systematically skewed towards the Global North, allowing wealthy countries to drain a net $2 trillion a year from low-income peers.... We need a dramatic transformation of this system to one that is rights-based, people-centered, democratic,

and transparent.... The wealthiest 1% have captured two-thirds of new global wealth created in the last two years, all while we are likely seeing the biggest increase in global inequality and poverty since World War II. Progressive taxes on extreme wealth starting at 2% would raise $2.5 to 3.6 trillion a year, and related proposals to crack down on tax dodging would significantly augment this. Global North leaders can show they are serious about this by starting with an initial '1.5% for 1.5°C' tax on extreme wealth and dedicating this to the new 'loss and damage' fund, and by agreeing to advance a universal and intergovernmental UN Tax Convention.... Even this initial redirection of harmful economic flows would have staggering impacts — it would be enough to close the universal energy access gap ($34 billion), fill the 'floor' of the 'loss and damage' fund ($400 billion per year), meet the overdue climate finance target fully with grants ($100 billion per year), and cover emergency UN humanitarian appeals ($52 billion per year) with plenty to spare."

10. World Council of Churches, Lutheran World Federation, Council for World Missions, and World Communion of Reform Churches.
11. In April 2023, the Climate Action Network International and partners published Seven Joint Principles for Finance System Transformation. https://tinyurl.com/ejnvnb4w. Accessed February 17, 2024.
12. Antonio Guterres, UN Secretary-General, at the launch of the global interfaith initiative, "Climate-Responsible Finance—a Moral Imperative and Responsibility to All Children and the Living World," May 9, 2022. https://tinyurl.com/4p2sv7n4.
13. Club of Rome website: https://tinyurl.com/5n8s2z6x. Accessed February 17, 2024.
14. Cited by Amitav Ghosh, *The Great Derangement* (Chicago: University of Chicago Press, 2016), 111.
15. The United Nations Environmental Programme's Faith for Earth illustrates.
16. On 9th May 2022, for example, the World Council of Churches (WCC), Faith for Earth of the United Nations, the Muslim Council of Elders, and New York Board of Rabbis launched the Climate Responsible Finance: A Moral Imperative towards Children initiative.
17. Frederique Seidel, Emmanuel de Martel, Eric Begaghel, *Cooler Earth—Higher Benefits*, 3rd ed. (Geneva: World Council of Churches, 2022), 7. https://tinyurl.com/42jnfwmb.
18. Morgan Simon, *Real Impact* (New York: Bold Type Books, 2017), 191.
19. Guterres, "Climate-Responsible Finance."
20. Bill McKibben, "The Most Dangerous Building in Town," *Sojourners*, February 2020, 16–17.
21. More details on investment statistics and analyses of specific banks can be found in Rainforest Action Network's Banking on Climate Chaos 2022 report and rankings. See also the Climate Justice Organizers' Toolkit at https://tinyurl.com/ye25ufh9, and https://tinyurl.com/4t2ekudf.
22. Arabella Advisors, *Measuring the Growth of the Global Fossil Fuel Divestment and Clean Energy Investment Movement*, September 2015. https://tinyurl.com/36y9efyx.
23. https://tinyurl.com/3z6v438p.
24. See https://tinyurl.com/cp6py4fy.
25. DivestInvest is "a global network of individuals and organizations united in the belief that by using our collective influence as investors to divest from fossil fuels,

and invest in climate solutions, we can accelerate the transition to a zero-carbon economy." https://www.divestinvest.org/about/.
26. The report goes on to say, "Since the movement's first summary report in 2014, the amount of total assets publicly committed to divestment has grown by over 75,000 percent. The number of institutional commitments to divestment has grown by 720 percent in that time, including a 49 percent increase in just the three years since the movement's most recent report."
27. William J. Ripple, Christopher Wolf, Thomas M. Newsome, Phoebe Barnard, William R. Moomaw, "World Scientists' Warning of a Climate Emergency," *BioScience*, 70, no. 1 (January 2020): 8–12, https://doi.org/10.1093/biosci/biz088.
28. Chris Flood, "Climate Change Poses Challenge to Long-Term Investors," *Financial Times*, April 21, 2019. https://tinyurl.com/yarya84d.
29. See an excellent account of divestment/reinvestment: Celia Bottger, Rachel Eckles, Bianca Hutner, Sarah Jacqz, Emily Thai, "The Reinvest Report" (Boston: The Solidarity Economy Initiative, 2018), iv.
30. https://neweconomy.net/.
31. "Tax justice refers to ideas, policies and advocacy that seek to achieve equality and social justice through fair taxes on wealthier members of society and multinational corporations. To this end, tax justice often focuses on tackling tax havens and curtailing corruption and tax abuse by multinational corporations and the super-rich.... Tax havens are key to understanding financial globalization and they expand the debate beyond tax into the areas of financial secrecy, financial regulation, criminal law, accountancy, economics and much more. Tax justice also refers to a growing global movement—the tax justice community—which the Tax Justice Network has helped pioneer." Uhuru Dempers, unpublished paper, "Talking Points for Presentation to NIFEA session in Bali, Indonesia on 11th to 13th October 2022."
32. This occurred at a tax justice workshop at the 11th Assembly of the World Council of Churches in Karlsruhe, Germany, from August 31 to September 8, 2022.
33. TJNA is a member of the Global Alliance for Tax Justice, a coalition led by people of the Global South.
34. "The State of Tax Justice 2020," released by the civil society group Tax Justice Network. Quotations in this paragraph are from https://tinyurl.com/mtwhhszh.
35. "The tax losses of countries around the world are equivalent to nearly 34 million nurses' annual salaries every year. Instead of blanketly applying one country's average annual nurse salary to the world, the global number of equivalent nurses' salaries lost is arrived at by first calculating how much each country's tax losses is equivalent to in local average annual nurse salaries in the country. Each country's equivalent in nurses' annual salaries is then summed to produce a global total the reflects nurses' annual salaries around the world. Countries' average annual nurse salaries are sourced from OECD data. For non-OECD countries, we use the average salary in the country, as reported by the International Labor Organization. Missing values in the OECD and ILO databases were calculated using the relation between the country's average salary and GDP per capita found in other countries." See n1 in https://tinyurl.com/4zmn3p28.
36. A lengthy July 2022 report called "Building Back with Justice: Dismantling Inequalities after Covid-19" by Christian Aid of London argues that responding to

the COVID crisis "presents an opportunity to mend a global tax system that was already deeply dysfunctional and regressive.... Plans to recover from the crisis should begin with a commitment to tackle tax abuse." See https://tinyurl.com/33h6zstm.

37. "Tax for the Common Good" (Evesham, UK: Church Action for Tax Justice), 3.
38. Council for World Mission, Lutheran World Federation, World Communion of Reformed Churches, World Council of Churches, World Methodist Council, "ZacTax Toolkit," 24. https://tinyurl.com/ycy33k46. Accessed February 17, 2024.
39. A wealth tax differs from an income tax in that the former taxes net worth and hence can get at income for which people can avoid paying income taxes.
40. Various forms of financial transaction tax have been proposed including the original proposal by Nobel Prize–winning economist James Tobin in what became known as the Tobin Tax on short-term trade in currencies; the Robin Hood Tax, which would tax a broader group of assets including stocks, bonds, mutual funds, derivatives; and the European Union Financial Transaction Tax. The former two have made more headway in Europe than in the US, with the Tobin Tax having been adopted in eleven countries and advancing in others. All three forms of transaction tax have been supported by civil society groups (including churches) who also propose using the revenues to combat poverty and climate change.
41. See for example: https://americansfortaxfairness.org/about/. See also on that website the sixty-seven organizations signing a letter to Congress encouraging a Billionaires Income Tax.
42. "Billionaire Wealth, U.S. Job Losses and Pandemic Profiteers," Inequality.org, October, 2020.
43. "9 ways to imagine Jeff Bezos' wealth," *New York Times Magazine*, 2022.
44. "Richest Americans—Including Bezos, Musk and Buffett—Paid Federal Income Taxes Equaling Just 3.4% of $401 Billion in New Wealth, Bombshell Report Shows," *Forbes*, June 2021.
45. "The Secret IRS Files: Trove of Never-Before-Seen Records Reveal How the Wealthiest Avoid Income Tax," *ProPublica*, June, 2021.
46. Robert Reich, personal email. Italics are mine. The world's richest ten men doubled their fortunes to $1.5 trillion during the pandemic, says Oxfam (MarketWatch, January, 2022). Other sources reporting the increase in billionaire wealth during the pandemic include Juliana Kaplan and Andy Kiersz, "American billionaires Added $2.1 trillion to Their Fortunes during the Pandemic," Business Insider, October 18, 2021: https://tinyurl.com/2nm86fuf; Jack Kelly, "The Rich Are Getting Richer During the Pandemic," *Forbes*, July 22, 2020; "Billionaire Wealth, U.S. Job Losses and Pandemic Profiteers."
47. https://www.finance.senate.gov/chairmans-news/wyden-unveils-billionaires-income-tax **and** https://americansfortaxfairness.org
48. In the UK for example, "The highest rate of income tax peaked in the Second World War at 99.25%. It was then slightly reduced and was around 90% through the 1950s and 60s. In 1971 (in England) the top rate of income tax on earned income was cut to 75%. A surcharge of 15% kept the top rate on investment income at 90%. In 1974 the cut was partly reversed and the top rate on earned income was raised to 83%. With the investment income surcharge this raised the top rate on investment income to 98%, the highest permanent rate since the war. This applied to incomes over £20,000 (£221,741 as of 2021)." https://tinyurl.com/mwxz9s4s.

49. For a history and assessment of the informal network of NGOs and churches that evolved into a more integrated but loosely affiliated coalition of groups collaborating on the Jubilee 2000 campaign, see Elizabeth A. Donnelly, "Proclaiming Jubilee: The Debt and Structural Adjustment Network," in *Restructuring World Politics: Transnational Social Movements, Networks, and Norms*, ed. Sanjeev Khagram, James V. Riker, and Kathryn Sikkink (Minneapolis: University of Minnesota Press, 2002), 155–58. **For summary of Catholic contributions see** Elizabeth A. Donnelly, "Making the Case for Jubilee: The Catholic Church and the Poor-Country Debt Movement." *Ethics & International Affairs* 21, no. 1 (2007). 107–33. doi:10.1111/j.1747-7093.2007.00063.x.
50. A report by a group of civil society groups led by Christian Aid (United Kingdom) describes the terrible outflows of money from African nations to service their international debt (paying money to lending institutions and governments of the Global North) that was accumulated through unjust means and now is being paid at deadly cost by Africa's people. Christian Aid estimates the equivalent of $50 billion annually from Africa, and writes, "The diversion of limited public funds to pay back expensive private debt acts like a chokehold on too many national economies in the global south. Money should be going to where it's most needed, like adapting farming to climate change and better health services." **Karimi Kinoti, Christian Aid's interim director of policy in Africa, in the report as described in** https://tinyurl.com/5yfmpcmp. **In the same report, the** Most Revd Albert Chama, Primate of Central Africa, asserts that public services are being cut in many African nations in order to service the debt ant that this meant that ordinary people "lose out on health care, education, and development projects which would give them a fair chance to thrive and build futures."
51. https://tinyurl.com/4rwb337a. Taylor goes on, "In his opening Nazareth sermon (Luke 4), Jesus cites the prophet Isaiah to proclaim 'the year of the Lord's favor,' a passage that evokes the ancient instructions for debt forgiveness, such as those found in Deuteronomy 15 ("Every seventh year you shall grant a remission of debts"). While biblical scholars can't confirm that these Jubilee injunctions were fully lived out, these instructions were understood to be a regular course corrective to extreme inequality and injustice. Other parts of the Bible flat-out forbid charging interest when the person seeking the loan is poor (Exodus 22:25, Leviticus 25:37)." See also https://tinyurl.com/53unx2mv.

CHAPTER TWELVE

1. Albert Pero Jr. "The Church and Racism," in *Between Vision and Reality: Lutheran Churches in Transition*, ed. Wolfgang Greive (Geneva: Lutheran World Federation, 2001), 262.
2. Isabel Wilkerson, *Caste: The Origins of Our Discontent* (New York: Random House, 2020), 151.
3. "Vanuatu Makes Historic Call for Treaty to End Fossil Fuel Era," EnviroNews Nigeria https://www.environewsnigeria.com/vanuatu-makes-historic-call-for-treaty-to-end-fossil-fuel-era/.
4. "Vanuatu Makes Historic Call."
5. https://fossilfueltreaty.org/history.

6. They go on to say that "Vanuatu's call builds on years of diplomatic efforts to curb fossil fuel production. Eight years ago, 14 Pacific island nations met in the Solomon Islands to consider a treaty that would ban new fossil fuel development for signatories and commit them to renewable energy targets. At the UN climate conference in 2017, Fiji underscored the importance of managing the phaseout of fossil fuels, and at COP26 in Glasgow last year, Tuvalu was at the forefront of pushing for reparations for damage caused by climate change."
7. "Vanuatu Makes Historic Call."
8. Kate Pickett and Richard Wilkinson, "From Inequality to Sustainability" (Rome: Club of Rome, 2021), 11.
9. https://tinyurl.com/mrxrwj2v. The report indicates that "Indigenous resistance to pipelines and other fossil fuel projects has saved the U.S. and Canada 12 percent of their annual emissions, or 0.8 billion tons of CO2 per year." See also: https://tinyurl.com/2kbzer7v, https://tinyurl.com/32vucfec, and https://tinyurl.com/99rhzted. The last of these organizations flowed from a campaign to convince the city of Seattle to divest from Wells Fargo, one of the major fossil-fuel funding banks.
10. In theological terms, "resisting the wrong" figures in the call to announce the inbreaking kinship of God on earth and denounce what thwarts it. Resisting the wrong is a form of denouncing.
11. This, they explain, was a communal effort, involving others who know the dangers faced by many Indigenous earth protectors.
12. Christopher Carter, *The Spirit of Soul Food: Race, Faith, and Food Justice* (Urbana: University of Illinois Press, 2021), 83.

CHAPTER THIRTEEN

1. This paragraph comes with slight revision from Moe-Lobeda, *Resisting Structural Evil*, chapter 9.
2. Among other recent fruits produced by the IEN is its Climate Finance Report, the first in the Network's Climate Justice Program Series. https://tinyurl.com/mr32cftn.
3. The network of Patriotic Millionaires promotes higher taxes for wealthy people like themselves and a livable living wage. In 2017 they "launched Tax the Rich! a public education and advocacy campaign to sway public opinion against the 2017 Tax Cuts and Jobs Act," and "three years later launched the Tax the Rich, Save America virtual roadshow with 3 Senators and 14 Members of Congress to engage lawmakers in public conversations about taxes, getting members of Congress on record in support of higher taxes for the wealthy." According to their website, they have been involved in in campaigns in nine states and WA DC to raise the minimum wage to $15.00 in those areas. https://patrioticmillionaires.org/history/.
4. https://tinyurl.com/y554jtz5.
5. For a comparison of worker-driven social responsibility and the more long-standing paradigm of Corporate Social responsibility (CSR), see https://tinyurl.com/ypkzwxh4.
6. https://tinyurl.com/5s9mffs2.
7. "From Florida to Fraserburgh: Can the Fair Food Programme Inspire A 'Fair Fish Programme'?," Fishing News, December 12, 2022.

Notes

8. Christine Feroli, "US Department of Labor Awards $2.5m Grant to Promote Human, Labor Rights in the International Cut Flower Supply Chains." February 14, 2023. https://tinyurl.com/2823hf4e.
9. See for starters: https://gofossilfree.org/.
10. George "Tink" Tinker, *American Indian Liberation: A Theology of Sovereignty* (Maryknoll, NY: Orbis Books, 2008), 161.
11. Sheryl Johnson, *Serving Money Serving God* (Minneapolis: Fortress Press, 2023), 81.
12. Pero, "The Church and Racism," 262.
13. Through practices of rematriation, cultural revitalization, and land restoration, Sogorea Te' Land Trust calls on Native and nonnative peoples to heal and transform the legacies of colonization, genocide, and patriarchy. https://sogoreate-landtrust.org/. The nonprofit collective Movement Generation (MG) organizes movements to build a Just Transition from an extractive economy to economies that are sustainable, equitable, and just for all. MG's work involves political education, movement building, and cultural strategy toward the liberation and restoration of land, labor, and culture. https://movementgeneration.org/.
14. The Land Trust and MG plan for this land to become a hub for organizers, healers, and others to build capacity for guiding their communities in "just transition" to an ecologically regenerative and socially just future.
15. Ta-Nehisi Coates, in his seminal 2014 article "The Case for Reparations" in the *Atlantic*, is clear about the need for white people, for example, to learn and acknowledge the history of theft from Black Americans. Kelly Brown Douglas in her "The Legacy of the White Lion" *Sojourners*, July 2020, calls for "anamnestic truth-telling," denouncing white privilege by which she means freeing selves and institutions from the benefits of white supremacy, and "proleptic participation," by which she means living in ways build more racially just spaces and societies.
16. See for example the declaration by the "Interfaith E-consultation on Just Finance and Reparations" held in October 2020 involving Bahá'í, Buddhist, Christian, Hindu, Islamic, Jewish, and Rastafarian voices. The statement, entitled, "Just Economics for Liberation and Life: Interfaith Message on Just Finance, Debt and Reparations," can be found at https://tinyurl.com/24sbnn2k or at the website of the International Network of Engaged Buddhists at https://tinyurl.com/d5yp26as. See also chapter 11 ("Move the Money.")
17. Christopher Carter, paper presented at American Academy of Religion, November 2022.
18. Many people see this as a modern manifestation of the Doctrine of Discovery extending its insidious tendrils into our day.
19. The national debts are for loans that were made over the years by predatory lending practices that benefited economies of the Global North but not the Caribbean people. The loan payments now draw huge sums of money out of the countries, money that then cannot be used for health care, education, and other basic needs.
20. To advocate for debt cancellation, see Jubilee USA Network at https://www.jubileeusa.org/.
21. Government efforts saw it fall from a high of 138% in 2012 to 80% in 2023.
22. Reparations Now Toolkit by M4BL at https://tinyurl.com/mwfkkef6.
23. See NAARC at https://reparationscomm.org/.
24. Douglas, "The Legacy of the White Lion," 25.

CHAPTER FOURTEEN

1. Emilie M. Townes, *Breaking the Fine Rain of Death* (New York: Continuum, 2001), 12.
2. Willie James Jennings, "My Anger, God's Righteous Indignation (Response to the Death of George Floyd)," *For the Life of the World* podcast, Yale Center for Faith and Culture, Yale Divinity School June 2, 2020. https://tinyurl.com/5n79dvkk.
3. Robin Wall Kimmerer, *Braiding Sweetgrass: Indigenous Wisdom, Scientific Knowledge, and the Teachings of Plants* (Minneapolis: Milkweed Editions, 2013), 377.
4. Gerald Manley Hopkins, "The Blessed Virgin."
5. St. Gregory the Great, *Morals on the Book of Job* VI:18 (London: Welter Smith, 1883), 325 cited in Ann Ulanov and Barry Ulanov, *The Healing Imagination* (New York: Paulist Press, 1991), 24.
6. Alice Walker, *The Color Purple*.
7. Martin Luther, "Sermons on the Gospel of John," in *Luther's Works*, ed. Jaroslav Pelikan (St. Louis: Concordia, 1957), 24:26. Luther, "That These Words of Christ, 'This Is My Body,' etc. Still Stand Firm against the Fanatics," *Luther's Works*, 37:57.
8. Christopher Carter, *The Spirit of Soul Food: Race, Faith, and Food Justice* (Urbana: University of Illinois Press, 2021), 125.
9. Walter Brueggemann, *Prophetic Imagination*, 40th anniversary edition (Minneapolis: Fortress Press, 2018), 41, 43, 43.
10. Townes, *Breaking the Fine Rain of Death*, 24, drawing upon Walter Brueggemann, "The Costly Loss of Lament," *Journal for the Study of the Old Testament* 36 (1986): 60.
11. Emmanuel Katongole, *Born from Lament: The Theology and Politics of Hope in Africa* (Grand Rapids: Eerdmans, 2017), 261. The other four citations in this paragraph are from xvi, xv, xv, 261.
12. SojoMail February 2, 2023. https://tinyurl.com/2csbbb37.
13. Both quotations are from Jennings, "My Anger, God's Righteous Indignation."
14. Jeffrey Stout, *Blessed Are the Organized: Grassroots Democracy in America* (Princeton, NJ: Princeton University Press, 2010), 65, 64.
15. Kimmerer, *Braiding Sweetgrass*, 377.
16. All quotations in this paragraph and the following three are from Kimmerer, *Braiding Sweetgrass*, 304–8.
17. Both quotations in this paragraph are from Kimmerer, *Braiding Sweetgrass*, 377.
18. The quotations from this paragraph are from Kimmerer, *Braiding Sweetgrass*, 376.
19. Christiana Figueres and Tom Rivett-Carnac, *The Future We Choose: Surviving the Climate Crisis* (New York: Alfred A. Knopf, 2020), xx.
20. Figueres and Rivett-Carnac, *The Future We Choose*, 100.

CHAPTER FIFTEEN

1. Vine Deloria, *God Is Red: A Native View of Religion*, 3rd ed. (Golden, CO: Fulcrum, 2003), 296.
2. Macarena Gomez-Barris, *The Extractive Zone: Social Ecologies and Decolonial Perspectives* (Durham, NC: Duke University Press, 2017), 136, 136.

3. There we discussed sacrifice zones as geographic areas or social groups whose well-being is "sacrificed" in the production of renewable energies. The term is used also for people and areas "sacrificed" in other efforts to gain profit for others.
4. Excerpted from the vignette in chapter 3.
5. The cruel reality is that five centuries of colonization sought at times explicitly to destroy Indigenous wisdom and ways of knowing, labeling it as superstition, demonic, heathen, and less than the intellectual paradigm of knowing that was elevated by Western epistemological norms. The nearly miraculous reality is that countless Indigenous peoples have maintained or refound those wellsprings of wisdom, and are building ways of living grounded in them. Regarding labeling as superstition or demonic, see Marilú Rojas Salazar, "Decolonizing Theology: Panentheist Spiritualities and Proposals from the Ecofeminist Epistemologies of the South," *Journal of Feminist Studies in Religion* 34, no. 2 (2018): 92–8 (93).
6. Gomez-Barris, *The Extractive Zone*, 133, 134.
7. "Tink" Tinker, *American Indian Liberation*, 161.
8. Gomez-Barris, *The Extractive Zone*, 135, 135.
9. Luis Cárcamo Huechante, "Mapuche Historians Write and Talk Back: Background and Role of ¡ . . . Escucha, winka . . . ! Cuatro ensayos sobre Historia Nacional Mapuche y un epílogo sobre el futuro (2006)," *Decolonial Gesture* 11, no. 1 (2014): 4.
10. Gomez-Barris, *The Extractive Zone*, 137.
11. Gomez-Barris, *The Extractive Zone*, 138.
12. Martin Luther King Jr., "Where Do We Go from Here: Chaos or Community?," in *A Testament of Hope: The Essential Writings and Speeches of Martin Luther King, Jr.*, ed. James M. Washington (New York: HarperCollins, 1991), 631.
13. King, "Where Do We Go from Here," 630.
14. Scholar of religion Myra Rivera calls us to "amplify voices that have been muffled" by various forms of domination. Myra Rivera, "What Is the Role of the Study of Religion in Times of Catastrophe," presidential address at AAR annual meeting 2022, Denver.
15. George "Tink" Tinker, "Walking in the Shadow of Greatness: Vine Deloria Jr in Retrospect," *Wicazo Sa Review* 21, no. 2 (Autumn, 2006): 167–77 (175).
16. Brene Brown documents the paralyzing impact of shame. See Brene Brown, *The Gifts of Imperfection* (Center City, MN: Hazelden Publishing, 2010), 40.
17. Kimmerer, *Braiding Sweetgrass*, 346, 10, 346–47.
18. Kimmerer, *Braiding Sweetgrass*.
19. Rich Heffern, "Cover Story: Thomas Berry," *National Catholic Reporter Online*, August 10, 2001. https://tinyurl.com/3ty9xv2k.

CHAPTER SIXTEEN

1. Ben Okri, *A Way of Being Free* (London: Phoenix House, 1997), 112 cited in Moana Jackson, "Where to Next? Decolonization and the Stories of the Land," in *Imagining Decolonization*, ed. Bianca Elkington et al. (Wellington, New Zealand: Bridget Williams Books, 2020), 154.
2. Christina Roberts, in public lecture as annual lecturer for the Naef Scholars Program at Seattle University.

3. Doyle Canning and Patrick Reinsborough, *Re-imagining Change: An Introduction to Story-Based Strategy*, 5. https://tinyurl.com/hnjhjbe8.
4. See Yuval Harari, *Sapiens: A Brief History of Humankind* (New York: Harper, 2015), 24–39.
5. David Korten, "Telling a New Story," in *The New Possible*, ed. Philip Clayton et al. (Eugene, OR: Cascade Books, 2021), 232.
6. Suzuki, *Sacred Balance*, 21.
7. Michael Pollan, *How to Change Your Mind* (London: Penguin Press, 2018).
8. "Not long ago a medical study showed that if heart doctors tell their seriously at-risk heart patients they will literally die if they do not make changes to their personal lives—diet, exercise, smoking—still only one in seven is actually able to make the changes." Robert Kegan and Lisa Laskow Lahey, *Immunity to Change* (Boston: Harvard Business School Publishing, 2009) 1.
9. Kegan and Lahey, *Immunity to Change*, x.
10. Kegan and Lahey, *Immunity to Change*, 59.
11. Likewise, the Club of Rome's Report "From Inequity to Sustainability" notes the ways in which ideology or worldview blocks our capacity to adopt policies that will reduce the wealth gap. Pickett and Wilkinson, "From Inequality to Sustainability," 9–10.
12. Kegan and Lahey, *Immunity to Change*, 222.
13. Canning and Reinsborough, *Re-imagining Change*, 5. It goes on to say, "Narratives can often function as a glue to hold the legitimacy of power structures in place and maintain the status quo. When working for social change, it is essential to understand specifically how these narratives operate. For example, when confronted with ongoing injustice, some people will say, 'that's just the way things are.' . . . This is one of the most common assumptions that normalizes existing power dynamics and makes them appear unchangeable" (7).
14. Václav Havel, "Address by the President of the Czech Republic": Forum 2000, Prague Castle, September 4, 1997.
15. Vijay Kolinjivadi, "Why a 'Green New Deal' Must Be Decolonial," Aljazeera, December 7, 2019: https://tinyurl.com/4fhhuzdx. The longer quotation reads, "Our development trajectory has been marred by the idea that humans are the overlords of the world, who have to tame nature and submit it to exploitation for their exclusive benefit. It implies that human civilization is somehow separate from nature, whose only role is to provide unlimited resources to feed and expand the human material world. . . . As long as we erroneously see ourselves as outside and above the rest of the living world, we will continue to contribute to its destruction. A decolonial GND, therefore, requires repositioning ourselves vis-à-vis nature as an integral part of it—just as many indigenous peoples have consistently sought to do in their historical and ongoing struggle for cultural autonomy and self-determination."
16. The theologian Willie James Jennings speaks of the "habits of mind and life that internalized and normalized [the colonial] order of things." Jennings, *Theological Imagination*, 8.
17. Francis Bacon, *The Works of Francis Bacon*, vol. 3, *Works Political* (London: C. Baldwin, 1819), 485 cited in Timothy Beal, *When Time Is Short* (Boston: Beacon Press, 1022), 29.

Notes

18. Thus was established the epistemological privilege of Euro-Western forms of knowing. Unseating that privilege and centralizing other forms of knowing is, of course, a central aim of some decolonial work. Walter Mignolo calls it "epistemic disobedience." Walter Mignolo "Epistemic Disobedience and the Decolonial Option: A Manifesto," *Transmodernity: Journal of Peripheral Cultural Production of the Luso-Hispanic World*, 1, no. 2 (2011). http://dx.doi.org/10.5070/T412011807.
19. Classical economic liberalism is not the same thing as "liberalism" commonly used to designate the contrast to conservativism.
20. Rodney Clapp, *Naming Neoliberalism: Exposing the Spirit of Our Age* (Minneapolis: Fortress Press, 2022) as cited in Frances Kitson, "In Review," *Christian Century*, July 27, 2022, 38.
21. What I have called *Homo consumens*. Cynthia Moe-Lobeda, *Healing a Broken World: Globalization and God* (Minneapolis: Fortress Press, 2002), 59–61.
22. Some sources attribute this quote to Arthur F. Burns. For discussion of the attribution, see https://tinyurl.com/5t4hd928.
23. Noted theorists argue that the driving force of advanced capitalism is consumption not production. Michel de Certeau, *The Practice of Everyday Life*, trans. Steven Rendall (Berkeley: University of California Press, 1984), referenced in William Cavanaugh, "Augustine and Disney on Coercion," paper delivered at the American Academy of Religion, Orlando, November 21, 1998, 2.
24. Victor Lebow, "Price Competition in 1955," *Journal of Retailing* (Spring 1955). https://tinyurl.com/yw8uwtej.
25. Johnston, *The Health or Wealth of Nations*, 50.
26. See Moe-Lobeda, *Healing a Broken World* for analysis of neoliberalism, its "free trade" agenda, and the impacts it has on thwarting the democratic principles of accountable and distributed power.
27. Kelly, *The Divine Right of Capital*, 7.
28. This assumption, asserts Jennings, is a terrible and consequential "loss." "This loss points . . . to an abiding mutilation of a Christian vision of creation and our own creatureliness." Jennings, *Theological Imagination*, 293.
29. Wilkerson, *Caste*, 268–69.
30. Lawrence Summers, then chief economist and vice president of the World Bank, and subsequently Harvard University president, in a World Bank memo, December 12, 1991..
31. As Raj Patel asserts, in order to maximize profit, the market needs society's institutions to turn more and more things into commodities to be sold and bought in the "free market." Raj Patel, *The Value of Nothing: How to Reshape Market Society and Redefine Democracy* (New York: Picador, 2009).
32. CBS Interactive Inc., December 4, 2015 at https://tinyurl.com/nh697ee4.
33. Linn Persson, "Outside the Safe Operating Space of the Planetary Boundary for Novel Entities," *Environmental Science and Technology* 56, no. 3 (January 18, 2022): 1510–21. https://tinyurl.com/7b7say7e.
34. Figueres and Rivett-Carnac, *The Future We Choose*, 110.
35. Okri, *A Way of Being Free*, 112, cited in Jackson, Where to Next?," 154.
36. Jackson, "Where to Next?," 154.

37. Sarah Lazarovic "Why 'Solarpunk' Gives Me Hope for a More Sustainable Future," *Yes Magazine*, Jan. 2021). https://tinyurl.com/583pahc2.
38. Figueres and Rivett-Carnac, *The Future We Choose*, 109.
39. For some time, scientists estimated that human cells were outnumbered 10 to 1 by microbial cells. That has been revised "so the current estimate is you're about 43% human if you're counting up all the cells." https://tinyurl.com/4zvmtsr2. If comparing genes rather than cells the microbiome genes outnumber human genes in far greater numbers. See also https://tinyurl.com/bdeab9fb and https://tinyurl.com/56kmv65s. "We are all of us walking communities of bacteria," note Lynn Margulis and Dorion Sagan in *Microcosmos: Four Billion Years of Evolution from Our Microbial Ancestors* (Berkeley: University of California Press, 1986), 191.
40. David Haskell, *The Song of Trees* (New York: Penguin Books, 2017), viii.
41. "He that encloses Land, and has a greater plenty of the conveniences of life from ten acres, than he could have from an hundred left to Nature, may truly be said, to give ninety acres to Mankind." John Locke, *Two Treatises of Civil Government* (London: J.M. Dent and Sons, 1924), 12.
42. In *Healing a Broken World*, I elaborate the claim of neoclassical economic theory that the human is primarily *Homo economicus*, argue that its neoliberal rendition is *Homo consumens*, and unveil the deceptions in that understanding of the human and the dangers inherent in continuing to enact it.
43. "An Interfaith Call for Justice and Compassion in Finance," statement issued by Interfaith Conference on Faith and Finance, hosted by World Council of Churches, Bangkok, Thailand, November 28–29, 2015. https://tinyurl.com/muytpjv2.
44. "Was wealth maximizing already naturally the most powerful human motive, or was it focused on and assiduously cultivated for two hundred years, until today we cannot imagine it as anything but natural?" Carol Johnston, *The Health or Wealth of Nations: Transforming Capitalism from Within* (Cleveland: Pilgrim Press, 1998), 48.
45. Helena Norberg-Hodge, in "Coming Back to Place," in Clayton, *The New Possible*, 232.
46. "Once evolution reaches the relationships between, and hierarchies within, groups, then nature's definition of 'fitness'—*i.e.*, natural selection—changes from choosing the best competitor to choosing the best cooperator. So, yes, 'survival of the fittest' remains true, but the definition of 'fitness' changes from the best competitor to the best cooperator, especially as complexification increases.... The 'selfish gene,' long bowed to as the sole driver of natural process, actually hands over its reins to cooperation when groups and hierarchies of groups step into play." Kurt Johnson, "Evolving toward Cooperation: David Sloan Wilson's New Evolutionary Biology," *Kosmos: Journal of Global Transformation* (Winter, 2028). Biologist E. O. Wilson and theoretical biologist Martin Novok also suggest that the evolutionary tendency toward cooperation—cooperation as innate in human being—includes cooperation within groups to make others into outsiders and to defend against the outsiders, what Wilson calls "tribalism." E. O. Wilson, *The Social Conquest of Earth* (New York: Liveright, 2012), 57.
47. Modernity separated fields of knowledge or inquiry into siloed disciplines.
48. John Powell, "Opening to the Question of Belonging;" Suzuki, *Sacred Balance*, 131; Barad, "What Flashes Up," 21–88; Harari, *Sapiens*, 32–37.

Notes

49. Jennings, *Beyond Whiteness,* 152, and Chryssavgis, *Cosmic Grace, Humble Prayer,* 218, 315, 28.
50. This and the following paragraph are adapted from Moe-Lobeda, "Method in Ecotheology: A Perspective from the Belly of the Beast," in *How Would We Know What God Is Up To?,* ed. Cynthia Moe-Lobeda and Ernst Conradie (Eugene OR: Wipf and Stock, 2022), 115–40.
51. Suzuki, *Sacred Balance,* 131.
52. Barad, "What Flashes Up," 21–88.
53. Harari, *Sapiens,* 32–37.
54. Timothy Beal, *When Time Is Short* (Boston: Beacon Press, 1022), 89.
55. Martin Luther.
56. "It" and "thou" are Martin Buber's terms distinguishing objects from subjects.
57. Kimmerer, *Braiding Sweetgrass,* 9.
58. Kimmerer, *Braiding Sweetgrass,* 9, 9, 9.
59. As cited by Jennings in *Theological Imagination,* 61.
60. Robert Macfarlane, "The Secrets of the Woodwide Web," *New Yorker,* August 7, 2016. https://tinyurl.com/4cymmz4w. See also https://tinyurl.com/4ay54v9p. https://tinyurl.com/3f3vhwbf. Some scientists have said that the theory is not yet adequately proven. Others refute that suggestion: https://tinyurl.com/2c5xzr65.
61. Jane Bennett, *Vibrant Matter: A Political Ecology of Things* (Durham, NC: Duke University Press, 2010).
62. Here, the psalmist declares, "The earth is full of the steadfast love of the Lord." Can this be true? The Hebrew word *erets* indeed refers to the earth, the land. The psalmist does not use a less earthy word that includes inhabitants of the earth. No, the psalmist says the earth itself, the land, is full of God's steadfast love.
63. Beal, *When Time Is Short,* 72.
64. Luther, "Sermons on the Gospel of John," 26.
65. Luther, the *Weimar Ausgabe* 23.134.34, as cited by Paul Santmire, *The Travail of Nature: The Ambiguous Ecological Promise of Christian Theology* (Philadelphia: Fortress Press, 1985), 129.
66. Luther, "That These Words of Christ," 57.
67. For a fuller account of freedom as market freedom, and the roots of this in classical liberalism, see Moe-Lobeda, *Healing a Broken World,* 53–61 and 63–65.
68. John McMurtry, *Unequal Freedoms: The Global Market as an Ethical System* (West Hartford, CT: Kumarian Press, 1998), 87.
69. Research on the birth of neoliberalism argues that the original neoliberal thinkers did not in fact see unbounded market freedom as consistent with democracy and the honoring of human rights. Rather they saw democracy and some political human rights as a threat to market freedom and sought to counter the rising twentieth-century push for widespread democracy. Historian Quinn Slobodian argues that the neoliberals strategized to "inoculate capitalism against the threat of democracy" (2). The "confrontation with mass democracy was . . . at the heart of the [twentieth] Century for neoliberals" (14). Their "project of thinking . . . offered a set of proposals designed to defend the world economy from . . . democracy" (4). For them, the world must be "kept safe from mass demands for social justice and redistributive equality" (16). Toward that end, for example "neoliberals helped craft a universal investment

code and bilateral investment treaties that they hoped would safeguard capital in "a world of rights" (22). Slobodian Quinn, *The Globalists* (Cambridge, MA: Harvard University Press, 2018.)

70. The following excerpts illustrate:
    - "Economic freedom is . . . an indispensable means toward the achievement of political freedom." Milton Friedman, *Capitalism and Freedom* (Chicago: University of Chicago Press, 1962), 12. Friedman is a foundational theorist of laissez-faire liberalism or the laissez-faire pole of neoclassical economic theory as developed in the University of Chicago school of economics. While commonly characterized as seeking to dismantle government intervention in the market, he actually "accepts government intervention, but not for the sake of equity" (Carol Johnston, *The Wealth or Health of Nations: Transforming Capitalism from Within* [Eugene, OR: Wipf & Stock, 2010, 101]). "We do not wish to conserve the state interventions that have interfered so greatly with our freedom, though of course we do wish to conserve those that have promoted it." (Friedman, *Capitalism and Freedom*, 8.)
    - "The kind of economic organization that provides economic freedom directly, namely competitive capitalism, also promotes political freedom" (Friedman, *Capitalism and Freedom*, 9.)
    - "Civil and religious freedom, progress, and the preservation of human rights are inextricably linked with economic freedom, with the right to own property, and with a minimum of state interference in economic affairs." Franky Schaeffer, "Introduction," in *Is Capitalism Christian?*, ed. Franky Schaeffer (Westchester, IL: Crossway Books, 1985), xvii, cited in Craig M. Gay, *With Justice and Liberty for Whom? The Recent Evangelical Debate over Capitalism* (Grand Rapids: Eerdmans, 1991), 73.
    - "If this freedom and flexibility [of the business corporation] are not protected, the entire society will suffer." Michael Novak, *On Corporate Governance* (Washington, DC, AEI Press), 31.

    These excerpts are consistent with the larger treatises and bodies of literature from which they are drawn. In previous work I bring also quotations from business coalitions, the OECD, and political theory. See Moe-Lobeda, *Healing A Broken World*, 54–55.

71. Adam Smith, *An Inquiry into the Nature and Causes of the Wealth of Nations* (Indianapolis: Liberty Fund, 1979), 266, 266, 266, 267, 267, 267, 267.
72. See Kelly, "The Rich Are Getting Richer."
73. See for example Vincent Gallagher, *The True Cost of Low Prices* (Maryknoll, NY: Orbis Books, 2006.)
74. Alternative notions of freedom have intellectual homes in political philosophy, the human sciences, theology, and more recently in the natural sciences and astronomy.
75. Kaplan and Kiersz, "American Billionaires Added $2.1 Trillion." Other sources reporting the increase in billionaire wealth during the pandemic include Kelly, "The Rich Are Getting Richer"; "Billionaire Wealth, U.S. Job Losses and Pandemic Profiteers"; and "The World's Richest 10 Men Doubled Their Fortunes."
76. Ripple et al., "World Scientists' Warning," 8–12. https://doi.org/10.1093/biosci/biz088. See also Phoebe Barnard et al., "World Scientists' Warnings into Action, Local and Global," *Science Progress* 104, no. 4 (2021), 1–32, page 20.

Notes

77. Fr. Travis Russell, SJ, "Budgets Are Moral Documents. Congress Should Treat Them Accordingly." https://tinyurl.com/4zkt7myx. Accessed February 18, 2024.
78. https://tinyurl.com/2s48ujun.
79. Kelly, *The Divine Right of Capital*, 142.
80. Pawl Hawken, *The Ecology of Commerce* (New York: HarperBusiness, 1993), 3. This and the two quotations below are on pages 2, xiv, 2.
81. For a somewhat fuller elaboration of this myth, see Moe-Lobeda, *Healing a Broken World*, 61–63.
82. Francis Fukuyama, *End of History* (Los Angeles: The Free Press, 2006), vx.
83. Fukuyama, *End of History*, xi.
84. A PRRI (Public Religion Research Institute) 2019 survey indicates that only 46% of Democrats and 79% of Republicans—when asked what it means to be "truly American"—indicated that "believing that capitalism is the best economic system is somewhat or very important for being truly American." See https://tinyurl.com/bdevx3su.
85. The New Economy Foundation. https://tinyurl.com/2bedr5w6. Accessed February 18, 2024.
86. Timothy Jackson, *Post-growth* (Cambridge, MA: Polity Press, 2021), 3, 106, 4.
87. I have elaborated this four-point critique of growth in my book *Healing a Broken World*, 48–53. For a book-length critique, see Jackson, *Post-growth*.
88. Senator Kennedy in a surprising speech during his presidential campaign decried blind allegiance to growth for precisely this reason. Growth counts as a good, he declared, "nuclear warheads and armored cars for the police to fight the riots in our cities.... It counts the television programs that which glorify violence in order to sell toys to our children.... It counts the loss of the redwood and the loss of our natural wonders." "Remarks at the Univeristy of Kansas," March 18, 1968. https://tinyurl.com/26afvnws.
89. United Nations Development Programme (UNDP), *Human Development Report 1997* (New York: Oxford University Press, 1997), 88–89. For example, since Mexico liberalized its economy in the mid 1980s, the number of billionaires has increased by 50%, pushing growth figures up, thus obscuring the significantly increasing number of people living in absolute poverty. See 88. The 1998 UNDP report (29) reports that in 1960, the wealthiest 20% of the world's population had thirty times the income of the poorest 20%, but that by 1995 that figure had increased to eighty-two times.
90. Figueres and Rivett-Carnac, *The Future We Choose*, xvii.
91. Ripple et.al, "World Scientists' Warning," 18. In measuring a nation's well-being, the GPI measures and accounts for the cost of environmental damage, the cost of crime, the value of unpaid caretaking and household labor, etc. Some nations and states of the United States are using GPI, including Maryland. GPI is not the only alternative measure that has been developed. Bhutan initiated the Gross National Happiness indicator, which includes measurement of health, education, and standard of living. The New Economics Foundation developed the Happy Planet Index. The Club of Rome confirms the necessity of such alternatives: "The transition to sustainability... will require that economic growth is replaced as a policy objective with a greater focus on increasing well-being." Pickett and Wilkinson, "From Inequality to Sustainability," 11. The Club of Rome is a nonprofit organization of

thought leaders from around the globe including one hundred business leaders, governmental leaders, scientists, economists, diplomats, and UN leaders. It issues occasional reports.
92. Ilhan Omar, press release. "Rep. Omar Introduces Guaranteed Income Bill and GDP Alternative Legislation," 2021.
93. Many are the constructive proposals regarding how to reduce emissions while enabling growth that is necessary to eliminate poverty and energy poverty in poorer nations where underconsumption not overconsumption is the problem. See for example https://tinyurl.com/529aev3p.
94. Aslan Runyan, Seattle University student in an ethics course, spring 2015.
95. Lahey and Kegan, *Immunity to Change*. Environmental studies scholar Robin Veldman also speaks to this interface between life-shaping narrative and practice: "My informants' attitudes... were embedded not only in their social world, but also in social practices whose intelligibility depended on a broader narrative." Robin Globus Veldman, *The Gospel of Climate Skepticism Book Subtitle: Why Evangelical Christians Oppose Action on Climate Change* (Berkeley: University of California Press, 2019), 115.
96. Michel Foucault, *The Hermeneutics Of The Subject: Lectures at the Collège de France, 1981–1982*, ed. Frédéric Gros (New York: Picador, 2006) xxiii–xxiv. Italics mine.
97. A seminal example of this exercise is Peggy McIntosh, "White Privilege: Unpacking the Invisible Knapsack," first published in *Peace and Freedom Magazine* (July/August 1989). Widely available online. One location is https://tinyurl.com/35cu3sbu.
98. This of course would entail the further public work of convincing the organization to take that stance. Some organizations are doing so.
99. Ulanov and Ulanov, *The Healing Imagination*, 23.
100. https://tinyurl.com/y5cevx3a. Accessed February 18, 2024.
101. Barbara Adams, "Art, Fabulation, and Practicing the Worlds We Want," https://tinyurl.com/4uu57sk7. Accessed February 18, 2024.

CHAPTER SEVENTEEN

1. Martin Luther, *Sermons of Martin Luther*, ed. John Nicholas Lenker (Grand Rapids, MI: Baker, 1992), 8:275.
2. Movement Generation, "Just Transition." An online resource at https://tinyurl.com/3d54mh4j.
3. Cited by Alexia Salvatierra and Peter Heltzel, *Faith-Rooted Organizing* (Downers Grove, IL: Intervarsity Press, 2014), 74.
4. Moe-Lobeda, *Resisting Structural Evil*, chapter 6.
5. Luther, *Sermons*, 8:275.
6. Walter Brueggemann, unpublished address at Fund for Theological Education's Conference on Excellence in Ministry, housed at Vanderbilt University, summer, 2001.
7. Walter Brueggemann, cited by Loretta Whalen, "Dear Colleague" letter from Church World Service Office on Global Education, October 31, 1998.
8. "Singer Mercedes Sosa: The Voice of the 'Voiceless Ones' Outlasts South American Dictatorships," TMCNET News, December 8, 2007. https://tinyurl.com/5yyx8by6.

Notes

9. This fact about "crime: poet" is according to Ulanov and Ulanov, *The Healing Imagination*, 5 who draw it from the introduction to Francis Padorn Brent, *Beyond the Limit* (Evanston, IL: Northwestern University Press, 1987), xii.
10. Both quotations are from Barbara Adams, "Art, Fabulation, and Practicing the Worlds We Want," UNHCR Innovation Service. https://tinyurl.com/mwk9ubsf.
11. Adams, "Art, Fabulation, and Practicing the Worlds We Want."
12. Gerald Manley Hopkins cited in Ulanov and Ulanov, *The Healing Imagination*, 22.
13. Gilio-Whitaker, *As Long as Grass Grows* (Boston: Beacon Press, 2019), 140.
14. Anne Elvey, *Reading with the Earth* (New York: T & T Clark, 2023), 136–38.
15. https://tinyurl.com/278kkd6v. Accessed February 18, 2024.
16. "What Was the Largest Landslide in the United States? In the World?" www.usgs.gov. Accessed February 18, 2024.
17. Paul Tillich, *Love, Power, and Justice* (New York: Oxford University Press, 1954), 9.

CHAPTER EIGHTEEN

1. Speaking as part of "Moral Revolution: An Interfaith Response to the Coronavirus Pandemic," April 9, 2020. https://tinyurl.com/4nuu48az.
2. In conversation, used with permission.
3. Pierre Teilhard de Chardin, *Toward the Future*, trans. Rene Hague (London: Collins, 1975), 55.
4. Cited in Bartholomew, *On Earth as in Heaven: Ecological Vision and Initiatives of Ecumenical Patriarch Bartholomew*, ed. John Chryssavgis (New York: Fordham University Press, 2012). Bartholomew is the world leader of Eastern Orthodox Christianity and the first global leader to call "crimes against the natural world" a "sin." (At Santa Barbara in November 1997, he declared: "To commit a crime against the natural world is a sin.")
5. Julia Vida Dutton Scudder was a late nineteenth century/early twentieth century Episcopalian churchwoman, professor of literature at Wellesley College, activist, Christian socialist, and leader in the Social Gospel movement.
6. Speaking as part of "Moral Revolution,"
7. The mining companies are based in Norway, Canada, and elsewhere. One mining project alone would directly impact 9,000 people, displacing 3,500. For a brief account of this situation, see Karen Bloomquist, ed., *Communion, Responsibility, Accountability: Responding as a Lutheran Communion to Neoliberal Globalization* Documentation No. 50 (Geneva: Lutheran World Federation, 2004), 39–40. For a longer account, see S. Khatua and W. Stanley, "Ecological Debt: a Case Study from Orissa, India" (2006) at http://www.deudaecologica.org/publicaciones/chapter5(125-168).pdf. Accessed February 18, 2024.
8. Nuns & Nones, "About the Land Justice Project," Nuns & Nones, n.d., https://tinyurl.com/bdh62uat. Accessed February 18, 2024.
9. Paraphrased from Penny Lernoux, *People of God: The Struggle for World Catholicism* (New York: Penguin Books, 1990).
10. One of the terms Rabbi Michael Lerner uses for God.
11. Of course, not all Christians and Jews agree with these claims.
12. Religious faith has en-spirited some of humankind's most noble moments—the civil rights movement in the US; Gandhi's movement of nonviolent resistance to

British colonialism in India; the South African antiapartheid struggle; the Buddhist resistance to imperial powers in Viet Nam; the abolitionist movement in the US; courageous freedom struggles in Central America, Chile, the Philippines, and elsewhere; and resistance to Hitler's fascism in the Scandinavian countries, France, and Germany.
13. Religion is defined in multiple ways; there exists no consensus among scholars about what constitutes religion. My use of the term is within the scope of various valid definitions.
14. Timothy Beal, *When Time Is Short* (Boston: Beacon Press, 2022), 6.
15. This is the meaning of the New Testament Greek word *pistis*, translated into English as "faith."
16. Irony permeates this understanding of religion. For millenia, people have misused religious faith to divide people, to set one faith group against another. This may be religion's greatest betrayal because religion could and should be the opposite—a source of communion and shared power to orient life around the widespread good.
17. That constellation of forces—both intentional and not—may be the most formidable in human history and includes the culture of consumption and the marketing that perpetuates it, the dependence on fossil fuels for the composition or production of our material world, the fierce commitment of the fossil fuel industry to continue extracting, the commitment of speculative finance to maximize short-term profit regardless of the long-term costs, the unwavering march forward of agribusiness with its attendant petrochemical industries, the influence of big money on democratic processes, and the magnetic pull of habit and momentum.
18. Grace Lee Boggs, *The Next American Revolution* (Berkeley: University of California Press, 2012), xxii.
19. This term comes from Denis Edwards, "Creation, Original Grace, and Original Sin," in *Just Sustainability: Technology, Ecology, and Resource Extraction*, ed. by Christiana Peppard and Andrea Vicini (Maryknoll, NY: Orbis Books, 2015), 166.
20. Karen Armstrong, *The Great Transformation: The Beginning of Our Religious Traditions* (New York: Anchor Books, 2007), xviii; as cited in Ulrich Duchrow and Franz J. Hinkelammert, *Transcending Greedy Money: Interreligious Solidarity for Just Relations*, New Approaches to Religion and Power (New York: Palgrave Macmillan, 2012), 46. Armstrong's emphasis was on this emergence in response to the increased violence made possible by Iron Age weaponry and how this history might enable contemporary people to counter war and violence.
21. Walter Brueggemann, "Faith Seeking Economic Justice," *Christian Century*, June 1, 2022, 15.
22. Brueggemann, "Faith Seeking Economic Justice," 15. In *The Prophetic Imagination* (Minneapolis: Fortress Press, 2001), Brueggemann explains in more detail that the religion of Moses arose to evoke and nourish a consciousness and way of life that was alternative to the dominant culture. "The ministry of Moses," he writes, "represents a radical break with" the dominant social, economic, and political order. That order included the politics and economics of oppression. The Moses alternative was a politics and economics "of justice and compassion" (22). However, that alternative order gradually was replaced by another imperial reign (of Solomon) that again built extravagant wealth for a few based on exploitation of many. The people in power

Notes

justified this order by claiming that they represented God. (Sound familiar?) The prophets of Israel, Brueggemann demonstrates, arose to counter that status quo and to energize people to live again according to a politics and economics of justice and compassion.

23. Michael Lerner, "Jewish Liberation Theology and Emancipatory Politics," in *Religion and Economic Justice*, ed. Michael Zweig (Philadelphia: Temple University Press, 1992), 130–31. Lerner goes on to explain that Moses leading the Jewish people out of enslavement under Pharoah is "the first recorded slave rebellion." With it, Judaism "insisted that there was nothing inevitable about the hierachies of the social world.... The most fixed and seemingly immovable powers of the world could be struggled against, that the power of ordinary people could triumph over the claims of the entrenched ruling elites" (131).

24. Brueggemann and Lerner make this claim in relationship specifically to the beginnings of Judaism, while Armstrong extends it to the other Axial Age religions and their offspring, Christianity and Islam.

25. Axial Age refers to the period during which the enduring religious traditions of Eurasian societies emerged (including Zoroastrianism, Buddhism, Confucianism, Hinduism, Daoism, Jainism, and Judaism with its later offspring of Christianity and Islam). The period is roughly defined as 500—300 BCE although some begin it as much as three centuries earlier.

26. Duchrow and Hinkelammert, *Transcending Greedy Money*, vii and 2. In more detail, they argue that beginning about 3000 BCE, the emerging urban powers began to demand labor from the agrarian tribal communities (9). By about the eighth century BCE, money, interest, and private property "spread widely in the Mediterranean, Ancient Near East, and Far East, leading to accumulation of land and other wealth for some and loss of land and debt slavery for others" (9–15). This economic oppression gave rise to the great prophets in the last part of the eighth and throughout the seventh century BCE. Amos, Hosea, Isaiah, Micah, Jeremiah, Ezekiel, and others called for justice and righteousness lost in the rise of new property rights and money mechanisms. They claimed that, with the cancellation of justice and the rights of the poor, Yahweh, the God of Israel, had also been abandoned (48). The authors go on to note, "This is the heritage that Jesus and his movement draw upon. He builds on the prophetic and Torah tradition" (52). This is precisely Bruggemann's assertion, and much New Testament scholarship (since Ched Myers's *Who Will Roll Away the Stone* in 1994) examines Jesus and the first-century Jesus movment as a moral-spiritual response to the oppression of the Roman political economy and a source of spiritual strength to live according to a politics of compaasion rather than a politics of oppression. Rev. William Barber says as much: "These faith traditions were born as response to terrible oppression by empire" (from the webinar "Moral Revolution").

27. See an account of this in Sheryl Johnson, *Serving Money, Serving God* (Minneapolis: Fortress Press, 2023). See also Cynthia Moe-Lobeda, "The Subversive Luther," in *The Forgotten Luther: Reclaiming the Social-Economic Dimension of the Reformation*, ed. Carter Lindberg and Paul Wee (Minneapolis: Lutheran University Press, 2016).

28. Cynthia Moe-Lobeda, "Love Incarnate: Hope and Power for Climate Justice," in *Ecotheology: A Christian Conversation*, ed. Kiara A. Jorgenson and Alan G. Padgett (Grand Rapids, MI: William B. Eerdmans Publishing Company, 2020).

29. The story and the quotation are from Kim Stanley Robinson, *The Ministry for the Future* (New York: Orbit, 2020), 254–5.
30. See Karenna Gore, "Ethical Call to Action on Climate Policy," *ICNY* (blog), July 1, 2020, https://tinyurl.com/yxmzwnfd.
31. Baraka Lenga, "Role of Fossil Fuels," repost, *GreenFaith*, 2023, https://tinyurl.com/yxxyxeuc. Accessed February 18, 2024.
32. Amitav Ghosh, *The Great Derangement: Climate Change and the Unthinkable*, The Randy L. and Melvin R. Berlin Family Lectures (Chicago: The University of Chicago Press, 2017), 159.
33. Ron Moe-Lobeda, sermon for University Lutheran Church, Seattle, 2010. Used with permission.
34. Vincent Miller, *Consuming Religion: Christain Faith and Practice in a Consumer Culture* (New York: Continuum, 2005), 107, 110; as cited by Erika Katske in "Augustine & Economic Desire: An Exploration of Sociological & Theological Approaches," Fall 2019 (unpublished).
35. Kathryn E. Tanner, *Christianity and the New Spirit of Capitalism* (New Haven, CT: Yale University Press, 2019), 7.
36. Tanner, *Christianity and the New Spirit of Capitalism*, 9.
37. Tanner, *Christianity and the New Spirit of Capitalism*, 8–9. Likewise, philosopher William Connolly writes that Christianity might help to craft a "counter-ethos of economic life . . . an ethos of egalitarianism, diversity, and care for future generations" (16). He calls for "larger imbrications between spiritual life, economic practice, and state politics," xi. See William E. Connolly, *Capitalism and Christianity, American Style* (Durham, NC: Duke University Press, 2008).
38. Armstrong, *The Great Transformation*, xviii as cited in Duchrow and Hinkelammert, *Transcending Greedy Money*, 46.
39. Rita Sherma, "Sustainability Studies: Beyond the Denial of Religion and Theology as Resources—an Introduction," in *Religion and Sustainability: Interreligious Resources, Interdisciplinary Responses: Intersection of Sustainability Studies and Religion, Theology, Philosophy*, ed. Rita Sherma, Puruṣottama Bilimoria, and Pravina P. Rodrigues (Cham, Switzerland: Springer, 2022), 5.
40. Rico Palaco Ponce, "Transformative Spirituality Is a Breath of Fire," World Council of Churches Website, March 23, 2012, https://tinyurl.com/bd6h8ncc.

CHAPTER NINETEEN

1. "1992 World Scientists' Warning to Humanity." https://tinyurl.com/5awphrvy.
2. Ghosh, *Great Derangement*, 159–61.
3. Rose Marie Berger, "Revealing Our Dignified Rage," *Sojourners Magazine*, November 2019, 16.
4. The village was Le Chambon-sur-Lignon. This story is documented in the film *Weapons of the Spirit*, produced by a Jewish man, Pierre Sauvage, who was rescued as an infant by the villagers.
5. The words and image are depicted in the film *Weapons of the Spirit*. The image and translation of the hymn are courtesy of Sauvage.
6. Many Christian theologians affirm that God is a communion (the Trinity of God the Mother/Father, God in Jesus Christ, and God as Holy Spirit) and that this

Notes

shapes how humans are to live in God's image. Human life is to take after the being of God. The church reminds people of this reality through hospitality, the Eucharist, baptism, songs, written liturgy, and more.

7. See chapter 3.
8. Howard Thurman, *Disciplines of the Spirit* (Richmond, IN: Friends United Press, 1963), 94.
9. Thurman, *Disciplines of the Spirit*, 94–95.
10. A related faith claim, stemming in Christianity from the second century, is that God's role in our lives is to continue guiding us toward the beings we are created to be.
11. Recall the dance to bless that land that occurred in this story in "Setting the Stage." It was a dance in communion with spirit ancestors.
12. A young Hispanic woman involved in the cooperatives' training program voices the global-local community links as she reflects on "other farmers from across the world who are doing exactly what I'm doing, trying to create an alternative to the industrial food system, and trying to feel the connection with those people." See Pamela Haines, "Feeding Children, Communities, and Souls," *Tikkun Magazine*, July 23, 2018, https://tinyurl.com/3vk8fskw, 48.
13. Haines, "Feeding Children, Communities, and Souls," 45.
14. Michael Tomasello, with Carol Dweck, Joan Silk Brian Skyrms, and Elizabeth Spelks, *Why We Cooperate* (Cambridge, MA: MIT Press, 2009), 99–100.
15. Edward O. Wilson, *The Social Conquest of Earth* (New York: Liveright, 2012), 57.
16. Denis Edwards, "Creation, Original Grace, and Original Sin," in *Just Sustainability: Technology, Ecology, and Resource Extraction*, ed. Christiana Z. Peppard and Andrea Vicini (Maryknoll, NY: Orbis Books, 2015), 168.
17. Edwards, "Creation, Original Grace, and Original Sin," citing Ernst Mayr, *What Evolution Is* (New York: Basic Books, 2002), 259.
18. We see it clearly, for example, in Jesus's meals with outsiders and despised people and his teachings of love for enemies. See, for example Luke 6:27 and Matt 5:44.
19. See Moe-Lobeda, *Resisting Structural Evil*. Paul Tillich also insists vehemently that love is not to be understood primarily as an emotion. Love "basically understood as emotion would be a sentimental addition . . . ultmatley irrelevant, unable to change . . . the structures of power." Paul Tillich, *Love, Power, and Justice* (Oxford: Oxford University Press, 1954), 24.
20. Navid Sabet, "Is Economic Justice Possible?" *The Bahá'í World*, September 17, 2020, https://tinyurl.com/yc8ddh6p, 2, 9, 11.
21. Paul Cloke, "Theo-ethics and Radical Faith-Based Practice in the Postsecular City," in *Exploring the Postsecular: The Religious, the Political and the Urban*, ed. Arie L. Molendijk, Justin Beaumont, and Christoph Jedan (Leiden: Boston: Brill, 2010), 210; cited in Julia Magdalena Berger, *Rethinking Religion and Politics in a Plural World: The Bahá'í International Community and the United Nations* (New York: Bloomsbury Academic, 2021), 127–38.
22. These include the World Council of Churches, the World Communion of Reformed Churches, the Lutheran World Federation, the Council for World Mission, the Alliance of Presbyterian and Reformed Churches of Latin America, and more.
23. Martin Luther King Jr., "Strength to Love," in *A Testament of Hope: The Essential Writings and Speeches of M. L. King, Jr.* (San Francisco: Harper, 1991), 48.

24. See Saint Basil, *On Social Justice*, ed. C. Paul Schroeder (Crestwood, NY: St. Vladimir's Seminary Press, 2009).
25. See one source for this quote is Upton Sinclair, ed., *The Cry for Justice: An Anthology of the Literature of Social Protest; The Writings of Philosophers, Poets, Novelists, Social Reformers, and Others Who Have Voiced the Struggle against Social Injustice* (Philadelphia: The John C. Winston Co., 1915).
26. For his language on economic exploitation as theft, see Martin Luther, *Large Catechism*, at https://tinyurl.com/3muwkb9e. Accessed February 18, 2024.
27. Luther, "Address to the Christian Nobility of the German Nation," *Luther's Works* 44: 213. For examples of Luther denouncing economic exploitation, see especially Luther's three treatises focusing on economic life: "The Short Sermon on Usury," *Weimar Ausgabe* 6, 1ff.; "Trade and Usury," *Luther's Works* 45:244–308; "Admonition to the Clergy That They Preach against Usury," *Weimar Ausgabe* 51, 325ff. See also Luther's comments on the seventh commandment in the *Large Catechism*. Luther also treats economic life in the following works whose primary focus is not economic life: "The Ninety-Five Theses," "The Blessed Sacrament of the Holy and True Body and Blood of Christ, and the Brotherhoods," "Address to the Christian Nobility of the German Nation," "Ordinance of a Common Chest" (this contains Luther's biblical rationale for social welfare and his descriptions of how a congregation ought organize its social welfare effort.).
28. Luther, *Large Catechism*.
29. Thurman, *Disciplines of the Spirit*, 96.
30. Imam Omar Suleiman, founder and president of Yaqeen Institute for Islamic Research, speaking as part of "Moral Revolution."
31. Nuns & Nones, "About Nuns & Nones," https://tinyurl.com/3ewdwtap.
32. Juan Carlos La Puente Tapia, "Hospitality and Friendship: Gleams of Collective Vocation," *Concilium International Journal of Theology* 5 (2022): 129–35.
33. Anne Hall, in conversation with me in 2024. Cited with permission.
34. Emilie M. Townes, "Ethics as the Art of Doing the Work Our Souls Must Have," in *Womanist Theological Ethics: A Reader*, ed. Katie Geneva Cannon, Emilie M. Townes, and Angela D. Sims (Louisville, KY: Westminster John Knox, 2011), 39–40.
35. Townes, "Ethics as the Art," 41–42. Philosopher Michael Foucault also reveals the necessity of inner work if we are to think, perceive, and imagine differently from how culture has trained us to think, perceive, and imagine. The ancient world, he notes, assumed that to access wisdom required spiritual development, deep inner work including "the practices we must undertake to transform ourselves, the necessary work of ourselves on ourselves in order for us to have access to truth." Foucault refers to this as spirituality. Michel Foucault, *The Hermeneutics of the Subject: Lectures at the Collège De France, 1981–1982*, ed. Frédéric Gros (New York: Picador, 2006), xxiii–xxiv. The linking of inner and outer work addresses a significant obstacle to transformative action toward "economies for life"—the fissure between cognitive knowing and spiritual development, a fissure constructed by the modern world. Foucault argued that modernity has split cognitive knowing off from the spiritual development that the ancient world assumed was necessary to access true wisdom. For wisdom to be found, he asserted, cognitive processes must be accompanied by a deep commitment to inner work. Most intriguing for our purposes here is Foucault's

Notes

sense that this work "on ourselves" includes seeking to understand how it would "be possible to think differently, instead of legitimating what one already knows" (xxvii). Thinking differently, for Foucault, is not a simple matter but rather a "matter of slow, sustained and arduous work." Thinking differently is at the heart of the transformation into the new economy. In this book series, we refer to this work as change in consciousness or worldview. It has two aspects: change in the individual's mindset and change in the collective consciousness or ethos of a society.

36. See http://www.becreaturekind.org/; http://www.jewishveg.org; and http://www.veganmuslims.com/
37. See https://greenfaith.org/.
38. Martin Luther, "Sermon on the 16th Sunday after Trinity," in *Sermons of Martin Luther*, ed. John Nicholas Lenker, vol. 8 (Grand Rapids: Baker Books, 1983), 275.
39. Rabbi Michael Lerner speaking as part of "Moral Revolution."
40. Panu Pihkala, "Eco-anxiety, Tragedy, and Hope: Psychological and Spiritual Dimensions of Climate Change," *Zygon* 53, no. 2 (June 2018): 545–69, https://doi.org/10.1111/zygo.12407.
41. Pihkala, "Eco-anxiety, Tragedy, and Hope," 563.
42. Emmanuel Katongole, *Born from Lament: The Theology and Politics of Hope in Africa* (Grand Rapids, MI: Eerdmans, 2017), 261. The other citations in this paragraph are from xvi and xv.
43. Beal, *When Time Is Short*, 104, 105.
44. Beal, *When Time Is Short*, 105–7.
45. Brock and Parker, *Saving Paradise*, 417.
46. Rabbi Mordechai Liebling, "Living in the Four Worlds," in *Rooted and Rising: Voices of Courage in a Time of Climate Crisis*, ed. Leah D. Schade and Margaret Bullitt-Jonas (Lanham, MD: Rowman & Littlefield, 2019), 5.
47. "Interview with Peniel Joseph, Author of *The Third Reconstruction*," *Forum* (KQED, June 19, 2023).
48. F. S. Michaels, *Monoculture: How One Story Is Changing Everything* (Kamloops, BC: Red Clover, 2011), back cover, 9, 131.
49. Scholars of religion tend to agree that one role of religion is to provide core stories that shape how we live, especially those that describe both human and cosmic purpose, origins, identity, and destiny (cosmologies and anthropologies). These are found especially in the creation stories of a people or a religion.
50. This helps to free the texts from the Hellenized and Westernized hierarchical dualism of Western worldviews that has been imposed on them.
51. OR *neh-fesh chay-yah*; נֶפֶשׁ חַיָּה.
52. *Nefesh*, often translated in this story as "soul," is equally well translated as "living being," "creature," or "breathing life." *Hayah* means living or alive. See Beal, *When Time Is Short*, 88–91.
53. Beal, *When Time Is Short*, 122–23. Typically, Beal notes, we have played down this Hebrew text "as mere poetry; we have simply ignored it, building a modern faith in dominion and human exceptionalism better suited to our interests in extraction and infinite growth."
54. This idea is rich in the Christian concept of "the Book of Nature," the idea that creation is the first book of revelation, with the Bible being the second. In a broad sense,

this idea is also present in the Islamic notion of *ayat* and in the Jewish teaching that the created world is "a commentary on Torah" (see n90). Of course, these religions also have served to denigrate the other than human parts of creation.
55. Her term *viriditas* may come from the two Latin words meaning "green" and "truth."
56. Rebecca Kneale Gould and Laurel Kearns, "The Tent of Abraham: The Emerging Landscape of Jewish, Christian, and Islamic Ecological Traditions," in *Bloomsbury History: Theory and Method Articles* (London: Bloomsbury Publishing, 2021), 6–7. https://tinyurl.com/5afwhdj8. Accessed April 11, 2024.
57. Suzuki et al., *The Sacred Balance*, 271.
58. Kearns and Gould, "The Tent of Abraham," 6–7.
59. Maurice Bloch, "Why Religion Is Nothing Special but Is Central," ed. Colin Renfrew, Chris Frith, and Lambros Malafouris, *Philosophical Transactions of the Royal Society B: Biological Sciences* 363, no. 1499 (June 12, 2008): 2055–61, https://doi.org/10.1098/rstb.2008.0007.
60. Ghosh, *The Great Derangement*, 128.
61. Tim Jackson, *Prosperity without Growth: Economics for a Finite Planet* (Washington, DC: Earthscan, 2011), 101, 102, 158.
62. This identity has additional power not discussed here. For example, it means that other people too are irrevocably beloved, and this says a great deal about how we are to treat them, interpersonally and through systems.
63. For example, when Emperor Constantine converted to Christianity and made it the religion of the Roman Empire, artistic depictions of Jesus Christ shifted from the lowly shepherd and teacher to an imperial, toga-wearing, crowned ruler.
64. As cited in chapter 13.
65. Ezra Chitando, "A Response to Christina Gschwandtner," in *T&T Clark Handbook of Christian Theology and Climate Change*, ed. Ernst M. Conradie and Hilda P. Koster (T&T Clark, 2020), 578..
66. Kimmerer, *Braiding Sweetgrass*, 383–4.
67. Liebling, "Living in the Four Worlds," 9.
68. William Cavanaugh, *Torture and the Eucharist* (Oxford: Blackwell, 1998), 14. Cavanaugh demonstrates that the ritual of the Eucharist became a counter act to the politics and practice of torture during Pinochet's regime in Chile. The "Eucharist built a social body capable of resisting the state's strategy of disappearance" and "torture" (251, 16). The Eucharist called Christians to "conform their practice to the Eucharistic imagination ... a vision of what is real," the reign of God, life as God would have it on earth. And this shaped the church's social practice or actions in society in the context of torture. He is clear not to idealize the church or to suggest that the Eucharist always had this impact because, as he says, the chuch is always flawed, imperfect, "constituted by foolish and sinful people" (14).
69. Chitando, "A Response to Christina Gschwandtner," 577–78.
70. Brock and Parker, *Saving Paradise*, 155–56.
71. See also Cynthia Moe-Lobeda, "Liturgy Reshaping Society," in *Ordo: Bath, Word, Prayer, Table: A Liturgical Primer in Honor of Gordon W. Lathrop*, ed. Dirk G. Lange, Dwight Vogel, and Edward Schillebeeckx (Akron, OH: OSL Publications, 2018), 164–87; and Cynthia Moe-Lobeda, "Liturgy for the 'Uncreators,'" *Studia Liturgica* 38, no. 1 (March 2008): 64–80, https://doi.org/10.1177/003932070803800105.

Notes

72. Timothy Gorringe, *The Education of Desire: Towards a Theology of the Senses* (London: SCM Press, 2001), 104.
73. Cyril, *The Works of Saint Cyril of Jerusalem*, trans. Leo P. McCauley, S.J and Anthony Stephenson (Washington, DC: Catholic University of America Press, 1970), 203.
74. Martin Luther, "The Babylonian Captivity of the Church," *Luther's Works* 36:58. In a contemporary Lutheran baptismal rite drawing upon this heritage, the cross is traced on the eyes with the words "receive the cross on your eyes that you may see the light of Christ, illumination for your way." See ELCA, *Holy Baptism: And Related Rites*, Renewing Worship 3 (Minneapolis: Augsburg Fortress, 2002), 27.
75. Christopher Morse, *Not Every Spirit: A Christian Dogmatics of Disbelief* (Valley Forge, PA: Trinity Press International, 1994), 43.
76. Perhaps this also is God's sage response to humans' pernicious proclivity to create God in our own image.
77. Brock and Parker, *Saving Paradise*, 14. They illustrate with the story of Jesus's disciples who, on the road to Emmaus, could not recognize the risen Christ in their presence until sharing the ritual of breaking bread at which point "their eyes were opened and they recognized him (Luke 24:31)" (145).
78. Brock and Parker, *Saving Paradise*, 146
79. Brock and Parker, *Saving Paradise*, 155
80. Brock and Parker, *Saving Paradise*, 145
81. Some religious rituals go beyond "reminding" of the presence of the Sacred to actually invoking it into and among the people gathered. For many Christian communities, for example, the Eucharist includes the *epiclesis*, invoking or calling down the very presence of the Holy one to be imbibed by the people. Cyril of Jerusalem (fourth century) called this the "Fire of compassion descending into the bread." "The communicants received the power of divinity in their own flesh, just as a body received energy from food." Brock and Parker, *Saving Paradise*, 144.
82. Randy J. C. Odchigue, "The Ecclesial Contribution to Sustainable Communities," in Peppard and Vicini, *Just Sustainability*, 176, 177.
83. Odchigue, "The Ecclesial Contribution to Sustainable Communities," 178.
84. Brock and Parker, *Saving Paradise*, 418–19.
85. World Council of Churches, "News Release: 'Just Economics for Liberation and Life' Statement Offers Faith-Rooted Vision," October 21, 2020, https://tinyurl.com/24sbnn2k.
86. World Council of Churches, "News Release." Previously, in 2015, a gathering of Christian, Muslin, and Buddhist leaders sponsored by the World Council of Churches issued an Interfaith Call for Justice and Compassion in Finance. See https://tinyurl.com/muytpjv2.
87. Inter-religious Climate and Ecology Network, "The Ice Network—Vision & Mission," https://tinyurl.com/5n7m2rpj.
88. The Inter-religious Climate and Ecology Network, "Home: Inter-Religious Climate and Ecology Network," n.d., https://www.ice-netwok.net/.
89. World Council of Churches et al., "Climate-Responsible Finance—a Moral Imperative towards Children" (World Council of Churches Publications, May 9, 2022), https://tinyurl.com/az5yrmaw.
90. See World Council of Churches, "Climate-Responsible Finance."

91. Additional resources from interfaith efforts to build climate justice and economic justice are in this book's online toolkit at https://buildingamoraleconomy.org/.

MOVING ON

1. This prayer in its original form begins with "O God," rather than "O Great Spirit," and ends with "through Jesus Christ our Lord." I have amended it slightly to be more accessible to people who may not identify as Christians. Known by many as the "Holden Village Prayer," it was written by Eric Milner-White, and first published in 1941 in Milner-White and G.W. Briggs, *Daily Prayer*. "See Nancy Winder, "A Prayer for Guidance," *Living Lutheran*, May 23, 2022. https://tinyurl.com/bdd3afx2.
2. Emily Kawano, in a presentation for "Decolonizing Economics: Third Annual Post-capitalism Conference." As noted in chapter 8, Kawano uses this metaphor more specifically to describe the "solidarity economy."

INDEX

Abundant Table, 135
Accord on Fire and Building Safety in Bangladesh, 144, 333n17
accountability, 29, 30, 57, 58, 136, 151, 155, 187, 223, 303n23, 304n25, 320n35, 327n49, 330n74, 351n7
Adams, Barbara, 240, 247, 350n101, 351n10
advertising, 28, 29, 88, 219, 220, 240, 302n13, 302n16
advocacy, 58, 65, 80, 89, 114, 124, 126, 138, 143, 150, 153, 155, 174, 188, 246, 262, 291, 337n31, 340n3
 electoral advocacy, 148, 150
 legal advocacy, 147
 legislative advocacy, 65
advocating congregation, 153
Afro-Indigenous farming, 134
Agrarian Trust, 135, 331
Ahimsa, 244
air travel, 25, 58
Alliance of Small Island States, 117
alternative, 91, 113, 124, 126, 130, 131–34, 137, 145, 176, 200, 208, 224, 227, 234, 266, 273, 314n43, 348n74, 349n91, 350n92, 352n22, 355n12
 alternative agriculture, 134–35
 alternative banking, 145, 176
 alternative finance, 67, 134, 241
 consciousness and perceptions, 77
 economic models, 62, 132
 economic vision, 89
Ambrose, Saint, 179, 276
anger, 22, 124, 161, 193, 195, 197–98, 201, 202, 276, 291, 342n2, 342n13

Arce-Valentin, Dora, 246
Archer, David, 161
Armstrong, Karen, 261, 262, 264, 266, 267, 352n20, 353n24, 354n38
art, 18, 35, 56, 57, 78, 80, 123, 129, 174, 187, 224, 240, 245–47, 249, 250, 261, 281, 297, 309n8, 350n101, 351n10, 351n11, 356n34
artificial intelligence, 132
Astudillo, Neddy, 175
Athanasius, 284
Atlas of the Future, 113, 313n34, 328n58
awe, 19, 40, 124, 194–95, 201, 202, 254

Bacon, Francis, 218, 344n17
Baker-Fletcher, Karen, 138, 332n20
Baldwin, James, 21, 56
Baptism, 259, 288, 355n6, 359n74
Barad, Karen, 38, 227, 305n6
Basil, Saint, 179, 276, 356n24
Bauxite, 177, 178, 255
B corporation(s), 62, 94, 316n8, 320n35
Beal, Timothy, 202, 230, 281, 344n17, 347n54, 349n86, 352n14
beauty, 12, 17, 19, 28, 44, 47, 51, 56, 63, 70–71, 98, 130, 194, 202, 222, 254, 257, 276, 289, 302n16
behavioral change, 46, 59, 73–75, 142, 299, 314n41
Beloved Community Incubator, 39, 124, 207
Benioff, Marc, 61, 62, 312n27
Bennett, Jane, 230, 347n61
Berger, Rose Marie, 269, 354n3
Berryhill, Nikkeya, 288

Berry, Thomas, 210, 300n7, 318n21, 343n19
Bezos, Jeff, 166, 300n6, 304n24, 338n43
Billionaire's Income Tax (BIT), 166, 328n55, 338n39, 338n41, 338n44, 338n45, 338n47
Black Church Food Security Network, 279, 314n40
Black Lives Matter, 47, 173, 288, 335n20
Bloch, Maurice, 284, 358n59
Boggs, Grace Lee, 352n18
Bonhoeffer, Dietrich, 181, 227
Boston Ujima Project, 114
bottom line, 62, 75, 94, 98, 111, 130, 157, 223, 318n21, 319n30
  financial bottom line, 62, 93, 152, 238
  triple bottom line, 62, 75, 93, 94, 98, 130, 152, 316n8
Bourdieu, Pierre, 101, 322n1, 334n7
boycott, 145, 173, 174, 317n24
Brandeis, Louis, 9, 95, 300n1
Bread for the World, 34
Brock, Rita Nakashima, 282, 289, 315n49
Brookings Institute, 26, 302n10
Brooks, David, 61, 312n25
brown, adrienne maree, 123, 330n1
Brown, Brene, 248, 343n16
Brown Douglas, Kelly, 41, 190, 221, 341n15
Brueggemann, Walter, 77, 195, 245, 262, 342n9, 342n10, 350n6, 350n7, 352n21
Buddhism, 259, 261, 262, 274, 353n25
buen vivir, 67
Burkett, Maxine, 116, 329n69
Bush, George H. W., 88, 265

California Worker Cooperation Act, 114
Callahan, David, 61, 302n11, 312n24
capitalism, 27, 49, 61 66, 96–98, 112, 115, 129, 198, 218, 221, 231, 265, 303n22, 304n28, 308n28, 311n22, 312n23, 312n30, 313n36, 313n37, 320n32, 322n46, 327n49, 327n52, 345n23, 347n69, 348n70, 349n84
  advanced global capitalism, 96, 234, 293, 303n22
  competitive, 126
  corporate-and-finance-driven capitalism, 31, 143, 313n37
  extractive capitalism, 208, 224
  finance-dominated capitalism, 31, 143, 266
  fossil-fueled, 30
  global capitalism, 96, 234, 285, 293, 303n22
  industrial capitalism, 47, 226
  neoliberal capitalism, 47, 57, 90, 98, 209, 220, 232
  predatory capitalism, 49, 51, 63, 136, 266, 273, 286
Carbon Brief, 325n34
carbon emissions, 58, 61, 67, 76, 87, 95, 97, 108, 119, 134, 149, 151, 184, 223, 304n23, 311n13, 319n27, 325n32, 334n8
carbon footprint, 27, 63, 76, 141, 142, 223, 316n14
carbon inequity, 57, 301n5
Carbon Majors Report (2017), 58, 310n10
carbon offset, 106, 109, 117, 118, 325n34
Carter, Christopher, 314n40, 320n36, 340n12, 341n17, 342n8
Cavanaugh, William, 345n23, 358n68
Center for Climate Justice and Faith, 180, 181
Center for Economic Democracy, 90, 114, 307n27, 332n12
Center for Story-based Strategy, 107, 213, 217
Certified B Corporations, 62
change the story, 124, 215, 225, 228, 231, 233–36, 239–41, 283, 284, 297
charity, 150, 263
Chitando, Ezra, 286, 287, 358n65, 358n69
Christian/Christianity, 49, 69, 132, 148, 152, 178, 179, 185, 195, 201, 216, 230, 245, 259, 261, 266, 271, 272, 274, 276, 281, 282, 285, 288, 289,

Index

292, 301n13, 301n23, 302n12, 304n27, 305n5, 309n4, 315n49, 316n9, 321n41, 328n64, 337n36, 339n50, 341n16, 342n19, 345n28, 351n4, 353n24, 353n25, 354n6, 354n35–354n37, 355n10, 356n27, 357n54, 358n63, 358n68, 359n81, 359n86, 360n1
Chryssavgis, John, 38, 306n9, 347n49, 351n4
Church Action for Tax Justice, 165, 338n37
Class Action, 67
Cleveland Cooperative Initiative, 113
Cleveland Model, 64, 86, 89, 312n34, 331n7
climate change, 9, 11, 13, 15, 21, 25, 28, 40, 43–45, 58, 61, 62, 64, 76, 81, 87, 102–5, 111, 115–19, 140, 142, 150, 153, 162, 172, 179, 188, 195, 201, 202, 205, 253, 263, 269, 279–82, 290, 291, 306n24, 311n16, 313n36, 322n5–323n9, 325n32, 326n40, 329nn70–74, 330n79, 338n40, 339n50, 340n6, 357n40
  and economic systems, 30
  efforts to mitigate, 47, 75, 97, 108, 110
  frame, 280
  and interfaith collaboration, 291
  IPCC released the synthesis report for, 45
  neoliberal capitalism and, 209
  poverty and, 66, 168, 282
  and predatory economy, 197
  wildfires induced by, 266
climate debt, 28, 116, 325n33
climate despair, 141, 145
climate gap, 103, 322n7
climate injustice, 16, 37, 101–4, 116, 163, 264, 321n45, 322n2
climate justice, 45–47, 49, 58, 63, 101–4, 109, 150, 173, 180, 240, 291, 293, 297, 308n29, 308n30, 311n16, 322n3, 323n10, 325n33, 330n74, 353n28, 360n91

Climate Justice Alliance, 90, 109, 124, 149, 210, 314n39, 324n26, 326n38, 335n20
climate refugees, 21, 55, 81, 103, 104, 116, 118
climate reparations, 94, 104, 115–19, 187, 311n16, 329n69, 329nn72–74, 330n82
climate warrior(s), 46, 64, 179, 291
Cloke, Paul, 275, 355n21
Club of Rome, 58, 61, 161, 173, 300n8, 303n19, 307n27, 308n31, 321n37, 340n8
Coalition of Immokalee Workers, 34, 144, 145, 333n11, 333n20
collective lives, 25
collective wisdom, 43, 278
colonialism, 28, 48, 58, 78, 118, 201, 207, 285, 309n38, 319n25, 330n79, 352n12
  blue colonialism, 103, 105, 106, 319n25, 321n45, 330n77
  green colonialism, 105, 106, 323n14, 324n19
colonization, 16, 49, 50, 105, 111, 117, 209, 218, 220, 257, 335n8, 341n13, 343n5
common good, 221, 267, 276, 293, 338n37
communion, 18, 19, 21, 33, 38, 49, 51, 69, 161, 175, 178–80, 190, 211, 216, 225, 227, 269, 272–74, 278, 282, 287, 291, 293, 301, 301n19, 309, 309n36, 313n38, 336n10, 338n37, 351n7, 352n16, 354n6, 355n11
community-based land trusts, 114, 135–36
community-based organizations, 114
community organizing / community organizer, 66, 148, 180, 181, 205, 279, 332n2
community-owned energy, 131, 135
community supported agriculture (CSA), 33, 134, 138, 141
community wealth building (CWB), 64, 67, 86, 87, 90, 113, 317n5, 328n59, 331n12

Community Wealth Ecosystem Building Program, 113
compassion, 10, 16, 17, 19, 27, 30, 41, 44, 56, 69, 72, 124, 125, 150, 166, 169, 178, 179, 181, 191, 202, 203, 209, 244, 248, 249, 254, 258, 262–64, 266, 267, 271, 274, 276, 278, 279, 289, 293, 296, 297, 346n43, 352n22, 359n81
compensation ratio, 25
complicity, 24, 49, 158, 171, 286
Concentrated Animal Feeding Operations, 33
consumer culture, 28, 302n12, 354n34
consumption, 24, 25, 28, 37, 42, 58, 89, 90, 91, 93, 106, 152, 160, 199, 200, 219, 222, 223, 226, 235, 265, 284, 285, 293, 300n5, 305n36, 307n26, 310n12, 319n26, 326n36, 345n23, 352n17
cooperation, 42, 45, 79, 227, 273, 274, 292, 307n27, 317n24, 346n46
cooperatives, 32, 39, 86, 87, 114, 126, 130, 132, 133, 136, 150, 207, 256, 273, 322n48, 331n4, 355n12
  employee-owned, 136, 331n5
  worker-owned, 67, 114, 130, 150, 332n14
COP 27, 117, 323n11
corporate social responsibility (CSR), 143, 179, 182, 340n5
Council for World Missions, 161, 336n10
counter narrative, 226, 284, 285
courage, 9, 10, 17, 21–24, 35, 51, 60, 68–71, 116, 124, 126, 164, 174, 177, 178, 184, 193, 195, 199–202, 209, 216, 242–45, 247, 250, 254, 258–61, 269–72, 277, 279, 289, 290, 295, 296, 298, 308n34, 352n12
  audacious, 73
  moral-spiritual, 48, 249, 261
  resistance, 245
Cowans, Gordan, 187–89, 285
Cox, Stan, 91, 92, 109, 318n18, 326n39
CreatureKind, 279

credit union, 67, 134, 161, 164
cultivating community, 179–81
Cyril of Jerusalem, 288, 359n73

Dakota Access Pipeline, 164
Daly, Herman, 67, 318n17
Davis, Mike, 300n11
Debt, 28, 104, 116–19, 159, 160, 167, 185, 187–89, 191, 292, 303n19, 318n14, 320n36, 325n33, 330n79, 335n8, 335n9, 339nn49–51, 341n16, 341n19, 341n20, 351n7, 353n26
  carbon debt, 119
  climate debt, 28, 116, 325n33
  debt cancellation, 119, 188, 189, 341n20
  debt injustice, 119
  ecological debt, 104, 351n7
decolonization, 46, 343n1
deep sea mining, 105, 106, 323n16
De la Puente, Juan Carlos, 13, 277, 278, 356n32
Deloria Jr., Vine, 229, 342n1, 343n15
democracy, 30, 46, 47, 61, 63, 87, 89, 95–98, 112–15, 150, 217, 221, 231, 234, 307n27, 324n26, 327n49, 327nn52–54, 328n56, 329n67, 332n12, 332n14, 335n15, 347n69
Democracy Collaborative, 65, 67, 86, 331n7, 332n12
democratic economy, 46, 90, 96, 98, 131, 300n3, 317n4, 321n44
democratic guidepost, 96
democratic socialism, 46, 97
democratization, 47, 115
denial, 23, 24, 26, 56, 145, 195, 198, 257, 280, 281, 308n33, 354n39
Descartes, Rene, 218
despair, 10, 19, 44, 55, 59, 71, 103, 141, 145, 280, 281, 289, 291
divestment, 160, 162–64, 169, 174, 183, 191, 337n26, 337n29
divine love, 69, 161
divine presence, 70, 289
Doctrine of Discovery, 16, 184, 185, 190, 341n18

Index

Dorrien, Gary, 328n63, 329n68
Doughnut Economics Action Lab, 67, 308n31
Duchrow, Ulrich, 262, 266, 352n20, 353n26, 354n38
Dulce Hogar, 39

earthling, 20, 59, 179, 225, 226, 244, 299n1
earth's agency, 230, 284
ecological guidepost, 93, 97
ecological healing, 49
ecological violence, 31, 201
economic democracy, 90, 96, 98, 112–15, 307n27, 328n54, 328n56, 335n15
economic freedom, 348n70
economic growth, 92, 221, 235, 320n31, 349n91
economic life, 31, 37, 38, 42–44, 67, 68, 72–74, 76, 78, 79, 82, 87–91, 119, 120, 123, 125, 221, 223–28, 238, 242, 244, 259, 263, 265, 269, 270, 273, 283, 286, 289, 290, 293, 295, 297, 303n22, 308n16, 354n37, 356n27
   alternative visions for, 89, 208
   equitable and ecological, 58, 60–63
   healing, 137, 138, 146, 155, 170, 176, 177, 181, 192, 205, 210, 249, 296
   purpose of, 74, 126, 224, 233–34
   rapid reorientation of, 43, 267
   as spiritual practice, 9–22
   transforming, 199, 258
economic moral vision, 88, 89
economics
   circular economics, 318n17
   decolonizing economics, 332n17, 332n18
   doughnut economics, 67, 68, 152, 308n31, 312n32, 318n17, 334n11
   ecological economics, 67, 318n17
   economics of justice, 353n22
   economics of oppression, 352n22
   just economics, 292, 318n14, 341n16, 359n85

neoclassical economics, 160
new economics, 318n17, 349n91
Windigo economics, 199
economic systems, 16, 25, 26, 27, 30, 31, 42, 50, 59, 66, 74–76, 87, 89, 90, 96, 98, 103, 120, 132, 136, 146, 185, 217, 226, 249, 273–75, 293, 296, 300n5, 307n26, 307n27, 311n22, 316n9
economic theory, 219, 318n17, 346n42, 348n70
economic transformation, 12, 16, 35, 44, 46, 47, 62, 63, 79, 140, 195, 201, 273, 297, 300n8, 307n27
economic violence, 10, 26, 27, 97, 140, 211, 258, 259, 263, 270, 281
economic vulnerability, 28
economy/economies
   climate justice economy, 46
   democratic economy, 46, 90, 96, 98, 131, 321n44
   ecological economy, 72, 150
   global economy, 27, 30, 49, 57, 75, 87, 112, 209, 219, 275, 292
   for life, 46, 73, 178, 195, 260, 295, 307n27, 326n36, 356n35
   local living economy, 46, 130
   low-carbon economy, 109–10
   low-emissions, 109–10
   moral economy, 32, 37, 42, 46, 47, 55, 66, 74, 78, 85, 89–91, 97, 98, 109, 138, 146, 155, 166, 168, 180, 181, 185, 190–92, 195, 198, 209, 235, 236
   new economy, 37, 46, 49, 67, 80, 90, 91, 98, 114, 123, 124, 131, 133, 138, 154, 164, 179, 205, 217, 224, 225, 236, 247, 273, 307n27, 309n6, 318n17, 321n44, 332n12, 357n35
   post-extractive economy, 111
   solidarity economy, 40, 46, 62, 65, 66, 130, 137, 224, 307n27, 314n43
   sustainable economy, 315n5
   wellbeing economy, 46, 307n27
economy of life, 20, 46, 66, 68, 95, 218, 224, 226, 299n1, 307n27, 314n38

ecosystems, 9, 50, 62, 91, 105, 107, 111, 233, 291, 300n5, 307n26
Ecumenical Patriarch Bartholomew, 253, 351n4
Elvey, Anne, 248, 351n14
employee-owned business, 12, 43, 80, 96, 131, 146, 306n17, 335n15
employee-owned cooperative, 136, 331n5
Employee Ownership Act, 114
environmental racism, 179, 324n26
equitable guidepost, 94
Escazu Agreement, 175
ethical values, 274
eucharist, 33, 201, 287–90, 355n6, 358n68, 359n81
Evergreen Cooperative Laundry, 65, 86
Evergreen Cooperatives, 86, 87, 317n6
exploitation, 10, 24, 27–30, 32, 34, 37, 38, 47, 57, 66, 78, 98, 104–6, 110, 115, 123, 134, 140, 142, 144, 149, 161, 162, 175, 179, 180, 187, 188, 205, 207, 218, 240, 263, 273, 277, 279, 285, 300n5, 306n20, 307n26, 325n31, 326n43, 333n13, 344n15, 352n22, 356n26
  Anti-Black, 190
  brutal, 29
  economic, 16, 28, 30, 63, 190, 234, 292
  and extraction, 14, 221, 297
  financial beneficiary of, 27, 47
  of natural resources, 104, 117
  sexual, 182
externalities, 111
Extinction Rebellion, 79, 173, 314n44, 317n26
extraction, 10, 14, 32, 37, 45, 63, 87, 92, 105, 106, 108, 109, 111, 142, 173, 174, 176, 184, 188, 190, 207, 209, 218, 221, 224, 235, 243, 277, 297, 308n30, 308n33, 357n53
extractive capitalism, 208, 224

Fair Food Agreement, 13, 34, 182
Fair Food Program, 34, 65, 140, 144, 182, 183, 340n7

Faith Action Network, 153
Farm Bill, 33
fear, 22, 28, 35, 41, 143, 166, 181, 193, 195, 200, 207, 230, 245, 254, 280, 284, 297
Figueres, Christina, 56, 79, 224, 309n4, 316n9, 317n26, 342n19, 342n20, 345n34, 346n38, 349n90
finance, 13, 31, 57, 58, 62, 75, 88, 114, 117, 118, 119, 136–38, 149, 152, 154, 160–62, 167, 169, 191, 211, 220, 221, 226, 241, 243, 254, 261, 266, 297, 303n22, 307n28, 313n37, 316n8, 328n53, 336n9, 336n16, 336n19, 341n16, 352n17
  alternative finance, 67, 134, 241
  finance institutions, 112, 118, 133, 152, 191
  socially responsible finance, 136
finance-dominated capitalism, 266
financial transaction tax, 166, 338n40
fingers on the hands of healing. See healing
fingers on the hands of liberative change, 120, 146, 202
food justice movement, 67
food sovereignty, 66, 180
  Black food sovereignty, 67, 135, 256, 314n40
Foote, Julia A. J., 278
fossil fuel industry, 13, 142, 162–64, 266, 308n33, 310n10, 352n17
Fossil Fuel Non-proliferation Treaty, 44–46, 172–74
fossil fuels, 15, 45, 58, 65, 92, 104–6, 110, 117, 119, 141, 157, 159, 162–64, 169, 173, 179, 243, 301n15, 306n24, 308n30, 308n33, 310n10, 336n25, 340n6, 352n17, 354n31
Foucault, Michael, 237, 308n32, 350n96, 356n35
Foy, Lawrence, 207
Francis, Pope, 25, 89, 313n36
freedom, 12, 15, 22, 27, 47, 48, 49, 50, 73, 82, 88, 111, 112, 115, 143, 144, 152, 157, 158, 214, 219, 221, 224,

Index

231, 232, 235, 237, 242, 245, 263, 264, 265, 267, 269, 270, 272, 285, 286, 293, 304n23, 308n28, 335n3, 347n67, 347n69, 348n70, 348n74, 352n12
- market freedom, 231, 347n67, 347n69
free market, 219, 231, 232, 345n31
Fukuyama, Francis, 234, 349n82
full-cost pricing, 111

Gandhi, M. K., 79, 244, 273, 278, 317n23, 317n24, 320n33, 326n43
Gebara, Ivonne, 58, 311n17
Genuine Progress Indicator (GPI), 236
Ghosh, Amitav, 56, 59, 60, 264, 269, 284, 309n3, 311n14, 311n18, 329n74, 336n14, 354n32
Global Alliance for Tax Justice, 110, 167, 337n33
global capitalism, 96, 234, 285, 293, 303n22
global economy, 27, 30, 49, 57, 75, 87, 112, 171, 209, 219, 275, 292
global warming, 45, 60, 92, 284, 308n33, 319n29, 322n6, 335n1
Gomez-Barns, Macarena, 205, 208, 342n2
Gore, Karenna, 264, 302n13, 354n30
Gould, Corrina, 186
gratitude, 124, 193, 194, 199–202, 210, 239
green and blue colonialism, 103, 105, 106, 319n25, 321n45, 330n77
Green Gulch Farm, 135
greenhouse gas emissions, 21, 25, 28, 46, 47, 81, 92, 104, 141, 153, 299n3, 310n12, 319n23, 322n6, 325n32
Green New Deal, 152, 318n18, 318n22, 319n24, 321n44, 324n20, 344n15
Gregory the Great, 194, 342n5
Greider, William, 112, 129, 327n48, 331n1
grief, 22, 43, 44, 70, 161, 195–97, 201–3, 259, 276, 281
gross domestic product (GDP), 67, 111, 189, 233, 235, 236, 311n13, 337n35, 350n92

Guterres, Antonio, 161, 162, 310n10, 330n80, 336n19

Ha'adam, 228, 283
Ha'adamah, 228, 283
Hadewijch of Brabant, 301n17
Hall, Anne, 356n33
Harai, Yuval, 77, 214, 344n4
Harari, Noah, 306n12, 317n20
Hardt, Michael, 46
Harrison, Beverly, 101, 198
Haskell, David, 346n40
Havel, Vaclav, 218, 344n14
Hawken, Paul, 180, 233
HEAL Act, 107, 108, 324n24, 324n25
healing, 12, 16, 17, 19, 21, 24, 27, 31, 37, 38, 46, 49, 50, 51, 55, 60, 63, 64, 68, 69, 71–73, 79, 82, 83, 88, 91, 101, 119–21, 123, 125, 127, 142, 144, 196, 202, 257, 258, 261, 270, 273, 277, 280, 281, 284–86, 289, 290, 291, 295–97, 304n25, 320n36, 327n49, 329n66, 342n5, 345n21, 345n26, 346n42, 347n67, 348n70, 349n81, 350n99, 351n9
- build new, 129–38
- build the bigger we, 177–92
- change rules, 147–55
- change the story, 213–42
- disease and, 37–40
- drink spirit's courage, 243–250
- economic life, 83
- gratitude, 199–201
- holy anger, 197–98, 201
- lament, 195–97, 201
- listen and amplify, 205–11
- live lightly, 139–46
- medicine, 120
- move money, 157–70
- practice awe, 194–95, 201
- of relationships, 120
- resist the wrong, 171–76
Hebrew prophets, 64, 80, 175, 179, 216, 259, 263, 271, 275, 278, 281
Henderson, Hazel, 67

Heschel, Rabbi Michael Joshua, 48, 193–95
Hildegard of Bingen, 284
Hill Collins, Patricia, 101
Hinduism, 259, 261, 353n25
Hinkelammert, Franz, 262, 266, 352n20
Hinkle-Rieger, Rosemarie, 136, 331n4
Homestead Act of 1862, 26
hope, 10, 11, 14, 22, 24, 29, 35, 44, 46, 47, 48, 55–57, 60, 61, 63, 69, 71, 109, 116, 120, 135, 162, 189, 193, 196–98, 201, 202, 231, 241–47, 255, 260, 264, 269, 270, 277, 278, 280–82, 289, 291, 295, 297, 304n25, 342n11, 343n12, 346n37, 353n28, 355n23, 357n40
　authentic, 281
　Christianity's, 196, 282
human exceptionalism, 218, 235, 357n53
human freedom, 111, 219, 221, 231
human relationships, 88, 245, 247, 249, 250
human rights abuses, 143, 144, 182, 309n7
hunger, 10, 13–15, 19, 23, 31, 39, 43, 55, 70, 129, 145, 150, 152, 166, 171, 181, 188, 189, 191, 199, 200, 255, 257, 269, 273, 296
　hunger, causes of, 31, 39, 150
　hunger, climate change and, 13, 15, 43

immunity to change, 216, 217, 344nn8–10, 350n95
Indigenous Earth protectors, 175, 340n11
Indigenous Environmental Network, 109, 174, 180, 210, 307n27, 325n35, 326n36
Indigenous people, 16, 26, 49, 62, 95, 102–4, 106, 107, 116–18, 126, 133, 174, 180, 184, 186, 199, 207, 208, 213, 222, 248, 254, 258, 291, 311n16, 313n37, 313n38, 324n21, 325n34, 326n36, 329n71, 330n74, 343n5, 344n15

Indigenous Women's Divestment Delegations, 163
inequity, 25, 26, 29, 57, 58, 150, 159, 166, 301n5, 310n12, 311n13, 312n23, 321n38, 329n67, 344n11
interdependence, 18, 47, 124
Interfaith Coalition on Food Justice, 34, 314n40
interfaith community, 187
Interfaith Movement for Human Integrity, 187, 190, 207, 287
Interfaith Power and Light, 292, 293, 309n35, 335n3
Interfaith Rainforest Initiative, 184, 293
International Accord for Health and Safety in the Textile and Garment Industry, 333n14
International Alliance for Localization, 317n25
International Monetary Fund, 291, 319n27
Inter-religious Climate and Ecology Network, 104, 292, 323n12, 359n27, 359n88
investment, 13, 15, 43, 75, 81, 92, 106, 114, 132, 143, 152, 153, 157, 159, 160, 162–64, 166, 168, 169, 178, 179, 182, 219, 220, 232, 240, 241, 254, 304n23, 321n44, 336n21, 337n29, 338n48, 347n69
　alternative, 67, 89, 132, 134, 236, 240, 241, 314n43
　speculative, 43, 75, 153, 166, 304n23
Irenaeus of Lyons, 216, 301n18
Islam, 259–62, 266, 274, 284, 289, 292, 341n16, 353n24, 353n25

Jackson, Moana, 224, 343n1
Jackson, Tim, 235, 284, 317n7, 358n61
Jara, Victor, 246
Jennings, Willie James, 38, 197, 198, 227, 305n5, 306n8, 342n2, 342n13, 344n16, 345n28, 347n49, 347n59
JewishVeg, 279, 357n36
Jha, Sonora, 215

Index

Johnson, Sheryl, 186, 341n11, 353n27
Johnson, Tore, 105
Joseph, Peniel, 283, 357n47
Jubilee Campaign / Jubilee 2000 Campaign, 167, 339n49
Jubilee USA Network, 168, 341n20
Judaism, 30, 38, 245, 258–60, 262, 274, 353nn23–25
justice-seeking, 14, 15, 17, 80, 185, 195, 231, 285
just transition, 45, 66, 90, 93, 94, 104, 107–10, 149, 172, 173, 183, 308n30, 310n9, 311n13, 314n39, 319n25, 321n45, 324n26, 325nn28–30, 325n32, 325n33, 325n35, 325n36, 326n37, 335n20, 341n13, 341n14, 350n2

Kane, Kristen, 39
Katongole, Emmanuel, 196, 281, 342n11, 357n42
Kaur, Valerie, 123
Kawano, Emily, 136, 296, 307n27, 332n18, 360n2
Kearns, Laurel, 358n56, 358n58
Kegan, Robert, 216, 237, 344nn8–10, 344n12, 350n95
Kelly, Marjorie, 113, 157, 220, 233, 253, 300n3, 317n4, 327n48, 327n49, 327n51, 331n1, 331n2, 335n14, 335n15
Keskitalo, Aili, 105
Kimmerer, Robin Wall, 85, 199–201, 229, 245, 300n9, 317n2, 342n3
King, Jr., Martin Luther, 96, 139, 197, 208, 275, 278, 332n3, 343n12, 355n23
Klein, Naomi, 9, 129, 300n3, 331n2
Korten, David, 213, 318n17, 344n5

labor, 11, 33, 47, 49, 57, 63, 87, 110, 139, 145, 150, 179, 232, 275, 300n6, 309n7, 324n26, 331n4, 333nn11–13, 341n13, 349n91, 353n26
    cheap, 25, 47, 232, 237, 307n28

child, 150, 179
    rights, 179, 183, 341n8
La foie et le Bien Commun, 293
Lakoff, George, 89
Lament, 124, 193, 195–97, 201, 202, 203, 220, 230, 246, 281, 282, 289, 291, 342n10, 357n42
landback movement, 67, 190
Land Justice Project, 255, 273, 351n8
land theft, 62
land trusts, 114, 129, 130, 131, 135, 136, 224, 256
Laskow Lahey, Lisa, 216, 237, 344n8
Laudato Si, 89, 313n36
Lazarovic, Sarah, 224, 346n37
Lebow, victor, 219, 345n24
Le Chambon, 354n4
Lenga, Baraka, 264, 354n31
Lent, Jeremy, 311n21
Lerner, Rabbi Michael, 69, 253, 262, 280, 351n10, 357n39
liberation theology, 206, 353n23
Liebling, Rabbi Mordechai, 282, 287, 301n14, 357n46
lifestyle change, 64, 76, 142, 144–46, 241, 332n8
Lim, Mary, 205, 206
Lincoln, Abraham, 96, 321n40, 321n42
listening, 11, 39, 64, 107, 123, 126, 130, 145, 184, 196, 205–7, 209, 210, 211, 231, 273, 291
liturgy, 123, 174, 286–88, 297, 355n6, 358n71
Liu, Eric, 32, 304n31
livable wage, 86, 223
living lightly, 140, 144, 146, 334n26
London Mining Network, 110, 326n45
loss and damage, 47, 116, 117, 118, 329n71, 329n73, 336n9
love story, 12, 16, 17, 20, 22, 35, 191, 260–61, 285
low-carbon economy, 109–10
Lukacs, Martin, 76, 316n12
Lutheran World Federation (LWF), 161, 309n36, 313n38

Index

Luther, Martin, 19, 70, 96, 139, 197, 208, 243, 244, 264, 275, 276, 279, 284, 288, 315n51, 332n3, 342n7, 343n12, 347n55, 350n1, 355n23, 356n26, 357n38, 359n74

Macfarlane, Robert, 229, 347n60
Mah-Hui, Lim, 25, 302n7
Mandlate, Bishop Bernardino, 167
Marciales, Kelly, 25, 139, 331n9
marketing industry, 25, 223
Matthews, Dylan, 147, 334n1
maximizing consumption, 28, 37, 160, 223
maximizing growth, 28, 89, 160, 219, 233
maximizing profit, 28, 48, 50, 59, 61, 74, 75, 79, 89, 94, 97, 179, 220, 222, 223, 226, 233, 236, 276
Mayr, Ernst, 274, 355n17
Mazaska Talks, 164
McKibben, Bill, 150, 157, 162, 335n1, 336n20
meat production, 25, 58, 243, 279, 301n4
metanoia, 80
Michaels, F. S., 283, 357n48
microorganism, 21, 194
Miller, Vincent, 266, 302n12, 354n34
Mills, C. Wright, 42
mindset, 35, 49, 74–79, 93, 111, 199, 214, 216, 217, 220, 226, 237, 316n9, 357n35
Mondragon Cooperative, 113, 136
moral courage, 9, 10, 48, 51, 199, 270, 279
moral economy. *See* economy/economies
moral imagination, 42–43
moral-spiritual agency, 245
moral-spiritual power, 35, 44, 48, 55, 56, 79, 195, 198, 201, 243, 248, 258, 259, 262, 287, 297
moral vision, 87–89, 175
Movement for Black Lives, 164
Movement Generation, 109, 186, 243, 307n27, 314n39, 324n26, 326n37, 341n13, 350n2
Mshana, Rogate R., 313n37

mud creature(s), 18, 301n18
multinational corporation(s), 24, 104, 171, 199, 320n35, 337n31
Munib, Bishop Younan, 174
Murdoch, Iris, 55, 309n1
Musk, Elon, 166, 300n6, 304n24, 338n44

narrative imagination, 40–42, 51, 77, 214
Nasheed, Mohammed, 23, 26
National African American Reparations Commission, 190
National Black Food and Justice Alliance, 135
Navarro, Angelica, 116, 117
NDN Collective, 210, 324n20
nefesh hayah, 283, 357n52
Negri, Antonio, 46
neighbor-love, 14–17, 19, 20, 21, 37, 76, 91, 116, 141, 144, 148, 166, 179, 185, 188, 191, 195, 239, 274, 275, 278, 290, 318n16
neoliberal economics, 94, 226, 313n37
assumptions of, 226, 227, 318n21
neoliberalism, 76, 112, 219, 220, 303n22, 316n12, 327n52, 345n20, 345n26, 347n69
Neruda, Pablo, 246
New Economics Foundation, 349n91
New Economy Coalition, 12, 80, 90, 114, 147, 154, 164, 224, 236, 307n27, 314n39, 318n15, 330n2, 334n3
new economy movement, 130, 273
New International Financial and Economic Architecture (NIFEA), 66, 160, 246, 307n27
Newton, Isaac, 219
Next System Project, 67, 308n31
Norgaard, Richard, 67, 318n17
numbness, 26, 195, 196, 197
Nuns and Nones, 255, 261, 273

Odchigue, Randy Calo (Randy J. C. Odchigue), 359n82

Index

oikonomia, 19, 38
oikonomos, 12, 20, 91
oikos, 12, 19, 38, 88, 308n30
Okri, Ben, 213, 224, 343n1
350.org, 64, 240, 314n44
Owens, Terri Hord, 253
Oxfam, 301n5, 304n24, 310n12, 328n55, 338n46

Pacific Blue Line, 323n15, 324n17, 324n18
Pacific Theological College, 208
Palaca Ponce, Rico, 267
Paradox, 10, 31, 40, 43, 44, 76, 125, 141, 142, 282
paradoxical imagination, 43–44
Parker, Rebecca Anne, 282, 289, 290, 315n49
Patel, Raj, 345n31
Patriotic Millionaires, 154, 340n2
Paul II, Pope John, 25, 301n6
Peralta, Athena, 313n37
Pero, Peter, 171, 186, 190
personal gain, 115, 265
Pew Research Center, 61, 311n22
Pihkala, Panu, 357n40, 357n41
plastics, 50, 74, 223, 243
political action, 141
Pollen, Michael, 216
Poor Peoples Campaign, 154
post-capitalist, 97, 307n27
post-extractive economy, 111
poverty, 10, 20, 23, 25–27, 57, 66, 95, 117, 130, 144, 147–50, 152, 165, 167, 168, 181, 187, 188–90, 206–9, 221, 235, 263, 274, 282, 290, 291, 305n4, 308n28, 313n37, 332n8, 333n11, 334n1, 335n7, 336n9, 338n40, 349n89, 350n93
Powell, John A., 58, 311n15
predatory capitalism, 49, 51, 63, 136, 266, 273, 286
privatization, 275
progressive taxation, 166, 275, 321n43
public bank/banks/banking, 67, 134, 150

public policy advocacy, 124, 126, 138, 147–50, 152–54, 291

racism, 28, 47, 58, 62, 96, 179, 217, 235, 305n4, 306n13, 306n20, 311n15, 323n16, 324n26, 326n39, 339n1, 341n12
radical reversal, 43
Rasmussen, Larry, 73, 315n1
Ratushinskaya, Irina, 246
Raworth, Kate, 37, 68, 94, 305n1, 312n32, 314n45, 318n17, 334n11
real-cost pricing, 111
rebuilding, 46, 79, 80, 98, 125, 285, 296, 300n5, 307n26
reclamation, 285
Reed, Melissa, 181, 189
Reich, Robert, 338n46
reinvestment, 132, 160, 162–64, 183, 337n29
religion, 14–16, 48, 49, 59, 70, 180, 201, 226, 245, 249, 253, 257–67, 269, 270, 273–75, 277, 279–84, 286, 287, 293, 297, 302n12, 303n21, 308n34, 309n35, 312n31, 313n36, 316n16, 323n13, 341n17, 342n1, 343n14, 352n13, 352n16, 352n20, 352n22, 353n23, 353n24, 354n39, 355n21, 357n49, 358n54, 358n59, 358n63. *See also* Buddhism; Christian/Christianity; Hinduism; Islam; Judaism
religious, 10–12, 38, 41, 43, 48, 60, 66, 69, 78, 88–102, 104, 159, 162, 165, 173, 179, 184, 187, 201, 206, 226, 227, 250, 253–65, 269–71, 274–76, 278–83, 285, 286–93, 299, 301n2, 302n16, 306n20, 315n3, 323n12, 348n70, 351n12, 352n16, 352n20, 353n25, 354n39, 355n21, 359n81, 359n87, 359n88
belief, 41
communities, 30, 49, 90, 163, 175, 256, 270, 274, 279, 280
faith, 261, 265, 269, 270, 276, 278, 281, 286, 291, 293

religious (*continued*)
  groups, 49, 264
  institutions, 15, 114, 162
  leaders, 10, 159, 165, 184, 206, 240
  rituals, 249, 289, 290
  teachings, 227
  traditions, 15–17, 30, 44, 66, 88, 245, 249, 258, 260–63, 271, 282, 283, 285, 293
renewable energy, 45, 46, 67, 75, 80, 92, 97, 105, 106, 108–10, 135, 163, 183, 306n24, 308n30, 326n40, 340n6
renewal, 69, 79, 255, 262
reparations, 47, 66, 94, 104, 115, 116–119, 184–191, 258, 285, 292, 306n24, 311n16, 318n14, 329nn72–74, 330n81, 340n6, 341n15
repentance, 80, 188, 196, 254, 286, 288
resistance, 48, 79, 80, 98, 138, 164, 174, 177, 178, 184, 200, 205, 206, 211, 245, 246, 255, 262, 269, 270, 272, 273, 278, 290, 296, 297, 315n5, 317n23, 334n27, 340n9, 351n12
Rieger, Joerg, 322n47
right relationships, 14, 116, 165, 185, 186, 187, 191, 275
Riis, Jacob August, 295
Rimington, Jess, 332n1
rituals, 174, 254, 270, 271, 286–91, 358n68, 359n77, 359n81
Rivera, Myra, 323n13, 343n14
Rivett-Carnac, Tom, 309n4, 316n9, 342n19
Roberts, Christina, 213, 343n2
Robin Hood tax, 153, 338n40
Roosevelt, Franklin D., 96
Roosevelt, Theodore, 326n47
ruach, 69, 244

sacred earth, 12, 284
sacrifice zone, 47, 57, 92, 97, 105, 109, 297, 319n25, 330n77, 343n3
Sami, 105–6
Sarsour, Linda, 152
Saulnier, Raymond, 219

Schlosser, Eric, 332n4, 333n13
Schut, Michael
Scudder, Vida, 253, 278
seeing, 11, 13, 22, 41–43, 55–56, 58–60, 63, 68–72, 75, 95, 98, 101, 105, 158, 175, 216, 284–85, 287–89, 336n9
self-love, 16, 19
"selves curved in on self," 264–66, 269, 270, 286, 291, 293
Sherma, Rita, 267, 354n39
Simon, Morgan, 162, 336n18
slavery, 49, 60, 123, 143, 150, 185, 187, 190, 218, 234, 272, 288, 307n28, 308n28, 333n12, 333n20, 353n26
Sloan Wilson, David, 226, 346n46
Smith, Adam, 98, 232, 348n71
Sobocienski, Meghan, 131
Sobrino, Jon, 23, 26, 305n4
Social Gospel movement, 115, 179, 351n5
socialism, 46, 61, 307, 311n22, 312n23. *See also* religion
  democratic, 97, 324n26, 327n49, 331n4
  state, 97, 129
  state-centered, 112
  state-dominated authoritarian forms of, 307n27
socially responsible investing, 134
Soelle, Dorothea, 56
Sogorea Te' Land Trust, 186, 341n13
Sojourners, 167, 197, 336n20, 341n15, 354n3
Solano Miselis, Jocabed, 175
Solidarity Economy Network, 65, 66, 114
Solnit, Rebecca, 76, 316n14
Sosa, Mercedes, 245–47, 350n8
Soul Fire Farm, 134
Southeast Center for Cooperative Development, 136, 331n6, 332n14
speculative investment, 43, 75, 153, 166, 304n23
speculative investment tax, 153, 166
spirit, 11, 15, 18, 24, 69–71, 82, 197, 207, 218, 231, 243–45, 247–49, 260, 266, 271, 273, 276, 279, 280, 282,

Index

289, 314n48, 329n74, 333n24, 343n5, 351n12, 353n26, 354n37, 355n11, 356n35, 360n1
Holy Spirit, 69, 148, 207, 354n6
Sacred Spirit, 15, 18, 69, 71, 244, 245
spirituality, 14, 15, 126, 130, 226, 237, 255, 258, 259, 261–64, 267, 270, 274, 279, 284, 286, 292, 354n40, 356n35
  of empathy and compassion, 262, 267
  of neighbor-love, 14–17, 19, 20, 37, 76, 91, 116, 141, 144, 148, 166, 179, 185, 188, 195, 198, 275, 290, 318n16
spiritual power, 35, 44, 48, 55, 56, 79, 161, 195, 198, 201, 244–46, 248, 249, 258, 259, 262, 287, 297
spiritual practice, 11, 14–16, 72, 73, 76, 82, 120, 149, 180, 185, 210, 211, 244, 247, 277, 295
Stanley Robinson, Kim, 322n48, 354n29
Stiglitz, Joseph, 147, 312n30, 334n2
Stout, Jeffrey, 198, 304n25, 342n14
structural change, 74, 75, 93–95, 126, 145, 191, 239, 315n3
Suleiman, Imam Omar, 150, 277, 305n4, 334n9, 356n30
sumac kawsay, 67
Summers, Lawrence, 93, 222, 345n30
sustainability, 75, 92, 105, 111, 180, 287, 303n19, 303n20, 317n5, 321n37, 321n38, 332n12, 340n8, 344n11, 349n91, 352n19, 354n39
Sustainable Economies Law Center, 300n5, 307n26, 330n2, 331n6, 334n7
2015 Suva Declaration, 45, 173
Suzuki, David, 214, 227, 305n6, 314n47
systemic change, 31, 46, 66, 125, 142, 296
systemic imagination, 42
systemic injustice, 29, 55, 71, 181, 272

Taiwo, Olufemi O., 329n72
Talia, Maina, 75, 117, 316n10

Tanaka, Aaron, 332n12
Tanner, Kathryn, 354n35
tax, 42, 46, 87, 111, 148, 152–54, 160, 186, 231, 241, 275, 300n6, 304n24, 312n33, 313n38, 328n55, 335n9, 337n31, 337n35, 338nn37–41, 338n44, 338n48, 340n3
  justice, 94, 110, 164–67, 235, 326n44, 337nn31–34
  reform, 165
Tax Justice Network, 164, 337n31
Tax Justice Network Africa, 164
Taylor, Adam Russell, 167, 197
Teilhard de Chardin, Pierre, 253, 351n3
Temple of Understanding, 293
teshuvah, 80
Thatcher, Margaret, 234
The "Great Work," 11, 300n7, 318n21
Thompson, Deanna, 29, 303n21
Thurman, Howard, 272, 278, 306n8, 355n8
Tillich, Paul, 249, 301n20, 351n17, 355n19
Tinker, George ("Tink"), 184, 207, 341n10, 343n7, 343n15
Townes, Emilie, 140, 193, 196, 278, 342n1, 356n34
transformative spirituality, 267, 354n40
triple bottom line, 62, 75, 93, 94, 98, 130, 152, 316n8
truth-telling, 43, 56–60, 72, 105, 289, 341n15
Tutu, Desmond, 148

Ujima Project, 114, 332n12
Union of Concerned Scientists, 308n34, 318n10
United Nations Alternative Economies for Transformation Programme, 67
United Nations Environment Programme, 292, 319n23
United Nations Framework Convention on Climate Change, 316n9, 329n70
United Nations Research Institute for Social Development, 62, 312n32, 314n43

United States Solidarity Economy
    Network, 65, 66, 114, 307n27,
    308n31
Urban *Adamah*, 135
urban farming, 134, 135
urban food desert, 14

Vaai, Maima, 322n3, 322n4, 323n10
Vanuatu, 44, 45, 172, 306n21, 306n22,
    306n24, 307n25, 339n3, 339n4,
    340n6, 340n7
Vasquez, Bianca, 39
Vegan Muslim Initiative, 279
Via Campesina, 117, 118, 135, 330n78,
    330n81
vision, 10, 32, 34, 39, 50, 55, 68–71, 81, 98,
    99, 124–27, 134, 148, 154, 164, 168,
    175, 178, 207, 208, 236, 240, 243,
    260, 269, 282, 288, 289, 296, 305n6,
    307n27, 308n34, 317n1, 339n1,
    345n28, 351n4, 358n68, 359n85
  for life-giving economies, 89–91
  of moral economy, 85
  morally empowering, 71
  mystical, 56
  power of moral, 87–89
vocation, 19, 356n32
Vurobaravu, Nikenike, 45, 172

wage theft, 39, 143, 182, 207, 333n11
Walker, Alice, 195, 342n6
Wallace-Wells, David, 119, 330n82
War on Want, 110, 326n45
wealth concentration, 40, 300n5,
    307n26
wealth gap, 26, 62, 64, 66, 91, 94, 302n10,
    308n28, 313n37, 320n31, 344n11
wealth inequity, 29, 166
Weapons of the Spirit, 354n4
Wellbeing Economy Alliance, 67
Wheatley, Margaret, 130
white superiority, 220, 222, 234, 235,
    237–40

white supremacy, 16, 41, 49, 51, 56, 107,
    209, 221, 243, 341n15
Wilkerson, Isabel, 171, 222, 339n2
Williams, Rowan, 165
Wilson, E. O., 274, 346n46
Windigo, 199, 200
wisdom traditions, 16, 244, 261
worker-driven social responsibility
    (WSR), 34, 65, 143, 182, 183, 191,
    340n5
worker-owned business, 39, 64, 67, 94,
    114, 131–33, 136, 138, 236, 241
worker-owned cooperative, 130, 150,
    332n14
World Bank, 93, 167, 168, 222, 291,
    320n32, 345n30
World Communion of Reformed
    Churches, 309n36, 313n38,
    338n38, 355n22
World Council of Churches (WCC), 66,
    79, 90, 102, 117, 150, 153, 161, 162,
    174, 246, 292, 307n27, 309n36,
    313n36, 313n37, 319n28, 326n44,
    330n79, 336n10, 336n16, 337n32,
    338n38, 346n43, 354n40, 355n22,
    359n85, 359n86, 359n89
World Inequality Lab, 301n22, 310n12
World Inequity Report, 58
world scientists, 58, 307n27, 316n9
World Scientists' Warning to Humanity,
    25, 89, 111, 299, 301n5, 318n10,
    354n1
World Trade Organization, 220
worldview change, 46, 73, 93–95, 299
worship, 33, 65, 66, 130, 187, 196, 230,
    237, 240, 254, 259, 271, 272, 274,
    279, 282, 288, 290, 305n5, 359n74

Yale Forum on Religion and Ecology,
    309n35
Yom Kippur, 254

Zacchaeus tax, 165, 166, 313n38